OXFORD CLASSICAL MONOGRAPHS

Published under the supervision of a Committee of the
Faculty of Literae Humaniores in the University of Oxford

The aim of the Oxford Classical Monographs series (which replaces the Oxford Classical and Philosophical Monographs) is to publish books based on the best theses on Greek and Latin literature, ancient history, and ancient philosophy examined by the Faculty Board of Literae Humaniores.

Flesh and Spirit in the Songs of Homer

A Study of Words and Myths

MICHAEL CLARKE

CLARENDON PRESS · OXFORD
1999

OXFORD

UNIVERSITY PRESS

Great Clarendon Street, Oxford OX2 6DP

Oxford University Press is a department of the University of Oxford.
It furthers the University's aim of excellence in research, scholarship,
and education by publishing worldwide in

Oxford New York

Athens Auckland Bangkok Bogotá Buenos Aires Calcutta
Cape Town Chennai Dar es Salaam Delhi Florence Hong Kong Istanbul
Karachi Kuala Lumpur Madras Melbourne Mexico City Mumbai
Nairobi Paris São Paulo Singapore Taipei Tokyo Toronto Warsaw

and associated companies in Berlin Ibadan

Oxford is a registered trade mark of Oxford University Press
in the UK and certain other countries

Published in the United States
by Oxford University Press Inc., New York

British Library Cataloguing in Publication Data

Data available

Library of Congress Cataloging in Publication Data

Clarke, Michael (Michael J.)
Flesh and spirit in the songs of Homer: a study of words and
myths / Michael Clarke.
p. cm.—(Oxford classical monographs)
Includes bibliographical references and indexes.
1. Homer—Criticism and interpretation. 2. Epic poetry. Greek—
History and criticism. 3. Mythology, Greek, in literature.
4. Spiritual life in literature. 5. Body and soul in literature.
6. Homer—Knowledge—Psychology. 7. Future life in literature.
8. Greek language—Etymology. 9. Psychology in literature.
10. Self in literature. I. Title. II. Series.
PA4037.C495 1999
883'.01—dc21 99-30884
ISBN 0-19-815263-9

1 3 5 7 9 10 8 6 4 2

Typeset by Joshua Associates Ltd., Oxford
Printed in Great Britain
on acid-free paper by
Bookcraft (Bath) Ltd., Midsomer Norton

For my father
and in memory of my mother

Chuaigh mé amach as an chathair go dtí an áit a mbíonn an chuid is tréine de na fir ag snámh, ag Cladach an Daichead Troigh. Ach bhí barraíocht daoine ansin agus chuaigh mé bunús míle thart an chuan go cladach Dheilginse . . . Bhi anál na farraige do mo neartú go millteanach, go dtí go raibh mé do mo mhothachtáil féin fiáin. Cuireann aer na farraige brí mhillteanach ionam, go háirithe i m'intinn. Is iomaí uair a smaoinigh mé dá dtigeadh an fonn orm agus mé cois farraige go scríobhfainn leabhar a shíobfadh ballóg na claigne den mhórchuid den chine daonna. Ach ní raibh fonn scríbhneoireachta ar bith an lá seo orm.

S. Mac Grianna, *Mo Bhealach Féin*

PREFACE

This book is based on work that I began in 1990 and continued intermittently during the eight years that I spent at the universities of Oxford, Cambridge, and Manchester. I owe special thanks to James Clackson, Michael Crudden, Stephanie Dalley, John Dillon, Pat Easterling, Mark Edwards, Roy Gibson, Jasper Griffin, Richard Hunter, John Killen, Matthew Leigh, Torsten Meissner, Reviel Netz, Trevor Quinn, Keith Sidwell, Christiane Sourvinou-Inwood, Oliver Taplin, and the late J. F. Procopé, who have been kind to me and have given me the benefit of their scholarship. Jasper Griffin in particular read countless drafts with great patience, and I would have done little without his acute learning and his relentless criticism. Torsten Meissner helped me without stint in my attempts to understand words, and Michael Crudden read the final draft and made many invaluable suggestions and corrections; while the meticulous work of Julian Ward and Georga Godwin was an unlooked-for boon during copy-editing and production. I am also very grateful to Judith Mossman and to my nephew, James Clarke, and his family, who lent me their homes to write in. Otherwise my chief debts are to all my family and friends, to the music of James Taylor, and to Regan's Tara Bar in Dublin, Clowns Café in Cambridge, and above all the New Excelsior Restaurant in Oxford, where they made the best coffee in England.

As the book is founded on a doctoral thesis, the reader may be surprised to find that I have allowed little space to complicated disagreements with published scholarship. So much is written about Homer that the student will be hindered rather than helped if he lets other people's theories distract him from the job of grappling with the substance of the poems, which remain bitterly hard to understand from line to line. By trying to let Homer's words speak for themselves I have developed a habit of arguing through glossed quotations, which sometimes makes for exhausted reading: but I hope the argument will be clear if the reader is patient. Certainly the book would have become unmanageable if I had discussed all my tussles with the books and articles that I had to read as I went along. Many times when I read something, I would be greatly helped by one of its observations but would leave aside many of the others: this applies particularly to Bruno Snell's *Discovery of the Mind*, David Claus's *Toward the Soul*, Thomas Jahn's *Zum Wortfeld 'Seele-Geist' in der Sprache Homers*, Jan Bremmer's *Early Greek Concept of the Soul*, Arbogast Schmitt's *Selbständigkeit und Abhängigkeit menschlichen Handelns bei Homer*, and Ruth Padel's *In and Out of the Mind*. A few recent books that seemed at first sight to belong in the same area, such as Hayden Pelliccia's *Mind, Body and Speech in Homer and Pindar* and Christopher Gill's *Personality in Greek Epic, Tragedy, and Philosophy*, turned out to be so remote from what I had already written that there was nothing to be gained by adding discussions of them to the final drafts; and although I have perhaps learnt more about Greek life and thought from Christiane Sourvinou-Inwood than from any other scholar alive today, I found myself at loggerheads with the Homeric chapter in her *'Reading' Greek Death*, which I first saw in draft form in 1992. (Conversation reveals that the difference is less between our conclusions than in the objects of our enquiries: see Ch. 1, n. 64.) Of all the studies of Homeric psychology the only one that I found really compelling was R. B. Onians's *Origins of European Thought*, but even there I have had to disagree with many of its brilliant and eccentric insights. If it and the other monographs are referred to only very briefly, this is not because I have ignored them but because the ancient evidence must take precedence at all times. I can only apologise for the multiplication of errors and omissions that will have been caused by this policy.

M.J.C.

Dalkey
September 1998

CONTENTS

Part III: Death and the Afterlife

Part IV: The Shaping of Myth

TEXTS, ABBREVIATIONS, AND COMMENTARIES

References to books of Homer are indicated by Roman numerals, small capitals for *Iliad* and lower-case for *Odyssey*. Standard abbreviations are used for all other ancient authors and works: see the lists in Liddell, Scott, and Jones, *Greek–English Lexicon* (9th edn., 1940) and the *Oxford Classical Dictionary* (3rd edn., 1996).

Principal texts

Bacchylides, *Carmina cum Fragmentis*, post B. Snell ed. H. Maehler (Leipzig, 1992).
Hesiodi Opera: Theogonia, Opera et Dies, Scutum, ed. F. Solmsen; *Fragmenta Selecta*, ed. R. Merkelbach and M. L. West, 3rd edn. (Oxford, 1990).
Homeri Opera, ed. T. W. Allen and D. B. Monro, 3rd edn. (Oxford, 1920).
Homeri Ilias, ed. T. W. Allen (Oxford, 1931).
Homeri Odyssea, ed. P. von der Mühll, 3rd edn. (Leipzig, 1961).
Pindar, *Epinicia*, post B. Snell ed. H. Maehler (Leipzig, 1987).
Scholia Graeca in Homeri Iliadem, ed. H. Erbse (Berlin, 1969–88).
Scholia in Homeri Odysseam, ed. G. Dindorf (Oxford, 1855).

Abbreviations

Bernabé   A. Bernabé (ed.), *Poetae Epici Graeci, Testimonia et Fragmenta*, i (Leipzig, 1987)
Boisacq   E. Boisacq, *Dictionnaire étymologique de la langue grecque*, 4th edn. (Heidelberg, 1950)

Chantraine	P. Chantraine, *Dictionnaire étymologique de la langue grecque* (Paris, 1968–80)
D	E. Diehl (ed.), *Anthologia Lyrica Graeca*, 3rd edn. (Leipzig, 1949–51)
D–K	H. Diels and W. Kranz (eds.), *Die Fragmente der Vorsokratiker*, 6th edn. (Berlin, 1951–2)
Frisk	H. Frisk, *Griechisches etymologisches Wörterbuch* (Heidelberg, 1954–72)
H	P. A. Hansen (ed.), *Carmina Epigraphica Graeca Saeculorum VIII–V a. Chr. n.* (Berlin, 1983)
KRS	G. S. Kirk, J. E. Raven, and M. Schofield, *The Presocratic Philosophers*, 2nd edn. (Cambridge, 1983)
LfgrE	*Lexicon des frühgriechischen Epos*, ed. B. Snell *et al.* (Göttingen, 1979–)
L–P	E. Lobel and D. L. Page (eds.), *Poetarum Lesbiorum Fragmenta* (Oxford, 1955)
LSJ	H. G. Liddell, R. Scott, and H. S. Jones, *A Greek–English Lexicon*, 9th edn. (Oxford, 1940)
M	H. Maehler (ed.), *Pindari Carmina cum Fragmentis*, ii: *Fragmenta* (Leipzig, 1989)
M–W	R. Merkelbach and M. L. West (eds.), *Fragmenta Selecta*, in *Hesiodi Opera*, 3rd edn. (Oxford, 1990)
N	A. Nauck (ed.), *Tragicorum Graecorum Fragmenta*, 2nd edn. (Leipzig, 1926)
OCD[2]	*Oxford Classical Dictionary*, 2nd edn. (Oxford, 1970)
OCD[3]	*Oxford Classical Dictionary*, 3rd edn. (Oxford, 1996)
P	D. L. Page (ed.), *Poetae Melici Graeci* (Oxford, 1962)
PEG	D. L. Page (ed.), *Epigrammata Graeca* (Oxford, 1975)
RE	*Paulys Real-Encyclopädie der classischen Altertumswissenschaft*, ed. G. Wissowa *et al.* (Stuttgart, 1893–)
S–M	*Fragmenta*, in *Bacchylidis Carmina cum Fragmentis*, post B. Snell ed. H. Maehler (Leipzig, 1992)

Ventris-   M. Ventris and J. Chadwick, *Documents in My-*
Chadwick *cenaean Greek*, 2nd edn. (Cambridge, 1973)
W   M. L. West (ed.), *Iambi et Elegi Graeci*, 2nd edn.
                  (Oxford, 1989–92)

Commentaries *(referred to by commentators' names)*

Aeschylus, *Agamemnon*, by E. Fraenkel (Oxford, 1950).
Aeschylus, *Choephori*, by A. F. Garvie (Oxford, 1986).
Aeschylus, *Prometheus Bound*, by M. Griffith (Cambridge, 1983).
Bacchylides, *Die Lieder des Bacchylides*, by H. Maehler (Leiden, 1982; *Mnemosyne*, Suppl. 62).
Euripides, *Alcestis*, by A. M. Dale (Oxford, 1954).
Euripides, *Bacchae*, by E. R. Dodds, 2nd edn. (Oxford, 1960).
Euripides, *Helen*, by A. M. Dale (Oxford, 1967).
Hesiod, *Theogony*, by M. L. West (Oxford, 1966).
Hesiod, *Works and Days*, by M. L. West (Oxford, 1978).
Homer, *Iliad*, by W. Leaf, 2nd edn. (London, 1900–2).
Homer, *Iliad* xxiv, by C. Macleod (Cambridge, 1982).
The Iliad: A Commentary, general ed. G. S. Kirk (Cambridge):
   vols. 1–2, bks. i–iv and v–viii, by G. S. Kirk (1985–90);
   vol. 3, bks. ix–xii, by J. B. Hainsworth (1993);
   vol. 4, bks. xiii–xvi, by R. Janko (1992);
   vol. 5, bks. xvii–xx, by M. W. Edwards (1991);
   vol. 6, bks. xxi–xxiv, by N. Richardson (1993).
A Commentary on Homer's Odyssey, general ed. A. Heubeck (Oxford):
   vol. 1, bks. i–viii, by S. West; bks. v–viii by J. B. Hainsworth (1987);
   vol. 2, bks. ix–xii, by A. Heubeck; bks. xiii–xvi by A. Hoekstra (1989);
   vol. 3, bks. xvii–xx, by J. Russo; bks. xxi–xxii by M. Fernández-Galiano; bks. xxiii–xxiv by A. Heubeck.
The Odyssey of Homer, by W. B. Stanford, 2nd edn. (London, 1958–9).
The Homeric Hymn to Demeter, by N. J. D. Richardson (Oxford, 1974).
Pindar, *Works*, by L. R. Farnell, 3 vols. (London, 1930–2).

A Commentary on the Fourth Pythian Ode of Pindar, by B. K. Braswell (Berlin, 1988).

Theognis, *Le Premier Livre*, by B. A. van Groningen (Amsterdam, 1966).

PART I
Prologue

I
Homeric Words and Homeric Ideas

> I am a little world made cunningly
>   Of elements and an angelic sprite,
>   But black sin hath betrayed to endless night
> My world's both parts, and oh both parts must die.[1]

John Donne writes as if it were self-evident that man is a combination of two things, first the 'elements' of the physical body and then the soul hidden inside it. In that belief he shows that he is steeped in Christian and classical tradition; and to this day in Europe and America the conventions of language, thought, and what remains of religion are shot through with this same twofold structure of body and soul, brain and self, flesh and spirit. My aim is to gain an inkling of the earliest knowable ancestor of this idea of the 'little world' of man, by asking how the Greeks of the early first millennium BC conceived of human identity in relation to the visible substance of the body. Facing the remnants of their culture we must put aside dualistic assumptions and pose the question on a more basic level. Where is the seat of man's sense of himself, as it were his 'I'? Is there a spiritual being hidden inside what others can see and touch, or are his meat and blood somehow identical with his thinking self? Above all, what is thought to happen when he dies: does one part of him go to the afterlife and another remain on the earth? If so, how are the two parts separated—and has the survivor in the afterlife also been a distinct component in his make-up during mortal life? If instead there is no such separation, how does the myth of an afterlife square with the fact that the corpse has been burnt or been put in the ground to rot? Such are the questions we will try to answer.

[1] John Donne, *Holy Sonnets* 5. 1–4.

Reading Homer in isolation

The *Iliad* and *Odyssey* are the oldest sustained documents of
Greek tradition, so they are naturally our main source.[2] In
them we will be concerned with two distinct things: first,
implicit concepts of how consciousness and mental life take
place in relation to the body, and then explicit narratives of the
process through which the dying man ceases to be a living body
and becomes something else, whether buried remains or the
inhabitant of a world beyond the grave. These two epics would
loom large in any study of this kind: but I propose to take the
more unusual step of treating them largely in isolation, shun-
ning the evidence of archaeology and of later Greek literature
and religion. This is an austere restriction, and it will lead us in
different directions from others who have moved in the same
field.[3] Its simplest justification is a practical one, that since any
culture is complex and many-faceted we cannot fully understand one of its constituent traditions if we filter it through
half-digested evidence from others. By doing that we might
ignore the gulf between the different settings in which the
culture expresses itself, and circular arguments would await us
at every turn. Let me illustrate this by glancing at two famous
passages from Homer, passages which would be prominent in
any study of life after death and especially of the vital word
ψυχή, which translators have been content to render as 'soul'.
Both passages will be discussed more fully in their place, and
for the moment I cite them only as examples of my approach.

First, in a twice-repeated passage of the *Iliad* the ψυχή

---

[2] Special problems attend the inclusion of *Iliad* x and the last portion of the
Odyssey under the heading of 'Homer'. In the former case I have been content
to assume that the author of the Doloneia was deep enough in the mainstream
tradition of ἀοιδή for his language and ideas to be included with those of
Homer proper (cf. Hainsworth in vol. 3 of the Cambridge *Commentary*,
p. 155). On the problem of the Second Nekuia in *Odyssey* xxiv see appendix
to Ch. 6.

[3] Notably Sourvinou-Inwood (1995), the latest sustained study. Previous
monographs have tended either to move back and forth between literary and
archaeological evidence for religious belief (e.g. Schnaufer (1970), Vermeule
(1979), Garland (1985)) or to restrict themselves to the study of words as
opposed to religion or ideas (e.g. Claus (1981), Jahn (1987)). On Sourvinou-
Inwood's incisive study see also n. 64 below.

departs from the dying man and flies to Hades, wailing in
lamentation as it goes:

ὣς ἄρα μιν εἰπόντα τέλος θανάτοιο κάλυψε·
ψυχὴ δ' ἐκ ῥεθέων πταμένη Ἄϊδόσδε βεβήκει,
ὃν πότμον γοόωσα, λιποῦσ' ἀνδροτῆτα καὶ ἥβην.

(xvi. 855–7 = xxii. 361–3)

To make sense of this we must convert the lines into a mental
picture of what they mean; but they are very lean,[4] with only a
few significant words to guide us: ψυχή, ἐκ ῥεθέων, πταμένη . . .
βεβήκει, γοόωσα, λιποῦσα. As we will see in due course, nearly all
these words are difficult and ambiguous.[5] As we try to flesh
them out evidence from the visual arts springs quickly to mind,
especially for πταμένη, 'flying'. A Boeotian *larnax* of Mycenaean date has a winged figure on it which was long ago
identified as one of the dead;[6] and several centuries later
classical Greek vases depict the moment of death with a little
birdlike soul flying away from the dying body.[7] Further afield
the Egyptians depicted the spirit of the dead (*ba*) as a small

---

[4] On the simile in the second Nekuia, where the image is extended by
comparing the ψυχή to a bat (xxiv. 5–10), see Ch. 6, pp. 193, 213–14, and App.,
pp. 227–8.

[5] See Ch. 5, esp. pp. 151–6.

[6] See Vermeule (1979), 65; Immerwahr (1995).

[7] On artistic representations of ψυχή as a bird see Vermeule (1979), esp. 8,
17–19, 65; and for a possible literary correlate from roughly the same period
see Soph. *OT* 174–8. An allied but distinct problem is posed by images on
pots depicting psychostasy, where the souls that are weighed are again
depicted in the form of birds. The myth of psychostasy is not Homeric, but
was developed in classical times on the analogy of the Homeric image of the
weighing of κῆρες (xxii. 209–13; also perhaps in the *Aethiopis*, on which see
Bernabé's apparatus to Proclus' summary, lines 14–15). For example, in
Aeschylus' Ψυχοστασία the souls of Memnon and Achilles were apparently
weighed on stage (see schol. A on viii. 70, schol. bT on xxii. 209, complaining
that Aeschylus perverted Homer's image of κῆρες into one of ψυχαί). Although
the weighing of souls is to all appearances an innovation within the Greek
tradition, it has a striking Egyptian correlate in the weighing of *ba*-spirits as
well as in the medieval Christian image of the weighing of souls in St
Michael's scales (see Boase (1972), 34, figs. 22, 23). Vermeule (1979: 159–
62, with 246 n. 22) notes in a useful discussion that Greek artistic representations of the weighing vary the pattern considerably and do not always depend
either on κήρ or ψυχή.

figure with wings,[8] while Mesopotamian texts imagine the dead
in the afterlife as beings with feathers:

> To the house where those who enter are deprived of light,
> Where dust is their food, clay their bread.
> They see no light, they dwell in darkness,
> They are clothed like birds, with feathers.[9]

This flotsam is fascinating in its way, but I am not sure it can
help us to understand the Homeric passage on its own terms.
The suggestion that the figure on the *larnax* is one of the dead
depends solely on modern scholars' interpretation of these
same passages;[10] the bird-souls on the fifth-century pots are
very likely based on a reminiscence of Homer that was little less
imaginative than those of modern readers; and there can be no
guarantee whatever that a coincidence of imagery between
Mesopotamian or Egyptian material and the Greek poets
reflects a real connection in the ways that the two cultures
conceived of death.[11] To understand this poetry we ought to try
to listen as its first audience would have done, and accordingly
it is *within* the Homeric corpus that we will look to draw
meaning from the key word πταμένη, which is the only real
suggestion of birdlike flight in our passage. As we will see (in
Chapter 5) there are two other contexts where the idea of flight
is evoked in similar ways: first, the winged words of Homeric

[8] Compared with the Greek ψυχή by Vermeule (1979), 74–6.

[9] *The Descent of Ishtar to the Underworld*, ll. 7–10 in Dalley (1991), 155.

[10] On the dangers of trying to extract evidence of death-mythology from
Minoan and Mycenaean artefacts see Sourvinou-Inwood's searching study of
the myth of Elysium (1995: 32–56).

[11] If we tried to use the Mesopotamian image as an aid to interpreting the
Homeric passages—rather than merely as an interesting parallel—we would
have to deal with the fact that the feathery inhabitant of the Mesopotamian
underworld seems to be conceived as the physical substance of the dead—in
effect, a mythologized version of the corpse—rather than as something that
departs from it at death. This means that the link between the two images is
indirect at best. (On Mesopotamian death-beliefs see esp. the collection of
essays in Alster (1980).) There is a similar objection to the parallel of the
Egyptian *ba*: despite the resemblance of the *ba* in the shape of a human-
headed bird to the classical image of the birdlike ψυχή, the *ba* is not something
that escapes from the body at death; instead, it dwells in the tomb with the
corpse and only leaves temporarily to flit unseen into the upper world in the
hours of daylight (see Spencer (1982), 58–9, 184.)

speech, ἔπεα πτερόεντα, and then a group of passages where gods are likened to, or transformed into, flying birds when they soar between heaven and the world of men. If we set aside all remoter parallels and turn instead to these kindred images, we can try to anchor ourselves in the verbal substance of Homer rather than the pictures evoked by one isolated image in the modern imagination; and if we can then read the passage with a new and more tenacious understanding of flight and its significance in myth, or indeed in cosmology, I hope we will come a step closer to understanding what really happens to Homeric man when he dies and passes into the afterlife.

My second example relates to a later stage in the process of death, the moment when the corpse is ritually cremated. The passage is one of the most striking in Odysseus' visit to Hades, where his mother's ghost explains why the dead like herself are strengthless and insubstantial:

> ἀλλ' αὕτη δίκη ἐστὶ βροτῶν, ὅτε τίς κε θάνηισιν·
> οὐ γὰρ ἔτι σάρκας τε καὶ ὀστέα ἶνες ἔχουσιν,
> ἀλλὰ τὰ μέν τε πυρὸς κρατερὸν μένος αἰθομένοιο
> δαμνᾶι, ἐπεί κε πρῶτα λίπηι λεύκ' ὀστέα θυμός,
> ψυχὴ δ' ἠΰτ' ὄνειρος ἀποπταμένη πεπότηται.   (xi. 218–22)

On the face of it she is talking about two things, the destruction of the corpse by fire and the flitting movement of the ψυχή: that much is clear, but very little more. The sequence of ideas is very difficult, and it is deceptively easy to interpret the whole passage through a neat scheme of religious history. On common sense grounds it is easy to assume that the burning of the corpse must be the pivotal moment of the soul's journey to the afterlife,[12] and then to filter the passage through the modern—or at least post-Homeric—idea that the burning of the corpse is imagined as enabling the spirit to escape from the body.[13] Speculation about cremation can easily be influenced

---

[12] See Nagy (1990a: 85–126) for an argument based on Indo-European parallels between Homeric and Hindu material which emphasizes the place of the burning in the afterlife journey in a way that is not justified by what I can find in the observable meanings of ψυχή and related words in the texts. This does not imply that Nagy's argument is invalid, only that in terms of our present approach it could be said to put the cart before the horse.

[13] See e.g. Rohde (1925), 18–22, and cf. Schnaufer (1970), 58–63. The theme is common in Roman renderings of the journey of death—as

by armchair anthropology, for which it is a perfect 'rite of passage', and even more insidiously by the controversy over cremation and inhumation which has been carried forward from imperial times and re-created (for example) through the Catholic Church's insistence on inhumation.[14] Then inferences from archaeology creep in. As is well known, Mycenaean burial practice is dominated by inhumation, while later Greek practice is dominated by cremation;[15] given that cremation is central to the funerals described by Homer, one can infer that Anticleia is expounding a post-Mycenaean belief that the body must be dissolved by fire in order to release the soul for its journey to Hades.[16] But archaeological evidence for ritual practices is no guide to what the ancients thought they were doing when they carried them out, if only because the relationship between belief and symbolic action is always fluid and unguessable.[17] For us, however, the most telling point is that in other references to cremation Homer implies that its purpose is to fittingly honour the dead person, rather than to achieve the soul's departure to Hades. Further, in the *Little Iliad*—perhaps post-Homeric, but from the same cultural horizon[18]—the story was told that Ajax was buried without cremation expressly in order to dishonour him for having insulted Agamemnon and

Propertius' 'luridaque evictos effugit umbra rogos' (4. 7. 2)—but its Greek exemplar is not normal death-lore but the extraordinary story of Heracles' immolation on Mt. Oeta. This story is not directly attested in Homer, but it is worth noting that in the earliest Greek accounts Heracles is burned *alive*, as in Sophocles' *Trachiniae*. See also Stinton (1990).

[14] The change from cremation to inhumation in the early imperial period of Rome cannot be satisfactorily explained in terms of beliefs about the afterlife, and there is no evidence that it was linked to the rise of mystery religions, tempting though it is to associate inhumation with the Christian doctrine of bodily resurrection. See Morris (1992), 31–42; also Nock (1972), with detailed documentation. On the wider issues Morris (1987) is particularly helpful, along with Huntingdon and Metcalf (1979).

[15] See Ch. 6 n. 56.

[16] See e.g. Dodds (1951), 136–7.

[17] See Morris (1992: ch. 1, esp. 15–17) for a subtle treatment of this issue.

[18] Given that in the Nekuia (xi. 543–62) Homer alludes to Ajax' suicide in a way that fits exactly with the surviving accounts of the *Little Iliad*, it seems reasonable to guess that the idea of dishonourable inhumation accords with Homeric attitudes to the γέρας θανόντων. On the inhumation of Ajax see further Ch. 6, p. 187 with n. 62.

then killed himself. With this in mind, when we grapple closely with the grammar of Anticleia's words we will see that she is not saying that the ψυχή is released from the body by the action of the flame: both events take place after death, but she makes no causal link between them. This will enable us to read the passage in a way that is honest towards the Greek, so that we can focus on the problem which will turn out to be the kernel of understanding it: if θυμός escapes from the bones of the dying person (221), how does this event relate to Anticleia's statement that a ψυχή flutters or flits about, πεπότηται (222)? Only by struggling with this will we be able to trace the connection of ideas in her speech—and, incidentally, to wipe away the seeming discrepancy between it and what is implied elsewhere in the poem and throughout the *Iliad*, where the loss of ψυχή is the gasping out of the last breath.

I hope this restricted approach will bring us a little closer than we might otherwise have come to the mental world of Homer and his audience. It seems to me that it provides the only sure path to an accurate reading, because it makes no assumptions about the links between different species of tradition and creativity or simply about the way early Greeks used words and pictures to express ideas. But by remaining within the narrow ambit of two long poems we face the danger that they are thoroughly dead and divorced from their original context, so that no-one will contradict us if we analyse them wrongly. This means we must start with a careful discussion of what we think we will be doing as we try to interpret them.

Religion and world-picture

The outstanding difficulty is that we will be using language and narratives as sources for the sort of thing that would nowadays be called religious ideas. Clearly it would be glib and lazy to take the text to bits and heap all the relevant fragments of words and ideas together as witness to a single monolithic body of beliefs.[19] It seems a good (if unprovable) rule that epic or any

---

[19] This problem constantly recurs (to me at least) in reading Tillyard (1943), perhaps the most celebrated English essay in studying a world-picture through a body of literature, in this case principally Shakespeare and other Elizabethan literati. By explaining every passage he cites as a reflection of

other Greek genre should be regarded not as *celebratory* but as *exploratory*.[20] In matters of religion in particular the artist in words does not simply reproduce revealed truths, rather he explores the possibilities that are offered within a much broader framework; and it is not easy, not necessarily possible, for the modern reader to enter this framework. Here it is worth citing the example of Christiane Sourvinou-Inwood's recent work on this problem of interpreting Greek religion.[21] For Sourvinou-Inwood, creativity takes place in the gaps, or 'interstices', offered within what she defines as 'the parameters of established belief'.[22] If what reaches the light of day within these parameters is somehow coherent, that need not mean that it is simple; and it may raise problems rather than solve them. Sourvinou-Inwood distinguishes deeply rooted beliefs, ideologies, and 'collective representations'[23] on the one hand from their literary, cultic, and artistic 'articulations' on the other. Where a given image or belief is concerned, individual works of art, rituals, stories, and poems can come to birth in different ways while ultimately depending on a single cultural unity: and this unity is borne out because each articulation emerges according to a generative pattern or 'schema' which is itself fixed in the culture.[24] Our search, similarly, must be for the common patterns which inform different articulations of a

'Elizabethan belief', Tillyard effectively reduces the author's ideas to platitudes. Arguably the same problem recurs in more elusive forms in some works of intellectual history in the modern French tradition (e.g. Ariès (1981); McManners (1981)).

[20] Funeral orations are the only exception known to me.

[21] Sourvinou-Inwood (1991), (1995).

[22] For a brief exposition see Sourvinou-Inwood (1995), 10–16.

[23] Durkheim's all-encompassing phrase: see Evans-Pritchard (1965), 53–69.

[24] 'After the analyses of the individual articulations have taken place these different articulations should be compared to each other; this will determine the parameters of variation in the meanings articulated in that myth or mythological nexus . . . When such analyses are conducted, the inescapable conclusion is reached that the different versions of a myth, for example the myths of father–son hostility, are all shaped by a basic underlying schema which structures (with variations) all variants. This scheme is itself structured by, and thus expresses as "messages", perceptions which correspond to the social realities and ideologies of the society which produced them' (Sourvinou-Inwood (1991), 19–20).

single idea about the nature of human identity; and since the disparate images which we will study are all set in a single poetic tradition, our success will depend on identifying the structures—the equivalent of Sourvinou-Inwood's 'schemata'—which the poet follows when he brings this world to birth in verse.

It follows that nothing is to be gained by trying to extract systematic doctrine from what Homer says. This is a point on which even an unconscious analogy between Greek lore and established modern religion can be very misleading. Let me take an example from the tradition in which I myself happen to be steeped. Mary McCarthy in her *Memories of a Catholic Girlhood* tells a good story about the school lesson where she was taught the doctrine of the Resurrection of the Body.[25] She challenged the teacher with the case of the cannibal: if the atoms of his victims' bodies are incorporated into his flesh one after another until he dies, who will be given which atoms when their bodies are resurrected on the Last Day? The question is interesting, and not only to a subversive child—as it happens, medieval frescos of the resurrection of the dead on Judgement Day pursue the same doctrine to the point of showing wild animals vomiting out the bodies of people they have eaten;[26] and it is very instructive that the teacher's answer was that 'these are difficult questions *and the Church has answers for them*' (my italics). If this Catholic doctrine of the afterlife claims to be complete, coherent, and self-sufficient, with no loopholes or grey areas, it can do so because it purports to depend on divine revelation channelled through a book and a human institution founded and presided over by divinity. Homer and his Muse claim a different kind of authority, the authority of traditional tales told in a traditional poetic language, and it is not their purpose to express a world-view that could be worked out in so schematic a way. Where does that leave us if we want to talk meaningfully about the view of the world that they do in fact communicate? This Homeric worldview, or indeed the whole corpus of early Greek lore about the world, must not be seen as a flat plane with a jigsaw pattern of interrelated doctrines but as something more complex and

---

[25] McCarthy (1957), 88–91.   [26] Boase (1972), 37 with fig. 26.

open-ended: in the words of one scholar, a 'structured array of cultural foci . . . round each of which cluster various ideas, images and narrative motifs':[27] but by accepting that, are we debarred from seeking some overarching unity in what is expressed there among words and images and stories?

It will be respectable, if no more, simply to follow the working hypothesis that *in some way or other* the Homeric poems bear witness to a single significant cultural unity. We will 'interpret Homer out of Homer',[28] but with the emphasis less on Homer as an individual personality (whatever that means) than on the controlling influence of the tradition of hexameter epic, ἀοιδή, which informs the epics that go under his name. ἀοιδή, according to the hypothesis, communicates a view of man and the world that is coherent, independent, and self-sustained. No doubt its elements entered it from disparate external sources, whether in song or religion or older narratives; but within the tradition they came together in a controlled unity which can only be understood in terms of ἀοιδή itself. The simplest justification of this approach is as a case of Occam's razor—it is better to seek a simple and ordered interpretation than a complex and disordered one. If we credit Homer with a coherent view of the world we will look more vigorously for meaning than we would have done if we assumed in advance that he is capable of contradicting himself.[29] For example: when we face an array of passages hinging on the word κήρ (Ch. 7, *passim*), and at first sight they seem to refer to different ideas of the causation of death, the best policy will be to seek to uncover some common idea linking the passages, rather than simply to say that the poet or poets responsible had no coherent idea of what fate is. In this case,

---

[27] Mondi (1990), 145; for different versions of the same point see Herington (1985: ch. 3), and Gould (1985), with the deeper soundings of Veyne (1983). Buxton (1994: 155–65), also discusses the problem of a religious system where what we call beliefs are moulded by the contexts where they are enunciated. As an example of how to cope with the problem, I have been much helped by Sourvinou-Inwood's essay on 5th-cent. votive *pinakes* from Locris (1991: 147–88), insisting that 'no aspect of a deity has any significance when separated from its organic context' (150) and then exploring 'the double point of reference, narrative-mythological and conceptual' (156).

[28] On the original meaning of Aristarchus' policy see Porter (1992), 70–85.

[29] Is this the principle of anthropological charity?

indeed, I hope to be able to show that our initial impression of vagueness has little to do with κήρ itself and much more to do with the cultural baggage that we ourselves carry around in words like 'fate', 'doom', or even 'death'. If it really is true that there is no unity in this or any other department of Homeric ideas, the best possible proof would be our failure to find it in over three hundred pages.

Words and ideas

On its own, however, that argument is not enough. In practice our problem of cultural unity will loom largest in the issue of the relationship between language and ideas. For example, when we study the journey to the afterlife we will first try to understand the word ψυχή and then to interpret the narratives where it comes most clearly into prominence. As a simple word, as we will see, it denotes the dying man's last breath; but when the ψυχή of Patroclus or Hector flies to Hades we move from words to myth. By this I do not mean myth as a species of narrative, the sense in which the word is normally used by classical scholars;[30] for our purposes myth or 'the mythical' must be defined more as a way of describing the furniture of the world and the events of human life so that they are imbued with shapes and personalities of a kind that everyday eyes cannot see. With the flight of the ψυχή Homer goes beyond the horizon of visible experience and enters this higher, imagined plane of unseen things that can only be seen with the privileged vision of the poet or the god. Once we are on that plane, we must begin an overall study of the lore of Hades. But is it reasonable to move in a single investigation from the linguistic meaning of the word ψυχή to the cosmological or religious meaning of the ψυχή's journey to the Beyond? The difficulty is in the attempt to work on several levels of communication at once, ranging from a single problem of word-definition to complex poetic imagery and finally to over-all beliefs about human identity and life after death. If those beliefs can be approached at all they must be part of a world-picture, a system of received ideas about the nature of man and

---

[30] See e.g. Graf (1993), 1–8; Buxton (1994), 15.

things. This implies some kind of unity, a single vista rather than a collection of random and unrelated images. The enquiry will only make sense if there really is a single picture to be extracted from these words and myths; but the sceptic can object that there is no reason to believe that this is so, and that when we draw them together in that way we over-simplify the Greek realities or fit them into an artificial structure of our own making.

In a way this problem of language and ideas has less to do with Homer than with the complexities of the culture that you and I live in today. For example, no anthropologist who wanted to analyse modern Western beliefs about life after death would try to infer a coherent body of ideas from the resources available in everyday speech to render mortality, burial and the afterlife. These resources cannot be studied as a single system, because they have strayed in from chaotically disparate sources and many of them are literary fossils. Consider the following justly famous attempt to render the idea *'This parrot is dead'* in as many ways as possible in 1970s English:

I know a dead parrot when I see one and I'm looking at one right now . . . he's stone dead . . . That parrot is definitely deceased. He's demised, he's passed on; this parrot is no more, he has ceased to be, he's expired and gone to meet his Maker, he's a stiff; bereft of life he rests in peace; if you hadn't nailed him to his perch he'd be pushing up the daisies; he's off the twig, he's curled up his tootsies, he's shuffled off this mortal coil, he's rung down the curtain and joined the choir invisible; he's snuffed it; *vis-à-vis* the metabolic processes he's had his lot; all statements to the effect that this parrot is a going concern are from now on inoperative; this is an ex-parrot![31]

Ideas are flying from countless directions—Judaic scriptures, Anglican liturgy; hackneyed metaphors drawn from candles, leaves, business ventures, 'all the world's a stage' and other Shakespearean tags; the euphemistic association of death with sleep; polite periphrases and East End whimsy. The parts do not need to cohere with each other because each of them originates in a separate context and system of ideas. Any one

---

[31] 'Dead Parrot Sketch', on the recorded version entitled *Monty Python Live at Drury Lane*.

of these systems may be alive in the mind of the speaker or listener but may equally belong in a cultural context that is now thoroughly forgotten; and because the speaker flits between them and combines them with products of his own time, he can communicate effectively even when his images contradict each other flatly in their superficial meaning. If we were to subject them to the kind of questions that we will be asking of Homer, every phrase would yield a different answer. Sometimes the identity of the dead parrot is tied to the body, as 'he's a stiff'; sometimes it is tied to his spirit, as 'he's shuffled off this mortal coil'; sometimes it has been annihilated, as 'this is an ex-parrot'. There is no need to apologize for using an example from comedy, because the same sort of chaos would emerge if we tried to put together all the different images of death implied by the language of tombstones in a single churchyard, or even that of a single poet or theologian. Not only would they lack internal coherence, they would also relate in no clear or tangible way to any one system of beliefs about death, least of all those of the speaker himself. Because such language is hybrid and many-faceted and enmeshed in an endless process of cultural development, in its products we cannot hope to find an easy marriage between the elements of the speaker's repertoire, or still less between his words and the ideas they combine to express.

Any reader would agree that Homeric Greek is different from that, but it is harder to say what the difference is. At this point it would be easy to take refuge in one or another version of the oral theory, which has dominated Homeric studies in English since the initial influence of Milman Parry. Without relying on more than what can be observed within the poems themselves, we can take it that Homer represents a tradition, best called by its Greek name of ἀοιδή, in which neither composition nor performance depended on writing,[32] and in

---

[32] Despite the elegance of modern theory (esp. Goody (1977, 1987)), I cannot pretend to understand orality; but one point is vital. The gulf between the arts of oral and written composition is not necessarily as decisive as was formerly supposed, and it would be dangerous to follow Lord (1960: 129) in assuming that 'the two [techniques] could not possibly combine to form another, a third, a "transitional" technique'. This means that when we consider Homer in terms of oral composition, we mean only that the poetry

which verses and narratives are built up out of traditional and more-or-less formulaic patterns and units. *Ex hypothesi*, these patterns and units operate in tandem at every level of the poet's art. For example, on the largest scale an extended narrative might have come into being either as the reproduction of an inherited story, or as the articulation of a new story along a traditional pattern, or as a combination of both in the remoulding of an old story for a particular narrative or rhetorical purpose;[33] the sequence of a single scene might be structured through the manipulation of a traditional pattern or template;[34] while on the smallest scale a single line of verse might be a unit inherited *in toto* from Homer's forebears, or it might be a new line built on a traditional framework, or it might be a combination of formulaic word-groups in a traditional shape.[35] In each

takes its creative techniques, its repertoire, and its aesthetic from the oral tradition, not that the *Iliad* and *Odyssey* necessarily took their final shape in a non-literate environment. On this point, see Edwards (1988); Pohlmann (1990), 11; Schwabl (1990); Taplin (1992), 35–7; Thomas (1992), 44–50; but cf. West (1990) and Janko (1992: 29–38), defending the dichotomy (at least in a limited form) by guessing that a recognizably fixed version of each epic could not have emerged without written exemplars. Janko's latest contribution (1998) suggests (to me at least) that the debate on this question is no longer likely to be fruitful; while Nagy's most ambitious formulation (1996: 29–63) is a reminder of the complexity of what may have happened when an oral text was disseminated.

[33] On this I have learnt much from the long series of articles on Homeric deployment of myths as *paradeigmata*. Earlier concern with distinguishing tradition from invention (e.g. Willcock (1964), Braswell (1971); for a critique of their approaches see Nagy (1992*a*)) has been replaced by the principle that Homer or his characters adapt and remodel existing myths along traditional structural patterns for *ad hoc* purposes, so that a given articulation can be simultaneously traditional and creative. See in particular Bremmer (1988), on Phoenix' use of the story of Meleager in the context of Achilles' withdrawal from battle (IX. 524–605).

[34] Particularly useful here has been Fenik's study (1968) of the typical structures of battle-scenes, and his briefer essay (1978*b*) on monologue speeches; also Taplin (1992: 74–82) on the structures shared by different episodes of visit and hospitality. Fenik emphasizes the fluidity of Homer's use of these 'structural templates' by stressing the point that they have no independent status and exist only in each of the variant forms under which they are brought to birth. 'The notion of a single, definitive (i.e. perfect) archetype is misleading, for it is a concept drawn from the literary history of another age and time' (1968: 36).

[35] On Homer's manipulation of structural formulae and ready-made word-

case, the tradition moulds the poet's creativity both by drawing him along set structural patterns and by providing him with ready-made units of composition. If the poetry is dominated by such structures it makes sense to suppose that the tradition is speaking *through* the poet, rather than to regard him as struggling to express himself within strict and cramping limits. Here, then, is a way to begin pinning down the difference between Homer and the man with the dead parrot: there is less reason to expect a tension between the thing expressed and the vocabulary for expressing it, because both alike are part of a single tradition or the stock-in-trade of a single Muse. The poet's imagination and invention are shaped by ἀοιδή, and it prescribes both the things that are sung of and the words in which those things take shape.

Here again, however, the problem of language and ideas emerges in a new guise. The more we emphasize the controlling and directing power of this tradition, the greater the temptation to regard it as restrictive of poetic freedom and precision. The balance is difficult. When the oral hypothesis is crudely applied, it is easy to say that the sequence of individual words in Homer is vague and woolly because the poet is hampered by the need to fit his thought into shapes that are unwieldy *because* they are formulaic. Parry himself began with the (wholly subjective) assumption that epithets must be semantically insignificant because they serve a mechanical function in building the line out to the end of the sixth foot;[36] and even after half a century commentators continue to assume that formulaic language is inherently vague, as if the poet were trying in vain to wield words

---

groups in composition which is both traditional and creative, the most useful recent study has been Martin (1989), esp. 164–6.

[36] Note especially M. Parry (1971 [1928]), 127: 'The fixed epithet . . . adds to the combination of substantive and epithet an element of grandeur, but no more than that . . . Its sole effect is to form, with its substantive, a heroic expression of the idea of that substantive. As he grows aware of this the reader acquires an insensibility to any possible particularised meaning of the epithet, and this insensibility becomes an integral part of his understanding of the Homeric style.' Parry moves effortlessly from the experience of 'the reader' or 'the student' to that of the original audience of the epics and back to the communicative act of the bard himself.

with the freedom and suppleness that pen and paper would provide.[37]

This assumption is hard to avoid, because its roots are deep in the way that the modern world thinks about language and expects words to communicate ideas. A recent writer on this problem[38] has neatly identified what he calls 'the conduit metaphor', the pattern by which people tend to imagine words as packages filled with ideas, parcelled up by the speaker and sent to his listener to be opened up and understood. We 'capture an image in a poem', we 'put an idea into words', we 'load a sentence with meaning', it is 'pregnant with unspoken thoughts', and so on. Words are imagined as containers or receptacles of meaning, and it follows from this that any restriction on free choice in the selection of words will be imagined as preventing the poet from 'fitting' his ideas into precisely the right verbal shapes. One who brings this to bear on his reading may tend to assume that an oral Homer, composing in performance under acute pressure of time, must have done this job less deftly than a literate poet with liberty to rub things out and revise them; and consequently that reader will be discouraged from listening to Homer's individual words as closely as he might.

This is why I want to follow a more flexible and positive model for Homeric communication, relying on the minimal assumption that the poet's ideas are not squeezed into words but take shape in and through those words, with the verbal signs corresponding precisely to the poetic meanings conveyed. On one level this can be well expressed in the words Phemius himself chooses to describe his inspiration, where the Muse has 'planted' the ways of song in his mind,

$$\theta\epsilon\grave{o}s \ \delta\acute{\epsilon} \ \mu o\iota \ \dot{\epsilon}\nu \ \phi\rho\epsilon\sigma\grave{\iota}\nu \ o\ddot{\iota}\mu\alpha s$$
$$\pi\alpha\nu\tau o\acute{\iota}\alpha s \ \dot{\epsilon}\nu\acute{\epsilon}\phi\upsilon\sigma\epsilon\nu \ . \ . \ . \quad (xxii. \ 347-8)$$

and it can equally be rendered in the more sober language of scholarship: as J.B. Hainsworth has recently written, 'the structures, patterns and other generative processes of the poetical grammar [are] primary and the formulas an incidental

---

[37] See now the shrewd critique by Bakker (1997: 13–15 and *passim*).
[38] Reddy (1993).

result of their use.'[39] The implication is that word and idea are tailor-made for each other. A version of the same principle has been formulated by Gregory Nagy:

The formulaic heritage of these compositions is an accurate reflection of their thematic heritage. Such a theory helps account for the problems raised by Parry's theory of the formula. Did the poet really *mean* this or that? Did he really *intend* such-and-such an artistic effect? My general answer would be that the artistic intent is indeed present—but that this intent must be assigned not simply to one poet but also to countless generations of previous poets steeped in the same traditions . . . The key is not so much the genius of Homer but the genius of the overall poetic tradition that culminated in our *Iliad* and *Odyssey*.[40]

In short, the poet is the master and not the slave of his inheritance, while at the same time his creativity is intimately united with the canons which the tradition prescribes; so that when he expresses a world-picture in words and stories, his own creative power is part and parcel of what that world-picture is. There is a perfect harmony between form and meaning, between the nuts and bolts of formulaic language and the ideas that the language aims to convey. Ideas take shape in words and words take shape in verse, so Homeric ideas cannot be considered in isolation from Homeric craft. Here, then, is one way to avoid the charge that the method is crude and simplistic: it will turn out that although Homer's scattered images of human identity and ψυχή are more than a patchwork, none the less they are not a seamless garment, because the coherence of the parts will reveal itself only when they are considered in terms of poetic creativity as well as beliefs and concepts as such.

[39] Hainsworth (1993), 3. There is now little support for the more dogmatic version of Milman Parry's contention that the mechanics of Homeric verse-making deprive certain words of active meaning. In particular, his basic argument about the interchangeability of name-epithet formulae has had to be much modified, and the claim that 'no noun-epithet formula which certainly forms part of a traditional system of noun-epithet formulae can contain an epithet whose meaning can be particularised' (1971 [1928]: 130) has been countered in many studies of the deftness with which Homer seems to choose between such epithets in practice (see e.g. Austin (1975), 1–80; Vivante (1980); Tsagarakis (1982); Sacks (1987); and cf. Hainsworth (1968), 9–11).

[40] Nagy (1979), 3; see also 78–9 and *passim*. Compare Latacz (1984), 17–20.

This point is worth comparing with the highly ambitious
theory of Homeric poetics advanced first by C. H. Whitman[41]
and later extended by M. N. Nagler.[42] Whitman approaches
the problem of unity from both ends: he argues first that
certain complex images and narratives are 'formulae acted
out',[43] that is manifestations on the largest scale of ideas that
are already implicit in the smaller units of the poet's repertoire,
and then moves to the largest level with the principle that a
single connection of ideas or images can be articulated in
different guises to create a single poetic meaning. In the
Iliad, for example, he shows that fire is associated with war
and warrior fury in contexts as diverse as single word-
meanings, formulae, similes, extended descriptions of warriors,
and the imagery used of the god Ares.[44] Nagler, moving
further from the ground, holds that a set of disparate
images, formulae, and meanings can arise from a single
embedded traditional idea, a 'preverbal *Gestalt*', which is
prior to each of the many manifestations ('allomorphs')
under which it appears on the surface of the poet's words.
The core of the argument is that meaning is generated
through, and not in spite of, the poet's willingness to mould
his lines and his narratives according to traditional patterns
and structural templates.[45] Such approaches offer one route to
unities behind the multiplicity of Homeric ideas and images,
but by definition the unities are remote and inaccessible. In
particular, Nagler's 'preverbal *Gestalt*' is prior both to any
form of words and to the sense it expresses, so that it becomes
impossible to pin down.[46] What remains fruitful (in my view

[41] (1958).

[42] (1967), (1974).

[43] (1958), 102–27, esp. 119.

[44] Ibid. esp. 128–53.

[45] In summary, Nagler (1974: 199) stresses 'the fact that so much of the oral
poet's meaning is deeply embedded in the generative impulses that underlie
his habits of poetic speaking, so that poetic meanings, for example, often
provide the most adequate definitions of the "deep structures" of his poetic
language'.

[46] See e.g. Nagler (1974: 33) on 'the dimensional network of potentialities
of sound, sense and even rhythm'. On the potential for vagueness and whimsy
of Nagler's and Whitman's approaches see Silk (1974), 63–70; Kahane (1994),
13–14. Of course, the fact that an interpretative strategy involves this danger
does not mean *ipso facto* that it is invalid.

at least) is the more limited point that ideas, words, and narratives are generated together and should not be separated out from each other: in Nagy's words again, 'form and content conceptually overlap'.[47]

Let me illustrate this with a glance at two well-known problems. When the Trojans attack the Achaeans' makeshift stockade Homer sounds as if he is describing something more like a siege at an elaborate city wall, made of stone and equipped with turrets, bastions, and the like (see e.g. XII. 52–9, 258–60, with VII. 336–43, 435–41); and the latest commentator explains this with the guess that the poet does not know any suitable formulae for describing a simple stockade.[48] My answering guess might be that the elevated rendering is part of the elevated depiction of the world which is the proper subject of poetry in Homer's tradition, so that if he *wanted* to describe it as a rickety stockade he would no longer be Homer. At the same time, the fact that he begins the narrative with a simple construction, but seems gradually to increase its scale and grandeur as the story-line progresses, is important as an example of the way Homeric ideas take shape in words.[49] Again, when Achilles defies the Embassy his complaint falls into a series of unanswered questions (IX. 334–43), and one scholar explains this on the grounds that the epic language is incapable of expressing anti-heroic ideas.[50] Instead, we might say that it is in the nature of ἀοιδή that the poet can go as far as Achilles goes, but no further, in producing a speech that rejects the

[47] (1992*b*), 27.

[48] See Hainsworth at XII. 54–7: 'That [sc. a stockaded earthwork] is the sort of structure the circumstances would demand and permit, yet the poet seems to describe a more substantial edifice, being constrained perhaps by the traditional diction for an assault on a city'. Hainsworth advances a similar argument to explain the apparent obscurities of the passage in which Odysseus builds a raft for himself (V. 243–61): 'Homer . . . has omitted various parts and operations. The reason for his doing so is possibly the fact that, having no traditional formulae for the construction of a raft, he borrows from a description of shipbuilding such as would be required for the story of the Argo' (note *ad loc.*).

[49] For the principle, compare the elaborate and even palace-like proportions which Achilles' encampment takes on during the visit of Priam (XXIV. 443–56).

[50] A. Parry (1956). For a critique of the argument, and especially the implied definition of 'language', see Reeve (1973); also Martin (1989), 146–61.

ethical canons of the heroic world. When his defiance of the
system is circumscribed as it is, the cause lies in the substance
of Homeric ideas as much as in the mechanics of how he can
clothe them in words. Tradition and originality are indistinguishable: the poet's identity is moulded by his inheritance, but
there is no tension in the union.

Poetic language and poetic ideas

The word 'poetry' continues to give trouble. When we say
that this language is poetic, that can easily suggest that it is
lyrical (in the modern sense) or allusive or otherwise less
straightforward an instrument of communication than was
(for example) the idiom of everyday speech in the Aegean
area in the eighth century BC. To generalize about the modern
English tradition, today the defining character of poetry tends
to be taken to be one or both of two things, metrical or verbal
music and the way language is wielded to express ideas. The
former cannot be our concern here, since the music of Homeric poetry is lost[51] and we cannot usefully guess at its
emotional effect on its audience, the Greek equivalent of the
feeling that made the bristles stand up on Housman's chin
while shaving.[52] Instead, our concern is with images, meanings, ideas; and under this aspect today's poetry is defined as
such by its departure from everyday idiom, by the fact that it
pushes words beyond the limits of what they do in normal
communication. 'Everyday' and 'normal' are loose words here,
but there is no avoiding them. When the poet goes beyond the
ordinary patterns of language he is supposed to create something new and individual, something in fact which his
language was not designed to express:

[51] For example, Kirk's essay (1985: 17–37) on what he calls 'the interplay
between diction and meaning' (17) cannot be presented as more than a
description of the structures observable in the *written* shapes of Homeric
sentences.

[52] Housman (1933). Housman makes a half-explicit attack on T. S. Eliot's
influence in his own generation when he denies that there is 'any such thing as
poetical ideas' and pins his sense of the poetic on something that is by
definition intangible and irreducible to verbal meaning.

> as imagination bodies forth
> The forms of things unknown, the poet's pen
> Turns them to shapes, and lends to airy nothing
> A local habitation and a name.[53]

Call this vague or romantic or self-inventing, but it remains with us whenever the word 'poetry' is used. The hallmark of creativity is the poet's *distortion* of language. Compare T. S. Eliot, writing about his sense of what his profession means:

Poets in our civilisation, as it appears at present, must be *difficult*. Our civilization comprehends great variety and complexity, and this variety and complexity, playing upon a refined sensibility, must produce varied and complex results. The poet must become more and more comprehensive, more allusive, more indirect, in order to force, to dislocate if necessary, language into his meaning.[54]

In our own generation even a poet as personally self-effacing as Seamus Heaney portrays himself in the same way:

The crucial action [in making a poem] is pre-verbal, to be able to allow the first alertness or come-hither, sensed in a blurred or incomplete way, to dilate and approach as a thought or a theme or a phrase. [Robert] Frost put it this way: 'A poem begins as a lump in the throat, a homesickness, a lovesickness. It finds the thought and the thought finds the words.'[55]

The principle that the meanings conveyed in poetic language are subtle, many-layered, and ambiguous, in the sense made famous by William Empson,[56] is simply a less lyrical way of expressing this same perception. The poet 'makes his words work harder and pays them extra': it is only by distorting and manipulating the norms of non-poetic language that he can ply his art, and correspondingly it is only by referring back to those norms that his readers or listeners can makes sense of his utterances. Since the poet rides on the back of the language of everyday communication, we could not appreciate his language without referring first to the lower register of contemporary prose or speech, and by the same token it would be

---

[53] Shakespeare, *A Midsummer Night's Dream* v. 1. 14–17.
[54] (1921), 65.   [55] (1980), 49.
[56] (1930), *passim*.

absurd to try to teach poets' English to foreigners as an independent language.[57]

But if Homer is poetry it is poetry of a different order. If it is an artificial dialect, a *Kunstsprache*, what does that mean? Evidently it is moulded not by an individual creative intellect but by a tightly organized tradition, and its purpose—ostensibly at least—is not to find words for the almost-inexpressible but to tell high tales in the appropriate high form.[58] If it is effective it is so because it tells them fully and clearly within the boundaries set by its proper expressive resources. It follows that Homeric language cannot have depended on the everyday language in the parasitic modern way. Certainly it must have drawn its elements from unmarked speech of different places and periods, but in itself it is complete and self-sufficient, and it must have been more fully and decisively marked off from everyday speech than is any kind of literary language current today. The tradition of composition must have been transmitted from teacher to apprentice bard, and a rigorous control of the metre, formulae, and the rules of word-building must have been necessary before anything like Homeric composition could have been achieved.[59] Consequently the extreme regularity of the epic diction is proof in itself of the strength and autonomy of the linguistic tradition which the author of our epics must have inherited from his teachers. Naturally the

---

[57] It is possible that a similar relationship exists between ordinary classical Greek and the artificially elevated language of Attic tragedy: as Aristophanes says of Aeschylus, the language of the poet is αὐθαδόστομος (*Frogs* 837). Perhaps the Greek of Homer sounded distant or elevated to 5th-cent. people in something like the same way; but that aesthetic sense should not be projected back to poet or even audience in the creative phase of the Homeric tradition.

[58] Cf. Martin (1989), 238: '[The Homeric poem] is an authoritative speech-act, initiated by a request for information, which is then recounted at length. The key word for this interpretation is the verb ἔννεπε, "tell"'. On the framing of cultural authority in the epic tradition see more generally Havelock (1963).

[59] Vital here, but beyond the scope of this study, is the strength of the poetic education that must have been passed from poet to pupil in something like the manner of the choral schools. See Nagy's thought-provoking treatment of the cultural implications of the development of γραμματικός education in the face of the old choral tradition (1990c); also cf. Robb (1994), esp. 183–213; and on the choral schools themselves see esp. Calame (1977), i. 385–411, and more generally Buxton (1994), 23.

dialect must have changed with changes in the spoken language, as otherwise it would have become unintelligible; but that need not have deprived it of its independent life.[60] Given all this, it makes sense to proceed on the assumption that within its metrical and aesthetic discipline it communicates just as directly, just as literally, as any ordinary species of language.

In fact this principle has always been familiar in studies of the nuts and bolts of epic language. The scholar who faces a hard word tries to infer its meaning on the strength of Homeric instances alone, then turns to other early hexameter verse, and only as a last resort does he look to other evidence in Greek or cognate languages. The implication is that the poet's word-hoard is locked away from the rest of language, and when he opens it his songs are distanced from all other utterances by the loftiness of dialect and metre as well as by the social role and heritage that gives him the authority of a teacher. Hence Homeric words have Homeric meanings, and they belong in a separate lexicon. If this is sound, it is only a short step to treat ἀοιδή as if it created not only its own language but its own view of the world. This principle applies most obviously to motifs and story-patterns, but can also be extended to ideas of the kind that our own culture might call religion. There is undoubtedly a two-way relationship between Homeric conceptions and early cultic practice, but external influences on the epic tradition need not have deprived it of its cultural autonomy. As for the possible influence of images from the visual arts, we can do no better than take the poet's own word for the relationship between sight and poetic evocation:

Ἔσπετε νῦν μοι, Μοῦσαι, Ὀλύμπια δώματ᾽ ἔχουσαι,
ὑμεῖς γὰρ θεαί ἐστε, πάρεστέ τε, ἴστε τε πάντα,
ἡμεῖς δὲ κλέος οἶον ἀκούομεν οὐδέ τι ἴδμεν . . . (II. 484–7)

---

[60] Cf. Janko (1992), 12: 'Not even the feeblest bards composed merely by stringing formulae together; poets always drew on their changing vernacular as they recreated and adapted the old tales, and the more striking or useful phrases entered the tradition, ultimately to become curious archaisms on the lips of singers hundreds of years younger'. But if a given poet was truly master of his craft, would these 'curious archaisms' have been any less meaningful to him and his peers than was the rest of his linguistic repertoire?

It is in this sense that Homer is blind:[61] he assimilates and re-creates tradition entirely within his hexameters, and what might be seen with the eyes bears only the dimmest relation to what comes to birth in language. If the tradition is strong and supple enough to exert a controlling power over the elements of imagery which it deploys, then our own interpretation must proceed in the same way, within the closed world of the hexameters.

The integrated study of Homer

Any argument that emphasizes the cultural unity of ἀοιδή will go against the grain of much Homeric scholarship, where the learned stress the fact that different elements have been culled from different sources in Greek and pre-Greek history to form a patchwork. Stock examples tend to come from matters of material culture. We know it would be pointless to try to describe (say) 'the Homeric shield' when art and archaeology show that the various names and descriptions of Homeric shields—ἀσπίς, σάκος, figure-of-eight shield, tower-shield, and so on—correspond to different kinds of shield used between early Mycenaean times and the time of composition.[62] But this point concerns the description in ἀοιδή of things that exist in the visible world, and it need not be extended to things that belong in the realm of the unseen and the imagined—religion, myth, psychology, everything that takes shape in word alone. Although we cannot talk about 'the Homeric shield' as a single kind of artefact, nevertheless we can hope for a coherent picture if we try to understand the ethics and psychology that Homeric characters exemplify when they defend themselves with those shields. If the poet is master of his language, or at the very least guided by the inheritance of language, ideas, and cultural authority that he calls his Muse,[63] then things that

---

[61] Cf. *h. Ap.* 172–3.

[62] See e.g. F. H. Stubbings in Wace and Stubbings (1962), 510–13. The analogy of the shield is cited by Sourvinou-Inwood (1995: 12–14) in defence of her willingness to analyse Homeric death-mythology with the prior assumption that it is an artificial amalgam (n. 64 below).

[63] On the Muse as a mythical embodiment of the poet's inheritance see Murray (1981: 100), arguing that the Muse is responsible not only for

belong in that inheritance alone will be fully in his power; so
that where those things are concerned it makes sense to follow
the belief that the poet or the tradition is speaking with a single
authoritative voice.[64] If there is unity in the Homeric conception of mental life or life after death or anything else, the
controlling harmony must lie in the independence and integrity
of the tradition of ἀοιδή itself. So we come full circle: if the
'Homeric world-picture' is coherent it is so because it is poetic,
not in spite of that fact.

I propose, then, that within the Homeric ambit linguistic,
literary, narrative, mythical, and religious elements are all
linked and do not belong in different categories of enquiry.
This need not lead to chaos, and it can enrich even the most
straightforward attempt to find meaning in words. Let me
illustrate this from an unusually clear example, similar in
kind to many that will appear in the following chapters.
Suppose I were trying to write about the Homeric view of
fear about the future. I might begin with the famous words in
which Nestor says that the battle by the ships may turn out in
disaster:

νῦν γὰρ δὴ πάντεσσιν ἐπὶ ξυροῦ ἵσταται ἀκμῆς
ἤ μάλα λυγρὸς ὄλεθρος Ἀχαιοῖς ἠὲ βιῶναι.   (x. 173–4)

Because the phrase 'on the razor's edge' has become proverbial
in Greek[65] and then in English tradition,[66] the sense of these

'inspiration' in an intangible or mystical sense but also for 'the technical
aspects of poetic creativity'. Cf. also Vernant (1985), 109–36; Gentili (1988),
ch. 1, esp. p. 8.

[64] In particular, this means that our assessment of the Homeric afterlife (in
Ch. 6) will differ radically from that of C. Sourvinou-Inwood in her recent
study (1995: esp. 76–94). Sourvinou-Inwood replaces the misleading traditional distinction between tradition and invention with the formulation that
the traditional poet innovates within the 'interstices' that exist within 'the
parameters of established belief', and goes on to distinguish two versions of
the afterlife, one in which the dead are as strong and substantial as the living
and one in which they are 'witless shades', taking it that the first of these
belongs in fossilized fragments inherited by Homer and the other corresponds
to the beliefs of Homer's own time. The opposition is not unlike that which I
will try to sketch between 'dead man as corpse' and 'dead man as wraith', but
with the difference that in this study I will regard the *intermingling* of the two
conceptions as the key to the whole scheme (see Ch. 6, pp. 207–15).

[65] See Simon. 12 PEG; Thgn. 557.

[*See p. 28 for n. 66*]

lines can seem deceptively simple. Once the cliché is forgotten
it becomes harder to grasp. Nestor is imagining two possibilities, one an abstract noun, the other an infinitive verb,
balanced on a sharp pivot (ξυροῦ ἀκμή) and about to fall in
one or other direction. Determined to interpret Homer out of
Homer, how can we shed further light on this? First, we recall
the scales that Zeus suspends over the battlefield to determine
the issue of a finely balanced combat: once when the two armies
struggle across the battlefield (VIII. 69–74), once when the
death-bringing κῆρες of Achilles and Hector are weighed
against each other (XXII. 209–13).[67] The latter is the more
famous example:

καὶ τότε δὴ χρύσεια πατὴρ ἐτίταινε τάλαντα,
ἐν δ' ἐτίθει δύο κῆρε τανηλεγέος θανάτοιο,
τὴν μὲν Ἀχιλλῆος, τὴν δ' Ἕκτορος ἱπποδάμοιο,
ἕλκε δὲ μέσσα λαβών· ῥέπε δ' Ἕκτορος αἴσιμον ἦμαρ,
ᾤχετο δ' εἰς Ἀίδαο . . .   (XXII. 209–13)

Zeus arranges, ἐτίταινε, the scales, then one pan falls down and
marks the destruction of the loser. Something that stands
wobbling on the ἀκμή of a ξυρός exactly corresponds to the
uncertain movement of the pans of a balance, and the match
between the two passages centres above all on the idea that
defeat or disaster is the falling of one of the two possibilities.[68]
The thought and the verb are identical when another character
looks forward to defeat in battle by saying that destruction will
'fall down' for the Achaeans, ἡμῖν δ' αἰπὺς ὄλεθρος ἐπιρρέπῃι (XIV.
99). This idea of perfect balance, the uncertain state before the
fall, is built up again under a different guise in an extraordinary
simile during the Trojan assault on the Achaean stockade:

ἔχον ὥς τε τάλαντα γυνὴ χερνῆτις ἀληθής,
ἥ τε σταθμὸν ἔχουσα καὶ εἴριον ἀμφὶς ἀνέλκει
ἰσάζουσ', ἵνα παισὶν ἀεικέα μισθὸν ἄρηται·
ὣς μὲν τῶν ἐπὶ ἶσα μάχη τέτατο πτόλεμός τε.   (XII. 433–6)

---

[66] I think the phrase has entered the language directly from Chapman's
translation: see *OED* s.v. 'razor'.

[67] Compare also XVI. 658, XIX. 223.

[68] Cf. Bianchi (1953), 77–85; Dietrich (1965), 294–6.

The deadlock between two sides is 'stretched out' like when a spinning-woman extends a pair of scales to weigh her wool.[69] We can dig still deeper into the bowels of the language. From an external point of view all these passages describe what in English would be called chance or fate or fortune, but from the psychological point of view they can be seen as externalized depictions of fear and uncertainty. Turning to Homeric verbs for fear, it is remarkable that δέδοικα seems (if no more) to be related etymologically to the root of δύο, 'two'.[70] The explanation is captured in something Odysseus says when he warns Achilles of the peril to the Greek ships from the Trojan onslaught:

> ἀλλὰ λίην μέγα πῆμα, διοτρεφές, εἰσορόωντες
> δείδιμεν· ἐν δοιῆι δὲ σαωσέμεν ἢ ἀπολέσθαι
> νῆας ἐϋσσέλμους, εἰ μὴ σύ γε δύσεαι ἀλκήν. (IX. 229–31)

Odysseus says the warriors fear, δείδιμεν, a future disaster because the safety or destruction of the ships is in δοιή, a state of 'doubleness': the *figura etymologica* bears out the verbal meaning.[71] Twin possibilities lie balanced and one or the other will lead to disaster if it is realized: it is hard to express the literal meaning of the Greek except by picturing them as lying in the pans of a balance or poised on the ἀκμή of a central pivot.

In this collection we have grasped—or can plausibly claim we have grasped—a single nexus of ideas manifested on four different levels of expression. The question of priority could easily be posed between them. The 'razor's edge' might be a miniature version of the scales of Zeus, or alternatively the latter might be a theological amplification of the former; the spinning-woman's scales might be a stylish variant on either of them; again, the three could be grouped together as different ways of working out the implications of the idea captured in the

---

[69] Similarly Zeus stretches out the battle equally on both sides, κατὰ ἶσα μάχην ἐτάνυσσε Κρονίων (XI. 336). Compare also the kindred simile of the carpenter's rule at XV. 410–13.

[70] See Benveniste (1971), 253–4.

[71] No consensus exists on the implications of lines where two cognate words seem to chime with each other in a so-called *figura etymologica*. Should the Homeric *figura etymologica* be classed as (*a*) a recognition of linked meanings between cognate words or (*b*) something akin to a pun? See most recently Reichler-Béguelin (1991), and cf. Hainsworth (1968), 36–8.

word δοιή, and hence be referred back to an ancient (and Indo-European, not merely Greek) identity between fear and 'doubleness'. But nothing in the evidence allows us to arrange these as if one caused or inspired the other, and to give priority to any one of them would be to ignore the internal complexity of the tradition. How, then, does the comparison advance our reading of Homer? If we are content to accept that our pieces of evidence are all closely related, and leave it at that, then we can safely use each to enhance our understanding of the others' meaning, if only because we now have a better sense of the mental picture that each sequence of words is meant to evoke. To put it another way, the links between them suggest that a certain set of abstract ideas is connected in the Homeric world in a way that might not make immediate sense in our own. Some cultural reality occupies the common ground between our passages, some underlying conception of what fear or uncertainty or doubleness *is*. This never takes shape directly on the surface of what is said, but its presence is felt in each of our passages, and we can gain some inkling of it by comparing them. Within the controlled discipline of ἀοιδή the things that our own culture would class as a myth, a metaphor, a simile, and a semantic field are mutually dependent ways of giving shape—Homeric, poetic, imagined shape—to a single idea of what happens in the moment when a conflict is evenly matched and its outcome is about to be decided. To use the terms which will appear throughout our discussion: the underlying idea is a *concept* of what uncertainty about the future means; and in different passages this concept is *articulated* or brought to birth in different ways. What is articulated in each case is an *image:* we grasp the image by following Homer's words, and we try to delve closer to the level of the concept by studying the observable links between disparate but kindred images. By identifying those links we come closer to the kind of sense that Homer's audience must have apprehended when they listened to each myth or figure or word within the framework of ἀοιδή, and so we aim ourselves to grasp something of the underlying unity. In this way, to return to the word that has been troubling me, the passages work together as witness to a single element of the Homeric *world-picture*.

Semantic reconstruction

The nub of what we have proposed is trust in the belief that epic poetry is an effective means of communication between poet and audience; and since our main concern will be to take words seriously as an index to ideas, to implement this trust we must begin our study of each department of Homeric ideas by looking with almost myopic closeness at the words that belong in it. Here I need to state a few points of policy that cannot be justified a priori. Faced with each question of interpretation we will prefer to treat the word in question as meaningful rather than the reverse. The fact that a word serves a mechanical function, for example as an epithet in part of a system of name-epithet formulae, will not stop us from trying to sketch its semantic range by comparing its various contexts.[72] More contentious will be our attitude to ill-attested words that defy translation. When we look at a word whose attestations cannot be fitted into a single semantic range that makes good sense in English, we will be unwilling to identify it as what has been called an 'iconym', that is a word whose sound or traditional associations make it appropriate to certain contexts but which fails to have any denotative meaning at all.[73] Similarly, we will

---

[72] Here there will be need of some juggling, because we must allow for the possibility that the semantic edges of a word may be blurred when it is assimilated into such a system. This point will prove important in our study of θυμός, φρένες, ἦτορ, and the related psychological entities: here Homeric practice suggests that each of these is identified with a distinct organ in the chest, while in the rendering of mental life their names are interchanged so freely that they are best understood as a system of virtual synonyms whose names denote a single process of psychological ebb and flow (Ch. 4, pp. 63–4).

[73] Silk (1983), 312: 'An iconym has no circle, no centre. It has only a few faint scattered connotations: a set of random associations, like ghostly rings, perhaps randomly overlapping, but largely unrelatable, and all in all leading nowhere. The random associations will consist partly of earlier literary contexts (from which the knowledge of the word presumably comes), partly, perhaps, of aural associations of the kind that we tend to read as "re-etymology". There is a diffuse reference, then, too diffuse to begin to derive a referent from it' (for a corresponding approach to—or escape from—interpretation see e.g. Chantraine, s.v. ἀμαιμάκετος). If Homeric poetry was produced for an audience and without drawing on pre-existing fixed texts which were no longer fully understood, it is difficult to see how any Homeric word could have operated as an iconym, except in the case of epithets and a

be slow to accuse the poet of having misunderstood or mis-
interpreted an item in his linguistic inheritance.[74] It makes
good sense to reserve such explanations for the last resort when
all other avenues of interpretation fail. Given the gulf of time
and cultural change between Homer and us, it will always be
possible that a Homeric word has a meaning whose coherence
is hidden by our ignorance or presuppositions.

In fact our main concern will be with words that pose just
that problem. If the lexical subtleties of an Homeric word can
be culturally significant in the same way as a formula or line or
story pattern, it follows that we will often want to plot the
range of meaning of a word and use that map as a pointer to a
significant unity in traditional ideas. But this will not be easy.
Lexical reconstruction is terribly difficult because our own
education—and perhaps even the way that English really
operates among those who use dictionaries—encourages us to
cope with a word by sorting it out into smaller categories of
meaning. A Liddell-and-Scott definition, for example, follows
a standard pattern based on cutting up the word into discrete
sections, labelled with numbers, but with the relationship
between them usually left unspecified. To each of these
sections other, smaller sections are joined, generally by words
like 'fig.', 'transf.', or 'metaph.', perhaps even 'hence'. The
whole system might be a group of islands, separated from each
other by deep water, and including some smaller offshore rocks
joined to the mainland by the bridges represented by 'transf.'
and similar. The problem, of course, is that nothing in the way
Greeks actually used the word can justify such a complicated
map. What has happened is that the modern scholar, guided by
the common sense of his own age, has cut the meaning up and

few other words which might (*ex hypothesi*) have served a purely ornamental
function.

[74] As in the work of Manu Leumann (1950). In many instances, including
the well-known κύμβαχος and παρήορος, Leumann's approach is based on what
would nowadays be seen as an extreme Analyst view of Homeric composition,
where a later composer is supposed to have misunderstood a word in an old
passage and used it in error when he put together his own new line. If the
epics are primarily created by oral composition and performance, and
especially if each is essentially a single work, it is hard to see how such
misunderstandings can have come about or been accepted into a developing
tradition. Cf. Ruijgh (1957: 103), parodying Leumann's strategy.

rearranged its parts so that they answer to associations which make sense in his own cultural world. In doing so, as likely as not, he has obscured the very connections and unities that gave the word its Greek meaning in the first place. If we turn away from the lexical habit and choose instead to see the meaning of the word as a single field, without artificial boundaries, then we will be much closer to understanding whatever cultural unities are embodied in it. We will also be better equipped to cope with the label 'metaphorical', because we will be ready to give a better-informed guess at what has happened in places where the word has genuinely been pushed beyond its normal meaning.[75]

Here, then, is the challenge. Homeric Greek is full of words that each combine two things that seem to be unrelated in English, and our task is to explain their internal unities. Let me begin with an especially strange example.[76] Describing the various things in Polyphemus' cave, Odysseus specifies how lambs and kids of different ages were segregated:

> διακεκριμέναι δὲ ἕκασται
> ἔρχατο, χωρὶς μὲν πρόγονοι, χωρὶς δὲ μέτασσαι,
> χωρὶς δ' αὖθ' ἔρσαι.   (ix. 220–2)

Translated with brutal literalism, Odysseus names first older animals, then mid-aged, and then *drops of dew*, because that is exactly what ἔρση/ἑέρση means.[77] It is unhelpful to say that the usage is metaphorical,[78] because the passage is one of plain

---

[75] I have discussed this principle at greater length elsewhere (1995a).

[76] See Benveniste (1973), 19–22; W. M. Clarke (1974), 69–73. Benveniste's full argument is more ambitious and includes the claim that ἄρσην, 'male', is from the zero-grade of the same root. Chantraine, s.v., denies this. Clarke speculates that ἔρος/ἔρως is literally identified with dew, semen, and kindred substances (note esp. Hes. *Theog.* 910). Note also the tradition that dew is the same as ἀμβροσίη, the food of the gods, which is only recorded after Homer (see e.g. [Hes.] *Shield* 395).

[77] The alternation between the two forms is Homeric (see XIV. 348, XXIV. 419, 757). Some deny that ἑέρση or ἔρση for dew is the same word as ἔρση for a young animal (see Leumann (1950), 258 n. 11; Beekes (1969), 64, 76–8), but without compelling evidence. Certainly the Greeks in the 5th cent. seem to have thought they were the same, as Aeschylus uses δρόσος (*Ag.* 141) for a young animal, and Sophocles has ψακαλοῦχος (< ψακάς, 'raindrop', fr. 725 N) for a mother animal (Benveniste (1973), 19–22).

[78] Thus LSJ s.v.

functional description where a creative metaphor would hardly
belong. After a longer look it can be argued that the word bears
witness to an ancient conceptual link between the vitality of
young newborn animals and that of life-giving dew, Homer's
τεθαλυῖα ἐέρση (xiii. 245) or θῆλυς ἐέρση (v. 467). Dew brings
about the growth and ripening of corn (see XXIII. 598, with p. 98
below) and it seems to be associated with sexual fertility when
it appears among the suddenly blossoming plants as Zeus and
Hera make love (XIV. 351); similarly it is identified with the
healthy life of humans when the dead Hector is supernaturally
protected from decay so that he looks ἐερσήεις (XXIV. 419, 757),
retaining the flourishing appearance of a living man.[79] It is not
necessary to say that Homer believes dew and lambs are one
and the same thing, which is plainly absurd; more modestly,
the evidence is that in Greek practice the word is not cut up
into parts as we have to do when translating it into English, and
that the link between dew and lambs is more intimate and more
literal than it seems from our modern perspective. If we treat
the word as a unity it may well help us to understand Homer's
conception of sexual generation—or, indeed, of moist things
that fall from the sky.

   That last example is perhaps marginal, since it relies on a
single passage; but the problem is no less stark with familiar
words and formulae. For example the word ὄζος is attested in
two contexts, first naming the branch or shoot of a tree and
secondly an epithet for warriors in lines like

   Λάμπον τε, Κλυτίον θ᾽, Ἱκετάονά τ᾽ ὄζον Ἄρηος.   (III. 147 = XX. 238)

No passage exists to explain how the two applications relate to
each other: so how does the reader cope with the problem that
Homer appears to think warriors relate to Ares in the same
sense as branches relate to a tree? Both Chantraine and Frisk
cut the word into two separate entries, one meaning 'branch'
and the other 'follower', and each backed up with a separate
guess at an Indo-European etymology. This empty guess does
no more than encourage the reader to avoid the labour of
working out how one meaning could be applicable to the two
kinds of referent. Liddell and Scott are more cautious and

[79] Cf. XXIII. 184–8.

admit that this is one word; but they cut it up into two sub-definitions, explaining ὄζος Ἄρηος as 'metaph., *offshoot, scion*'. This brings us little closer to the Greek realities, because the English metaphor in 'offshoot' or 'scion' makes sense because of a symbolic meaning attached to growing plants in an English system of ideas which (in all likelihood) has little or nothing in common with the Greek. More generally, the mechanism of metaphorical transference implied by the entry is peculiar to literate English tradition—indeed, to a particularly mannered and rarefied version of that tradition. There is every reason to think that the patterns of Greek word-usage were different. Consequently, the only way to give a useful account of ὄζος would be to study the full range of meanings that Homer attaches to the growth or vigour of plants and that of human beings in general and warriors in particular, trying to establish how the life of the one is assimilated to the other: in which case useful evidence might be found in the pattern of thought that enables Odysseus to compare Nausicaa to a palm-tree (vi. 160–9), or in the Iliadic similes associating the deaths of warriors with the deaths of trees,[80] or simply in the range of meaning of words like θάλλω/θαλέθω, applied to the flourishing of both trees and young men, or ἄνθος, which refers both to growing vegetation and growing facial hair.[81] Whether or not those particular parallels would be enough to account for ὄζος Ἄρηος in Homeric terms, the exercise would exemplify the general principle that the task of understanding individual words belongs in the larger labour of using the full range of evidence to understand the world picture of their users.

When we try to make sense of the Homeric vocabulary for mental life and life after death it will be easy to distort the words by breaking up the unity of each one according to the range of English words that we have to use to translate it. This will be our problem in Chapter 4 when we grapple with the word θυμός, which in different contexts can be taken to refer to air in the lungs and to the locus of mental activity; and subsequently when we turn to ψυχή, which can usually be twisted into 'soul' but occasionally needs to be glossed 'life',

---

[80] See e.g. IV. 482–7, V. 560, XIII. 178–81, XVII. 53–60, XVIII. 55–9, 437–40, and cf. xiv. 175. Cf. Nagy (1979), 18 ff.

[81] See M. J. Clarke (1995b), n. 49.

'breath', or some other word no less vaguely related to the first. For every Greek word of this sort it is easy to separate out the various English equivalents and take one of them as the basic sense of the word and the others as extensions in one or other direction—metaphor, metonymy, or some other kind of figurative use. But if we do that we violate the real meaning, because the word has been distorted in two ways. First, it has been passed through the filter of modern expectations about how language works: specifically, expectations about the ways in which meanings are first mapped by individual words and then extended in creative directions by poets. Secondly, it has been broken up along lines of division laid down by modern words, words whose meanings were framed in terms of a culture utterly different from Homer's. To interpret the verbal data we have to arrange them in a pattern, and the pattern will be worse than useless if it is determined uncritically by our own upbringing. In short, the problem that faces us concerns not only the Homeric words but also the late twentieth century ideas that organize our linguistic sensibilities when we read them. This calls for a pause.

The Categories of Body and Soul

Asking the right questions

A person is a mass of living flesh who also thinks and feels and calls himself 'I'. That is the only universal fact about the structure of human identity, and any further elaborations are products of particular cultures and traditions: and because the ideas in question are intangible, and their expression often difficult and oblique, when we face an alien world-picture there is a temptation to pass its ideas through the filter provided by our own. I begin with a cautionary tale. Here is Frazer in the *Golden Bough*—a book that is still in print—with an anecdote to illustrate primitive beliefs about body and soul:

Addressing some Australian blacks, a European missionary said, 'I am not one, as you think, but two.' Upon this they laughed. 'You may laugh as much as you like', continued the missionary, 'I tell you that I am two in one; this great body that you see is one; within that there is another little one which is not visible. The great body dies, and is buried, but the little body flies away when the great one dies.' To this some of the blacks replied, 'Yes, yes. We also are two, we also have a little body within the breast.' On being asked where the little body went after death, some said it went behind the bush, others said it went into the sea, and some said they did not know.[1]

I have no idea what the Australians really believed or what they thought the missionary meant, but their answers—and above all their laughter—suggest that his talk of body and soul did not make sense to them. The most striking thing is that Frazer cites the story as evidence for the Aborigines' own beliefs, when in fact all it illustrates is the missionaries' failure to communicate with them. The story shows how easy it is to conjure up

[1] (1922), 179.

evidence of non-existent beliefs by asking questions that do not make sense except in the very words that the questioner uses. The danger is that of adopting what has been called an 'introspectionist psychology'—reliance, that is, on the beliefs and categories and intellectual pigeon-holes that our peculiar modern experience has imposed on us.[2]

There is a useful comment on this in one of the essays of Lucien Lévy-Bruhl, who produced increasingly subtle refinements of his own theory of 'primitive' soul-belief[3] before he took the further step[4] of accepting the insidious danger of framing one's questions in terms of modern Western schemes:

Almost all the observers assume, without reflecting on the question and as if no other hypotheses were possible, that the primitives have beliefs comparable to their own, and that in their eyes the human individual is made up of a body and a soul: that is to say, two entities quite different from each other which happen to be joined together in this life.[5]

What, then, happens when the investigator confronts the so-called primitives with such talk? 'To ask them about it would be useless at least . . . Their answers would clearly show only one thing: that the meaning of the question had escaped them.'[6]

[2] Evans-Pritchard (1965), ch. 1, and see also Lienhardt (1966), 150–2.

[3] The most important is in Lévy-Bruhl (1918), a work whose influence on classical scholars has been insidious ever since (see Ch. 4 nn. 4, 5, 32). Throughout the first half of the 20th cent., over-simplified doctrines of the primitive mentality continued to work their insidious way into English studies of early Greek language and lore, just as Hegelian models of *Geistesgeschichte* lie in the background of Snell's analyses of the Homeric view of man. For a trenchant early critique of the intellectual atmosphere which this created, see Barfield's discussion of 'that luckless dustbin of pseudo-scientific fantasies, the mind of primitive man' (1928: 56).

[4] Lévy-Bruhl (1963 [1927]).

[5] Ibid. 128.

[6] Lévy-Bruhl (1963 [1927]), 1. The insights quoted here supersede Lévy-Bruhl's earlier treatment of soul-belief (1918: 81–93), where he had condemned the 'Doppelgänger' theory of Tylor and his successors (see below, n. 34) on the grounds that certain cultures ascribe several souls to man (cf. Arbman (1926–7); Böhme (1929), *passim* and esp. 114–26; Bremmer (1983), *passim*), but fell short of rejecting the notion of 'soul' itself. He was later to modify his theory of the primitive mentality almost out of existence: see esp. Lévy-Bruhl (1931), the theory in its more modest form, then his 'Palinode' (1952) and finally the subtleties of his last work, the *Carnets* (1949). His

In the same way, if we now ask the wrong questions of Homer or his words there will be no lack of wrong answers to mislead us. But we face an added peril, a peril that Frazer's missionaries did not face among the Aborigines: because our poet is dead and silent he cannot laugh back at us, so when we ask the wrong questions it may never be obvious that we are on the road to nowhere.

Dualism of body and soul is insidious

Above all, if we think like lexicographers or word-for-word translators we will be liable to create false categories and make associations that do not exist for Homer. Words like 'soul', 'mind', and 'self' lack concrete or verifiable referents, so they have an especially insidious power over the categories of our thought.[7] In particular, because learners of Greek are taught to translate ψυχή as 'soul', and because that word and its translations have persisted through the history of religion and philosophy, it is very easy to assume that the Homeric ψυχή is more or less the same thing as what one might talk about nowadays in a discussion of psychology or selfhood or the soul. To do that is to avoid the issue of working out what that word really means and how it belongs in the early Greek view of man: as Ruth Padel has written on the equivalent problem in the language of tragedy, 'When we choose a word to translate [ψυχή], we tilt each passage with a particular load of ψυχή's semantic heritage, picking over the debris of centuries of reflection accumulated between the early Greeks and ourselves.'[8]

Short of relying on endless doubt, is there any sure way to

lasting contribution was the negative side of his approach, the all-important first step of recognizing that the sort of cultures that he called 'primitive' see the world in different ways from his own and ours (see also Evans-Pritchard (1965), 82 ff.; Lloyd (1990), esp. 1–5).

[7] Cf. Gill (1996: ch. 1) on the problem that modern definitions of 'self-hood', 'personality', and similar can contaminate the study of Greek ideas of psychological identity (see esp. 1–3).

[8] Padel (1992), 32; the same point is made by Bremmer (1983), 4. Contrast Vermeule (1979), 118: 'The Greeks understood that body and soul parted in death, of course . . . They never quite accepted it, however, and, as strongly as any other people, felt that the link endured'.

break out of the framework of late twentieth-century assumptions? If nothing else, we can at least begin by looking more closely at some of the patterns of thought involved, so as to put ourselves more clearly on guard against becoming trapped in this maze of modern ideas about human identity. Very crudely stated, the Western tradition in religion, philosophy, and ordinary language alike dictates that a person is divisible into two things: on the one hand there is the body, and on the other hand there is something else, something that might variously be called the *soul, the spirit, the mind, the self, das Ich, der Lebensträger, le soi,* or any of many such names.[9] To invoke this dichotomy, however covertly, is to enter a skein of ideas which enmeshes the history of religious, philosophical, and popular ideas about man. Christian dualism of body and soul is only the most overt modern working-out of this tradition. 'Noli foras ire,' writes Augustine, 'in teipsum redi: in interiore homine habitat veritas.'[10] So stated, the Christian model shades imperceptibly into the Cartesian, and 'Cogito ergo sum' is only another way of working out Augustine's principle. Since Descartes, the effect of what Gilbert Ryle has called the myth of 'the ghost in the machine'[11] has been to separate body from mind and identify the true self with the latter. The structure is the same when the Christian moralist directs his mental and moral life at the salvation of his immortal soul, or when a schoolboy is urged to have a healthy mind in a healthy body, or when a poet's imagination distinguishes his true self from what others see:

> An aged man is but a paltry thing,
> A tattered coat upon a stick, unless
> Soul clap its hands and sing, and louder sing
> For every tatter in its mortal dress.[12]

[9] On this point, and the sketch which follows here, I have been guided by Ryle (1949: esp. 11–24) and Taylor (1989: esp. 3–210). Each is concerned primarily with presenting a historical analysis as background to his own theories, so it is natural that both tend to collapse the distinction between the history of philosophy and of everyday beliefs and language.

[10] Aug. *De vera religione* 39. 72 (quoted by Taylor (1989), 129). See also Bernstein (1993), 327–33.

[11] Ryle (1949), 15–16 and *passim.*

[12] W. B. Yeats in 'Sailing to Byzantium', from *The Tower* (1928). On the image of the soul in Yeats see esp. Nalbantian (1977).

Such dualism remains pervasive in the present generation, where (for example) a singer-songwriter can distinguish his true self from his body when he faces the prospect of death,

> Lord, my body has been a good friend,
> but I won't need it when I reach the end, . . .[13]

while another pins his identity on his soul:

> I dreamed I was dying:
> I dreamed that my soul rose unexpectedly
> and looking back down at me
> smiled reassuringly,
> and I dreamed I was flying . . .[14]

Perhaps there is something self-consciously religious, even archaic, in Paul Simon's talk of his soul here. In the world most readers will have been brought up in, the key word is more likely to be 'self': as Charles Taylor remarks in the prosaic terms of the academic philosopher, 'we naturally come to think that we have a self in the same way that we have legs and arms.'[15] The concept of the self can be endlessly undermined by intellectuals, but it remains pervasive; and the gulf between it and the body is invoked every time words come together in a form like the opening of a letter to an agony aunt, 'I *have* a good *body* but I don't feel happy *inside myself*'. In each case human identity is pinned on a spiritual core which is within and distinct from the physical stuff of the body. This is not the place for a potted history of the concepts of self, soul, and person; the crucial point is that different forms of the same dualism have trickled into ordinary language and assumed the status of a kind of popular dogma. As soon as I speak of the soul or the body the shades of men like Descartes, Augustine, St Paul, and Plato himself lurk in the background. My words are laden with the tradition, and if I use them uncritically I remain its prisoner.[16]

[13] Cat Stevens, 'Miles from Nowhere', on the album *Tea for the Tillerman* (1970).

[14] Paul Simon, 'American Tune', on the album *There Goes Rhymin' Simon* (1973).

[15] (1989), 112.

[16] Gill (1996) is likewise concerned to remove Cartesian assumptions from his approach to Greek ideas of the self, but addresses a different aspect of the

Dualistic words and categories constrain scholarship

In its simplest form this difficulty is well illustrated by Thomas
Jahn's recent study of the 'semantic field of soul and spirit' in
Homeric Greek.[17] Jahn's approach is to restrict himself to the
lexical definition of the Homeric words which answer to the
categories of *Seele und Geist* in his own language: and although
his investigation of the dictional characteristics of some of these
nouns will prove very useful to us in due course, a question
mark hangs over the idea of the semantic field itself.[18] The idea
of a field of meaning is useful only if its external boundaries
and its internal subdivisions are drawn up in some way that
does not distort the Greek realities.[19] But by concentrating on
two words in his own language to draw up the ground-lines,
Jahn implies that the Homeric words and ideas must occupy
the same field of meaning as is covered by 'soul and spirit'.
That this should hold good over two so widely separated
cultural horizons is not obvious nor even likely.[20] The shortcomings of the system are clearest when Jahn turns to the word
$\psi v \chi \acute{\eta}$,[21] some of whose most striking appearances we have
already observed in Chapter 1 above. This word names the
shade of the dead man in the Underworld, it names something
lost at death, and it is also a sign of the life which is hazarded
when one risks death. The central problem of $\psi v \chi \acute{\eta}$ is the
relationship between those three senses and the precise implications of the third. Jahn assumes first that those three

orthodoxy, not body–soul dualism but the 'subject-centred' model of man
that posits an undivided independent self as autonomous psychological agent
(see esp. 6–11).

[17] Jahn (1987). In the following notes I have translated Jahn's German.

[18] Jahn relies on the 'Wordfield' theory of Jost Trier (1931), originally
framed in a study of developments in psychological vocabulary in medieval
German.

[19] See in particular Jahn's tabular classification (1987: 119–23). His
assumption of a correspondence between Greek and German conceptual
structures is never questioned or justified, even when Jahn accepts in passing
that the constituents of his Wordfield are 'in no way a homogeneous unity' (9).

[20] Once the determining categories are imposed willy-nilly on the Greek
material, I see no reason to expect Homer's view of man to follow a pattern
which 'shows a structure of the psychic sphere which is meaningful, internally
logical and therefore plausible' (Jahn (1987), 122).

[21] Ibid. 27–38.

senses must refer to a single entity with an 'existence of three phases',[22] and proceeds to assess it according to the criteria that define his idea of a psychological centre: Is it an 'inner faculty', and is it responsible for 'soul-spirit life' or a subdivision of that life? Answering each of these questions in the negative, but continuing to assume that it must be somehow *seelisch-geistig*,[23] he gives it a definition of its own: 'Carrier of life, vital principle; part of the human being that survives after death . . . in our own area of ideas: "soul" as a transcendent, religious idea'.[24] That he is able to come full circle in this way is the result of working through definitions based on a priori assumptions rather allowing himself to be guided by the way Homer uses his language in practice.[25]

A different version of the same difficulty is illustrated by Jan Bremmer's study of early Greek soul.[26] Instead of attempting to fit Homeric concepts into the categories provided by contemporary Western ideas, Bremmer imposes a paradigm lifted from Ernst Arbman's paradigmatic scheme of primitive soul-belief based on the Vedas.[27] Putting all his trust in the comparative method Bremmer proceeds on the assumption that early Greek beliefs can be mapped onto Arbman's model, according to which the primitive believes that man is equipped with 'a free soul representing the individuality of a person and the body-souls endowing a person with life and consciousness.'[28] The problem is that even if the world-pictures of early

---

[22] Ibid. 38.

[23] Jahn (1987: 32) simply assigns ψυχή to 'a quite different district within the soul-spirit Wordfield from the six other inner centres'.

[24] Jahn (1987), 121. Cf. the equivalent formulation on p. 30.

[25] To be fair to Jahn, he concludes his sketch with a disclaimer: 'The purely semantic analysis of ψυχή in the framework imposed on this work is hereby concluded: further investigations towards a detailed understanding of the image that associates itself with the word ψυχή in Homer's ideas, would be the topic of an enquiry into religious development, cultural history, and anthropology, for which the present work . . . can supply only the lexical foundations' (1987: 38). But the real question of word-meaning remains unanswered if 'semantic analysis' is allowed to proceed without addressing cultural questions at the same time.

[26] Bremmer (1983). See also M. L. West's review (1985*b*).

[27] Arbman (1926–7). For an earlier attempt to fit Homer's ψυχή into Arbman's scheme, see Böhme (1929), 114–26.

[28] Bremmer (1983), 11.

Greek epic and of the Vedic hymns share a common ancestor in the same way as their two languages, the archetype would lie so far back that we could not assume in advance that a significant structure is shared by the cultures embodied in the existing literatures.[29] To map the one onto the other is to confuse the ancestry of ideas with the shape they actually take in a living system.[30]

These two studies illustrate two pitfalls that lie before us: first, the tendency to fit Homeric words to definitions that make sense only in our own language and time, and secondly the temptation to fit Homeric ideas onto frameworks lifted from other cultures or from invented universal models. The interplay between those two strategies is again illustrated by the series of attempts to define an early Greek doctrine of the soul that was launched by Erwin Rohde's analysis in *Psyche*.[31] Rohde tried to define the ψυχή as a spirit which is dormant during life but underlies all psychological activity and is finally released at death to go to Hades:

Both the visible man (the body and its faculties) and the indwelling ψυχή could be described as the man's self. According to the Homeric view human beings exist twice over: once as an outward and visible shape, and again as an invisible 'image' which only gains its freedom at death.[32]

[29] The same criticism applies to G. Nagy's essay (1990*a*: 85–121) analysing Homeric ψυχή, μένος, and θυμός in the light of Vedic mythology. Nagy's argument depends first on assuming that a complex doctrine of the soul is obliquely referred to in the episode of Patroclus' ghost (XXIII. 65–108) in particular, and secondly on extrapolating sophisticated lore not from Homer but from the Vedic cognates of a few Homeric formulae (notably μένος ἠΰ (XXIV. 6)). I cannot attempt a full critique here because I cannot read Vedic; for present purposes, it suffices that the evidence *within Homer* for the doctrine proposed by Nagy is slight, so that his arguments about the Indo-European ancestry of words and ideas do not easily translate into analyses of the shape they take in Homeric tradition proper.

[30] At one point Bremmer (1983: 10) seems more cautious about the practical usefulness of his study for the Greek material: 'It seems reasonable to apply [Arbman's] method to the problem of Greek soul-belief *in order to establish its usefulness* for the study of archaic Greek soul-belief' (my italics). In practice, however, Bremmer seems less concerned with applying Arbman's methodology than with forcing his theory onto the Greek evidence.

[31] Rohde (1925), ch. 1, esp. 4–10. The argument is reviewed in the first part of Regenbogen (1948); and see also Claus (1981), 1–7.

[32] Rohde (1925), 6.

If this pushes ancient ideas through a mill of logic, it is because
Rohde wanted to fit his analysis into the fashionable theory that
explained primitive soul-belief [33] through the doctrine of the
Doppelgänger, a shadowy second self which is dormant in the
living man and leaves the body at death. [34] To justify this he had
to rely on a fragment of Pindar (131b M) for the mysterious
doctrine that a wraith (αἰῶνος εἴδωλον) is imprisoned in the body
during the waking hours and escapes during sleep. [35] Nothing
in Homer's depiction of man and ψυχή suggests such sharp
dualism, and Pindar's revelations almost certainly emerge from
a very different traditon: with hindsight Rohde's insistence on
the *Doppelgänger* looks like slavery to the intellectual fashions
of his own day. In reaction W. Otto[36] proposed a definition in
two parts, whereby the primary meaning of the word was 'life',
and its name was transferred to the part of man that survived
death—the word for 'life' stood also for what replaces life.[37]

[33] On the lure of the concept of the primitive cf. Nilsson (1941) and (1967),
40–4.

[34] Rohde (1925: ch. 1) avowedly aims to fit Homeric death-belief onto the
Doppelgänger model (see esp. p. 6, citing Herbert Spencer). Cf. Frazer (1922),
189–94; Tylor (1903), i. 428–9, for a model of 'primitive philosophy'
maintaining that dreams and the problem of the corpse led to the appearance
of the supposed primitive belief in the soul as a second self; also Lévy-Bruhl
(1918), 7–19, 81–2; (1963 [1927]), 161–9; and on the history of the concept of
the *Doppelgänger*, which acquired a spurious orthodoxy in anthropology and
psychology alike, see Rank (1971).

[35] Rohde (1925), 7. On this fragment see Epilogue, pp. 310–12.

[36] Otto (1923). For the point that Pindar's αἰῶνος εἴδωλον is not Homeric see
pp. 15–21. In his concepts of 'life-soul' and 'death-soul' (θυμός and ψυχή
respectively) Otto was applying another model of 'primitive thought', drawing
on the early work of Lévy-Bruhl (see esp. Otto (1923), 13–15). Otto says (21)
that his method is to advance the Homeric evidence first and only then turn to
a 'comparison with the beliefs of primitives'; but this does not seem to inform
his practice, which depends on over-compensating for Rohde's shortcomings
by forcing every example of ψυχή into the category either of 'death-soul' or
'life', with no middle ground.

[37] See Otto (1923), 23–31; and cf. Rohde (1925), 28–30. Otto pushes 'life' as
a translation for ψυχή even when it is lost in swoons (see below, Ch. 5, pp. 140–
3). Nehring (1947) extends the argument in the same vein; Warden (1971) is
equivocal on whether the word 'life' is a meaningful equivalent for ψυχή. Claus
(1981) is the latest scholar to follow this course. He makes ψυχή one of a group
of words, otherwise dominated by θυμός, which each refer sometimes to
individual acts of thought and emotion and sometimes to 'a force or energy
on which the "life" of a man depends' (15). Facing the fact that Homeric ψυχή

46 — Prologue

This was not far from 'Lucus a non lucendo', and others were quick to object to the theory that a single word meant such different things.[38] E. Bickel[39] maintained that Homeric man 'dies twice', once when he expires and once when he is cremated, with the ψυχή as a soul which leaves only at cremation;[40] then J. Böhme[41] argued that ψυχή was a 'death-soul' which was lost at death alongside the θυμός as 'life-soul'.[42] All these theories—schematic, almost catechetical—were

is not used in these ways, he argues that Homer artificially avoids using the word in these senses because a semantic clash would be caused by the prominence in the epics of the other role of the ψυχαί as shades of the dead. Apart from the fact that it is hard to imagine such a course being followed in a living language, it is impossible to get to grips with the theory because Claus does not explain what a 'life-force' is: the word appears in his opening discussion of αἰών—' "life-force" in a not very precisely defined sense' (12)—but it is not explained any further. Discussing some of the problematic passages in which he would translate ψυχή as 'life-force', he takes refuge in a reference to 'language which is transparently metaphorical and . . . should warn against literal interpretation of any of these phrases' (64), which is again hard to understand. See also Ch. 4, p. 68.

[38] Esp. Bickel (1926), 32–4. See also Regenbogen (1948), 3–5.

[39] (1926). Bickel's concept of the 'living corpse' draws on some of the same materials as I will in my discussion of the relationship between ψυχή and νέκυς/νεκρός (Ch. 6), but he works through a model dependent on equating Greek with Israelite and Egyptian ideas (see esp. his pp. 12–15). His theory of the 'second death' (on which see also our Ch. 6 n. 68) is a good example of the pitfalls of looking for organized doctrines where none ought to be expected (see esp. 82–6). His methodology involves a particularly insidious Analyst approach, taking Homeric death-lore as a patchwork of elements from different periods: he sets up his own 'living corpse' model as the *Urform* (see esp. 6–12) and explains everything that contradicts as intrusions reflecting the (equally arbitrarily defined) animism of later Greek thought. Bickel's animism turns out to rely on another universal construct, no more Homeric than Rohde's *Doppelgänger* and drawing on theories of the doctrine of transmigration and divinity of the soul (see esp. 100–33, on soul as δαίμων).

[40] Bickel (1926), *passim*. Bickel seems to have been the first to build on the fact that ψυχή is described in imagery drawn from breath and the lungs (see esp. 48–50), something others had tended to ignore in their concern with doctrines as opposed to plain facts of language.

[41] (1929), esp. 102–6.

[42] Böhme's study of ψυχή is the least openly dependent on universal models of primitive thought, though it involves applying Arbman's model of death-soul and multiple life-souls (114–26), in much the same way that we saw it forced onto Homer in Bremmer's book (see above, p. 43).

replaced by the more incisive formulation of O. Regenbogen,[43] who defined the ψυχή as a sort of substratum of life, mentioned most often in the context of death but remaining as an underlying essence, the '*conditio sine qua non*' of mental activity and consciousness.[44] Regenbogen's definition is both the clearest and the most influential, and we must keep it in mind as we proceed: but it once again invites the objection that it sets up a lexical definition that is not justified by the facts of Homeric language. We will be able to show that the definition glosses over the fact that in practice the word is not used in the context of life as lived, but only with reference to its end in death or in the loss of consciousness that comes with a swoon. To define ψυχή in Regenbogen's way is effectively to identify it as the soul of man: by emphasizing what seems logical rather than what Homer actually says, the scholar allows himself to fall back on dualism of the familiar twentieth-century kind.

The quest ahead

It takes a very long time to read those books, and their enduring lesson is that the only way forward is to throw away every crutch and let the Homeric words speak for themselves. This will amount to advancing a sustained hypothesis by trying to fit the Homeric evidence into a single structure of ideas, a structure which should be plausible if it fulfils four criteria. It should be reasonably simple; it should explain the relevant words of the texts in a plausible way; it should not rely on any gaping assumptions that are never backed up by the text; and it should include *everything* that Homer says about human identity into a single overarching analysis. Inevitably, within the prescribed framework some of our interpretations of words and phrases will be obvious and some will claim to be no more than plausible, but I hope that some will draw out meanings that have hitherto gone

---

[43] (1948).

[44] 'the *conditio sine qua non* for θυμός, μένος etc.' (Regenbogen (1948), 11–12). Where Homer is concerned there is little real difference between Regenbogen's and Rohde's versions of the theory that ψυχή dwells in the living: 'The final proof of the idea that the ψυχή must have been living in man is the fact that it is separated from him in death' (Rohde (1925), 30).

unnoticed; and if any of them carry credibility it will be as parts of a larger whole.

The starting-point, as we have suggested, will be to cast aside the crutch of the modern assumption that man is a thing of two parts. There are three especially dangerous traps ahead. The first would be to assume that the activity of thought and emotion must imply the possession of something that can be separated off from the body in the way that our own culture separates off the thing we call the mind; the second, correspondingly, would be to assume that the survivor in the afterlife must be imagined as spirit which dwelt in the body of the living man and escaped from it at death. The third snare is more subtle. A system which distinguishes the body both from the thinking mind and from the survivor in the afterlife will inevitably associate these two with each other, since both alike will be thought to partake of spirit as opposed to body.[45] Here nothing is more influential on our assumptions, and more dangerous to the present enquiry, than the semantic range of the word 'soul'. Consider the example with which I began this book, Donne's declaration that there is a divine spirit inside the material 'elements' that make up his body. If this spirit is what he elsewhere calls his soul, then it is in one sense the seat of thought and emotion and in another sense the carrier of his identity in the Christian afterlife. Hence he can distinguish body from soul when he woos a woman,

> T' our bodies turn we then, that so
> Weak men on love revealed may look:
> Love's mysteries in souls do grow,
> But yet the body is his book, . . .[46]

and likewise when he imagines the resurrection of the dead for the Last Judgement:

> At the round earth's imagined corners, blow
> Your trumpets, angels, and arise, arise
> From death, you numberless infinities
> Of souls, and to your scattered bodies go.[47]

---

[45] On the identification of thinking mind with immortal soul in Catholicism after Descartes, see McManners (1981), chs. 5 and 6, esp. 120–6, 148–66.

[46] 'The Ecstasy', ll. 69–72 in *Songs and Sonets*.

[*See opposite page for n. 47*]

Ideas and words alike are moulded by the structure of soul and body, inner and outer, which folds up mental life with life after death. Nowadays there is nothing exclusively Christian about this: for example the classical scholar E. R. Dodds, whose influential theories of ψυχή will be noted later in this book,[48] makes exactly the same connection in a Yeatsish poem of his own, 'The Moon Worshippers':

> We are the partly real ones
>> Whose bodies are an accident,
>> Whose half-born souls were never meant
> To fix their insubstantial thrones
> Inside a house of blood and bones.[49]

His fantasy accidentally makes explicit the skein of ideas and connections in which anyone may be enmeshed when the word 'soul' creeps into a discussion about life after death; and it seems to me that in Dodds's scholarly writings his enthusiasm for cross-cultural comparisons between Greeks and 'Borneo and the primitive past'[50] did little to remove the insidious influence of his own upbringing. My hope lies rather in vigilant self-consciousness: by refusing to rely on the concept of soul in the first place it should be possible to read the Homeric data without assuming that there is a close association between psychological life and life after death, or that the essential part of man should be the same in both those environments. This is my policy as we enter the meadow of Homeric words—

$$πολέες \ δ' \ ἔνι \ μῦθοι$$
$$παντοῖοι, \ ἐπέων \ δὲ \ πολὺς \ νομὸς \ ἔνθα \ καὶ \ ἔνθα. \quad (\text{XX. } 249)$$

---

[47] *Holy Sonnets* 7. 1–4.

[48] See Ch. 3 n. 1, Ch. 6 n. 98.

[49] In L. Robinson (1927), 201–2. Compare his poem 'When the ecstatic body grips . . .' (ibid. 91–2), which evokes a similarly sharp dichotomy of body and soul in an erotic context reminiscent of Donne's 'The Ecstasy' quoted above.

[50] (1951), 13.

PART II

The Language of Thought and Life

3
The Breath of Life and the
Meaning of ψυχή

The shape of Homeric man

Our concern is with the words and images with which Homer goes behind the external shape of man to express or imply a relationship between the consciousness—as it were the 'I'—and the visible stuff of the body. Along the story-line these fall into three groups. First is the rendering of consciousness—thought, emotion, introspection—where this 'I' thinks and feels while the bodily man stands or moves. Next come narrations of and allusions to the moment of death, where the conscious self must depart or be extinguished or undergo some other transformation along with the collapse of the visible man; and finally we move to the depiction of Hades, where an imagined life (or half-life) goes on when the bodily man has been buried or otherwise put away from sight. In each of these areas we enter a complex territory of language and ideas, and we cannot pick a path through it unless we begin by identifying landmarks. In all three terrains the most prominent feature is a closely knit group of nouns: and although we will deal in practice with processes no less than things, our first priority is to pin-point the meanings of these nouns.

A bald summary will give us our co-ordinates (see Fig. 1). In mental life the significant words are θυμός, φρήν/φρένες, ἦτορ, κῆρ, κραδίη, and πραπίδες, with the kindred but distinct νόος. It will be convenient to refer to these together as 'the θυμός family', treating νόος as a distant cousin and reserving its full treatment for later in the discussion. The roles and functions of all these things are bound up together, so that we will be less anxious to draw up their individual definitions than to pin down the single pattern in which they participate. For this

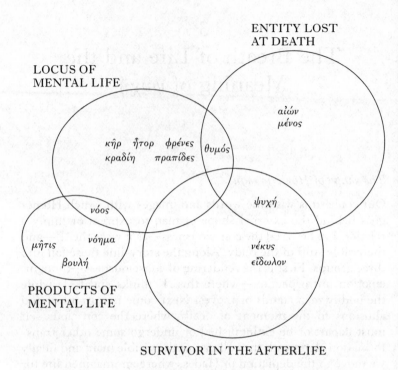

FIG. 1. The provinces of the major nouns to be studied.

purpose the label of 'family' is conveniently vague and allows us to begin with a question mark over the exact relationship between them. At the moment of death ψυχή, alternating with θυμός and very occasionally ἦτορ, comes to the fore when the dying man gasps out his final breath or his killer takes it from him. Here μένος or αἰών may also be the name of the life which is lost. Finally, in Hades the carrier of the dead man's identity is by turns called νέκυς or νεκρός—roughly translatable as 'corpse'—and ψυχή or more rarely εἴδωλον, a wraith or counterfeit image which represents the bodily appearance of the dead man.

There is clearly a problem: at a glance the noun ψυχή seems to break down the division into three areas, because it names first what is lost at death and then the survivor in the afterlife.

This is the point on which scholars have been apt to seize: seeing that something called ψυχή escapes the body at death, and something called ψυχή lives a dreary life in Hades, it is very easy to infer that this is the name of the Homeric soul. As I suggested in my discussion of Regenbogen and other scholars in the last chapter, that analysis invites suspicion because it makes the Homeric realities seem to fit so snugly into the highly idiosyncratic structure of body and soul that we have in our own culture. My approach will be to remove that structure from the framework of my interpretation and ask a series of different questions, some seemingly perverse, in an attempt to grasp what this word really means. One question will be how the ψυχή lost at death relates to the ψυχή of the afterlife. Normally, as we will see, the meaning and associations of the word are fundamentally different in those two environments, the one among the visible events of this world, the other in the unseen world of myth. The few passages where the ψυχή flies to Hades after leaving the dying man will turn out to be difficult and creative articulations that arise from other and simpler ideas. But I begin with a still more fundamental question invited by the ψυχή: if it is what departs at death, is it also present in man during life? When Homeric man loses consciousness for ever, does his body give up a soul or animating principle that identified him as a man?

Does the living man have a ψυχή?

The only way to answer the question is to look at how Homer actually uses the word: so for the moment we will lay aside all the instances of ψυχή that refer unambiguously to death or to survival in Hades, reserving them for full discussion in due course, and take a closer look at the residue. As we do so the crucial fact will emerge that ψυχή appears only in the context of life lost or threatened, never of life held and enjoyed.[1]

---

[1] With the argument that follows compare Böhme (1929), 110–13; also, more vaguely, Dodds (1951), 16: 'The only recorded function of the ψυχή in relation to the living man is to leave him.' Wilamowitz's simple formulation (1931: 370) remains the most apt, taking ψυχή as 'the cold breath of death' in sharp distinction to the inhaled breath which underlies life. Snell (1953: 8–9)

Two images built up by Achilles will direct us towards an answer. In one he develops the idea of the final loss of ψυχή in uniquely vivid terms:

> ληϊστοὶ μὲν γάρ τε βόες καὶ ἴφια μῆλα,
> κτητοὶ δὲ τρίποδές τε καὶ ἵππων ξανθὰ κάρηνα,
> ἀνδρὸς δὲ ψυχὴ πάλιν ἐλθεῖν οὔτε λεϊστὴ
> οὔθ’ ἑλετή, ἐπεὶ ἄρ κεν ἀμείψεται ἕρκος ὀδόντων.   (IX. 406–9)

Men can lose and acquire cattle and prizes as they will, but when the ψυχή is lost it is lost for ever.[2] Since the implication is that the return of the ψυχή would imply the return of life, Achilles' words suggest that the ψυχή which is lost at death carries a meaning which *might* be extended further to link it to the life that men live and enjoy; but this potential is not brought to birth in what he says, and the idea of its return is seen as something absurd or impossible. Compare this with another image in the same speech:

> οὐδέ τί μοι περίκειται, ἐπεὶ πάθον ἄλγεα θυμῶι,
> αἰεὶ ἐμὴν ψυχὴν παραβαλλόμενος πολεμίζειν.   (IX. 321–22)

Achilles says that nothing has been gained by 'casting his ψυχή about' when he has risked his life in the fray. The image may suggest gambling, casting the ψυχή around as one rattles lots in an urn,[3] or more simply it may refer to the loss of ψυχή which occurs when a man is wounded, exhausted, or finally dying.

is cautious on the ψυχή of the living, but his argument is not entirely clear. He sees that 'life' is only a contextual gloss for ψυχή and that ἀϋτμή is used instead of ψυχή when the sense is positive, concluding that Homer 'has a concept of "the breath of life"', a statement which appears to make no claims about ψυχή as such; but it is not clear how all this relates to the assertion that 'ψυχή is the force which keeps the human being alive' (8).

[2] On this passage and its train of thought see esp. Taplin (1992), 196.

[3] Martin (1989: 192–3), sees this image as a metaphor drawn from gambling, suggesting that it is akin to εὖχος ἐμοὶ δώσειν, ψυχὴν δ’ Ἄιδι κλυτοπώλωι (v. 654 = XI. 445, XVI. 625): the latter image, he says, 'reduces "boast" and "soul" to counters in a game of war advantage.' Jahn (1987: 29) glosses ψυχή in IX. 322, iii. 74, and ix. 255 as 'life seen as a possession', and similarly at XXII. 338. In terms of my argument that ψυχή is precisely the same as expired breath (see Ch. 5, *passim*), it may simply be that ψυχὴν παραβαλλόμενος expresses in a simple and non-figured way the idea that breath is cast about when a warrior gasps or groans in exhaustion, unconsciousness, or finally death.

The context of both passages is a speech of peculiar introspection: and it is interesting that ψυχή comes to the fore as it does when Achilles is reflecting on his own feelings in the light of the prospect of death: it is when he is most aware of himself and most isolated that his ψυχή begins to take on something like an existential role.[4] But although he invokes it at a time when his mood has been dictated by yielding to his passions in the most intense self-awareness, even here the core of the images is that the ψυχή will be lost in death, not that it underlies emotion, thought, or active life. This is borne out later in the same scene: when Achilles does mention vitality in a fully positive sense he calls it ἀϋτμή, a word for any warm billowing substance[5] which has no special significance either for mental life or for the life lost at death:

> . . . φρονέω δὲ τετιμῆσθαι Διὸς αἴσῃ,
> ἥ μ' ἕξει παρὰ νηυσὶ κορωνίσιν, εἰς ὅ κ' ἀϋτμὴ
> ἐν στήθεσσι μένῃ καί μοι φίλα γούνατ' ὀρώρῃ.
>
> (IX. 608–10; sim. X. 89–90)

What this suggests is that it is not enough to gloss ψυχή as 'the breath of life': in fact it is that breath only in so far as it is dissipated.

That gives us our cue: the loss of ψυχή is the dividing line between life and death, so it becomes a sign of life lost or

---

[4] On Achilles' introspective use of language see Martin (1989), 146–230 *passim*, with bibliography of earlier studies; in particular 192–3 on the images of ψυχή at IX. 322, 401 as 'another example of the shift toward an interior language.'

[5] ἀϋτμή (occasionally ἀϋτμήν) is what is hot and billowing or flowing: for example the warm fragrance of melted oil (XIV. 174), the blast from Hephaestus' bellows (XVIII. 471), the steam of boiling water (XXI. 366), the panting of a runner (XXIII. 765), the burning stuff that comes from Polyphemus' eyeball (ix. 389), the furious blast of winds (xi. 400), the smell of cooking meat (xii. 369), and smoke (xvi. 290, xix. 9, 20). In its movement ἀϋτμή closely resembles θυμός, but the latter is specifically mental or emotional in the living man. ἀϋτμή in the passage I quote here is the force behind bodily movement, propelling the limbs, whereas the vigorous θυμός of a mentally energetic man can be opposed to his physical weakness (e.g. at IV. 313–14). ἀϋτμή is very probably built from the same root as is the verb ἄημι < *ἀϝημι, 'blow', just as with πνεῦμα and πνέω (see *LfgrE* s.v.): formally the correspondence resembles that between τίω and τιμή or χαίρω and χάρμη (Risch (1974), §19b). See also Hainsworth at IX. 609–10.

threatened. When Achilles chases Hector around the walls, they are said to be struggling not for an ordinary prize but for Hector's life or death, περὶ ψυχῆς θέον Ἕκτορος ἱπποδάμοιο (XXII. 161). After most of Penelope's suitors have been killed, the remaining brave few fight to the death, περὶ . . . ψυχέων (xxii. 245); Odysseus considers every plan for getting out of Polyphemus' cave because his life is at stake, ὥς τε περὶ ψυχῆς (ix. 423); and in the scene discussed above Achilles says that the treasures of Troy are not worth dying for, οὐ . . . ἐμοὶ ψυχῆς ἀντάξιον (IX. 401).

In each of the passages we have observed, ψυχή is defined as the issue in the mortal combat: by an easy shift the word has been extended from its simple sense as the thing whose loss is tantamount to death. Similarly Hector begs mercy of Achilles by invoking three apparently heterogeneous things:

> λίσσομ᾽ ὑπὲρ ψυχῆς καὶ γούνων σῶν τε τοκήων,
> μή με ἔα παρὰ νηυσὶ κύνας καταδάψαι Ἀχαιῶν . . .   (XXII. 338–9)

How does ψυχή belong here? Hector is asking Achilles to remember the things that bring a sense of moderation or self-restraint to Homeric man:[6] his parents, his knees, and his mortality. Achilles is not being asked to 'look into his soul' but to remember the prospect of death.[7] Compare another speech where Agenor reminds himself that Achilles is mortal:

> καὶ γάρ θην τούτωι τρωτὸς χρὼς ὀξέϊ χαλκῶι,
> ἐν δὲ ἴα ψυχή, θνητὸν δέ ἕ φασ᾽ ἄνθρωποι
> ἔμμεναι.   (XXI. 568–70)

This passage, more than any other, has prompted scholars to believe that the holding, as well as the loss, of ψυχή defines it as the basis of life.[8] The context is clearly one of rhetorical

---

[6] On themes in Homeric supplication see Gould (1973); also Richardson ad loc.

[7] Compare Theoclymenus' words when he supplicates Telemachus: λίσσομ᾽ ὑπὲρ θυέων καὶ δαίμονος, αὐτὰρ ἔπειτα | σῆς τ᾽ αὐτοῦ κεφαλῆς καὶ ἑταίρων (xv. 261–2). κεφαλή is many times invoked as a metonymic sign for life at risk: see Ch. 6 nn. 29, 30.

[8] Otto (1923: 25), uses the passage to prove that ψυχή can mean 'life': cf. also Richardson ad loc., with Snell (1953), 9; Adkins (1970), 14. Böhme (1929: 111) is closest to the mark when he specifies the reference as 'life in contrast to death'.

expansion rather than simple statement, but nevertheless it prompts the crucial question: if Homeric man dies by losing his ψυχή, does it follow that he lives by holding it? But the context shows that Agenor's point is solely that Achilles can die, so that here again ψυχή stands for the distinction between life and death, and the basis of the image is its loss, just as in Achilles' own image of the ψυχή that can pass only once out of his mouth. If the ψυχή is 'in' the man, it is there only as something that will be lost.

The same principle applies in the proem of the *Odyssey*, where Odysseus is defending or protecting his ψυχή amid perils:

> πολλὰ δ' ὅ γ' ἐν πόντωι πάθεν ἄλγεα ὃν κατὰ θυμόν,
> ἀρνύμενος ἥν τε ψυχὴν καὶ νόστον ἑταίρων. (i. 4–5)

Is the metonymy significant to the point that when Odysseus is ἀρνύμενος his ψυχή he is thereby providing himself with ψυχή as 'breath of life' in an active spiritual sense? The best clue to the imagery here is provided by a few similar references to ψυχή at risk when men are at sea, when life is not vaguely losable but actively set at hazard in the perils of sailing. Twice in the *Odyssey* pirates are described as ψυχὰς παρθέμενοι (iii. 74 = ix. 255), risking their lives just as the suitors are σφὰς . . . παρθέμενοι κεφαλάς (ii. 237) when they court disaster by their crimes. The precise image in ψυχὰς παρθέμενοι becomes less mysterious if we compare it with the passage where death by drowning is actually imagined as gaping open-mouthed and gasping out breath, πρὸς κῦμα χανὼν ἀπὸ θυμὸν ὀλέσσαι (xii. 350). It is in this sense that Odysseus is protecting himself from the loss of ψυχή when he is in the sea, ἐν πόντωι: he is warding off the final gasping-out of life that comes with a death by drowning. The image is essentially the same as what Achilles deploys when he describes himself as ψυχὴν παραβαλλόμενος, casting around his ψυχή, when he risks death in battle.

All other Homeric instances of ψυχή refer to its departure or to its role as a wraith in Hades. After this survey I hope it is clear that the evidence gives no encouragement to the supposition that ψυχή is the substratum of mental life and consciousness: in fact it has meaning only in a negative sense, in so far as life is lost or liable to be lost. In due course we will see that ψυχή is closely identified with the last gasp of breath exhaled by the dying man. Athough its meaning is extended metonymically so that it becomes a potent symbol of life lost or at risk, it never ceases to be the same as the cold breath which passes into the air at the moment of death. To see it as the basis of life as lived and enjoyed would be to step beyond the Homeric depiction of man, and to do so in a way that would map Homeric ideas willy-nilly onto those of our own culture. As we proceed now to study the depiction of thought, emotion, and will, we can be confident that the mental life and identity of Homeric man are not pinned on ψυχή.

4
Mental Life and the Body

θυμός and its family

In this chapter we will try to understand the basis of Homeric thought, emotion, and consciousness: so we turn to the nouns θυμός, φρήν/φρένες, ἦτορ, κῆρ, κραδίη, πραπίδες, and νόος, answering to the mysterious group of things which we have called 'the θυμός family'. The sum of the argument will be that these things are manifestations in action of an indivisible human whole, a whole where the complexities of mental life make sense best if apprehended without trying to divide man into mind and body. This will send us to the relationship between the ψυχή, the corpse, and the 'I' of the dead man armed with an important insight: if Homer's understanding of mental life involves no concept of a spiritual core distinguishable from the body, it will make good sense to avoid imposing the same model on his view of what happens at death.

The idea of psychological identity

From the start the question at issue can easily be distorted by denying the common-sense assumption that Homeric man is an autonomous psychological agent. In one of the more poetic analyses of Homeric psychology, H. Fränkel[1] drew on the fact that verbs of seeing and knowing tend to include both the mental act and the corresponding physical action in a single word, suggesting that the emotional sphere is not distinguished from the cognitive, nor that in turn from the sphere of action: 'there are no boundaries, there is no cleavage between feeling and the corporeal situation.'[2] Fränkel then went on to link this

---

[1] (1975), 75–85.
[2] Ibid. 79. Cf. Onians (1951), 13–22; Seel (1953), 302–9; Snell (1953), 1–4; Schwabl (1954), 58–9. On the assumptions about selfhood and the

with the way Homer describes the intervention of gods in human thought. Just as mind and body are not distinguished in the psychological process proper, so there is no practical distinction between independent mental life and the promptings imposed from outside by specific gods or the indefinite δαίμων.[3] Fränkel generalizes in the manner of the armchair anthropologists of his generation[4] by denying that Homeric man has a mental life fixed by the limits of his human frame:

If man is, as it were, a field of energy, whose lines extend into space and time without limit or restraint, then external forces, for their part, operate in him without hindrance, and it is meaningless to ask where his own force begins and where that from outside ends . . . In the *Iliad*, then, man is completely a part of his world. He does not confront an outside world with a different inner selfhood, but is interpenetrated by the whole, just as he on his part by his action and suffering penetrates the total event.[5]

This is a striking idea, even a Romantic one, but it can hardly be taken literally. Regardless of the deeper meaning of divine intervention, Homeric language implies a sense of the psychological life that goes on in the bodily whole that we call a man. Take Phoenix' words when he warns Achilles against stubborn anger:

history of ideas that tend to underlie such analyses see Gill (1996), 29–93 *passim*.

[3] Fränkel (1973), 80. For the association of Homeric psychology proper with the question of divine intervention cf. Dodds (1951), 13–18; Snell (1953), 23–42; Seel (1953), 307–9; Schwabl (1954), esp. 48 f.; Lesky (1961), 1–11. A. Schmitt (1990: 126–73) argues at length (126–173) that Homeric language does indeed distinguish reflective thought from reactions to external promptings, but not in the terms applied by Snell and other scholars of the time. His critique is mostly concerned with the scholars' own intellectual background and its influence on their categories of interpretation.

[4] Although Fränkel does not cite Lucien Lévy-Bruhl by name, the resemblance to the theories in that savant's *Les Fonctions mentales dans les sociétés inférieures* is unmistakable (see above, Ch. 2, pp. 38–9 with nn. 3–6). There is a very similar version of the 'open field' theory of Homeric man in Dodds (1951: 8–18), relying like Fränkel on the place of divine intervention in Homeric psychology. Dodds acknowledges his debt to Lévy-Bruhl: see his reference to Lévy-Bruhl (1918) and to the theory of participation (1951: pp. viii and 40).

[5] Fränkel (1975), 80. Cf. Lévy-Bruhl (1963 [1927]: 133–50), another version of an 'open field' theory of the primitive self.

Mental Life and the Body 63

ἀλλὰ σὺ μή μοι ταῦτα νόει φρεσί, μηδέ σε δαίμων
ἐνταῦθα τρέψειε, φίλος . . . (IX. 600–1)

A question mark hangs over the relationship between divine
prompting and Achilles' own act of will; but that question is a
matter of myth and cosmology, and irrespective of its answer
we must look on a lower and simpler plane of ideas to find out
what Homer means by the words σὺ μή μοι ταῦτα νόει φρεσί.
What are φρένες, what does the verb νοέω mean? Where and
how is mental life believed to be going on?

The mental apparatus has many names but is undivided

When I talk of 'the θυμός family' I choose a label that cannot
be taken literally, because the relationship between the entities
in question is very difficult to grasp. I have argued (Ch. 1,
pp. 15–22) that the formulaic theory of Homeric diction
should not allow us to believe that his words are vague and
woolly in meaning, and throughout this study I trade on the
basis that all words—including epithets—carry meaning as
distinctly and precisely as they would in the most straightforward and prosy language. None the less, we can accept that
Homer's vocabulary includes systems of interchangeable
words which are switched for the sake of metrical conveni-
ence, and that the semantic edges of a particular word may be
blurred when it functions in this way. A familiar example of
such a system is the array of collective names for the
Greeks—Ἀχαιοί, Δαναοί, Ἀργεῖοι, and so on—where the poet
can switch between the names in the course of a short passage
referring to a single host of warriors. In an important study
T. Jahn has shown that the names of θυμός, φρήν/φρένες, ἦτορ,
κῆρ, κραδίη, and πραπίδες are interchangeable in exactly this

---

[6] (1987), 182–246. In the cases of θυμός, φρένες, ἦτορ, κῆρ, κραδίη, and
πραπίδες, Jahn documents this pattern exhaustively: by collating passages and
formulae referring to each of 37 species of emotional and intellectual activity,
by comparing disparate references to the anger of Achilles against Agamemnon, which he takes as a test case, and by comparing successive lines or
formulae in descriptions of single mental acts. Jahn's finding is based primarily on passages in which the psychological noun has a 'pleonastic function' and
is not crucial to the grammar of the sentence, but passages in which the noun

way,[6] exhibiting the characteristics of 'range' and 'economy' that Milman Parry identified in his pioneering study of name-epithet formulae.[7] (νόος is a special case, with a peculiar identity of its own, but in practice it plays its part in the system along with the other nouns.[8]) Jahn's finding leads us to a view of Homeric psychology which has no parallel in our own language: in a given type of context there may be a tendency for one or other of the nouns to be used particularly often—θυμός, for example, is especially connected with passionate emotion[9]—but there is no firm distinction, and the nouns are freely interchanged across different passages or even within the description of a single act of thought.[10] This does not mean that they are semantically identical, just as an adjective does not necessarily become meaningless when it is part of a system of name-epithet formulae; but it indicates convincingly that in practice Homer treats them as interchangeable labels for a single apparatus.[11]

A simple fact corroborates this. Nowhere do the entities in the family behave in opposition to each other, in the way that (for example) reason and passion or the heart and the mind might be opposed in our own language; and likewise a complex

is more closely integrated seem to follow the same pattern of broad interchangeability (Jahn's 'pregnant functions', 212–46).

[7] Jahn (1987), 247–98.

[8] See below, n. 148.

[9] Caswell (1990: 49–50), corroborates Jahn with a useful summary of the patterns by which each of θυμός and its cousins predominates in certain types of context but acts elsewhere as a 'functional synonym' of the others.

[10] Jahn's pioneering work enables us to go further than Claus (1981), who spends much effort on assigning distinct meanings to the different nouns in this group (ch. 1 *passim*), and Bremmer (1983), who assumes a priori that θυμός, φρένες, and the others are to be taken as a group of distinct entities; similarly Cheyns (1985) tries to distinguish the meanings of ἦτορ, κῆρ, and κραδίη and contrives extremely subtle definitions for each. Darcus Sullivan (1988) and Caswell (1990) restrict themselves to a single noun, φρένες and θυμός respectively, and perhaps limit themselves as a result.

[11] Many of the earlier studies of Homeric psychology (e.g. Halkbart (1796), Helbig (1840), Schrader (1885)) aimed to identify differences in meaning between the nouns in the θυμός family: for summary sketches see Jahn (1987), 124–81. Böhme (1929) was the last full study of this kind; he sought to assign a particular species of emotional and intellectual activity to each of the members of the family (37–87), and concluded that Homer has no sense of a psychic whole (*Gesamtgemüt*) because they all exist and act separately.

thought or succession of thoughts is never expressed in terms of a complex relationship between them.[12] Homeric man can change his mind in the course of a single soliloquy, and he and his θυμός may waver between alternatives, but changing or conflicting thoughts are never assigned to separate mental centres. θυμός (for example) may be ἐν στήθεσσι, νόος may be ἐν θυμῶι, thought may be carried out κατὰ φρένα καὶ κατὰ θυμόν (I. 193, etc.), or a single thought may be τόνδε νόον καὶ θυμόν (IV. 309); but here the nouns are co-ordinated rather than contrasted, and the mental apparatus acts as a single unit.[13] Likewise a sudden change of mind may be ἕτερος . . . θυμός (ix. 302); one gives a gift willingly but with an unwilling mental apparatus, ἐκὼν ἀέκοντί γε θυμῶι (IV. 43), and a man can listen to his own θυμός and then disagree with it;[14] but such change is never produced by a conflict between θυμός and some other part of the mental anatomy.

This is driven home by the way Homer describes decision-making. When two simultaneous thoughts or ideas are in conflict, the image is one of twofold division, δίχα, within a single θυμός, ἦτορ, or κραδίη. Zeus describes himself wavering between two courses of action, διχθὰ δέ μοι κραδίη μέμονε φρεσὶν ὁρμαίνοντι (XVI. 435), and when Nestor ponders indecisively there is twofold division in the place where his thought goes on, ὥρμαινε δαϊζόμενος κατὰ θυμόν | διχθάδια (XIV. 20–1). Similarly the mental apparatus thinks doubly, ἐν δέ οἱ ἦτορ | στήθεσσιν λασίοισι διάνδιχα μερμήριξεν (I. 188 f; sim. xvi. 73, xxii. 333), and

---

[12] The nearest approach to such an opposition that I can find is in Helen's description of her own feelings: αὐτὰρ ἐμὸν κῆρ | χαῖρ', ἐπεὶ ἤδη μοι κραδίη τέτραπτο νέεσθαι (iv. 259–60). In fact, however, it is very doubtful whether the functions of κῆρ and κραδίη are opposed to each other: since what is described is a single harmonious movement from decision to resultant happiness, it seems rather that the same mental act or apparatus is given two slightly different names in succession. Otherwise, the only approaches to such oppositions lie outside the θυμός family proper, as the following: ἀλλά τέ οἱ βράσσων τε νόος, λεπτὴ δέ τε μῆτις (of a man who must think on his own, x. 226); κραιπνότερος μὲν γάρ τε νόος, λεπτὴ δέ τε μῆτις (of a young man's rashness, XXIII. 590).

[13] Cf. Jahn (1987: 18), who draws up an interesting, if very schematic, diagram arranging στήθεα, φρένες, θυμός, κῆρ, κραδίη, and ἦτορ in concentric circles.

[14] e.g. XI. 407 = XVII. 97 = XXI. 562 = XXII. 122 = 385.

the θυμός is broken up: ὡς καὶ ἐμοὶ δίχα θυμὸς ὀρώρεται ἔνθα καὶ ἔνθα (xix. 524). In each of these instances the thoughts in question are then listed in sequence, linked by ἤ . . . ἤ . . .: connected thoughts follow a linear progression, and there is no sense in which different thoughts or impulses are assigned to several centres or organs distinguished by differing names.[15]

Mental agents and functions are one

What, then, are these things that form the mental apparatus? Evidently θυμός and the others are within the boundaries of the body—they are ἔνδοθι (e.g. I. 243) or ἔνδον (e.g. xi. 337)—and their processes are those that would nowadays be assigned to the mind: thought, emotion, self-awareness, will. If that is so, does it not follow that in some plain sense they are the mental core of man? In Homeric language as in any other there is naturally a distinction between the thinker and what he thinks. 'I' must be different from something that can be called one's own, φίλον ἦτορ (v. 364; i. 60, etc.) or φίλος θυμός (xi. 407; xiii. 40) or φίλον κῆρ (i. 491; i. 341).[16] εἶδος is opposed to φρένες (e.g. iii. 44–5; iv. 264, xi. 337, xvii. 454) or φυή to φρένες (see

---

[15] On the linear progression of thought in sequences like these see Arend (1933), 106–15; Voigt (1934), *passim*, with full collections of passages; Snell (1978), 82–3. Adkins (1970: 23), follows Snell on the point that the pattern with μερμήριξε allows only a straight sequence of alternatives, while more complex decision-making is liable to be rendered in terms of divine intervention.

[16] In the meaning of φίλος it is very difficult to disentangle the idea of affection from that of mere ownership. Those two things seem to be inextricably united in Homeric thought: for example, follow Achilles' train of thought when he explains why he loved Briseis: 'just as any sound man loves and cares for the woman who is his own (τὴν αὐτοῦ φιλέει καὶ κήδεται), so I loved (φίλεον) her, spear-won though she was' (ix. 341–3). Achilles' point is that possession and affection imply each other—in a nutshell, one φιλέει what is φίλον. A great deal has been written about this word. Most recently, D. Robinson (1990) argues that Homeric φίλος is always affectionate rather than merely possessive and suggests that φίλον ἦτορ, φίλα γούνατα, and the like are found especially often in contexts where life is threatened. He holds that in monologues like those quoted in these pages, θυμός is personified as a friend. Such an interpretation may be going too far: compare Hooker (1987), arguing that the possessive and affectionate senses need not be sharply distinguished in the first place; and see also Landfester (1966: 13–34), plotting distinctions between φίλος as what is owned, what is loved, and what is 'inalienable'.

esp. viii. 168–81), just as ἔργον might be opposed to ἔπος. The most extreme manifestation of this contrast comes when Odysseus must strive to restrain his urge to rise up against the suitors. His κραδίη groans or growls, ὑλάκτει, like a bitch defending her whelps from attackers, and the hero's mental apparatus is virtually personified as he urges it to endure as it did in Polyphemus' cave:

> τέτλαθι δή, κραδίη· καὶ κύντερον ἄλλο ποτ' ἔτλης
> ἤματι τῶι ὅτε μοι μένος ἄσχετος ἤσθιε Κύκλωψ
> ἰφθίμους ἑτάρους· σὺ δ' ἐτόλμας, ὄφρα σε μῆτις
> ἐξάγαγ' ἐξ ἄντροιο ὀϊόμενον θανέεσθαι. (xx. 18–21)

The hero seizes what is in his breast, and as he writhes to and fro it remains steadfast:

> ὣς ἔφατ', ἐν στήθεσσι καθαπτόμενος φίλον ἦτορ·
> τῶι δὲ μάλ' ἐν πείσηι κραδίη μένε τετληυῖα
> νωλεμέως· ἀτὰρ αὐτὸς ἑλίσσετο ἔνθα καὶ ἔνθα. (xx. 22–4)

How does the man himself—αὐτός—relate to ἦτορ or κραδίη here? If ἦτορ or κραδίη is what endures and thinks, if it is what escaped from Polyphemus' den, then it sounds very like a psychic self, a 'ghost in the machine'.[17] The impression is similar when the begrudger gives a gift willingly but with an unwilling mental apparatus, ἑκὼν ἀέκοντί γε θυμῶι (IV. 43). Unless there is a simple dichotomy between body and spirit, where does the thinker stand in relation to the apparatus in renderings like these?

An answer to this problem lies a little further afield. The most challenging examples of introspection come when a character moves along a train of thought through an extended dialogue with his mental apparatus. A hero in battle begins a soliloquy by addressing his θυμός thus,

> ὀχθήσας δ' ἄρα εἶπε πρὸς ὃν μεγαλήτορα θυμόν, . . .

and goes on to describe his ideas as an address by his θυμός to himself:

> ἀλλὰ τίη μοι ταῦτα φίλος διελέξατο θυμός;[18]

---

[17] Cf. Gill (1996), 183–90.

[18] Soliloquies are arranged in this way at XI. 403–11, XVII. 90–105,

As Dodds boldly puts it, θυμός acts here with an 'independent inner voice'.[19] However, the most remarkable thing about the 'inner voice' is that in a single train of thought it begins as an address by the man to the θυμός, but as his thoughts develop he sees them going in the opposite direction from the θυμός to himself.[20] How can this make sense? Here we can build on D. B. Claus's[21] useful observation that in Homer the entities in the θυμός family can stand both for that which thinks and for that which is thought: 'The chief emotional agents could not be thought of in Homer without some feeling that the "life" of a man was dependent upon their activities, and . . . intellectual agents could not be imagined without a constant ambiguity with contextually determined "thought"'.[22] This point is vital. The semantic range of each noun in the θυμός family varies between two poles: from actor to activity, from agent to function, from the entity that thinks to the thoughts or emotions that are its products. Nor is there any gulf between those two:[23] the range is fluid and continuous from one extreme to the other, and every stage along the way is represented. This will prove crucial for my final argument. Taking the first six books of the *Iliad* as our sample, we will now trace the range of ways in which the entities in the group relate to mental

XXI. 552–70, XXII. 98–130. On the psychological and linguistic patterns see esp. Scully (1984); and more generally Fenik (1968), 96–8, 163–5; (1978b), 68–90; and for some further psychological points see Sharples (1983).

[19] (1951), 16–17; cf. Russo and Simon (1968), 42–8; also the acute discussion by Burnett (1991).

[20] Inner debate of this kind is not to be confused with decision-making of the διάνδιχα μερμήριξεν type (see above, n. 15), where the relationship between 'I' and θυμός or φρένες is constant.

[21] Claus (1981), ch. 1. Claus's overall argument is otherwise very different from mine (see above, Ch. 2 n. 37).

[22] Claus (1981), 16. For the bridging of the gap between agency and function, see also Snell (1953), 15. For detailed expositions of the attested examples see also Darcus (1979b) for φρήν, Darcus (1980) for νόος, Darcus Sullivan (1980, 1981) for θυμός, Darcus Sullivan (1987) for πραπίδες, and Darcus Sullivan (1988), 37–175 for φρήν/φρένες.

[23] It is perhaps a pity that Claus goes on to fit the psychological entities into a rigid division of categories, forcing each instance to be taken *either* as an agent *or* as a function. As I argue in this chapter, it makes better sense to collapse the distinction between concrete and abstract, so that the distinction between life-forces and organs ceases to be relevant. This is enough to do away with many of the complexities of Claus's analysis.

activities: sometimes they think, sometimes man thinks in, by, with, or through them, and sometimes they stand for the resultant thought itself. In this light it will be easier to understand that in sequences of extended introspection the locus of the psychological process seems to swing startlingly from one pole to the other.

The sliding scale of agency and function in Iliad I–VI

At one extreme the entity named by θυμός and the other nouns behaves like an independent agent. It is tantamount to the man himself, so that it acts as a periphrasis for his name, Πυλαιμένεος λάσιον κῆρ (II. 851). It desires to eat or drink, πιέειν ὅτε θυμὸς ἀνώγοι (IV. 263), similarly οὐδέ τι θυμὸς ἐδεύετο δαιτὸς ἐίσης (I. 468 = I. 602 = II. 431). It holds ideas or skills, θυμὸς ἐνὶ στήθεσσι φίλοισι | ἤπια δήνεα οἶδε (IV. 360–1); one imagines it as forgetting a thought or emotion, φαίην κε φρέν᾿ ἀτέρπου ὀϊζύος ἐκλελαθέσθαι (VI. 285); it carries out organized thought, ἐν δέ οἱ ἦτορ | στήθεσσιν λασίοισι διάνδιχα μερμήριξεν (I. 188–9); it desires a particular course of action, θυμὸς ἐπέσσυται ὄφρ᾿ ἐπαμύνω (VI. 361; sim. I. 173) and a particular activity is dear to it, φίλα φρεσί (I. 107). By its own act it practises an emotion: it is eager or hasty, μαίμησε δέ οἱ φίλον ἦτορ (V. 670), and it floats or swells unrestrainedly in arrogance, ὁπλοτέρων ἀνδρῶν φρένες ἠερέθονται (III. 108).

At a slightly reduced level of independence, it is passively subjected to emotional experience: it is filled with anger, μένεος δὲ μέγα φρένες ἀμφὶ μέλαιναι | πίμπλαντο (I. 103–4), and it is struck or broken up by terror, κατεπλήγη φίλον ἦτορ (III. 31) or ὀρίνθη θυμός (V. 29). In like manner it is penetrated or entered by emotions and sense-impressions. Grief arrives at it, ἄλγος ἱκάνει | θυμὸν ἐμόν (III. 97–8); a divinity throws an emotion into it, θεὰ γλυκὺν ἵμερον ἔμβαλε θυμῶι (III. 138); passion envelops it, ἔρως φρένας ἀμφεκάλυψεν (III. 442); exhaustion goes around it, πόνος φρένας ἀμφιβέβηκεν (VI. 355); an insult bites it, δάκε δὲ φρένας Ἕκτορι μῦθος (V. 493); one helps it by favourable acts, ἤ ἔπει ὤνησας κραδίην Διὸς ἠὲ καὶ ἔργωι (I. 395); an arrow-wound hurts it, κῆδε δὲ θυμόν (V. 400).

Similarly, the apparatus can be persuaded or moved to thought or emotion by a person or god. To encourage people is to raise it up in them, Τρωσὶν θυμὸν ἐγεῖραι (v. 510); a goddess gives one an idea in it, τῶι γὰρ ἐπὶ φρεσὶ θῆκε θεά (I. 55); another person persuades it of something, τῶι δ' ἄρα θυμὸν ἐνὶ στήθεσσιν ἔπειθε (VI. 51; sim. IV. 104), or urges or prompts it, ὄτρυνε μένος καὶ θυμὸν ἑκάστου (V. 470 = v. 792 = VI. 72). One vexes or disturbs it, θυμὸν ἐνὶ στήθεσσιν ὄρινε (II. 142, III. 395, IV. 208), or turns it in a new direction, τράπε θυμὸν Ἀθήνη (v. 676; sim. VI. 61), or even takes it away by making the person behave foolishly, Γλαύκωι Κρονίδης φρένας ἐξέλετο Ζεύς (VI. 234).

So far, our instances have suggested that the psychological agent acts or suffers on its own, which could simply imply that it is tantamount to the thinking person as a whole. However, it can also impel the person to a course of action, αὐτῶν θυμὸς ἐποτρύνει καὶ ἀνώγει (VI. 439; sim. VI. 444). It can drive him on to rash action, as οὔ θήν μιν πάλιν αὖτις ἀνήσει θυμὸς ἀγήνωρ | νεικείειν βασιλῆας (II. 276–7), or to piety, σὲ δ' ἐνθάδε θυμὸς ἀνῆκεν | . . . Διὶ χεῖρας ἀνασχεῖν (VI. 256–7). These last examples seem to take the mental apparatus as something that the person owns and holds inside himself; and the name of the person himself often stands beside it in the dative or genitive case. The construction is common when its quality or character is referred to, as when one wishes another's physical strength were like his mental strength,

εἴθ', ὡς θυμὸς ἐνὶ στήθεσσι φίλοισιν,
ὥς τοι γούναθ' ἔποιτο. (IV. 313–14)

Often an expression on this pattern occurs with a descriptive adjective, as when Agamemnon wishes that there was a particular kind of mentality *to* ('possessed by') everyone, τοῖος πᾶσιν θυμὸς ἐνὶ στήθεσσι γένοιτο (IV. 289). Likewise one accuses another of cowardice, σοὶ δὲ κακὸς μὲν θυμός [sc. ἔστι] (v. 643), and Homer imagines how it would be if he had a heart of brass, [εἰ] χάλκεον . . . μοι ἦτορ ἐνείη (II. 490; sim. III. 60); likewise there is no secure mental apparatus in a fool, τούτωι δ' οὔτ' ἄρ νῦν φρένες ἔμπεδοι οὔτ' ἄρ' ὀπίσσω | ἔσσονται (VI. 352–3). Similarly the mental apparatus *of* kings is large, θυμὸς δὲ μέγας ἐστὶ διοτρεφέων βασιλήων (II. 196). It is in the same way that a person can be described as something like 'greathearted', μεγαλήτωρ (II. 547, 641, V. 468, 674, 785, VI. 283, 395).

Again, the person can be said to hold or possess the mental apparatus or the experience of thought: τόνδε νόον καὶ θυμὸν ἐνὶ στήθεσσιν ἔχοντες (IV. 309) or τλήμονα θυμὸν ἔχων (V. 670) or θυμὸν ἔχων ὃν καρτερόν, ὡς τὸ πάρος περ (V. 806). Achilles says a coward has the mental stuff of a hind—κυνὸς ὄμματ' ἔχων, κραδίην δ' ἐλάφοιο (I. 225). The apparatus is subordinated to the person still more decisively when he experiences an emotion by doing something to it. He puts an emotion in it, χόλον τόνδ' ἔνθεο θυμῶι (VI. 326); he afflicts it with grief, ἔνδοθι θυμὸν ἀμύξεις (I. 243); he represses it in self-control, χόλον παύσειεν ἐρητύσειέ τε θυμόν (I. 192) or ἐπιγνάμψασα φίλον κῆρ (I. 569); by adopting a mood of courage he picks it up, as ἄλκιμον ἦτορ ἕλεσθε (V. 529).

At the next stage, the mental apparatus loses its autonomy: the personal agent thinks or feels in his own right and the apparatus's name is used to qualify or localize the action. He is angry, μάλα θυμὸν . . . χολώθη (IV. 494) or χωόμενος κῆρ (I. 44), or grieved, ἀκηχεμένη φίλον ἦτορ (V. 364) and κῆρ ἀχέων (V. 399); and hurtful words are experienced in the same way, as when Paris tells Helen not to assail him with insults, μή με . . . χαλεποῖσιν ὀνείδεσι θυμὸν ἔνιπτε (III. 438). The pattern is the same when an emotion arrives to the person in or at or with respect to the apparatus, constructed with a double accusative. Thus grief comes, μιν ἄχος κραδίην καὶ θυμὸν ἵκανεν (II. 171); likewise sorrow, τί δέ σε φρένας ἵκετο πένθος; (I. 362) and joy, χαρείη δὲ φρένα μήτηρ (VI. 481) or ὁ δὲ φρένα τέρπετ' ἀκούων (I. 474) or simply γηθόσυνος κῆρ (IV. 272 = 326).[24] In the same way when a deity impels mortals to valour she rouses strength for each of them with regard to his heart, ἐν δὲ σθένος ὦρσεν ἑκάστωι | καρδίηι (II. 451–2).

We reach a further degree of the same subordination when the person thinks or feels emotion in or through or along the apparatus, usually with the preposition κατά. In this way Homer renders anger, χωόμενον κατὰ θυμόν (I. 429); fear, δείδοικα κατὰ φρένα (I. 555); pondering, τὰ φρονέοντ' ἀνὰ θυμόν (II. 36) or μερμήριξε . . . κατὰ φρένα καὶ κατὰ θυμόν (V. 671) or ταῦθ' ὥρμαινε . . . κατὰ φρένα καὶ κατὰ θυμόν (I. 193). In this way a

---

[24] Similarly one woman is compared to another 'in respect of' her mental and physical qualities: οὔ ἑθέν ἐστι χερείων | . . . οὔτ' ἄρ φρένας οὔτε τι ἔργα (I. 114–15).

decision manifests itself, ἥδε δέ οἱ κατὰ θυμὸν ἀρίστη φαίνετο βουλή (II. 5), and one apprehends knowledge, ἥιδεε γὰρ κατὰ θυμόν (II. 409) or τάδε οἶδα κατὰ φρένα καὶ κατὰ θυμόν (IV. 163, VI. 447) or τὸ οἶδε κατὰ φρένα (V. 406). Conversely, one who is ignored or disliked is excluded from the mental process, ἀπὸ θυμοῦ | μᾶλλον ἐμοὶ ἔσεαι (I. 562–3).

Next, the person acts independently with the mental entity in the dative case, as the location or instrument of his thought. This is especially so with affective or reactive emotions: one offers love through the apparatus, θυμῶι φιλέουσά τε κηδομένη τε (I. 196 = I. 209), or accords honour, μοι περὶ κῆρι τιέσκετο Ἴλιος ἱρή (IV. 46)[25] or enmity, τοι ἀπέχθωνται [sc. certain cities] περὶ κῆρι (IV. 53). Similarly one is angry, θυμῶι κεχολωμένον (I. 217; cf. II. 241), and one rejoices, ἄλλοι τε Τρῶες μέγα κεν κεχαροίατο θυμῶι (I. 256); a gift is given unwillingly, ἀέκοντί γε θυμῶι (IV. 43); and in the same way one grieves, μή. . . λίην ἀκαχίζεο θυμῶι (VI. 486), or feels reverently abashed, σεβάσσατο γὰρ τό γε θυμῶι (VI. 167, 417), or holds miseries, ἔχω δ' ἄχε' ἄκριτα θυμῶι (III. 412).

Knowledge and cognitive activity take place in the same way, in or by means of the apparatus. One plots evil there, κακὰ μήσατο θυμῶι (VI. 157), or holds thought or disposition, φρεσὶν . . . ἥιδη (V. 326), or conceals knowledge, σὺ σῆισιν ἔχε φρεσίν (II. 33, 70); and Thersites keeps unpleasant thoughts or sayings in the apparatus, ἔπεα φρεσὶν ἧισιν ἄκοσμά τε πολλά τε ἥιδη (II. 213). Similarly spirit or determination arises in or through the apparatus, μετὰ φρεσὶ γίγνεται ἀλκή (IV. 245); one who is yearning or raging is θυμῶι μεμαώς (V. 135) or ὀλοιῆισι φρεσὶ θύει (I. 342); one dares or endures to do something by means of the apparatus, οὔτε λόχονδ' ἰέναι . . . | τέτληκας θυμῶι (I. 227–8).

At the final extreme, the apparatus can simply be the place *within* which the person does his thinking or feeling. Martial spirit lodges there, as in the phrase οὐκ ἔστι βίη φρεσὶν οὔτε τις ἀλκή (III. 45); it is there that one one feels spite, κοτέοντο νεμέσσηθέν τ' ἐνὶ θυμῶι (II. 223), or fury, ἐν θυμῶι μεμαῶτες (III. 9); likewise one ponders, σὺ δ' ἐν φρεσὶ βάλλεο σῆισι (I. 297 = IV. 39 = V. 259), or knows something in the apparatus, ἔγνω ἧισιν ἐνὶ φρεσί (I. 333; sim. II. 301).

---

[25] I take περί as an adverb rather than a preposition here.

In this way the range between agency and function turns out to be smooth and continuous. The entity represented by the nouns in the θυμός family stands in no fixed relationship with the human being, since it is sometimes the source of thought, sometimes its mode or instrument, and sometimes merely the locus of the thought-process. It is this fluid definition which enables states of indecision to be imagined where the situation moves from man addressing θυμός to θυμός addressing man, or—as in the *Odyssey* passages quoted above—where the urge of the θυμός and the action of the bodily self are contrasted with each other. Given this continuum between agency and function, it would be misleading to take those passages in isolation as illustrating a permanent dichotomy between θυμός as 'mind' and αὐτός as 'body'. Homer's language does not allow us to distinguish whether they are the agents, the instruments, or the results of those processes. Although from a modern point of view there may be an easy distinction between psychological agents and psychological functions, between that which thinks and that which is thought, we cannot readily apply that distinction to Homer. Our final response to this problem belongs later, but for the present it will serve to warn us from applying any easy translation-word like 'mind' or 'heart' to explain the area covered by our nouns. Like those words they name something that is inside the body, but its life is not like the abstract autonomous life that a language like English gives to the mind.

Mental life is in the breast

The next, and crucial, aspect of this psychological system is that it has nothing to do with the head or the brain. The head, κεφαλή or κάρη or κάρηνον, is a sign of life and identity, especially from another person's point of view,[26] but the seat of thought and consciousness is the upper torso: the θυμός is in the breast, ἐν στήθεσσι, and when an act of thought is described the words ἐν στήθεσσι are equivalent to ἐν θυμῶι or ἐνὶ φρεσί:[27]

---

[26] The main significance of the head is its symbolic association with life threatened and life as opposed to death, on which see Ch. 6 nn. 29–30.

[27] Jahn (1987) documents this fully: see esp. the tables on pp. 255–8.

ἐν δέ οἱ ἦτορ
στήθεσσιν λασίοισι διάνδιχα μερμήριξεν. (I. 188–9)

He thinks in his θυμός, his φρένες, his ἦτορ, he thinks in his hairy chest.[28] Yet the intellectual processes undertaken there are the same as what we would assign to the mind: thinking, emotion, awareness, reflection, will. If these things are in the chest, so also are the lungs and the heart and other things of flesh and blood; and our most glaring problem is the relationship between the two.

The crux of the problem is that when anatomy rather than psychology is in question, each of φρήν, ἦτορ, κραδίη, κῆρ, πραπίδες is the name of a solid physical part of the body. This is best illustrated when warriors are cut open in the mayhem of battle: a man is wounded or pierced in the ἦτορ, his φρένες are cut open through a wound, a spear pierces his κραδίη, his φρένες slip out of a gash in his torso, another is struck in the liver below the πραπίδες, another is pierced in the place 'where the φρένες are enclosed around the dense κῆρ' (XVI. 481).[29] There is an interesting reflex of this in the famous passage where Achilles tries to embrace the ghost of Patroclus and finds that he cannot touch it:

ὢ πόποι, ἦ ῥά τίς ἐστι καὶ εἰν Ἀΐδαο δόμοισιν
ψυχὴ καὶ εἴδωλον, ἀτὰρ φρένες οὐκ ἔνι πάμπαν. (XXIII. 103–4)

What he has realized is not that the ghost had no mind or wits—what it said was very lucid—but that there was no physical substance in the breast when he flung his arms around it.[30]

---

[28] λάσιον obviously refers to the visible breast as shaggy or hairy (cf. XXIV. 125; ix. 433). Note also the curious Πυλαιμένεος λάσιον κῆρ (II. 851; sim. XVI. 554), a periphrasis of the proper name of the same kind as ἱερὴ ἲς Τηλεμάχοιο and similar (on which see esp. below, pp. 110–15).

[29] The clear cases of this are conveniently collected by Jahn (1987), 9–19; see also Ireland and Steel (1975). Briefly: a man is pierced, βεβλαμμένον, in his ἦτορ (XVI. 660) and another is δεδαϊγμένον in his ἦτορ (XVII. 535); one is struck ἔνθ' ἄρα τε φρένες ἔρχαται ἀμφ' ἀδινὸν κῆρ (XVI. 481); a spear is pulled out from a wound, προτὶ δὲ φρένες αὐτῶι ἕποντο (XVI. 504); a spear pierces a man's κραδίη (XIII. 442); a man is struck in his ἧπαρ ὑπὸ πραπίδων (XI. 579 = XIII. 412 = XVII. 349); a foe could be struck πρὸς στῆθος, ὅθι φρένες ἧπαρ ἔχουσιν (ix. 301).

[30] In antiquity this interpretation was offered by Aristophanes. Another

If that were all, one might think it enough to say that each of the words in the θυμός family has 'two meanings', a part of the body or a part of the mind, so that the psychological uses are somehow 'metaphorical'—the English word 'heart' makes for a suitably trivial analogy. But the Homeric facts cannot be tamed in that way. The foundations of an understanding of the θυμός family were laid by R. B. Onians[31] with his brilliantly imaginative insight that the φρήν/φρένες are the lungs, the θυμός is the air breathed into them, while each of ἦτορ, πραπίδες, κραδίη, κῆρ are specific organs in the chest. The pivot of the theory is that the ongoing process of thought is conceived of as if it were precisely identified with the palpable inhalation of breath and the half-imagined mingling of breath with blood and bodily fluids in the soft, warm, flowing substances that make up what is behind the chest wall. If this is right, the life of the organs in the chest is exactly the same thing as what we would call the life of the mind; and it follows naturally that the organs of thought can be seen and touched when the body is pierced.

It is not hard to see why classical scholars have nearly always treated Onians's theory with suspicion or downright scorn. By imposing stark anatomical translations—lungs, blood, chest wall—he seemed to reduce Homeric psychology to something grotesque. Take one of the dramatic moments of the *Iliad*, when Agamemnon first rises up in rage:

> τοῖσι δ᾽ ἀνέστη
> ἥρως Ἀτρεΐδης εὐρὺ κρείων Ἀγαμέμνων
> ἀχνύμενος, μένεος δὲ μέγα φρένες ἀμφὶ μέλαιναι
> πίμπλαντ᾽, ὄσσε δέ οἱ πυρὶ λαμπετόωντι ἐΐκτην. (I. 101–4)

With Onians the underlined words ought to mean that 'his lungs were filled and darkened by blood'. So translated, the explanation of the apparent *non sequitur* was the tradition that the dead are incapable of thought, which is referred to several times in the Nekuia of the *Odyssey*. But this tradition is one that appears and disappears even within the Nekuia itself, and it plays no part whatever in Patroclus' ghost's dealings with Achilles, so that it would be very weak as an explanation of the present passage. See Richardson ad loc., with refs. to scholia, and Ch. 6 below, pp. 206–7.

[31] Onians (1951), 13–83 and *passim*. The problem is also touched on by Böhme (1929), but with the bodily and psychological identity of each noun firmly separated from each other (see esp. 29–36).

words sound crude and primitive, impossible to square with the reader's intuition that Homer's portrayal of the king's mental state is deep and subtle and sophisticated. The theory would have us believe that the psychological subtleties of Agamemnon's changing moods are purely and simply the movement of breath and oozing liquids—the very substances, in fact, that Achilles would see if he sliced the king open with his sword. Like many of his generation Onians was captivated by the idea that ancient ideas could be illuminated by the study of modern non-Western cultures, but that enterprise came to grief when classical scholars like him chose to draw on theories of 'primitive thought' and the 'prelogical mentality' that made the peoples studied seem naïve or absurd.[32] In this case, Onians gladly assumed that the early Greeks resembled the 'primitives' of armchair anthropology in that they were unable to think in terms of abstract ideas or figurative language.[33] Despite the rigour and subtlety of his reading of the Greek evidence, he was foolish or humble enough to let it be influenced by half-understood analyses of people he had never met, *obscurum per obscurius*, so that Homer's language was forced into a strait-jacket of brutally literal interpretation.

This means that although in what follows I will draw greatly on Onians's insights, I will also try to address the nagging question: does Homer imagine a 'mind' which is no more a part of the body than what we today think of as the organs of the upper torso? If θυμός is precisely what our language calls breath in the lungs, as Onians supposed, then how could it make sense for Homer to describe it behaving as an autonomous agent of

---

[32] Onians (1951) acknowledges the inflence of Lévy-Bruhl's theory of the primitive or prelogical mentality in its early, crude form: see in particular p. 19, quoting from the first edition of *Les Fonctions mentales dans les sociétés inférieures*.

[33] (1951), 51: 'At the stage of thought at which these beliefs emerged, there was difficulty in conceiving anything except material entities'. The other side of the coin is that Onians made no move to set aside the a priori assumption that the θυμός family act as a localized soul or mind. Consider the categories of his first sentence: 'What is the nature of the mind? What are its processes? What is the soul? . . . This book began in an attempt to discover the earliest answers of the Greeks and the Romans to these fundamental questions, the beliefs which for centuries satisfied their minds and governed their actions' (ibid., p. xi).

thought and emotion? We will see that this simple one-to-one identification is less than the whole truth, since the relationship between the bodily and mental identity of these entities is subtle and elusive, with no equivalent in either the psychological or the anatomical language familiar today. Similarly *νόος*, which we will examine in detail in due course, is never spoken of as if it were a part of the body, yet it is a product of the processes that go on in *θυμός* and the others.[34] Seeing that Homer's psychological system allows abstract ideas to arise from entities which are wholly and solidly part of the body, it is clear from the start that unless Homer's culture is naïve and stupid—a supposition that I will never admit—then this psychology is not easily reducible to what we can apprehend on the basis of our modern understanding of the physical body.[35]

The 'concreteness of the innards', in Ruth Padel's phrase,[36] is confirmed in several directions at once by Homer's words, once we proceed from the minimum hypothesis that *θυμός* is breath inhaled deep into the lungs,[37] and *φρήν/φρένες* are the lungs themselves.[38] These basic identities are unmistakable.

[34] See Onians (1951), 82–3; Jahn (1987), 46 and 46–118 *passim*; and note examples of *νόος* in the pattern of ebb and flow discussed below.

[35] Compare Austin (1975: 103–13), who denies completely that *θυμός* is ever identifiable with a part of the body, on the grounds that it is 'too versatile' in its role and behaviour. Cf. also Vivante (1956), 113–20.

[36] (1992), esp. ch.2. In Padel's work on concepts of 'inner' and 'outer' in tragedy, one of the central themes is the need to approach the language of psychological life by setting aside modern distinctions between literal and metaphorical and between body and spirit. To that extent her approach has much in common with mine here. However, she approaches the language of Homer and that of the tragic poets as one, on the grounds that 'Tragedy's language of consciousness rests on Homer' (18). This means that much of the imagery she discusses is not relevant to my treatment here, since in fact the range of psychological metaphor found in tragedy is much more varied and more figurative than the patterns recognizable in Homer. A full discussion of this problem would be out of place here. On the psychological imagery of the tragedians, see also Webster (1957); Sansone (1975); and cf. Handley (1956) on Aristophanes.

[37] Onians (1951), 44–61, esp. 50; Harrison (1960); Caswell (1990), 16–21 and *passim*; Padel (1992), 29–30.

[38] Onians (1951), 23–30; see also Darcus Sullivan (1988), 7–9, 21–9. Darcus Sullivan usefully surveys earlier theories identifying *φρένες* with lungs, diaphragm, and pericardium, but draws a sharp distinction between the

Odysseus lies breathless with exhaustion, ἄπνευστος καὶ ἄναυδος, then recovers his breath: ἄμπνυτο καὶ ἐς φρένα θυμὸς ἀγέρθη (v. 458; sim. IV. 152, XXII. 475, xxiv. 349), and he is θυμηγερέων (vii. 283), that is he inhales and gathers breath into his lungs, just as in the opposite event an exhausted man has little breath, ὀλίγος . . . θυμὸς ἐνῆεν (I. 593), while a dying man exhales it in a final groan, θυμὸν ἄισθε καὶ ἤρυγεν (XX. 403) or breathes it out, θυμὸν ἀποπνείων (IV. 524); similarly one groans with a deep breath, μέγα δὲ στεναχίζετο θυμῶι (VII. 95).[39] Now θυμός is ἐνὶ φρεσίν as well as more vaguely ἐν στήθεσσι, and many epithets of θυμός are themselves compounds in -φρων;[40] similarly, θυμός is often the subject of an active verb of thinking, while φρένες never are. When a man thinks, therefore, θυμός may be the active agent,[41] but φρένες are the place or instrument in which such thought is carried out.[42] All this makes sense if θυμός is breath which is held in φρένες when thought goes on. The φρένες themselves are in the chest, στήθεα; they must be in front of the μετάφρενον, which is evidently the back of the torso (see II. 265, V. 56, etc.); they are indeterminately singular or plural, φρήν or φρένες, and θυμός can 'blow in two ways' in them, δίχα . . . ἐνὶ φρεσὶ θυμὸς ἄητο (XXI. 386). When a man groans, ἀνεστενάχ-ιζε, and expels breath from his mouth the φρένες shake, τρομέοντο δέ οἱ φρένες ἐντός (X. 9–10). The apparatus of breathing fits the language exactly; and the fact that when a man is cut open the φρένες but *not* the θυμός can be seen accords well with the fact that the breath would be gasped out at that moment.

bodily and the psychological meaning. Rather than assigning specific bodily meanings to θυμός and φρένες, she prefers the vaguer label 'indefinitely corporeal'. Similarly Ireland and Steel (1975) identify θυμός and the others in terms of the physiology of the chest in less precise terms than Onians. Snell (1978: esp. 53–60), argues closely against a sharp distinction between the anatomical and psychological identity of φρένες. Cf. Chantraine, s.v. φρήν, with refs. to earlier theories.

[39] Once one forgets woolly English expressions like 'to groan in spirit', these words are untranslatable unless θυμός is the source or essence of the gasping. Compare ὀλοφύρεται ἐν φρεσὶ θυμός (VIII. 202; sim. XVI. 450, XXII. 169), where the mental apparatus is the agent of the gasp.

[40] These epithets are usefully collected by Darcus (1977).

[41] On this aspect of θυμός, see esp. Cheyns (1981), esp. 140; Cheyns (1983); Padel (1992), 27–9.

[42] On this aspect of φρένες, see esp. Snell (1978), 53–4; Darcus Sullivan (1988), 71–112.

As we try to picture what goes on inside the breast, there is little to be gained by assigning precise anatomical identities to each of κῆρ, κραδίη, ἦτορ, πραπίδες. Probably the κῆρ is the heart, since the φρένες are wrapped around it (XVI. 481), and the cognate word κραδίη presumably names the same or a kindred organ;[43] the ἦτορ must be somehow connected to the θυμός if the phrase μεγαλήτορα θυμόν is to be meaningful;[44] and the πραπίδες are something that sits above the liver.[45] Such speculations can be multiplied, but they are not our concern here. Onians's insight combines well with Jahn's formular analysis if we accept that since Homer does not think in terms of X-rays and neat textbook diagrams, the organs of the chest will naturally be less sharply defined for him than for us, so that the distinctions between different organs and processes will necessarily seem blurred. The passages in which men are cut open and their organs revealed are enough to show that each of these names corresponds to some physical organ, but in psychological language it is difficult to distinguish between them. Thus although they are the names of separate bodily parts, it is not illogical that when they refer to intangible mental activity they are virtually synonymous.

Mental life ebbs and flows as breath and fluids

Let us pursue the hypothesis that θυμός is breath drawn into the lungs. In origin the word corresponds exactly to Latin *fumus,* Sanskrit *dhuma-,* and Lithuanian *duma,* 'smoke':[46] and although that etymology is no index to its active meaning in Greek, it encourages the claim that θυμός is billowing gaseous breath. Within Greek, closely related words suggest more clearly what sort of phenomenon is involved. First, observe

[43] κῆρ and κραδίη are reflexes of a single root, which in prehistoric Greek might have looked like *kr̥d-. The best indication that the referent is the anatomical heart is provided by cognates in other languages, as Latin *cor(d-),* Irish *cride* (see Chantraine s.v.).

[44] Onians (1951: 81–2) holds that the ἦτορ is a collection of blood-vessels near the lungs, at least when the word is not simply a virtual synonym of φρένες and θυμός.

[45] See n. 29 above.

[46] See Chantraine, s.v., who accepts the equation but surprisingly thinks it 'difficile pour le sens'; compare Renehan (1975), s.v. θυμός; *LfgrE* s.v. θυμός.

θύ(ν)ω, the verbal reflex of the same root,[47] which denotes the violent surging of wind and water, air and fluid: a river rushes along in swollen flood, ἐπέσσυτο οἴδματι θύων (XXI. 234; sim. 324), likewise the swollen sea groans under the winds, ἔστενεν οἴδματι θύων (XXIII. 230; sim. xiii. 85); a wind rushing in storm is λαίλαπι θύων (xii. 400, 408, 426), and the floor of a room after slaughter is awash with blood, αἵματι θῦεν (xi. 420, xxii. 309, xxiv. 185). The word is further used of a man who rushes about in wild fury, θῦνε (v. 250, XI. 342 = XX. 412, XXII. 272; xxiv. 449, etc.),[48] and Homer says that such a one resembles a flooding

[47] Harrison (1960) offers a brilliantly perceptive sketch of this relationship. See also Chantraine (1933: 132–4), taking θυμός from θύω as one of the class of verb-based action nouns that is represented also by such forms as θωμός/τίθημι, χυμός/χέω. Interestingly, the parallel with Sanskrit *aniti* 'blows' suggests that Greek ἄνεμος may be formed in the same way. A further group of words built on the same stem answer in various ways to the idea of producing smoke, vapour, or fragrance. Attested early are the verbs θυμιάω, 'make to smoke' (first in Hipponax *175 W) and θυόω in the participle τεθυωμένον, meaning something like 'anointed, fragrant' (XIV. 172); the adjectives θυόεις (XV. 153), θυώδης (v. 264, etc.), θυήεις (VIII. 48, XXIII. 148, viii. 363), all referring to the rising of smells and the like into the air; and above all the verb θύω for offering sacrifice. This θύω is already well attested in Homer (IX. 219; ix. 231, etc.) with several associated nouns, notably θύσθλα as instruments of sacrificial ritual (VI. 134) and θυηλή or θύος as the thing burnt in sacrifice (VI. 270, IX. 220, 499). θύος is also attested as a fragrant substance. (τύφω 'produce smoke', whose perfect middle τέθυμμαι shows that the present is *θύφω distorted by Grassmann's law, seems to be on the same horizon.) When θύω refers to sacrifice the offering is always burnt, and the defining element of the ritual is the rising-up of the smoke: see esp. the clear (if possibly post-Homeric) account at VIII. 547–52. The semantic link between the members of this group, and between the group as a whole and θυμός, becomes irresistible when we find βωμὸς θυήεις (VIII. 48, XXIII. 148; viii. 363), an altar from which the smoke of sacrifice is raised, and θυόεν νέφος (XV. 153), a billowing cloud. Similarly θύος, which for Homer is something burnt in sacrifice, is attested in Linear B for aromatic spices (*tu-we-a*, Pylos Un08: see Ventris–Chadwick, pp. 223–4). Although the movement of billowing smoke unites all these words, in the case of the verb θύω itself it remains difficult to unite 'offer burnt sacrifice' and 'surge along' (or the like) within the ambit of a single lexeme with a single range of meaning, so it seems that the two words must be separate in practice in the Homeric vocabulary. All we need definitely conclude of the whole array of words is that they offer *historical* corroboration for the argument that θυμός is vaporous, smokelike, and billowing.

[48] I do not know what significance, if any, attaches to the appearance of a nasal infix in the imperfect and once in the present imperative (v. 250): cf. Risch (1974), § 99b.

river, θῦνε ... ποταμῶι πλήθοντι ἐοικώς (v. 87). This is the bodily movement of the whole man: but Achilles describes a more psychological movement when he says that the raging Agamemnon surges along with a wild mental apparatus in his breast, ὀλοιῆισι φρεσὶ θύει (I. 342). Since what surges in these φρένες is literally θυμός, here there is a perfect semantic match between verb and noun. Linked to this in turn is the idea that when a man is impelled to action or decision, θυμός itself rushes forward impetuously, ἔσσυται (x. 484) or ἐπέσσυται (I. 173, VI. 361, IX. 42, 398). We are now able to move on from our first, clumsy equation of θυμός with smoky billowing breath: it is specifically breath that is vigorous, active, self-propelling, with the strong swift movement that marks the actions of both warrior and thinker.

The idea of violent windy-and-watery movement reappears in the noun θύελλα, a raging tempest, which corresponds to θύω in the same way as ἄελλα does to ἄημι with very similar meanings.[49] The implications of this link are writ large in imagery that Homer applies to θυμός in mental life. As C. P. Caswell has shown, many of the verbs that render its movement are used identically of gusts and storms—ὀρίνω, ἀνίημι, ἐποτρύνω, ἐπισσεύομαι—and on the larger scale several similes liken confusion and indecision in the θυμός to tempests at sea.[50] The clearest example is when Nestor cannot decide how best to help his comrades in the battle by the ships:

> ὡς δ' ὅτε πορφύρηι πέλαγος μέγα κύματι κωφῶι,
> ὀσσόμενον λιγέων ἀνέμων λαιψηρὰ κέλευθα
> αὔτως, οὐδ' ἄρα τε προκυλίνδεται οὐδετέρωσε,
> πρίν τινα κεκριμένον καταβήμεναι ἐκ Διὸς οὖρον,
> ὣς ὁ γέρων ὥρμαινε δαϊζόμενος κατὰ θυμὸν
> διχθάδια ... (XIV. 16–21)

Similarly, weariness and confusion among the Achaean warriors is like a turbulent sea stirred up by conflicting winds:

[49] On ἄελλα, ἄημι, ἀήτης, see Chantraine (1933), 252.
[50] (1990), esp. 51–64; and cf. Onians (1951), 45–6.

ὡς δ' ἄνεμοι δύο πόντον ὀρίνετον ἰχθυόεντα,
Βορέης καὶ Ζέφυρος, τώ τε Θρήικηθεν ἄητον,
ἐλθόντ' ἐξαπίνης· ἄμυδις δέ τε κῦμα κελαινὸν
κορθύεται, πολλὸν δέ παρὲξ ἅλα φῦκος ἔχευεν,
ὣς ἐδαΐζετο θυμὸς ἐνὶ στήθεσσιν Ἀχαιῶν.   (IX. 4–8)

The movement of breath as thought and passion is mirrored in the equally vital and equally intangible flow of squalling winds and churning waves in the world at large; and the singular ἐδαΐζετο θυμός suggests that the confusion is within each individual man rather than between factions.[51] Similarly anguish batters the θυμός, θυμὸν ἐρέχθων (v. 83 = v. 157) just as a storm-battered ship is ἐρεχθομένη (XXIII. 316–17). In tighter words the conception is the same when strife among the gods makes their θυμοί blow in contrary directions, δίχα δέ σφιν ἐνὶ φρεσὶ θυμὸς ἄητο (XXI. 386), and again when a goddess's μέγας ... θυμός drives her to impetuosity that blows like wind, θάρσος ἄητον (XXI. 395); while the adjective ἀεσίφρων and the noun ἀεσιφροσύνη, referring to recklessness or folly, probably combine the root of ἄημι with that of φρένες and φρονέω:[52] thought is the same thing as fierce blowing breath.

[51] Note also a simile (II. 143-9) where division of opinion in the assembly is likened to the movement of waves on a stormy sea. Here the same verb describes their mental state, τοῖσι δέ θυμὸν ἐνὶ στήθεσσιν ὄρινε (II. 142); but the following simile hangs on the verb κινήθη, with the assembly moved or stirred like choppy waves, and it is unclear whether the comparison is with their mental state or their physical movement or both. Similarly, a more complex simile (XV. 624–9) likens Hector's attack on the Achaeans to a storm falling on a ship at sea, and the sailors' terror corresponds to the Achaeans' dismay, again ἐδαΐζετο θυμός: but it is difficult to tell how complex is the binding-together of ideas between simile-image and narrative, and it is not clear that what is happening in the Achaeans' θυμοί is being compared to the turmoil of the winds as well as the sailors' terror.

[52] To be ἀεσίφρων is to be a reckless fool, and ἀεσιφροσύνη is childish naïvety (XV. 470). In such a compound the second element is normally the object of the verbal idea expressed in the first element: compare ἀρτίφρων (XXIV. 261), which embodies the root of ἀραρίσκω—the sound thinker settles or fixes his thought-stuff (cf. Risch (1974), §§ 70–1). On that analogy ἀεσίφρων is simple enough: the person's thought proceeds as a gusty blowing. However, ancient and modern scholars have sometimes read ἀασίφρων and ἀασιφροσύνη, whose first element would embody the root seen in ἀάω and ἄτη rather than that in ἄημι. In some at least of the attestations the folly in question is less serious than what might be called ἄτη, and this strengthens the case for reading ἀεσι-; on the other hand, when one who is φρεσὶν ᾗσιν ἀασθείς holds his anger in his

If we are willing to regard the similes of storm not as isolated decorations but as a serious reflection of Homer's conception of mental life, we can seize on them as a representation writ large of how thought is imagined to proceed. Just as rushing wind moves over the face of the sea, so the inhaled breath rushes along towards the oozing stuff at the base of the lungs; and just as the dark flowing sea is churned up with the winds in the tempest, so this breath mingles with blood and the other ebbing and flowing liquids of the expanding chest; and once we add the point that in practice each of the nouns in the θυμός family can stand for the whole phenomenon, then Homer's psychological imagery will fall into a subtle and consistent pattern.

What goes on in φρένες? The activity must be what is represented by the verb φρονέω, which is derived from the noun by way of the compounds in -φρων.[53] Usually this verb seems translatable by psychological words like 'think' or 'ponder': but there are a few places where it is unavoidable that we interpret 'drawing into the φρένες' as inhalation.[54] When a fighting animal or a furious warrior is μέγα φρονέων[55]

ἀεσίφρονι/ἀασίφρονι θυμῶι (xxi. 301–2), it is very tempting to read ἀασι- for the sake of the *figura etymologica*. It remains possible that one of the two formations was introduced during the transmission of the text, or even that the ambiguity goes back to the living epic tradition. (See *LfgrE* s.v. ἀασίφρων; Chantraine s.v. ἀάω; Fernández-Galiano at xxi. 302. I am indebted to T. Meissner for advice on this intriguing problem.)

[53] On the sequence of word-formation from φρήν via -φρων to φρονέω, see Leumann (1950), 114–16; Ruijgh (1957), 105–6; Snell (1978), 53–5. Whatever the historical sequence of development, Homer's own words show that for him the semantic connections run in both directions. The words τῶι δὲ φρένας ἄφρονι πεῖθεν (iv. 104) make nonsense if ἄφρων here means 'without φρένες': rather, the adjective must be taking its meaning from the verb, so that a close translation would be 'she persuaded his φρένες, and he was not himself φρονέων'. (For a conceit of a somewhat similar kind, compare Eurycleia's words when she tells Penelope not to trouble Laertes: μηδὲ γέροντα κάκου κεκακωμένον, iv. 754.) However, since the relationship between φρήν and φρονέω does not answer to one of the regular patterns of word-formation there can be no guarantee that it is as active in the Homeric lexicon as is (e.g.) that between πνέω and πέπνυμαι, where the correspondence is regular and transparent between two parts of the paradigm of a single verb (below, pp. 84–5 with nn. 57–9).

[54] The examples of this are subtly demonstrated by Lockhardt (1966).

[55] Beasts, XI. 325, XVI. 758, 824; warriors, VIII. 553, XI. 296, XIII. 156,

as he surges into the fray, he is not thinking deep or complex thoughts: apparently Homer means that he is gulping in air, just as he might elsewhere describe advancing warriors as μένεα πνείοντες, experiencing the onset of warlike passion as the gulping in of breath (III. 8, XXIV. 364, etc.), while likewise μένος, θάρσος, and suchlike are breathed in or thrust in, ἔμπνευσε or ἔμβαλε, when a man is impelled to valour or high spirits by a god.[56] There is a similar suggestion when a speech in the assembly is introduced by the line

$$ὄ σφιν ἐϋφρονέων ἀγορήσατο καὶ μετέειπεν . . . \quad (\text{I. } 73 = 253, \text{ etc.})$$

The sense fits the context best if we take it that the speaker's lungs are filled with the breath of thought, ἐϋφρονέων, when he projects his voice. Similarly Priam contrasts Hector's coming death with the prospect of his own survival: when his son lies dead the old man will be ἔτι φρονέοντα, not 'still pondering' but still breathing as a living and thinking man (XXII. 59).

If when I φρονέω I draw air into the lungs, in the next stage of the process it makes sense that the key verb for sound reflective thinking is πέπνυμαι, 'I have inhaled'. Scholars have been surprisingly unwilling to accept that πέπνυμαι is the perfect middle of πνέω, 'I breathe', but the identification makes straightforward sense.[57] In the specially precise meaning

XVI. 258, XXII. 21. Of course μέγα φρονέω could be taken to mean that the breast is swollen with violent expanded thought, which is itself spoken of as breath; but it is striking that the words occur every time when the beast or warrior is moving headlong, either advancing to battle or actually attacking, when he would be engaged in action not thought.

[56] For ἔμπνευσε μένος, see e.g. X. 482, XV. 60, XV. 262 = XX. 110, XVII. 456; for ἔμβαλε μένος and similar, see III. 139, X. 366, XIII. 82, XVI. 529, XVII. 118; XIX. 10, xix. 485, etc.

[57] See Chantraine s.v.; Frisk s.v. The lexicographers' objections seem to be grounded in nothing but semantic common sense (note esp. Chantraine *ad fin.*), and I see no reason to resist the plain conclusion that πέπνυμαι relates to πνέω in the same way as (for example) κέχυμαι relates to χέω (see Risch (1974), § 120a). Beyond that, all that need be said is that the perfect πέπνυμαι denotes specifically—even exclusively—thinking as a result of inhaling, while the other forms of πνέω imply nothing but the gulping in of air; and this narrowing of the semantic range in the perfect leads to a specially precise meaning for the participle πεπνυμένος. (Compare Ruijgh (1957), 134–5, also Nehring (1947); and more extravagant speculations by Onians (1951), 57–61).

carried by the perfect πέπνυμαι, this inhalation is identified with wise thought, as when the shade of Tiresias alone among the dead retains wisdom:

> τῶι καὶ τεθνηῶτι νόον πόρε Περσεφόνεια
> οἴωι πεπνῦσθαι. (x. 494–5)

Here νόον is closely correlated to πεπνῦσθαι: when the sage thinks wisely he fills his lungs with thought (sim. xxiv. 377). The word is used especially often with reference to the maturing Telemachus,[58] and it is striking that he is described as πεπνυμένος almost exclusively when he is speaking aloud, as in the familiar line τὸν δ' αὖ Τηλέμαχος πεπνυμένος ἀντίον ηὔδα: could this refer directly to the deep breath that would begin such a speech?[59] Similarly the man who speaks wisely speaks deep-breathed things, πεπνυμένα βάζεις (ix. 58; sim. xix. 352), and when Telemachus asserts himself to his mother she accepts his μῦθον πεπνυμένον (i. 361 = xxi. 355). In essence, however, the act is deeper than merely vocal: observe how he explains that he has not yet attained full maturity:

> αὐτὰρ ἐγὼ θυμῶι νοέω καὶ οἶδα ἕκαστα,
> ἐσθλά τε καὶ τὰ χέρεια· πάρος δ' ἔτι νήπιος ἦα.
> ἀλλά τοι οὐ δύναμαι πεπνυμένα πάντα νοῆσαι. (xviii. 228–30)

The shift is natural from the deeply breathing thinker to the deeply-breathed thought. By a further shift the verb can be used to refer not to an individual act of speech or thought but

---

[58] i. 361 = xxi. 355, and very often throughout the *Odyssey*. This trait of his is especially Odyssean: note the echo at the climactic moment of Odysseus' recognition by Penelope, when he tells him that he should not be angry at her stratagem because he is a man of unrivalled intelligence, ἐπεὶ τά περ ἄλλα μάλιστα | ἀνθρώπων πέπνυσο (xxiii. 209–10).

[59] The great majority of instances of πέπνυμαι are in contexts where wisdom is shown forth in speech: the formulae introducing speeches by Telemachus and others are only the most common example of this pattern (see esp. III. 148, 203, VII. 347; iv. 204–6, xix. 350–2). However, any interpretation of this must be doubtful: at the opening of a speech, for example, we cannot tell whether πεπνυμένος is to be taken adverbially or adjectivally: either 'With a deep breath Telemachus spoke . . .' or 'Telemachus the sound thinker spoke . . .'. The rigidity of the formulaic language confounds us. Austin (1975: 74–9) explores the psychological connotations of πέπνυμαι and notes that the participle is specially appropriate at the beginning of a speech, but he skips over the connection with breathing.

to wisdom fixed in the character: the intelligent man is πεπνυμένα μήδεα εἰδώς (ii. 38; sim. iv. 696, 711, xxiv. 442, etc.) or simply πεπνυμένος (III. 148; iii. 52, 328, iv. 190, viii. 388, xviii. 65, 125, etc.).

This leads us to a further group of cognates: the adjective πινυτός, the noun πινυτή, and the verb ἀπινύσσειν.[60] To be πινυτός is to be wise by character, while πινυτή is wisdom that enters the lungs, φρένας ἵκει (xx. 228)—in other words, it is breath.[61] The range of meaning of the negative ἀπινύσσω[62] captures the idea clearly: on the one hand it is used of one unable to catch his breath, ὁ δ' ἀργαλέωι ἔχετ' ἄσθματι κῆρ ἀπινύσσων (xv. 10), and on the other of one who seems not to lack wisdom or intelligence, δοκέεις δέ μοι οὐκ ἀπινύσσειν (v. 342, vi. 258).

As breath is drawn into the mental apparatus in the breast, it combines with bodily fluids in the deepening and concentration of thought. To ponder something is to cast it around within, ἐν φρεσὶ βάλλομαι or ἐν θυμῶι βάλλομαι;[63] and when

[60] Most scholars seem to agree that there is some relation between πνέω and/or πέπνυμαι and these words, but it is not clear what it is: see the varying expressions of acceptance, doubt, and equivocation by Chantraine s.v., Frisk s.v., Schulze (1892), 322–5, Ruijgh (1957), 134–5, Risch (1974), §105b, and the more detailed (if impenetrable) defence of the connection by Nehring (1947), 111–12. Seemingly the scholars' main problem is again late 20th-cent. common sense. Formally, the difficulty is the relation between -πνυ- and -πινυ-. Simple anaptyxis is uncharacteristic of Greek and cannot be offered as a stopgap explanation of the ι in -πινυ-. However, T. Meissner has suggested to me that there is a tentative parallel in an alternation seen in forms in -νη- that are attested for certain verbs, as κίρνημι for κεράννυμι, πίτνημι for πετάννυμι, σκίδνημι for σκεδάννυμι. Here the nasal should imply that the attested form comes from the zero-grade of the root: but there is no straightforward explanation of the form with ι either as a development of that zero-grade or as an extension by levelling from the aorist form, which is normal e-grade in each case (see Sihler (1995), §473b). What we see, then, is the unexpected appearance of an ι between the two consonants of a verbal stem derived from a zero-grade, just as with our forms in -πινυ-. The similarity is especially close in κίρνημι, with its sequence of stop + resonant.

[61] For the adjective πινυτός, see i. 229, iv. 211, xi. 445, xx. 131, xxi. 103, xxiii. 361; for the noun πινυτή, VII. 289; xx. 71, 228.

[62] Positive πινύσσω/πινύσκω is not attested in Homer, as the isolated ἐπίνυσσεν (XIV. 249) probably makes better sense if we take it from ἐπινύσσω (see Janko ad loc., with MS support), but it appears in Aeschylus (Pers. 830) and possibly Simonides (508. 2 P; but cf. Ch. 5 n. 19).

[63] The formula ἄλλο δέ τοι ἐρέω, σὺ δ' ἐν φρεσὶ βάλλεο σῆισι is common in both

Penelope reflects on her life her thoughts are whirled around inside her, τόδε θυμὸς ἐνὶ στήθεσσι φίλοισι | πόλλ' ἐπιδινεῖται (xx. 217–18). Here the movement perhaps suggests that of stormy wind, recalling the similes noticed above; but as we move into the mingling of breath with bodily fluids the crucial clue in those similes is provided less by the wind than by the stormy waters, which correspond *ex hypothesi* to the fluids—especially blood—that ebb and flow in the breast as breath is drawn into it. The θυμός is μελιηδής or μελίφρων, like honey in the φρένες.[64] If thought flows as an oozing fluid[65] and the inner recess of the breast is liquid, it makes sense that Homer renders pondering and doubting by the verb πορφύρω (XXI. 551; iv. 427 = iv. 572 = x. 309), which we have already seen used in a psychological simile to denote the turbulent heaving of the sea (above, p. 81).[66] Consider then the remarkable image in κακὰ βυσσοδομεύω (iv. 676, viii. 273, ix. 316, xvii. 66, xvii. 465 = 491 = xx. 184), which is always used of

epics (i. 297 = xi. 454, etc.). Compare νόστον . . . μετὰ φρεσὶ . . . βάλλεαι (IX. 434–5); ἐν θυμῶι δ' ἐβάλοντο ἔπος (xv. 566); ἐν θυμῶι βάλλονται ἐμοὶ χόλον (XIV. 50); τοιαῦτα μετὰ φρεσὶν ἔργα βάληται (xi. 428). On the depth of the thought brought into the φρένες, see also Snell (1978), 83–5.

[64] Similarly anger is sweeter than dripping honey (XVIII. 109) and a man can be γλυκύθυμος (XX. 467).

[65] πευκάλιμος (VIII. 366, XIV. 165, XV. 81, XX. 35) is an epithet of φρένες which has often been explained as a derivative of πεύκη, a pine-tree (see Chantraine s.v., Frisk s.v.). Because φρένες are πευκάλιμαι when one falls asleep (XIV. 165–6), it is attractive to guess that the link with pine-trees lies in the oozing of pine resin: compare μελίφρων ὕπνος (II. 34); but for a neater solution see below, p. 89 with n. 75.

[66] πορφύρω is a fine puzzle. The psychological instances clearly refer to doubt or pondering, and the verb is also used of the heaving action of the sea. The latter association naturally recalls the adjective πορφύρεος, which is often used of the deep, dark colour of sea as well as of blood, clouds, and suchlike (see Gipper (1964) and Moreux (1967: 263–8), on the colour πορφύρεος). Despite this, Chantraine (s.v. πορφύρω) holds that the adjective and the verb come from different roots: he suggests that it is through a confusion of senses that both are used of the sea. This seems to me too easy: is it possible that πορφύρεος simply covers both an area of colour and a type of movement, 'dark and flowing', in the same way as ἀργός means indeterminately white and swift-moving, and ξουθός means both nimble and emitting a trilling sound? (Dale at Eur. *Hel.* 1111). See further Cestuignano (1952); Irwin (1974), 19 n. 31, with further refs.; and compare the intriguing verb καλχαίνω (Soph. *Ant.* 20; Eur. *Heracl.* 40).

deep or deceitful plotting: the thinker is building in the depths of the sea, βυσσοί.[67] The word applies the image of the heaving ocean to what could be described in more lean language as 'hiding one's thoughts' in the mental apparatus, as when Achilles describes the deceitful or disingenuous man who conceals his thoughts deep in his breast, ὅς χ' ἕτερον μὲν κεύθηι ἐνὶ φρεσίν, ἄλλο δὲ εἴπηι (ix. 313).[68]

Inside the breast the stuff of thought ebbs and flows. When one's mental state is wise or reasonable, αἴσιμος,[69] it is in equilibrium, held in φρένας ἐΐσας (xi. 337, xiv. 178, xviii. 249); similarly a strong and wise man is well fixed in his thoughts, φρεσὶν ἦισιν ἀρηρώς (x. 553),[70] just as one fortified by food has filled his θυμός with good things, πλησάμενος . . . θυμὸν ἐδητύος ἠδὲ ποτῆτος (xvii. 603), and has settled and strengthened what is in his breast, ἤραρε θυμὸν ἐδωδῆι (v. 95 = xiv. 111).[71] Similarly a firm intention or idea is fixed or settled in the mental apparatus, μῦθος . . . ἐνὶ φρεσὶν ἤραρεν ἡμῖν (iv. 777), and a wise person is

[67] The first element must refer to the depths of the sea, βυσσοί (thus *LfgrE* s.v., and both Chantraine and Frisk, s.v. βυθός). As such the metaphor (as it seems to be) is unusual in Homer for its extravagance (see Russo at xvii. 66). Its implications are startlingly extended by Aeschylus, whose image of the thinker as a diver in the deep sea (*Supp.* 407–9) reinterprets the idea of mental βυσσοί in a characteristically heightened manner.

[68] For κεύθω in this sense, see esp. I. 363 = XVI. 19; viii. 548, xviii. 406, xxiii. 30, xxiv. 474. Compare κλέπτω: μὴ κλέπτε νόωι (I. 132) evidently refers to deceit (thus Kirk ad loc.; cf. ἔκλεψε νόον, XIV. 217). Compare also νόον σχέθε τόνδ' ἐνὶ θυμῶι (xiv. 490).

[69] For αἴσιμος, αἴσιος, or ἐναίσιμος as the best quality of θυμός and the others, contrasted with emotional excess and unruliness of the thought-stuff, see XXIV. 40; ii. 231 = v. 9, vii. 309–10; for the same contrasted with foolishness or dissipation of the thought-stuff, see xviii. 220 (the same formula as XXIV. 40), xxii. 14; contrasted with its hardness (σιδήρεος), v. 191; and see also xiv. 433.

[70] Here the quality is denied to the weak Elpenor.

[71] The opposite state is apparently what is expressed by the curious image of the forlorn, despairing man who cannot or will not taste food and drink and eats the stuff of thought in his breast, θυμὸν ἔδων and ὃν θυμὸν κατέδων (VI. 202; ix. 75 = x. 143, x. 379); similarly σὴν ἔδεαι κραδίην (XXIV. 129). Ignoring the superficial resemblance to something like 'eating his heart out' in English, the idea seems to be that the absence of food or drink entering the breast leads the fasting man instead to consume what is already inside it—in other words, to devour his θυμός. See esp. XXIV. 129, x. 379, where the connection with failure to eat is made explicit. Perhaps the connection of ideas is that as he fasts he falls more and more into despair, so that on both counts his θυμός is diminished.

fixed in his thinking, ἀρτίφρων (xxiv. 261): the adjective is a compound in -φρων built on the same stem as in ἤραρε.

Correspondingly, with deep thought or emotion the stuff in the breast is compressed. The key adjective is πυκ(ι)νός, dense or concentrated.[72] Those who are thoughtful or troubled are thinking concentratedly, πύκα . . . φρονεόντων (IX. 554, XIV. 217), and they have dense thoughts, πυκινὰ φρεσὶ μήδε' ἔχοντες (XXIV. 282, 674; xix. 353); Odysseus is πυκινὰ φρονέων when he outwits Polyphemus (ix. 445), and the plan of Zeus is Διὸς πυκινὸν νόον (XV. 461). Similarly Penelope describes her troubles as dense in her mental apparatus, πυκιναί . . . ἀμφ' ἁδινὸν κῆρ | ὀξεῖαι μελεδῶναι (xix. 516–17). ἁδινός here is a virtual synonym of πυκνός (see also XVI. 481),[73] and subtle thoughts and plans are themselves πυκινά,[74] densely wrought, just as crafty schemes and plots are spun or woven in the thoughts, with the verbs ὑφαίνειν and ῥάπτειν (see Ch. 7, pp. 251–2 with n. 49). When φρένες are described as πευκάλιμαι (VIII. 366, XIV. 165, XV. 81, XX. 35) the adjective explains itself best as a cousin of πυκνός: the stuff in the breast is thickly concentrated.[75]

---

[72] Examples of πυκ(ι)νός of things that are close-packed or concentrated: warriors in battle formation (IV. 281, V. 93, etc.), doors snugly fitted (XIV. 339, etc.), a dense forest (XVIII. 320, etc.), a hail of weapons thrown (XI. 576), the dense roots of an uprooted tree (XXI. 245, etc.), stones fitted to a wall (XVI. 212) and stakes holding one together (XXIV. 453); the layers of hide covering on a shield (XIII. 803–4), armour strong enough to resist blows (XV. 529), a thundercloud (V. 751, XVI. 297–8), wings (repeatedly beating?) (XI. 454). The meaning is less clear when the adjective is applied to bedclothes (IX. 621, etc.) or a house (XII. 301, etc.), but the general shape of the meaning is precise. The cognate verb πυκάζω and the adverb πύκα are used in the same way. Chantraine (s.v. πύκα) considers it 'peut-être possible, mais pas très satisfaisant' that 'dense' and 'intelligent' should be in the same semantic field, but he sees no alternative. Both Boisacq and Frisk (s.v.) speculate to explain the link. Cf. Vivante (1982), 115–16, 118; Darcus Sullivan (1988), 137–8, 169 n.

[73] T. Meissner points out to me that ἁδινός plainly relates to ἁδρός, 'dense', in the same way as κυδνός to κυδρός, with the characteristic intrusive -ι- of a Caland system. See also Chantraine (1933), 100–1.

[74] Examples of πυκ(ι)νός applied to the products of thought: βουλή (II. 55), ἐφετμή (XVIII. 216), δόλος (VI. 187), ἔπος (XXIV. 75) μύθεα (iii. 23). The astute slave Eurycleia is πυκιμηδής (i. 438), and good advice is given πυκινῶς (i. 279).

[75] I am indebted again to T. Meissner for pointing out this correlation on the analogy of such pairs as κυδρός and κυδάλιμος (see also Risch (1974), § 37). Cf. Darcus Sullivan (1988), 90–1; Onians (1951), 30–4.

New emotions flow into the mental apparatus

In accordance with this system, the access of any strong or violent emotion is the entry of new, oozing liquids into the breast. Emotion arrives there—ἵκανεν, ἵκετο, and similar—and covers over the φρένες as blood and other fluids flow in the chest. A few especially vivid renderings show clearly what is imagined. When Agamemnon is enraged his lungs become blackened and swollen with μένος, perhaps specifically identified with blood:[76]

μένεος δὲ μέγα φρένες ἀμφὶ μέλαιναι
πίμπλαντο . . .　(ι. 103–4; also iv. 661–2)[77]

Achilles' breast is filled with the same volatile stuff when he rushes against his foe in the wilder circumstances of battle:

ὡρμήθη δ' Ἀχιλεύς, μένεος δ' ἐμπλήσατο θυμὸν
ἀγρίου . . .　(XXII. 312–13)

Similarly Zeus describes how passion—this time sexual—has been poured into his breast and has overcome his θυμός:

οὐ γάρ πώ ποτέ μ' ὧδε θεᾶς ἔρος οὐδὲ γυναικὸς
θυμὸν ἐνὶ στήθεσσι περιπροχυθεὶς ἐδάμασσεν.　(XIV. 315–16)

Passion covers over Paris' φρένες as never before:

οὐ γάρ πώ ποτέ μ' ὧδέ γ' ἔρως φρένας ἀμφεκάλυψεν.　(III. 442)

Similarly warlike bravery fills them in a warrior:

ἀλκῆς καὶ σθένεος πλῆτο φρένας ἀμφὶ μελαίνας.　(XVII. 499)

Grief strikes one deep in the φρήν:

. . . τὸν δ' ἄχος ὀξὺ κατὰ φρένα τύψε βαθεῖαν.　(XIX.125)

In an extended version of this image grief touches or feels its way into the θυμός, ἐσεμάσσετο . . . θυμόν (XVII. 564; cf. xi. 591). On entering the φρένες it swells them, makes them dense:

---

[76] See further Padel (1992: 23–6), who closely identifies μένος and χόλος with the flow of blood into the chest. On μένος see also below, pp. 110–11.

[77] On this passage see esp. Combellack (1975), who emphasizes the anatomical reference.

Ἕκτορα δ' αἰνὸν ἄχος πύκασε φρένας ἀμφὶ μελαίνας.

(XVII. 83; sim. VIII. 124 = VIII. 316)

Likewise when a man actively increases his grief he rouses it up in himself,

. . . ἐν μὲν κραδίηι μέγα πένθος ἄεξε.   (xvii. 489)

So far, all this answers very literally to the conception that the deeper part of the mental apparatus ebbs and flows like the stormy sea in the psychological similes discussed earlier in this chapter. However, in a few instances Homer pushes this phenomenon of covering, entering, and seizing by these fluids onto a more figured level of language. A man is said to have put on bravery in his φρένες like a garment, φρεσὶν εἱμένος ἀλκήν (XX. 381), similarly θοῦριν ἐπιειμένοι ἀλκήν (VII. 164 = VIII. 262);[78] in a different image grief gnaws inside, μευ καταδάπτετ[αι] . . . φίλον ἦτορ (xvi. 92), while strife eats at the mental apparatus: it is θυμοβόρος ἔρις (VII. 210).[79]

All this makes sense if the emotion is a substance flowing or oozing into the base of the breast. To understand this conception it is worth comparing Homer's rendering of the effects of drinking wine, which physically enters the breast and psychologically makes a man drunk. Because Homer does not distinguish the lungs in particular from the lower breast as a whole, the digestive and respiratory processes go together.[80] Hence the

---

[78] Compare the image of a man clothed in shamelessness, ἀναιδείην ἐπιειμένος (I. 149, IX. 372). The same idea is suggested in later literature when Theognis describes a tipsy man as οἴνωι θωρηχθείς (470, 842, etc.; sim. Pindar, fr. 72 M): the wine covers over what is inside his breast in the same shape as a breastplate would do outside. A similar image is suggested by the epithet in Aeschylus' μελαγχίτων φρήν (*Pers.* 115; see Onians (1951), 27), where black blood oozing in the φρήν has covered it as a garment in the process that Homer more simply renders when he describes Agamemnon's anger, μένεος δὲ μέγα φρένες ἀμφὶ μέλαιναι | πίμπλαντο (I. 103–4).

[79] Compare δάκε δὲ φρένας Ἕκτορι μῦθος (V. 493), and θυμοδακής . . . μῦθος (viii. 185). In the same constellation is the idea that fire eats what it burns, πῦρ ἐσθίει (XXIII. 182). As often, it is impossible to tell whether the range of meaning of each verb has been deliberately extended into a metaphorical sense of 'devouring': certainly the image is less extravagant than the tragic πυρὸς γνάθος (*PV* 370), which probably looks directly to Homer's πῦρ ἐσθίει.

[80] This goes against the grain of modern common sense, but it is irresistible. In Homer the clearest proof is the expression πλησάμενος . . .

entry of wine into the body exactly parallels the entry of emotion in the form of breath and blood. Wine seeps into the φρένες in an oozing, honey-like flow, it is μελίφρων (VI. 264; vii. 182, etc.); it goes around them, Κύκλωπα περὶ φρένας ἤλυθεν οἶνος (ix. 362), it holds them, σε οἶνος ἔχει φρένας (xviii. 331 = 391); in a drunk man they are overwhelmed, and he is δαμασσάμενος φρένα οἴνωι (ix. 454; cf. ix. 516) or he is burdened in them by the wine, βεβαρηότα . . . φρένας οἴνωι (xix. 122; sim. iii. 139); and the drunk man makes his φρένες wild, φρένας ἄασεν οἴνωι (xxi. 297). If anger and passion swell the breast in the same way, the inference must be that they are identified no less fully and literally as a rushing movement of fluid into the breast.

The flow of bile, χόλος

Because of the nature of the story-line in our two surviving epics, it is very often dangerous or violent emotions that are described as flowing into the mental apparatus. This comes most to the fore in the rendering of heroic pride and folly. Achilles, characteristically, produces the most striking rendering of this phenomenon when he rails against the anger of his quarrel with Agamemnon, anger which is at at once disastrous and sweet as dripping honey:

> ὡς ἔρις ἔκ τε θεῶν ἔκ τ' ἀνθρώπων ἀπόλοιτο,
> καὶ χόλος, ὅς τ' ἐφέηκε πολύφρονά περ χαλεπῆναι,
> ὅς τε πολὺ γλυκίων μέλιτος καταλειβομένοιο
> ἀνδρῶν ἐν στήθεσσιν ἀέξεται ἠΰτε καπνός.   (XVIII. 107–10)

The new emotion surges in, and the breast is in turmoil. In their different ways, billowing smoke and flowing honey participate in the kind of flowing movement that Homer sees

θυμὸν ἐδητύος ἠδὲ ποτῆτος (xvii. 603), where food and drink go into the breathing apparatus; similarly the *Homeric Hymn to Demeter* describes grazing cattle as filling the φρήν with fodder, κορεσσάμενοι φρένα φορβῆι (l. 175); and when Alcaeus urges someone to drink he tells him to wet his lungs, τέγγε πλεύμονας οἴνωι (fr. 347 P). For the connection between the two types of filling or concentration of the chest, by nutrition and by improved thought, see x. 456–65.

in the life of the psychic substances that are inside the breasts of men.[81]

χόλος here is an emotion and a psychological force, but by the same token it is a substance in the body, produced by the organs in the abdomen known as χολάδες, which are concrete enough to slide out when a man's torso is sliced open (IV. 526 = XXI. 181). 'Bile' is probably the truest translation.[82] Although Achilles' imagery is uniquely vivid, it is consistent with what is said of χόλος throughout Homer.[83] When a man grows angry χόλος enters his breast, ἔμπεσε θυμῶι (IX. 436, XIV. 207, 306), ἵκοι (XVII. 399); he puts it there, ἔνθεο θυμῶι (VI. 326); it is in his φρένες (II. 241); he casts it around within, ἐν θυμῶι βάλλονται . . . χόλον (XIV. 50); it enters the φρένες and seizes him, ἔδυ (XIX. 16), λάβεν (I. 387, VI. 166, XVI. 30), ἥιρει (IV. 23; viii. 304). His breast can hold it in check, ἔχαδε στῆθος χόλον (VIII. 461). When his anger deepens he keeps it guarded there, φυλάσσει (XVI. 30); he foments it inside him and makes it moistly swollen like ripened fruit, πέσσει (IV. 513, IX. 565), καταπέψηι (I. 81);[84] conversely when he relents he releases it,

---

[81] Taplin (1992: 199) suggests that this simile 'arises perhaps from the practice of smoking bees'; for earlier and equally imaginative interpretations of it see Edwards ad loc., and Moulton (1979), 285.

[82] For the tangible identity of χόλος, note the passage where Achilles imagines the frustrated Myrmidons telling him that his mother reared him on this substance instead of milk (XVI. 203). Padel (1992: 23–4) points out that mothers smear this bitter substance on their nipples to wean babies, so that the image evokes a very real irony as well as referring directly to the substance that is identified with Achilles' mood.

[83] On the swollenness of Achilles' anger see also Gill (1996), 190–204.

[84] πέσσω and compounds are hard words in Homer. The basic idea seems to be of ripening, as when the breeze blowing on fruit-trees makes some grow while it ripens others: τὰ μὲν φύει, ἄλλα δὲ πέσσει (vii. 119). In psychological language, the verb refers to brooding on anger or sorrow without acting upon it. The clearest example is where Calchas fears that Agamemnon will suppress his anger for the moment but give vent to it later: εἴ περ γάρ τε χόλον γε καὶ αὐτῆμαρ καταπέψηι, | ἀλλά τε καὶ μετόπισθεν ἔχει κότον, ὄφρα τελέσσηι, | ἐν στήθεσσιν ἑοῖσι (I. 81–3). Similarly, Meleager, his thoughts already full of sullen wrath, lies by his woman nursing his anger, χόλον θυμαλγέα πέσσων (IX. 565); much the same words describe Achilles sulking (IV. 513); likewise Priam says that he grieves impotently for Hector, κήδεα μυρία πέσσω (XXIV. 639); and after Niobe is turned to stone she continues her sorrow, κήδεα πέσσει (XXIV. 617). With such images there seems to be a close analogy with the ripening fruit-plants: just as the moist flesh of the fruit increases, so

μεθέμεν (I. 283, XV. 138), μεθήσει (i. 77), ἔα (IX. 260), μεθίεν χαλεποῖο χόλοιο (xxi. 377), and in some less clear sense he turns his mental apparatus away from it, ἐκ χόλου ἀργαλέοιο μετασ- τρέψηι φίλον ἦτορ (X. 107).

The flow of χόλος and kindred emotions looms especially large when the plot of the *Iliad* deepens and Achilles' anger is expressed and criticized at length. He describes how his mental apparatus is being swollen by this substance:

> ἀλλά μοι <u>οἰδάνεται</u> κραδίη χόλωι, ὁππότε κείνων
> μνήσομαι. (IX. 646–7)

The same image appears when Phoenix tells how anger swelled Meleager's thought in his breast:

> ἀλλ' ὅτε δὴ Μελέαγρον ἔδυ χόλος, ὅς τε καὶ ἄλλων
> <u>οἰδάνει</u> ἐν στήθεσσι νόον πύκα περ φρονεόντων . . . (IX. 553–4)

To resist stubborn pride is to curb or compress what swells in the breast, ἀέξεται ἠΰτε καπνός (XVIII. 110). Thus Odysseus reports Achilles' refusal to yield, saying that he will not quell[85] his anger but is filled still more with fury:

the χόλος swells and thickens and grows more moist in the mental breast. The two remaining Homeric instances are more obscure. Thersites sarcastically urges that Agamemnon be left alone with the gifts he has refused to part with, αὐτοῦ ἐν Τροίηι γέρα πεσσέμεν (II. 236–7); and Hector urges that the Achaeans be harried as they board their ships so that each of them will have a wound to nurse at home, ὥς τις τούτων γε βέλος καὶ οἴκοθι πέσσηι (VIII. 513). Both of these instances suggest the action of holding something to oneself and cradling it, something like Latin *foveo*, and this works well in the light of the psycho- logical image of keeping χόλος close in the breast; but in these same two passages it seems impossible to find an idea of ripening or digesting. (For unsatisfactory attempts at such explanations see Kirk ad locc.)

[85] The standard translation of σβέννυμι seems to be 'extinguish', and this can be misleading if it is taken to refer specifically to putting out a fire. Although the verb is often found with reference to fire it is equally common with other kinds of controlling or quiescence. Thus to kill men in battle is ἀνθρώπων σβέσσαι μένος (XVI. 621), and ἔσβη | οὖρος (iii. 182–3) means that the wind died down. The metaphors would be odd and Homerically unique if the images here were referring to fire. Similarly the adjective ἄσβεστος is used of μένος (XXII. 96), shouting (XI. 50, etc.), laughter (I. 599; viii. 326, etc.), and fame, κλέος (vii. 333), and only more rarely of fire. Shouting, lamentation, and rumour are occasionally said to blaze, δεδήει (II. 93, XII. 35; xx. 353), so at a pinch ἄσβεστος might be taken as an image from fire when it is applied to

οὐκ ἐθέλει σβέσσαι χόλον, ἀλλ᾽ ἔτι μᾶλλον
πιμπλάνεται μένεος. (IX. 678–9)

Similarly Phoenix urges Achilles to control himself, to overcome his θυμός:[86]

ἀλλ᾽, Ἀχιλεῦ, δάμασον θυμὸν μέγαν· οὐδέ τί σε χρὴ
νηλεὲς ἦτορ ἔχειν. (IX. 496-7)

In the same spirit Odysseus recalls Peleus' parting advice to his son, that he should restrain or keep checked what is in his breast:

. . . κάρτος μὲν Ἀθηναίη τε καὶ ῞Ηρη
δώσουσ᾽ αἴ κ᾽ ἐθέλωσι, σὺ δὲ μεγαλήτορα θυμὸν
ἴσχειν ἐν στήθεσσι. (IX. 254–6)

Ajax describes how a man curbs his mental apparatus when he accepts compensation for a wrong done him:

τοῦ δέ τ᾽ ἐρητύεται κραδίη καὶ θυμὸς ἀγήνωρ
ποινὴν δεξαμένωι. (IX. 635–6)

Phoenix recalls his own youthful impatience, when he refused to do this:

ἔνθ᾽ ἐμοὶ οὐκέτι πάμπαν ἐρητύετ᾽ ἐν φρεσὶ θυμός. (IX. 462)[87]

At the beginning of the Wrath Achilles had seen the possibility of such restraint when he considered whether to kill Agamemnon or to repress his rage, χόλον παύσειεν ἐρητύσειέ τε θυμόν (I. 192);[88] and when he finally rises up from his

---

utterances; but since wind, κλέος, μένος, and χόλος are nowhere else described in terms of fire, it seems best to suppose simply that the meaning of σβέννυμι is broader than the dictionary translation suggests. The reference is to quelling and subduing anything given to vigorous vital movement. If this is right σβέσσαι χόλον is not a metaphor at all.

[86] Odysseus in Hades uses the same image in urging Ajax to unbend and speak to him: δάμασον δὲ μένος καὶ ἀγήνορα θυμόν (xi. 562).

[87] For the distinct but similar notion of restraining not the swelling that comes with anger but the dissipation that comes with fear, note Idomeneus' image of the coward whose θυμός cannot stay compressed in order to prevent him from flight, οὐδέ οἱ ἀτρέμας ἧσθαι ἐρητύετ᾽ ἐν φρεσὶ θυμός (XIII. 280).

[88] Similarly, there is fear that when Priam sees Hector dead he will not curb his anger, χόλον οὐκ ἐρύσαιτο (XXIV. 584).

sullenness this is exactly what he does, mastering and curbing what is in his breast:

> ἀλλὰ τὰ μὲν προτετύχθαι ἐάσομεν ἀχνύμενοί περ,
> θυμὸν ἐνὶ στήθεσσι φίλον δαμάσαντες ἀνάγκηι.   (XVIII. 112–13)

In the *Odyssey*, this same restraint is characteristic of the hero. Thus Odysseus says that if disaster strikes, he will control his feelings:

> τλήσομαι ἐν στήθεσσιν ἔχων ταλαπενθέα θυμόν.   (v. 222)

Similarly he restrains himself from rash violence, φρεσὶ δ' ἔσχετο (xvii. 238); and the suitors are urged to do likewise, ἐπίσχετε θυμὸν ἐνιπῆς | καὶ χειρῶν (xx. 266—7).

Conversely, a person yields to the swelling when overcome by excessive emotion, as when χόλος enters the chest and swamps the thoughts. In this way Nestor accuses Agamemnon of causing the Wrath through his stubbornness, by yielding to his θυμός,

> σὺ δὲ σῶι μεγαλήτορι θυμῶι
> εἴξας ἄνδρα φέριστον, ὃν ἀθάνατοί περ ἔτεισαν,
> ἠτίμησας.   (IX. 109–11)

Similarly Phoenix recounts how Meleager fought after indulging his passion,

> ὣς ὁ μὲν Αἰτωλοῖσιν ἀπήμυνεν κακὸν ἦμαρ,
> εἴξας ὧι θυμῶι.   (IX. 597–8)

In the same way, a woman who yields to lust is ὧι θυμῶι εἴξασα (v. 126), and those who are rash and greedy are ὕβρει εἴξαντες (xiv. 262). As Achilles moves deeper into wildness and anger this psychological pattern is repeated in what Apollo says about his mistreatment of the dead Hector:

> ὧι [sc. Ἀχιλῆϊ] οὔτ' ἄρ φρένες εἰσὶν ἐναίσιμοι οὔτε νόημα
> γναμπτὸν ἐνὶ στήθεσσι, λέων δ' ὣς ἄγρια οἶδεν,
> ὅς τ' ἐπεὶ ἄρ μεγάληι τε βίηι καὶ ἀγήνορι θυμῶι
> εἴξας εἶσ' ἐπὶ μῆλα βροτῶν . . .   (XXIV. 40–3)

The wrathful hero will not curb the idea or intention, νόημα, in his breast, refusing to keep it bent or compressed, γναμπτόν:[89]

---

[89] With γναμπτόν in Apollo's speech compare ἐπιγνάμψασα φίλον κῆρ (I. 569),

to say that he has yielded to his θυμός is to say that the liquids flowing into his breast are filling it unchecked.

The stuff of thought alternately softens and coagulates

This deepening and compression of what is in the breast leads us to a further set of images referring to the hardening and softening of the mental apparatus. Here the bloody wetness of the anatomical heart and the neighbouring innards must be the basic anatomical phenomenon. Weakness or yielding, or simply joy, is softness or moistness in the breast. Penelope's surrender to grief and misery is a melting of the θυμός:

> ὦ γύναι αἰδοίη Λαερτιάδεω Ὀδυσῆος,
> μηκέτι νῦν χρόα καλὸν ἐναίρεο μηδέ τι θυμὸν
> τῆκε πόσιν γοόωσα. (xix. 262–4; cf. III. 176)

The commonest image of this kind is with ἰαίνω, to melt or soften or make warm:[90] the θυμός melts, ἰαίνεται, when joy comes after stubborn anger (see XXIV. 321; xv. 379, xxii. 58–9, etc.).[91] This is the pivot of a revealing simile during the

Hera repressing her anger in silence. Also honour appeases men, ἐπιγνάμπτει νόον ἐσθλῶν (IX. 514). The idea in γναμπτός and γνάμπτω is of something bent, or capable of being bent, back on itself: as of limbs (XI. 669, etc.), a fishing-hook (iv. 369, xii. 332), and vessels of curling shape, ἕλικας (XVIII. 401). The compounds ἐπιγνάμπτω, περιγνάμπτω, ἀναγνάμπτω are similar in sense to the simple verb. In psychological contexts γνάμπτω and γναμπτός might arguably be taken to refer to the *redirection* of ideas under persuasion, somewhat as in formulae like στρεπταὶ μέν τε φρένες ἐσθλῶν (XV. 203; see below, pp. 123–4); but every non-psychological instance suggests bending back rather than bending away, and it is most accurate as well as most suited to our argument to take the psychological image as one of bending back, restraining, compressing (for this view see also Chantraine s.v.).

[90] ἰαίνω in non-psychological contexts refers at once to heating and to melting or softening: bronze (viii. 426), water (x. 359), wax (xii. 175); also the unfurrowing of the brow of a worried person (xv. 102–3).

[91] This would corroborate Chantraine's view (s.v. ἰαίνω), shared by Frisk, that the dominant meaning 'échauffer, amollir par la chaleur' stems from an (original) sense 's'agiter, se répendre'. Latacz (1966: 220–331) develops this view of ἰαίνω and demonstrates that its application to emotional activity is not a metaphor but the description of a real process imagined as happening in the θυμός.

Funeral Games, when Menelaus' anger is appeased by recompense and apology:[92]

$$τοῖο δὲ θυμὸς$$
$$ἰάνθη ὡς εἴ τε περὶ σταχύεσσιν ἐέρση$$
$$ληΐου ἀλδήσκοντος, ὅτε φρίσσουσιν ἄρουραι·$$
$$ὡς ἄρα σοί, Μενέλαε, μετὰ φρεσὶ θυμὸς ἰάνθη.$$ (XXIII. 597–600)

Here, it seems, the moist rain or dew is thought of as softening and becoming part of the ripening and swelling ears,[93] just as the passing-away of anger is the melting of the thought-stuff.[94] On the same basis a consolation or mitigation of unhappiness is θαλπωρή (VI. 412, X. 223, i. 167), a warming of the innards, the noun being cognate with the verb θάλπω.[95]

The exactly opposite process is named when Menelaus, withdrawing from the fray before a redoubled onslaught, is likened to a lion repelled from a farmstead by armed men:

$$τοῦ δ' ἐν φρεσὶν ἄλκιμον ἦτορ$$
$$παχνοῦται, ἀέκων δέ τ' ἔβη ἀπὸ μεσσαύλοιο.$$ (XVII. 111–12)

His mental apparatus is in the state of πάχνη, frosty frozen rain or dew. The easy parallel with English expressions like 'frosty-

[92] On the psychological situation from which this image arises, see Taplin (1992), 256–7.

[93] Richardson ad loc. suggests that the drops are imagined as evaporating. This would weaken the simile, as ἰαίνω would no longer link the image of the dew with what is happening to Menelaus: anger might 'evaporate' in English, but if something like the same thing happened to a θυμός in Greek it would mean that the man swooned or became faint (see Ch. 5, pp. 139–43). Homeric rain or dew is a life-giving substance, τεθαλυῖα ἐέρση (xiii. 245), and the droplets falling on the hairy beard fertilize and ripen and make moist what is within. On the simile see also Taplin (1992), 257 n. 11, and on the fertilizing character of dew see Boedeker (1984), *passim*. In early Greek the most striking evocation of the idea is Aeschylus' image when Clytaemnestra, rejoicing in the spattering of drops of blood from Agamemnon's wound, compares herself to the crop rejoicing in the fall of dew or rain when the sheath is in its birth pangs: χαίρουσαν οὐδὲν ἧσσον ἢ διοσδότωι | γάνει σπορητὸς κάλυκος ἐν λοχεύμασιν (*Ag.* 1391–2).

[94] In post-Homeric literature τέγγω appears in the same sense: to make the psychological apparatus moist is to appease, placate, induce gentle feelings (e.g. *PV* 1008; Eur. *Hipp.* 303; Ar. *Lys.* 550). The principle is the same as when wine moistens the lungs and creates feelings of bonhomie: τέγγε πλεύμονας οἴνωι (Alcaeus fr. 347 P). See also Epilogue, p. 289.

[95] Chantraine s.v.

hearted' does not help: so far as I know Homer nowhere else imagines the mental apparatus as cold,[96] and it would be an odd metaphor as well as an anatomical impossibility if that were the idea here. The clue, as often, comes from a glance at the root behind πάχνη, which is the same as in the verb πήγνυμι, to stick fast or make stiff.[97] Thus Homer says that in cheese-making fig-juice curdles and solidifies, συνέπηξεν, the milk to which it is added (v. 902). Since what determines the meaning of πάχνη is not so much the coldness as the stiffness of the thickened liquid, this suggests that when the mental apparatus παχνοῦται, its ebbing liquid coagulates and solidifies. This is then the exact reverse of the man's experience when he yields to placation so that his mental apparatus melts and is liquefied, ἰάνθη. The only other instance of παχνόω in this sense neatly illustrates the contrast: Hesiod describes a thief as experiencing some negative emotion, which ἐπάχνωσεν φίλον ἦτορ (*WD* 360), and contrasts this with one who gives freely and rejoices, χαίρει τῶι δώρωι καὶ τέρπεται ὂν κατὰ θυμόν (358).[98]

[96] Arguably an exception is thrown up by the verb ῥιγέω, which translates as 'I fear' but also refers in some way to coldness—the combination is neatly borne out by the cognate adjective in the comparative form ῥίγιον, indeterminately translated as 'colder' and 'more to be feared' (xvii. 191, with I. 325, XI. 405, etc.; see Chantraine s.v., and compare the Latin cognates *frigus*, *frigeo*). What, then, does Laertes mean when he says αἰεί μοι θυμὸς . . . ἐρρίγει (xxiii. 216), referring to long foreboding? The link between the two senses is usually taken to be the idea of shuddering: when I ῥιγέω I shrink away with a shiver, either because I am cold or because I am afraid. If this is right, the similarity to ἦτορ παχνοῦται is merely superficial, because the two verbs are associated with coldness in quite different ways. A better parallel for Laertes' experience is provided by expressions like τρομέοντο δέ οἱ φρένες ἐντός (X. 10), where the quivering or shaking is that of the physical act of groaning and sighing (see Ch. 5, pp. 139–40). In this last example, when the mental apparatus quivers the emotion in question is one of continued fear and mental trouble over an extended space of time, just as in the case of Laertes' dread, whereas in the παχνοῦται simile the lion's experience must be of some more sudden and volatile emotion. Outside the Homeric ambit, Sappho has ψῦχρος ἔγεντ᾽ ὁ θυμός (42. 1 L–P), apparently describing fear felt by doves. Here the idea of coldness is clearly present, either as an extension of the ἦτορ παχνοῦται idea or by transference from the idea of the expulsion of ψυχή as cold breath (see Ch. 5, pp. 144–7).

[97] See Chantraine s.v. Homer does not provide an example of πήγνυμι for the freezing of water, but it is common later: see Aesch. *Pers.* 496; Alcaeus 338. 2 L–P, etc.

[98] Aeschylus has Electra describe herelf when she weeps as κρυφαίοις

Stern or unflinching emotion is a further extreme of hardness and rigidity, a conception that is writ large in Paris'
comparison of Hector's mental apparatus to an axe:

αἰεί τοι κραδίη, πέλεκυς ὥς, ἐστιν ἀτειρής,
ὅς τ' εἶσιν διὰ δουρὸς ὑπ' ἀνέρος, ὅς ῥά τε τέχνηι
νήϊον ἐκτάμνηισιν, ὀφέλλει δ' ἀνδρὸς ἐρωήν·
ὡς σοὶ ἐνὶ στήθεσσιν ἀτάρβητος νόος ἐστίν.   (III. 60–3)

It is because his mental state is ἀτάρβητος, never to be frightened, that what is in his breast is ἀτειρής, never worn away or
reduced:[99] contrast with this the idea that debilitating pains are
those that wear away at a wounded person's mental apparatus,
αἵ μιν τείρουσι κατὰ φρένας (xv. 61). The idea is similar when the
θυμός, ἦτορ, or κραδίη of a stern or unyielding person is
described as a thing of iron, σιδήρεος (see XXII. 357, XXIV. 205,
iv. 293, v. 191, xxiii. 172), and when the μένος of a fierce fighter
is likened to iron, αἴθωνι σιδήρωι (XX. 372; sim. xii. 279—80).[100]
Just as Penelope's emotional collapse was a melting of the
θυμός, so conversely Telemachus complains that her κραδίη is
harder than stone, στερεωτέρη . . . λίθοιο (xxiii. 103), when she
hesitates before yielding to Odysseus. The hero himself later
describes her mental apparatus as a κῆρ ἀτέραμνον (xxiii. 167),
and the adjective again embodies the root seen in τείρω: the
stuff of her thought cannot be worn down, melted, or dissipated.[101]

πένθεσιν παχνουμένα (*Cho.* 81–3): here the 'thickening' appears to be what
follows from the gorging of her mental apparatus with grief.

[99] I am not sure that there is any need for the more complex and allusive
explanations that have been offered for this image (see Moulton (1977), 91,
and Kirk ad loc.).

[100] This interpretation of σιδήρεος is very tentative, because other uses of the
word show that the associations of iron in Homer's world are utterly different
from those it holds in ours: the force of fire (XXIII. 177), the uproar of battle
(XVII. 424), and the sky (xv. 329 = xvii. 565) are all σιδήρεος in senses that
cannot now be clarified.

[101] I am grateful to T. Meissner for pointing out this explanation of
ἀτέραμνος to me. We can also compare the less easily visualized images with
ἀπηνής, which perhaps refers to hardness when it describes the θυμός or νόος of
an overbearing or stubborn person (xv. 94, XXIII. 484, 611; xviii. 381, xxiii. 97,
230). Note especially XVI. 33–5, where Patroclus rails against Achilles'
stubbornness: he describes him hyperbolically as the child of the sea and
the sea-cliffs, on the grounds that he has a νόος ἀπηνής. Many have analysed

In folly the stuff of thought is dispersed

If passionate and deeply felt thought and emotion is a deepening and thickening of what is in the breast, the converse follows that the thoughts of the fool are loose and dissipated, with the breast emptied of its concentrated stuff.[102] A light-headed or dispirited person has wholly or partly lost what is in his breast: where the wise man is ἐχέφρων (see esp. xiii. 332) his opposite is ἄφρων[103] or ἀφρονέων (XV. 104) or ἄθυμος (x. 463) or has an ἄφρων θυμός (xxi. 105), just as when Hecuba thinks Priam has fallen into folly and she asks where his φρένες have gone to, πῆι δή τοι φρένες οἴχονται; (XXIV. 201).[104] It is possible, if no more, that the adjective ἀκήριος expresses the same phenomenon as the absence of κῆρ.[105] Similarly, the mental substance of the fool

ἀπηνής as referring in its proper sense to the person as a whole rather than to their mental apparatus, making it an image of averting the face, ἀπ-ηνης from *ἀνος, ῆνος, 'face'. See *LfgrE* s.v.; Chantraine is unconvinced by this. The key passage for this word is the speech where Penelope contrasts the reputation of an ἀπηνής person with that of one who is ἀμύμων (xix. 329–34): but the latter word remains as difficult as the former (cf. A. A. Parry (1973), 110–16). Blanc (1985) associates ἀπηνής with ἀναίνομαι and takes it to refer to refusal or unwillingness to co-operate.

[102] On folly as loss of φρένες see esp. Snell (1978), 62–9.

[103] ἄφρων (III. 220, IV. 104, V. 761, 875, XVI. 842; vi. 187, viii. 209, xvii. 586, xx. 227, xxi. 102, 105, xxiii. 12) and ἀφροσύνη (V. 110; xvi. 278, xxiv. 457) refer to folly rather than cowardice.

[104] Note, however, that the difficult expression τῶι δὲ φρένας ἄφρονι πεῖθεν (IV. 104, XVI. 842) will not make sense if ἄφρων means that the φρένες are empty: the meaning must rather be that the activity is not proceeding in them, the person is not φρονέων (see above, n. 53).

[105] Fear is δέος ἀκήριον (V. 812, 817, XIII. 224) and feeble and immobile men are ἀκήριοι (VII. 100), as are sailors in peril from the monster Scylla (x. 98, xxiii. 328). If ἀκήριος is to be taken from κήρ rather than κῆρ (on this ambiguity see *LfgrE* s.v. ἀκήριος), then the adjective is presumably formed by prefixing ἀ- privative to the noun. If this is right, in each of these instances it refers to the loss or dissipation of κῆρ as the stuff of thought. However, when it is said that the blow of a weapon will make a man ἀκήριον (XI. 392, sim. XXI. 466) this must mean that it will make him dead. Both one who dies and one who becomes breathless with fear could be said to lack θυμός, so that if we attribute a similar meaning to the lack of κῆρ all our instances of ἀκήριος will make good sense. Other early attestations (Hes. *WD* 823; *h. Merc.* 530; Semonides, fr. 4 W) cannot easily be fitted to the same pattern, so the word remains obscure: some at least of the instances must be formed with intensive ἀ (< *sm̥) or with κήρ, or both.

is loosened and released and left slack: he is χαλίφρων or χαλιφρονέων or full of χαλιφροσύνη (iv. 371, xvi. 310, xix. 530, xxiii. 13);[106] dull-wittedness or immaturity leads to thin, insubstantial thought, λεπτὴ μῆτις (x. 226, XXIII. 590), and the lungs of a rash young man are distended and floating, φρένες ἠερέθονται (III. 108).[107]

Likewise, in cowardice and misery the stuff of thought becomes diffuse and insubstantial. The simplest form of this is in indecision, when it is divided in two directions, δαίεται ἦτορ (i. 48; above, pp. 65–6), but the experience of sustained grief and misery is similar, as when Odysseus describes himself as αἰεὶ φρεσὶν ᾗσιν ἔχων δεδαϊγμένον ἦτορ (xiii. 320).[108] More violently, in grief and shame and such negative emotions the mental apparatus is shattered, κατεκλάσθη φίλον ἦτορ (iv. 481, x. 198, etc.); the one who grieves is breaking it up, θυμὸν ἐρέχθων (v. 83 = 157) or he rends it apart, θυμὸν ἀμύσσει (I. 243);[109] and by dismaying another person one scatters it apart in confusion, θυμὸν ὄρινε (II. 142; sim. v. 29, IX. 595, XXIV. 585, etc.).[110] Note also the perfect ὀρώρεται, which is

---

[106] χαλιφρονέων is derived from χαλαρός in a Caland form, embodying the root seen in χαλάω: see Risch (1974), §79.

[107] The verb is related to ἀείρω: on the form see Kirk ad loc. Kirk calls this phrase 'a brilliant metaphor', but the imagery is not unusual.

[108] δαΐζω means 'rend apart', as when a man's garments are rent by an attacker (II. 416, XVI. 841) or the man himself is cut open (XI. 497, XVIII. 236, etc.); similarly, as one rends the hair in grief (XVIII. 27) or cuts meat into portions (xiv. 434). (Cf. Cheyns (1979: 605–7) for discussion of these passages.) Twice the words ἐδαΐζετο θυμός refer to doubt and confusion which is compared to squalls at sea (IX. 8 = xv. 629); but at XIV. 20–3 the verb seems to refer simply to doubting and indecision between alternatives, with the ἤ . . . ἤ . . . construction usual for μερμηρίζειν. Within the semantic range of this verb, hesitation and anguish might be seen as two forms of the same mental disarray. Note also that one suffering the anguish of a mortal blow is δεδαϊγμένος ἦτορ (XVII. 535): it is hard to tell whether this refers only to the physical piercing of his belly (XVII. 518–19) or also to his mental woe.

[109] For the meaning of ἀμύσσω note its application to the action of tearing or beating the breast in grief (XIX. 284): the visible manifestation of the emotion corresponds exactly to what happens inside.

[110] The exact sense of ὀρίνω is illustrated from non-psychological contexts: storm rouses the sea to tempest (II. 294, XI. 298, etc.), a river rouses itself to flood (XXI. 235, 313), soldiers scatter in flight (IX. 243, etc.), and the suitors scatter before Odysseus' wrath (xxii. 23, 360). Both Chantraine and Frisk (s.v.) suggest that it is related semantically to the cognate ὄρνυμι in the sense

closely tied to ὀρίνω:[111] the breath of thought is broken up and scattered by worries, ὀρώρεται ἔνδοθι θυμὸς | κήδεσιν (xix. 377–8), just as it is divided by sorrow and indecision, ἐμοὶ δίχα θυμὸς ὀρώρεται ἔνθα καὶ ἔνθα (xix. 524). Misery and fear churn up what is in the breast, συγχεῖ θυμόν (IX. 612, XIII. 808, etc.) so that thoughts are thrown into disarray, νόος χύτο (XXIV. 358).[112] Similarly terror or distraction is the loss of mental substance, as when a hero is killed and his charioteer, frozen in terror, has the contents of his φρένες knocked out of him:

> ἐκ δέ οἱ ἡνίοχος πλήγη φρένας, ἃς πάρος εἶχεν,
> οὐδ᾽ ὅ γ᾽ ἐτόλμησεν, δηΐων ὑπὸ χεῖρας ἀλύξας,
> ἂψ ἵππους στρέψαι.

> (XIII. 394–6; sim. XVI. 403–4, XVIII. 225)

Again, Paris the coward has his mental apparatus struck down out of him, κατεπλήγη φίλον ἦτορ (III. 31) when he shrinks from the Achaean host, and when Telemachus cannot think deep-breathed thoughts it is because the suitors have brought on the same loss of mental substance in him:

> ἀλλά τοι οὐ δύναμαι πεπνυμένα πάντα νοῆσαι·
> ἐκ γάρ με πλήσσουσι παρήμενοι ἄλλοθεν ἄλλος
> οἵδε κακὰ φρονέοντες . . . (xviii. 231–2)

In effect they have mentally winded him and emptied his breast.

'rouse up' rather than 'scatter'; our non-psychological examples involve both actions. See also Caswell (1990: 48–9, 53–5), showing that ὀρίνω is used in similar ways of sea, wind, and θυμός.

[111] On the link between ὀρώρεται and ὀρίνω, see Rix (1965); Chantraine, s.v. ὀρίνω; Risch (1974), §120c.

[112] In this connection the verb ἀχεύω also gives us pause: one who grieves or is dismayed is θυμὸν ἀχεύων (V. 869, XVIII. 461, etc.) or ὀδυρόμενος καὶ ἀχεύων (XXIV. 128, etc.). No context gives a clear indication of the associations of this verb, other than that it is characteristic of grief, and it is normally analysed as a derivation from ἄχος (see Chantraine s.v.; Frisk s.v.). However, it is hard to believe that χέω in its psychological sense is not somehow associated with it in Homeric practice: consider esp. the close consonance between the two in the line μή μοι σύγχει θυμὸν ὀδυρόμενος καὶ ἀχεύων (IX. 612). In addition χώομαι, as in χωόμενος κῆρ (I. 44, IX. 551; xii. 376), is obscure in precise meaning but clearly refers to anger or mental turmoil in general; since antiquity it has been associated with χέω (see Chantraine s.v.; Frisk s.v.; and cf. Adkins (1969), 13–18).

When this spreading and dissipation lead to the expulsion of the stuff of thought from the breast, the experience can be made manifest as sighing or groaning. φρένες shake with fear, ἐπτοίηθεν (xxii. 298), and they are made to tremble when a man groans out in misery:

> ὣς πυκίν' ἐν στήθεσσιν ἀνεστενάχιζ' Ἀγαμέμνων
> νείοθεν ἐκ κραδίης, τρομέοντο δέ οἱ φρένες ἐντός.
>
> (x. 9–10; cf. xv. 627)

In the same way, when Penelope plans to make the suitors fear her, her hope is to make their θυμός expand and dissipate:[113]

> ὅπως πετάσειε μάλιστα
> θυμὸν μνηστήρων . . .   (xviii. 160–1)

The verb that might elsewhere be translated 'make to flutter' or 'make to fly' must refer here to the escape of θυμός expelled from the mouth in a groan[114]—just as when an animal groans in death its θυμός flies away, ἀπὸ δ' ἔπτατο θυμός (x. 163 = xix. 454, Ch. 5, pp. 152–3). Twice, this conception creates a strikingly extended image. Agamemnon, describing his own fear, says that his breast has been emptied and his κραδίη has leapt out of him:

> οὐδέ μοι ἦτορ
> ἔμπεδον, ἀλλ' ἀλαλύκτημαι, κραδίη δέ μοι ἔξω
> στηθέων ἐκθρώισκει.   (x. 93–5)

Similarly the thought-stuff of frightened men falls at their feet:

> τάρβησαν, πᾶσιν δὲ παραὶ ποσὶ κάππεσε θυμός.   (xv. 280)

The breath of thought is expelled, vanishes, falls away: the image takes no liberties with what fear is literally conceived to be.

In this way the phenomena of fear and light-headedness are the opposite of the mental inhalation indicated by πεπνῦσθαι. The principal bodily phenomenon is breathless gasping, but it

---

[113] Jasper Griffin suggests to me that her (or Athena's) intention is rather to make the suitors erotically inflamed, to place a higher value upon her. The story-line is consistent with this: but the verb used is one which seems definitely to stand for confusion and mental dissipation.

[114] See Russo ad loc.

is accompanied by the accelerated beating of the heart. The two phenomena need not be sharply distinguished, as the verbs πατάσσει and πάλλεται will suggest. First, consider Idomeneus' description of a coward in battle:

ἐν δέ τέ οἱ κραδίη μεγάλα στέρνοισι πατάσσει
κῆρας ὀϊομένωι, πάταγος δέ τε γίγνετ᾽ ὀδόντων.   (XIII. 282–3)

His heart knocks against the wall of his breast. Similarly Hector is daunted:

Ἕκτορι δ᾽ αὐτῶι θυμὸς ἐνὶ στήθεσσι πάτασσεν.
(VII. 216; sim. XXIII. 370)

From our own language it might be natural to refer πατάσσει to the rapid beating of the heart and to distinguish that sharply from the behaviour of breath in the lungs. However, Homeric evidence suggests that those two are inextricably merged. When Melantho mockingly tells the disguised Odysseus that if he is not drunk he is φρένας ἐκπεπαταγμένος (xviii. 327–32), she is suggesting that he is a fool or a madman: the participle can only mean that his φρένες are emptied of mental substance, in other words that his breast is emptied of the breath of thought.[115] Similarly, when Andromache grows weak with fear she describes her ἦτορ as rising and quivering in her throat:

ἐν δ᾽ ἐμοὶ αὐτῆι
στήθεσι πάλλεται ἦτορ ἀνὰ στόμα, νέρθε δὲ γοῦνα
πήγνυται.   (XXII. 451–3)

We should not be misled by the superficial resemblance of Andromache's words to the English hyperbole 'her heart is in her mouth'. As she rushes out she is quivering within, παλλομένη κραδίην (XXII. 461), and finally she gasps out her breath, ψυχή, in a swoon (466–7). Now πάλλω in non-psychological language is the action of agitating something and scattering it abroad:[116] clearly, then, what she experiences

[115] For ancient suggestions of such an interpretation see Russo ad loc.

[116] πάλλω is a difficult verb with no English equivalent. It appears most often when one flourishes or brandishes a missile weapon prior to throwing it (III. 19, XXII. 320, etc., of spears; v. 304, of a stone); when a man dandles a baby in his arms (πῆλε, VI. 474), and possibly when one trips up and stumbles (πάλτο, XV. 645). Backward–forward agitation is evidently the common factor. The clearest indicator of its meaning is in the casting of lots, where πάλλω is

is a trembling or knocking in the breast which leads directly to the flow of the stuff of thought out of her lungs. Because this stuff is the seat of mental life it follows that after its escape she collapses on the ground: through different levels the diminution of mental substance in terror shades into the loss of consciousness itself, which we will consider in the next chapter.

Homeric psychology is a seamless garment

We have seen that Homer's understanding of thought and emotion revolves around a close-knit group of phenomena: the ebb and flow of breath, the flow of fluids into and out of the breast, and the soft liquidity of the organs around and below the lungs. If my explanations of individual words and passages have seemed plausible, the overall analysis should confirm the hypothesis that the Homeric 'mind' is the same thing as the life of physical substances in the breast. We can now return to the problem posed at the beginning of this chapter, when we saw that this kind of account of Homeric psychology runs the risk of seeming intolerably crude and naïve. It turns out that it is a little less than the whole truth to say baldly and bluntly that φρένες are the lungs and θυμός is the air in them. Although the mental apparatus is tied to what is literally and solidly in the chest, it is not limited or constrained by that dependence, and the system is subtle, expressive, and self-consistent in a way that has no parallel in the jumbled and allusive imagery of the mind that characterizes our modern languages. The clarity and elegance of the system was illustrated most clearly by the Wrath of Achilles and its aftermath, where every nuance of his and Agamemnon's changing emotional states was expressed in terms of the alternate swelling and dissipation of χόλος and kindred emotional fluids. Because we have been able to fit *every*

---

the action of the one who shakes the helmet containing the lots: they whirl round inside, and one of them leaps out (III. 324–5, VII. 181–2, etc.). The combination of vibrating and leaping out exactly corresponds to the image in our psychological passages, where the rapid beating of the heart goes with the gasping out of breath. On the combination of vibrating and leaping out, see Chantraine s.v.; and on the psychological imagery, cf. Onians (1951), 50. On the difficult πάλτο in XV. 645, which may be from the rare verb παλέω, see Janko ad loc.; also a strange dissection by Leumann (1950: 60–4).

significant fragment of description applied to the θυμός family into the same process of inhalation, ebb and flow, liquefying and coagulation, we can accept that the system is complete, self-sufficient, and indivisible: and when mental life and the life of these organs are inseparably bound up together, it is pointless to ask where one stops and the other begins.

This being so, questions like 'What is the meaning of θυμός?' are only half-answered if we consider the word itself in isolation from the patterns of description in which the whole conception of θυμός is brought to birth. It would be especially misleading to say that these patterns are metaphorical, that they are a feature of poetic creativity rather than of abiding ideas.[117] Any metaphor worthy of the name involves a transfer of imagery, a yoking-together of things that in themselves are imagined to be distinct.[118] In Homer, metaphors in this strict sense are surprisingly thin on the ground, and they fall into two classes: either formulaic images roughly equivalent to epithets, or more extended flourishes that nearly always appear in speeches. In both types there is an obvious gulf between the metaphorical image and the thing to which it is compared, and apprehension of the meaning depends on recognizing a structural analogy between them. In principle it is always possible that as a metaphor is developed its image

[117] For our argument on this point see also Padel (1992), esp. 9–11. Padel emphasizes the need to break down the modern distinction between literal and metaphorical before approaching the ancient psychological vocabulary (but cf. n. 36 above). A closely similar problem has been addressed in an interesting way in biblical scholarship, where there is naturally a particularly pressing need to distinguish figurative language from the non-figurative essence of thought and belief. For useful discussions of areas of language—including psychology—in which such distinction becomes impossible, see in particular Farrer (1972), and Caird (1980), esp.64–8.

[118] In the absence of a full-length study of Homeric metaphor, the most useful is Moulton (1979); also Edwards (1987), 111–13; (1991), 48–53. The principal earlier discussions of Greek metaphor are M. Parry (1971 [1933]), Stanford (1936). For general purposes, the theoretical discussion of Black (1955) serves as a good warning against the fallacy of trying to understand single metaphors as isolated verbal tricks distinct from the substance of poetic ideas. See also Kittay (1989), ch. 1, for a survey of approaches. Interaction in metaphorical imagery in post-Homeric verse is studied at length by Silk (1974), esp. 3–56. His treatment is not directly relevant here, as his concern is with the 'local significance' of metaphors in their immediate context rather than with broader systems of image-making (see esp. 4).

can be drawn into the depiction of the thing to which it is applied, so that the two become organically fused, but in practice interactive metaphors of this kind are almost unknown in Homer.[119] In the first group, for example, when the war-leader at the head of his host is called the shepherd of the people, ποιμένα λαῶν (e.g. I. 263, II. 85), or when fertile Argos is called the udder of the plain, οὖθαρ ἀρούρης (IX. 141 = 283; sim. *h. Cer.* 450), alongside the precise parallel there is a clear overall contrast between the narrative image and its metaphorical twin, between the *tenor* and the *vehicle*.[120] In a particular example the latter may draw on associations which elsewhere come to light under different forms, most obviously in similes, but the metaphor itself remains an excrescence in its context.[121] The principle is the same in metaphors of the more creative or rhetorical type, as for example when Hector threatens the dandified Paris that if he were put to death in punishment

---

[119] Only once in Homer is an explicit metaphor developed at length in this way. In a speech urging that the warriors be fed before they go to battle, Odysseus likens war to harvest: αἷμά τε φυλόπιδος πέλεται κόρος ἀνθρώποισιν, | ἧς τε πλείστην μὲν καλάμην χθονὶ χαλκὸς ἔχευεν, | ἄμητος δ' ὀλίγιστος, ἐπὴν κλίνῃσι τάλαντα | Ζεύς, ὅς τ' ἀνθρώπων ταμίης πολέμοιο τέτυκται (XIX. 221–4). Although the exact correspondences are disputed, it is clear that several links are being drawn at the same time: the καλάμη strewn on the ground is parallel with the fallen warriors, the bronze of the reaping-hooks with the bronze of weapons, and so on. Thus argument seems to be proceeding *through* metaphor. On these and other possible correspondences in the metaphor see Combellack (1984) and Moulton (1979: 284–5), reviewed by Edwards ad loc.

[120] These terms framed by I. A. Richards are helpfully adapted to early Greek examples by Silk (1974), 3–26.

[121] A striking example of such interaction on the local scale is the passage in which the metaphorical image νέφος . . . πεζῶν is immediately followed by a simile likening the advancing army and their waiting foes to a storm-cloud and a terrified farmer observing its advance (IV. 274–82). More distantly, the formulaic metaphor ποιμένα λαῶν bears comparison with similes where the war-leader is compared to a shepherd and the host of warriors to a flock (XIII. 491–5 is the closest analogy; cf. also XII. 451–6, XVI. 352–7, XVIII. 161–4). In the same way, the epithet ὄζος Ἄρηος (II. 540, 704, etc.) makes more sense if it is taken in the light of numerous similes which compare a youthful warrior to a growing tree (see Ch. 1, p. 35 with n. 80). On the cumulative effect of groups of thematically similar similes see Moulton (1977), esp. 18–49. Somewhat similarly, C. H. Whitman (1958: 128–153) studies the association of war with fire throughout the *Iliad* as a symbolic system of which similes are only the most obvious manifestation (compare also Taplin (1992), 226–7). On the perils of Whitman's approach see also above, Ch. 1, pp. 20–1.

for his crimes he would 'don a tunic of stones', λάϊνον ἕσσο
χιτῶνα (III. 57). Similarly, the distinction is unambiguously
marked out when Alcinous describes oars as the wings of ships,
εὐήρε' ἐρετμά, τά τε πτερὰ νηυσὶ πέλονται (xi. 125 = xxiii. 272) or
when Penelope speaks of ships that act as men's horses, νηῶν
ὠκυπόρων . . . αἵ θ' ἁλὸς ἵπποι | ἀνδράσι γίγνονται (iv. 708–9).
Explicit metaphors like these are not comparable with the
rendering of mental life, because in that system there is no
sense in which heterogeneous things have been brought
together by poetic art. The whole of Homeric psychology is
shot through with the imagery of bodily ebb and flow, and the
one does not exist without the other: there is no metaphor, no
transference or extension, no extraneous imagery which we can
separate off from what thought and emotion are literally
conceived to be.[122] We would be thinking as translators, not
interpreters, of Homer if we sought to distinguish body from
spirit, mind from organs, air in the lungs from abstract
thought: in this language they are one and the same, so for
Homer man thinks and lives as a unity in which mental life and
the life of the body are one and indivisible.

The defining factor can be in movement not substance

Consequently, we can easily obscure the Homeric realities if
we attempt to draw up a strict definition for any of our nouns.
It is especially misleading to arrange the word's meaning into
a series of sub-definitions in the manner of Liddell and Scott.
To assign (say) a given instance of φρένες either to 'lungs' or to
'mind' would be to ignore the fact that for Homer they are
both at the one time: and if we break its range of meaning into
the subsections dictated by our own language, we impose a

---

[122] On this view the Homeric rendering of mental life could be likened to
what cognitive scientists call a 'conceptual schema' or a 'cognitive metaphor',
that is a coherent system of image-making which determines the shape of
language and thought on a given subject (see esp. Lakoff and Johnson (1980);
Lakoff and Turner (1989); Turner (1991); Gibbs (1996)). However, the major
difference remains that our system depends on a clear and literal conception of
what happens inside the breast, while the metaphors or schemata of the
cognitive scientists lack definite referents and develop autonomously in
language and thought.

distinction that makes sense only in terms of our modern assumptions, idiosyncratic as they are, and so robs the Homeric words of their internal logic. The problem of definition is best approached by examples: and a very neat and instructive example is offered by μένος.[123] As we have seen, it is one of the substances that ebb and flow in the mental apparatus, most often by entering the φρένες (e.g. I. 103, XXI. 145) or θυμός (XXII. 312), so that it can seize or possess the person, as μένος ἔλλαβε θυμόν (XXIII. 468). So far, this enables us to take it as a species of what comes to the fore when the inhalation of breath is followed by its combination with liquid substances flowing through the breast. However, beyond psychological language proper other vital fluids are also included as μένος, as for example when tears or mucus burst from the nose:

$$\text{ἀνὰ ῥῖνας δέ οἱ ἤδη}$$
$$\text{δριμὺ μένος προῦτυψε.}\quad\text{(xxiv. 318–19)}$$

Again, when Athena tells Telemachus that he will succeed in emulating his father if this substance has 'dripped down' from Odysseus into him, εἰ δή τοι σοῦ πατρὸς ἐνέστακται μένος ἠΰ (ii. 270–2), the words are easily fathomed if μένος refers to semen.[124]

Tears, semen, blood in the breast: if the essence of vigorous life is in these fluids it makes sense that a man's μένος can be tantamount to his identity, as in periphrases like Πριάμοιο μένος or ἱερὸν μένος Ἀλκινόοιο. The word ἱερός is revealing here. This is not the only instance where the word can hardly mean 'holy' or 'of the gods' in any normal sense of those English words: on the analogy of other problematic uses, ἱερός here seems to mean that the μένος of the man is imbued with vitality and rushing

---

[123] On the difficulty of categorizing μένος, cf. Jahn (1987), 39–45. μένος is difficult for Jahn in his account of *Seele-Geist* words, since it acts in mental life as one of the θυμός group but can also be breathed in from outside, and again it can simply be the force of motion in an inanimate object.

[124] Similarly Archilochus' λευκὸν μένος is his semen (fr. 196a. 52 W). For the *Odyssey* passage cited here, compare Pindar's words when he has Zeus explain to Polydeuces that Castor was conceived separately from his brother by the seed of a mortal man: τόνδε δ' ἔπειτα πόσις σπέρμα θνατὸν ματρὶ τεᾷ πελάσαις | στάξεν ἥρως (*Nem.* 10. 80–2). In the sexual act the father makes his semen drip down into the mother, and the semen is tantamount to the child himself.

movement.[125] This points us to a further aspect of μένος, without which its definition is incomplete. Alongside its role as a tangible part of a human being it can also be the force of violent self-propelled motion in something non-human: for example wind (v. 524; v. 478), a river (XXI. 383), the sun (x. 160), fire (VI. 182, XXIII. 238 = XXIV. 792; viii. 359, xi. 220), or a flying spear (XIII. 444 = XVI. 613 = XVII. 529).[126] How can we include the extremes of its meaning in a single definition for a single word? The clue is that as a quality of character or mood, μένος represents a furious urge to action that can tend eventually to frenzy and self-destruction (see esp. VI. 100–1, 407, XVII. 20–3).[127] The core of its definition is not a particular thing but a particular type of activity: vigorous, self-propelled, thrusting movement. The mood of the fell warrior is one of impetuous motion; the vital fluids of the body provide the capacity for that motion; the god incites the hero to surging aggression when he impels him to battle; flying missiles, blazing fire, rushing water, and sunbeams embody thrusting motion again in their less complex ways. Given this almost abstract character it makes sense that unlike other mental substances μένος can also be communicated from outside when a god breathes it into a man, ἔμπνευσε μένος (e.g. XV. 262 = XX. 110, XXIV. 442; more vaguely VIII. 335, XV. 594, XVI. 529). In short the unifying characteristic of μένος is not a substance but a process, a verbal rather than nominal idea, and one whose scope is clearly and precisely defined.

If this argument seems whimsical it can be bolstered by two close analogies in the shape of the words ἴς and αἰών. First, ἴς

---

[125] See most recently M. J. Clarke (1995*b*).

[126] This formulaic line is tantalizing. In each case the spear strikes something, quivers, and then Ares takes its mobile force away, ἀφίει μένος ὄβριμος Ἄρης. Given the special character of references to Ares in the language of battle (Ch. 8, pp. 269–72), this is ambiguous: it might simply mean that the driving force of the spear was dissipated, or it might look back to some old belief about the personalities of weapons (see Janko at XIII. 444). Either way, however, μένος here must refer to vigorous motion or the impetus behind it.

[127] It is worth noting that μένος is cognate with words in other languages that approximate to 'mind': Latin *mens*, Irish *menmae*, Sanskrit *manasa*. In Greek the word appears to have shifted in meaning so that it refers to fierce, vigorous motion of various kinds, including volatile psychological movement of the kind that can tend to ferocity or madness, μανία, another reflex of the same root. See now the acute observations of Hershkowitz (1998), 142–60.

(= ϝίς) and the plural ἶνες (= ϝῖνες) make a classic lexical problem. ἴς in the singular is the strength of motion and of the active body in particular. The force of a river rushing in spate is ἶς ποτάμοιο (XXI. 356), similarly the force of a gale is ἶς ἀνέμοιο (XV. 383; ix. 71, etc.). It is also what enables a man to hurl weapons, run, wrestle, and the like (v. 244–5, VII. 269, XI. 668–9, XII. 320–1, XXIII. 720; ix. 538, xi. 393, xviii. 3, xxi. 283) and what enables the fingers to knead wax (xii. 175). A man's ἴς, like his βίη or his μένος, can be tantamount to his identity, as ἱερὴ ἴς Τηλεμάχοιο (ii. 409, xvi. 476, etc.). The instrumental ἶφι and the adjectives ἴφιος and ἴφθιμος, which are possibly cognate, refer in the same way to the force of motion and muscular strength (see Ch. 6, pp. 176–7). Add to this the fact that a word with accusative ἶνα and plural ἶνες names muscles and tendons. Thus Anticleia's shade describes the wraiths' feebleness, when the sinews no longer hold flesh and bone together: οὐ γὰρ ἔτι σάρκας τε καὶ ὀστέα ἶνες ἔχουσιν (xi. 219). Similarly Apollo obscures the sun to delay the decay of Hector's corpse,

$$μὴ πρὶν μένος ἠελίοιο$$
$$σκήλει᾽ ἀμφὶ περὶ χρόα ἴνεσιν ἠδὲ μέλεσσιν. \quad (XXIII. 190–1)$$

A simile describes a man cutting through the muscle of an ox's neck, ἶνα τάμηι διὰ πᾶσαν (XVII. 522); and ἰνίον, presumably cognate, is the large muscle of the human neck (v. 73, XIV. 495). At first a gulf seems to yawn between the two meanings, abstract strength and solid bodily parts: but we make a bridge if we observe that when ἴς in the singular is human strength, it is closely identified with the muscular flexibility of the limbs, being ἐνὶ γναμπτοῖσι μέλεσσιν (XI. 668–9; xi. 393–4, xxi. 283). Similarly, κρατερὴ . . . ἴς Ὀδυσῆος (XXIII. 720) is his strength in wrestling; one who throws a stone pushes his ἴς behind it, ἐπέρεισε δὲ ἶν᾽ ἀπέλεθρον (VII. 269; ix. 538); and men surging into battle—muscles taut, strength advanced—are ἶν᾽ ἀπέλεθρον ἔχοντας (v. 245). This means that the distinction between 'strength' and 'muscles, tendons' is one which Homer's use of the word ἴς does not allow us to make: although the declension ἴς, ἰνός is odd it is not unparalleled,[128] and the

---

[128] Cf. Ζεύς, Ζηνός; ῥίς, ῥινός. Chantraine, Frisk, and *LfgrE* each list two separate words, meaning 'strength' and 'tendon' respectively, but note the

evidence invites us to take it as a single word whose range of meaning extends from the vigour of motion in the broadest sense down to the parts of the body that are its particular agents.

Turning to a last example, αἰών answers somehow to life and vitality. At death it disappears with the last breath, τόν γε λίπηι ψυχή τε καὶ αἰών (XVI. 453; sim. v. 685, vii. 224), and to die is to be deprived of it, φίλης αἰῶνος ἀμερθῆις (XXII. 58; sim. ix. 523) or ἀπ' αἰῶνος νέος ὤλεο (XXIV. 725). Since αἰεί, 'always', is closely cognate and αἰών in later Greek generally denotes a period of time, it is easy to assume that the Homeric meaning must involve the idea of the time or span of one's life: so when it is said that a hero was short-lived, μινυνθάδιος δέ οἱ αἰών | ἔπλετο (IV. 478–9 = XVII. 302–3), the reference to time at first seems straightforward. But elsewhere this adjective is applied not to the period of time but the person who exists for that period, as for example a man who dies young is himself μινυνθάδιος (e.g. I. 352, XXI. 84; xi. 307, xix. 328).[129] αἰών here sounds less like a time span than a substance tantamount to vitality—'his αἰών will be short-lived'. In just this way when Achilles imagines the prospect of a long life, ἐπὶ δηρὸν δέ μοι αἰών | ἔσσεται (IX. 415–16), he says literally that there will be αἰών in (or 'to') him for a long time. A doubtful passage of the *Iliad* also reads well in this sense. Describing the killing and dishonouring of Patroclus, Achilles fears that worms will fester in the dead man,

ἀεικίσσωσι δὲ νεκρόν—
ἐκ δ' αἰὼν πέφαται—κατὰ δὲ χρόα πάντα σαπήηι. (XIX. 26–7)

Taking πέφαται from θείνω,[130] the parenthesis translates as something like 'his αἰών has been killed out of him'—an expression which would be odd, and unparalleled in Homer, if the αἰών were a period of time. It must instead be some thing or essence that is tantamount to vitality.[131] The plot thickens

possibility of an etymological link between the two ('possible, non plus', Chantraine).

[129] Similarly μινυνθαδιώτερον ἄλγος is 'less long-lasting grief' (XXII. 54).

[130] Thus Chantraine s.v. θείνω, followed by Edwards ad loc. The mutation of the labio-velar has caused trouble since antiquity and some have taken πέφαται here from φαίνω, which makes for bigger difficulties.

[131] Cf. Edwards ad loc.

when αἰών is identified as the substance of tears. Odysseus weeps and his αἰών flows down:

$$οὐδέ ποτ' ὄσσε$$
$$δακρυόφιν τέρσοντο, \underline{κατείβετο δὲ γλυκὺς αἰὼν}$$
$$νόστον ὀδυρομένωι. \quad (v. 151–3)$$

A few lines later Calypso tells him not to let this stuff waste away from him, μηδέ τοι αἰὼν | φθινέτω (v. 160–1). Penelope describes weeping in the same way when she hopes for a gentle death that will end her lamentations:

$$ἵνα μηκέτ' ὀδυρομένη κατὰ θυμὸν$$
$$\underline{αἰῶνα φθινύθω.} \quad (xviii. 203–4)$$

In the *Homeric Hymn to Hermes* αἰών is the moist stuff under a tortoise's shell (42, 119) and there is some evidence that the word also names bone marrow.[132] The picture that emerges is of something visible and tangible, the vital moist stuff that characterizes the living body; yet in the temporal sense, as we saw from αἰεί, this same word names something entirely abstract, the duration of a life. The common ground of meaning is not in a particular static thing but in the ongoing *process* of living, which can be seen and encapsulated in different contexts by a length of time or by an oozing liquid.[133]

The lexical structure that informs these three words—ἴς, αἰών, μένος—is analogous to the conceptual structure that informs Homer's rendering of mental life. At first it seemed hardly to make sense that Homer encompasses tangible bodily parts and the intangible essence of life and thought within the

---

[132] Solmsen (1979) argues that σύμφυτος αἰών is the bone marrow that surges or rules (ἀνάισσει, ἀνάσσει) in the bodies of the chorus of Aeschylus' *Agamemnon* (*Ag.* 76–7, 106). Hesychius has the tantalizing gloss ὁ ἐν παντὶ τῶι σώματι μυελός, though it is of course possible that this represents a guess no better informed than our own. On Pindaric αἰών see Epilogue, p. 311.

[133] On αἰών as 'time of life' and as 'essence of life', see most recently Claus (1981), 11–13, and Bremmer (1983), 15–17. Onians (1951: 200–6), boldly identifies αἰών with tears, marrow, and cerebro-spinal fluid. Degani (1961: 17–28) surveys the uses of αἰών in Homer and suggests that 'forza vitale' is the original meaning, transferred sometimes to marrow as a symbol of that force. Nikitas (1978: 75–86) argues that the association of αἰών with the marrow and the spine is post-Homeric, and compares the Homeric examples. On the development of αἰών into the temporal sense familiar in later Greek, see Benveniste (1937); Festugière (1949); Degani (1961), *passim*.

meanings of individual words and throughout the imagery where those words express ideas; but it turns out that the system is clear and meaningful because the life of Homeric man is defined in terms of processes more precisely than of things. Because the oozing, flowing, billowing life of breath and the organs in the breast is dynamic rather than static, it expresses the flow of mental life clearly and naturally, with at least as much depth and subtlety as does the language of the mind in our own culture.

The body and the self are one

The implication of all this is that Homer does not oppose mental life to the life of the body but takes them as an undifferentiated whole. There is no 'ghost in the machine': Homeric man does not *have* a mind, rather his thought and consciousness are as inseparable a part of his bodily life as are movement and metabolism. If that is right, then by the same token he will not *have* a body: the thing that English calls 'the body' will be exactly coterminous with and identical to the mass of blood, bones, and consciousness that is a human being. We now turn to establish whether or not this is the case: and the results of this second enquiry will allow us to end our chapter with a more definite sketch of the relation between the physical and psychological identity of Homeric man.

Body and not-body

Just as H. Fränkel held (above, pp. 61–3) that Homeric man draws no line between the inner self and the outer world, so B. Snell[134] advanced the bold theory that Homer has no unified concept of man's mental identity, that the entities in the θυμός family represent jumbled fragments of mental life that do not add up to a 'psychic whole'. I hope that the discussion in this chapter has been enough to show that that is not the full truth, at least on the word-by-word level. What remains challenging in Snell's essay is an observation about Homer's attitude to

---

[134] Snell (1953), 8–17. On the intellectual background of Snell's preoccupations, see MacCary (1982), 3–34; A. Schmitt (1990), 12–71, 117–25.

the body, that he sees it not as a unity but as a collection of parts:

Our phrase 'his body became feeble' would be the Homeric λέλυντο γυῖα; 'his whole body trembled' would appear as γυῖα τρομέονται. Where we might say 'sweat poured from his body', Homer has ἵδρως ἐκ μελέων ἔρρεεν; 'his body was filled with strength' is πλῆσθεν δ' ἄρα οἱ μέλε' ἐντὸς ἀλκῆς . . . How would we translate [into Homeric Greek] 'He washed his body'? Homer has χρόα νίζετο. How would Homer say 'The sword pierced his body'? Here again he uses the word χρώς: ξίφος χροὸς διῆλθε.[135]

On its own this tendency might simply be seen as a matter of style rather than ideas;[136] but the argument rests more solidly on the observation that Homer has no one word to denote the living body, and hence by extension that he has no conception of the body as a single thing. This is the point on which we must fasten.

    Snell relies in the first place on the observation attributed to Aristarchus that in Homer σῶμα always refers to a corpse.[137] The facts are the following.[138] σῶμα is attested for human bodies (VII. 79 = XXII. 342; xi. 53, xii. 67, xxiv. 187) and those of animals (III. 23, XVIII. 161, XXIII. 169), and every human σῶμα is definitely a corpse.[139] Of the three instances applied to

---

[135] Snell (1953), 5–6.

[136] Irrespective of the question of underlying ideas, there is undoubtedly a stylistic tendency as well: see e.g. viii. 134–6, xviii. 67–9.

[137] Cited in Apollodorus, *Lexicon Homericum* 254.

[138] σῶμα has no secure etymology. On the problem of its Homeric meaning, see Herter (1957); Koller (1958); Krafft (1963), 26–30; Renehan (1979); also some (perhaps glib) remarks by West at Hes. *WD* 540 (see Epilogue, p. 285). Herter (1957) holds that a σῶμα may be living or dead, on the grounds of the passage in the *Shield* (see n. 140 below) and the supposition that Asiatic lions do not eat carrion, and he prefers to define the σῶμα as the body as opposed to the head, like German *Leib*; though he accepts (216–17) that there may be deeper implications in the fact that Homer does not use the word of living human bodies. Koller (1958) avoids the issue by maintaining that σῶμα is cognate with σίνεσθαι, and that in the lion similes it is 'what is mauled or attacked' and in other contexts 'corpse'. Renehan (1979) reviews the debate and is content to accept that in practice, at least, Homer does not use any one word for the living human body; he is unwilling to draw any firm conclusions from this, but concludes with a suggestion similar to my own argument here, holding that Homer does not speak of the body because he recognizes no division of man into body and not-body (278–80).

animals, one refers to flayed corpses, δρατὰ σώματα (XXIII. 169), but the other two are doubtful. Both occur in lion similes, where the σῶμα is the lion's prey: it is plausible at least that these are also corpses, as there is no good reason to think that Homer's lions are averse to carrion.[140] Although this cannot be certain, we can follow Aristarchus and Snell to the extent that in practice Homer does not apply this word to the living human body. Other candidates for a word for the body are equally unsatisfactory.[141] For example δέμας, like the less common φυή, refers to one's shape or appearance rather than the body as a concrete thing.[142] The word occurs nearly always as an accusative of respect[143]—typically when a disguised god resembles someone in shape, for example εἰσάμενος Κάλχαντι δέμας καὶ ἀτειρέα φωνήν (XIII. 45; compare XVII. 323, ii. 268, etc.), or to explain that an adjective refers to someone's appearance:

---

[139] The only debatable instance is at xii. 67, where men's σώματα are washed away after they are shipwrecked in the Clashing Rocks. It is (technically) arguable that they might have not drowned immediately; though it is implied that they are now lost permanently, so that the reasonable interpretation is that they are dead.

[140] One of the two similes (III. 23–7) closely resembles a passage in the Hesiodic *Shield of Heracles* (426–32), where the σῶμα is clearly that of a living animal; if it were assumed that the epic language is the same in both instances, the Iliadic similes might be taken as referring to living beasts (see Herter (1957)). We will see later (Epilogue, pp. 315–19) that σῶμα is used in new and different senses in post-Homeric Greek, and that this change is reflected when Hesiod himself uses σῶμα of the living body in *WD*. Hence the *Shield* passage need not be taken as an index of the Homeric usage.

[141] Vivante (1955) usefully surveys the claims of γυῖα, ἅψεα, μέλεα, ῥέθεα, χρώς, σῶμα, δέμας, εἶδος, and φυή to the title of the Homeric word for 'body', and shows that none of these fits the bill.

[142] δέμας is cognate with δέμω, 'build', so that it seems to denote the shape or form in which a person is made (see *LfgrE*, Chantraine s.v. δέμας; Frisk s.v. δέμω).

[143] See Ruijgh (1971), 865. There is one arguable exception. Penelope describes the decline of her beauty: ἦ τοι ἐμὴν ἀρετήν, εἶδός τε δέμας τε, | ὤλεσαν ἀθάνατοι (xviii. 251–2 = xix. 124–5). Does this mean that the gods have destroyed her 'ἀρετή and appearance and body' or that they have destroyed her 'ἀρετή in respect of appearance and form'? There is nothing to choose between the two translations, except that the latter would be more regular statistically.

οὔ ἑθέν ἐστι χερείων,
οὐ δέμας οὐδὲ φυήν, οὔτ' ἆρ φρένας οὔτε τι ἔργα.

(I. 114–15; sim. XXIV. 376, iii. 468, xiv.
177, etc.)

Hence δέμας behaves less like a noun than an adverb, qualifying an adjective or a verb expressing a comparison. Similarly it can act as a preposition introducing a simile, as ὡς οἱ μὲν μάρναντο δέμας πυρὸς αἰθομένοιο (XI. 596 = XIII. 673 = XVIII. 1; sim. XVII. 366). δέμας, then, names not the body but the manner in which something is shaped or constructed.

Revealing here is the passage where Odysseus describes finding his companions turned into swine by Circe:

οἱ δὲ συῶν μὲν ἔχον κεφαλὰς φωνήν τε τρίχας τε
καὶ δέμας, αὐτὰρ νοῦς ἦν ἔμπεδος ὡς τὸ πάρος περ.   (x. 239–40)

When Homer tries to render the difficult and unique idea that the men look like beasts but have their own human identity, δέμας moves close to denoting the substance of the body as opposed to the thinking man. The fact that the usage is unique to this passage, with its extraordinary situation,[144] confirms the impression that Homeric language does not reflect a distinction between body and not-body in the make-up of the living man. Similarly, even if it is possible in the Homeric lexicon for σῶμα to denote the living body, still the fact that Homer never does use it in this sense must be significant—especially if we recognize how difficult it would be in English to describe things like hand-to-hand combat or heroic physique without using the equivalent word.

Snell adduced the lack of a word for 'body' as proof that for Homer 'the physical body was comprehended not as a unit but as an aggregate.'[145] In the light of the argument in this chapter a simpler solution presents itself: to seek a word for 'body' is to ask Homer a wrong and unanswerable question. That a man

---

[144] Compare the other references to Circe's transformations, which do not involve anything like a concept of body *qua* body: the transformed men are ὡς τε σύες (x. 283) or σιάλοισιν ἐοικότας ἐννεώροισιν (x. 390), and similarly when they change back to human appearance: τῶν δ' ἐκ μὲν μελέων τρίχες ἔρρεον . . . ἄνδρες δ' ἀψ ἐγένοντο (x. 393–5). The shape-changing of Proteus is described in much the same way (iv. 416–24, 455–61).

[145] (1953), 6.

should have a body makes sense only if he has another part to be distinguished from it: soul, mind, the ghost in the machine. Since we saw from the θυμός family that for Homer there is no mental part of man that can be distinguished from the body, it follows now that the body is indistinguishable from the human whole. A spear strikes a man's head or hand or foot or more generally it strikes the man, and that is all. Both in psychological life and in the life of the flesh, the bodily and spiritual continuum can be identified unambiguously in many ways—ἄνθρωπος, αὐτός, Ἀγαμέμνων, and so on—and there is no place for a name for either half of a dichotomy that does not exist. In this way the problem of σῶμα and δέμας corroborates the theory that the undivided unity of human nature is all that stands behind the activity of θυμός and its family.[146]

As νόος the product of thought goes beyond the apparatus in the breast

We saw at the beginning of this chapter that θυμός and its family have an indeterminate status between mental agents and mental functions or phenomena. At the latter extreme they can occasionally be identified with the products of thought rather

[146] Such a revision of Snell's argument about the 'fragmented self' has been made under various forms in German studies: for a succinct statement of the debate and its resolution, see A. Schmitt (1990), esp. 178–82. The point was first articulated clearly by Lanig (1953), see esp. 39. Something similar is briefly suggested by Herter (1957), 206–8, with bibliography of other revisions of Snell's argument; see also Vivante (1955), 47–8, and Renehan (1979), 279. Adkins (1970: 21–7) closely follows Snell on the idea of a lack of psychic unity, but comes closer to my argument here when he mentions that 'there is no word for the [psychic] whole *apart from the implications of the personal pronouns*' (22, my italics). Austin (1975: 82–5) shows in a brief sketch that received ideas about primitive mentality and language underlie Snell's theory: 'To concentrate exclusively on isolated words . . . produces an erroneous impression since, in fact, Homer is being judged according to his understanding of later general concepts' (84–5). The same point has been re-emphasized in more philosophical terms by Gaskin (1990). Compare Lesky's suggestion (1950: 99–100), in his review of Snell's book, that Homeric language may reflect a unified concept of self without having a word to correspond to that concept (also Lesky (1961), 7–9; followed by Darcus Sullivan (1988), 2–7); and for a more oblique approach to 'unity in multiplicity', see Padel (1992), 44–8.

than the ongoing process.[147] This explains why it is often implied that the mental entity is something that exists only temporarily: throughout this chapter many of our examples have illustrated this, as when one is affected by a new thought, ἕτερος θυμός (ix. 302), or when fear or folly amounts to the loss of mental substance, as in the question to one who seems to have gone mad, 'where have your φρένες disappeared to?' (XXIV. 201–2; see also e.g. VI. 352, XIII. 394, and see above, pp. 101–2). When an appeal to courage is expressed as ἄλκιμον ἦτορ ἕλεσθε (V. 529), the image is not figurative in the same way as an English expresssion like 'take heart'. It is in the same way that Nestor, after expounding his favoured battle-plan, can say that in former times men fought τόνδε νόον καὶ θυμὸν ἐνὶ στήθεσσιν ἔχοντες (IV. 309; cf. XVI. 265) or that men acting and thinking in unison are ἕνα φρεσὶ θυμὸν ἔχοντες (XIII. 487) or ἕνα θυμὸν ἔχοντες (XV. 710, XVI. 219, XVII. 267; iii. 128). All this makes sense if our nouns stand not for the thinker or the process but for its results.

νόος here is an important case in point.[148] It is associated primarily with intellectual rather than emotional activity,[149] though this is not a watertight rule—note the phrase χαῖρε νόωι (viii. 78)—and we have seen in many examples that it participates in the pattern of ebb and flow shared by all the θυμός family: in particular it tends to be the contents of the flow, as when anger expands it, οἰδάνει νόον (IX. 554) or appeasement compresses it, ἐπιγνάμπτει (IX. 514); in someone wise it is dense, as Διὸς πυκινὸν νόον (XV. 461);[150] and a foolish

---

[147] This observation is perhaps the most useful part of Claus's contribution (above, p. 68).

[148] Jahn (1987: 46–118) has an exhaustive and very useful survey of νόος, which begins by dividing the definition in two—νόος 1 is the 'instrument or subject' of mental life, νόος 2 is the 'mobile product of thought'. He eventually collapses the distinction and sets νόος apart from the other mental entities because of its 'character as a δύναμις' and its peculiar status as the 'result and consequence of rational activity' (117–18). The grammatical data about νόος as object or product of thought are usefully collected by Darcus (1980), 33–9. Cf. also Onians (1951), 82; Claus (1981), 19–21.

[149] On this see also von Fritz (1943), answering Böhme (1929), who had maintained (52–63) that νόος was exclusively intellectual; and on the relationship between θυμός and νόος see also Marg (1938), 43–6.

[150] Similarly cunning plans are weavings of thought, κακορραφίαι νόοιο (ii. 236).

person has an ἄνοον κραδίην (XXI. 441), a mental apparatus with no ideas in it. Although it does not necessarily act as a full synonym of θυμός and the others, it is closely linked to them. For example, when Paris describes Hector's disposition he begins by talking of his κραδίη,

αἰεί τοι κραδίη πέλεκυς ὥς ἐστιν ἀτειρής, . . . (III. 60)

but when he finishes his description its name has become νόος:

ὥς σοι ἐνὶ στήθεσσιν ἀτάρβητος νόος ἐστί. (III. 63)

It is also possible for νόος to be assimilated to the main mental apparatus, as in the doublet τόνδε νόον καὶ θυμόν (IV. 309). It differs, however, in that it is not a part of the straightforward anatomy of the body—no-one's νόος is ever visible, and it is not described as air breathed into the lungs like θυμός. In view of this, could it be identified as a kind of spiritual self, an immaterial centre of psychological life?[151]

Here the exception proves the rule. νόος, along with the kindred νόημα, differs from the other psychological identities because it is not the source or instrument of mental life but the

---

[151] A theory in this direction is advanced by A. Schmitt (1990), 188–221, esp. 211–21. Seeking to identify a single entity unifying the functions of the members of the θυμός family, he proposes νόος as the 'true self' of Homeric man. In this argument, as throughout his book, he is concerned less with the body–mind question than with the categories into which mental life is to be divided: specifically, whether a structure can be found in Homeric psychology which would answer to the distinction beween reason, will, and emotion in modern philosophy. From this starting-point he is led to define νόος as the rational force which imposes order on the disordered passion represented by θυμός. Because Schmitt tends to argue through general principles or through the terms of later Greek philsophy, it is difficult to get to grips with his ideas about the realities of Homeric thought and language. If we accepted the contrast between θυμός and νόος which he proposes it would be very hard to explain passages where the two are ostensibly one and the same (e.g. IV. 309). More generally, there are two simple difficulties with his approach. First, no Homeric passage actually mentions a conflict between θυμός and νόος or, indeed, an opposition of any kind between νόος and any of the nouns in the θυμός group (cf. esp. 188–9; and see above, pp. 64–6). Secondly, Schmitt sidesteps the possibility that the νόος of his chosen passages is a temporary phenomenon, an act of thought rather than a permanent substratum (see esp. 176–8); so that it can still be argued that the value of his argument lies in distinguishing types of mental activity or mental products, rather than in identifying one or other source of thought as the 'true self'.

conclusion of the thinking process,[152] the product of the act named by the cognate verb νοεῖν or νοεῖσθαι.[153] So it is that a νόος can be virtually identified with a plan or stratagem, as in the doublets νόος καὶ μῆτις (VII. 447, XV. 509; XIX. 326)[154] and βουλή τε νόος τε (ii. 281, iv. 267, xi. 177). When it is said that Odysseus πολλῶν ἀνθρώπων ἴδεν ἄστεα καὶ νόον ἔγνω (i. 3) it is misleading to translate that he 'knew the minds' of men: the straightforward meaning is that he learnt their plans and policies, the same claim that Menelaus makes more plainly about his own wanderings:

ἤδη μὲν πολέων <u>ἐδάην βουλήν τε νόον τε</u>
ἀνδρῶν ἡρώων, πολλὴν δ' ἐπελήλυθα γαῖαν.

(iv. 267–8; cf. viii. 559)

Likewise a νόος is produced by the act of planning, as οὐ γὰρ δὴ τοῦτον . . . ἐβούλευσας νόον αὐτή (v. 23 = xxiv. 479), or by the act of thinking, νοεῖν:[155]

οὐ γάρ τις <u>νόον</u> ἄλλος ἀμείνονα τοῦδε <u>νοήσει</u>
οἷον ἐγὼ <u>νοέω</u>.   (IX. 104–5)

Here what is produced by νοεῖν is something objective, a scheme or idea, just as elsewhere it is an utterance, μῦθον . . . νοῆσαι (VII. 358 = XII. 232; sim. I. 543). Likewise Zeus does not bring men's intentions to fulfilment, ἀλλ' οὐ Ζεὺς ἄνδρεσσι νοήματα πάντα τελευτᾷ (XVIII. 328; sim. X. 104–5); one can know (or not know) another's thoughts or plans, οὐ γάρ πω σάφα οἶσθ' οἷος νόος Ἀτρεΐωνος (II. 192). When a man reveals others' plots he recounts their νόος, πάντα νόον κατέλεξεν Ἀχαιῶν (iv. 256; sim. XVIII. 295); and one who has become foolish has been led away from it, παρὲκ νόον (X. 391; cf. XX. 133).

[152] Cf. Onians (1951), 82; Vivante (1956), 128–30; Claus (1981), 19–20.

[153] On the relationships within this family of words, see von Fritz (1943); Krischer (1984). Von Fritz suggests that νόος, νοέω, and νόημα refer to differing stages in 'the realisation of a situation' (91), a suitably vague definition; Krischer modifies this to 'the disposition of a person . . . that determines his behaviour' (147; cf. Snell (1975), 19–25). For the proposal of A. Schmitt (1990) about the relation of νόος to θυμός, see n. 151 above.

[154] Compare the more distant pairings at X. 226, XXIII. 590; also note νόος καὶ αἰδώς (XV. 129).

[155] For νόος clearly marked out as the product of thought, see e.g. VII. 447, XIII. 732, XV. 509, 699, XXII. 185, XXIV. 367; ii. 124, 281, iv. 493, xiv. 490.

All this suggests that the *directional* aspect of thought is at the heart of the meaning of νόος.[156] The most remarkable indication of this is a simile where the swift movement of a god between heaven and earth is like the movement of a man's thought:

> ὡς δ' ὅτ' ἂν ἀΐξηι νόος ἀνέρος, ὅς τ' ἐπὶ πολλὴν
> γαῖαν ἐληλουθὼς φρεσὶ πευκαλίμηισι νοήσηι,
> "ἔνθ' εἴην, ἢ ἔνθα", μενοινήηισί τε πολλά,
> ὣς κραιπνῶς μεμαυῖα διέπτατο πότνια Ἥρη.

(xv. 80–3; sim. *h. Ap.* 448, *h. Merc.* 43–6)

The man stays still but the places he remembers are shifting: the image only makes sense if the νόος is not in the thinker but in the things at which his memories are directed. The action denoted by νοεῖν is a movement out of the self to the external objects of his mental activities. It follows that in this aspect the νόος itself is not a thing but a process. Hence ships can be swift as a wing or a thought, νόημα (vii. 36; sim. *h. Ap.* 186);[157] the νόος of an ineffective man is of short reach, βράσσων (x. 226), while that of a rash young man is too swift, κραιπνότερος (XXIII. 590). It is particularly revealing that when Athena beguiles the suitors she misdirects their thoughts, παρέπλαγξεν . . . νόημα (xx. 346; sim. *h. Ven.* 254), just as one might divert the flight of an arrow (e.g. xv. 464); while to think erroneously is to aim inaccurately and miss the goal of thought, νοήματος ἤμβροτεν ἐσθλοῦ (vii. 292). Similarly the careful thinker is controlling the movement of his thought, νόον πολυκερδέα νωμῶν (xiii. 255; sim. xviii. 216). The principle is the same when thought is less overtly depicted in terms of aiming and directing: by persuasion one turns another's mental apparatus,

---

[156] A fascinating sidelight is thrown on this by Douglas Frame's theory (1978: *passim*) that νόος is a reflex of the root seen in the verb νέομαι and is also co-ordinated on some level with νόστος. Although the ultimate shape of Frame's argument is beyond the scope of this study, on the verbal level it chimes neatly.

[157] Seemingly this is what Odysseus refers to when he tells Achilles that he is wiser than him: 'I would cast further than you in thinking', ἐγὼ δέ κε σεῖο νοήματί γε προβαλοίμην | πολλόν (XIX. 218–19). It is not sufficient to gloss the verb with an English metaphor like 'surpass', because there is no Homeric authority for that extension of meaning.

ἔτρεψεν . . . φρένας (VI. 61; sim. IX. 600–1, X. 45, XV. 52, iii. 147, iv. 259–60, vii. 263, xix. 479, etc.). Men who are ἐσθλοί yield to persuasion, and as such their φρένες are turnable, στρεπταί (XV. 203). If νόος travels to the object of thought it makes sense that a man of sound mind is one who touches things mentally, ἐπιψαύηι πραπίδεσσι (viii. 547).[158] In short, νόος is the abstract, intangible thing that emerges from the tangible stuff in the breast, and behind any one νόος this stuff is the unity of the human being as psychological agent.

This is a fine distinction and it must not be pushed too far. Since the thought-process naturally produces thoughts, ideas, mental pictures that form the permanent make-up of the personality, νόος can move closer than anything else in Homer's vocabulary to being an intangible mental essence. Witness the way Theoclymenus includes it along with bodily members in a list of his own attributes:

> εἰσί μοι ὀφθαλμοί τε καὶ οὔατα καὶ πόδες ἄμφω
> καὶ νόος ἐν στήθεσσι τετυγμένος οὐδὲν ἀεικής.   (XX. 365–6)

A still clearer example of this kind is the passage describing Odysseus' men turned into swine, where we have already observed the unique substantive use of δέμας:

> οἱ δὲ συῶν μὲν ἔχον κεφαλὰς φωνήν τε τρίχας τε
> καὶ δέμας, αὐτὰρ νοῦς ἦν ἔμπεδος ὡς τὸ πάρος περ.
> (X. 239–40; compare XVIII. 419 f.)

Although νόος here seemingly refers to the thoughts or conceptions made by the men, rather than to some non-bodily portion of their make-up, it is easy to see how a forced contrast between the shape of the body and the thinking self might prompt the idea that νόος is a disembodied entity, the fixed mental centre of man. If so, however, that idea has not been brought to birth in the Homeric depiction of man.

This tendency is implied in a subtle way when a νόος is imagined as an agent of thought or planning. One considers whether it will achieve anything, εἴ τι νόος ῥέξει (XIV. 62); it can have its own intentions, νόος δέ οἱ ἄλλα μενοινᾶι (ii. 92 =

---

[158] On the ambiguity in this expression see Hainsworth ad loc. Somewhat similar is the image of the θυμός of a greedy man reaching out for gifts, δώρων ἐπεμαίετο θυμός (X. 401).

xiii. 381); it hides secrets, τί . . . νόος ἔνδοθι κεύθει; (xxiv. 474).[159]
Here the νόος is not an independent mental agent inside the
man: rather, it is the things *produced* by the human agent that
are taking on a life of their own. There is an illuminating
parallel here with μῆτις, which we have already seen closely
merged with νόος in doublets (VII. 447; xix. 326, etc.). The
independent νόος is exactly paralleled by the autonomous plan
or scheme, μῆτις, that Odysseus imagines almost as a personal
being when it led him out of Polyphemus' cave:

$$\ldots \text{ὄφρα σε } \underline{\mu\hat{\eta}\tau\iota\varsigma}$$
$$\hat{\epsilon}\xi\acute{\alpha}\gamma\alpha\gamma' \hat{\epsilon}\xi \text{ ἄντροιο ὀϊόμενον θανέεσθαι.} \quad \text{(xx. 20–1)}^{160}$$

Although this speech is complicated by the chime between μή
τις and his ploy with the word οὖτις (ix. 366–7), the words make
sense only if his plan or stratagem is dimly personified as a
being who led him out of Polyphemus' cave (sim ix. 414). The
image may even suggest something like the personal Metis who
slept with Zeus, became Athena's mother, and was swallowed
by her consort.[161] Although this is not an Homeric story it is
undoubtedly a very ancient one: and because food enters the
same apparatus in the breast as does the stuff of thought
(above, pp. 88–9), when Zeus swallows Metis his action is
equivalent to what a thoughtful mortal does when he puts a
stratagem in his breast, μῆτιν ἐμβάλλεο θυμῶι (XXIII. 313).[162] For
us, the crucial point is that a μῆτις is something produced or
invented by thought, as when one weaves or spins it, μῆτιν
ὑφαίνει (see Ch. 7, n. 49). If we accept that νόος and μῆτις are
closely akin or overlapping, the parallel suggests that in our last
group of νόος images it was the result or product of mental
activity, rather than the agent behind it, that was close to taking
on an independent localized existence.

With this we reach the limits of our argument for the

[159] The more usual tendency is to see the secret as hidden in or by the
thought: witness μὴ κλέπτε νόωι (I. 132), μὴ κεῦθε νόωι (I. 363; sim. viii. 548).
[160] Compare ii. 279, ix. 414, xxiii. 124–5.
[161] The earliest source is Hes. *Theog.* 886–900. See also Hes. fr. 343 M–W
(dub.); Stesich. fr. 233 P; Ibyc. fr. 298 P; *h. Hom.* 28.
[162] Beyond this suggestion is difficult to tell how closely the personal Metis
is tied to Zeus' identity as thinker or planner, μητίετα Ζεύς, though it is
interesting (albeit in a probably late source) that that epithet is applied to Zeus
in *h. Hom.* 28. 4 in the context of Athena's parentage.

dependence of mental life on the body. The abstract or non-bodily aspect of Homeric psychology is the special province of νόος alone among our nouns, and it is so in virtue of the fact that νόος is bound up with the production of ideas, νοεῖν, so that it passes beyond the continuum of agency and function which we have sketched. Behind these products, mental life is rooted in the bodily unity of man; and that unity is the immediate source of every act of thought, of all that is νόος.

We have now observed the relationship between the body and mental activity from three standpoints. First, we saw that the stuff of thought and emotion is one with the stuff of the physical body. Moving to the other end of the telescope, as it were, we then observed that Homeric language recognizes nothing that can be called the body: nothing, in other words, which is flesh and blood as opposed to mind or spirit. Neither category can be translated from our language to that of Homer. Lastly, we have now seen that in practice the relationship between the θυμός group and the 'I' of Homeric man varies in such a way that only the results of thought, not their source, can be decisively distinguished from the flesh and blood which lurk behind them all. It is the bodily reality of those mental acts, free of any concept of an abstract or spiritual self, which identifies θυμός and the other nouns in relation to man. When these points are combined, Homeric man stands revealed as a continuum in whom the sources and processes of his mental life are inseparably united with the substance of what we would nowadays call the body.

PART III

Death and the Afterlife

5
The Dying Gasp and the
Journey to Hades

Loss of ψυχή is not departure of soul from body

We have seen that for Homer mental life is the inhalation of breath and its mingling with blood and kindred fluids in the breast, and hence that no part of the living man can be separated off as a mind imprisoned in the body. If man lives and has consciousness as an indivisible unity, what happens when he dies? Here we return to ψυχή. There are many allusions to the loss of something of this name at the moment of death, and in a few passages it is described as going to the Underworld. The classic text is the lines that narrate the deaths of Patroclus and Hector:

> ὣς ἄρα μιν εἰπόντα τέλος θανάτοιο κάλυψεν,
> ψυχὴ δ᾽ ἐκ ῥεθέων πταμένη Ἀϊδόσδε βεβήκει,
> ὃν πότμον γοόωσα, λιποῦσ᾽ ἀνδροτῆτα καὶ ἥβην.
>
> (XVI. 855–7 = XXII. 361–3)

Whatever the ψυχή is, here it leaves the hero's youth and manhood behind and flies off, bemoaning the grim prospect of the land of the dead. Similarly the proem of the *Iliad* describes how the Wrath sent ψυχαί to Hades and left the men themselves as carrion:

> πολλὰς δ᾽ ἰφθίμους ψυχὰς Ἄϊδι προΐαψεν
> ἡρώων, αὐτοὺς δὲ ἑλώρια τεῦχε κύνεσσιν
> οἰωνοῖσί τε πᾶσι. (I. 3–5)

It is easy—too easy—to map these images onto the dichotomy of body and soul that informs modern language and beliefs, so as to say that here the immortal part of Homeric man departs from his corpse. We know that the name ψυχή also belongs to the wraith or ghost, the image of the dead man that will live on in the shadowy afterlife in Hades. What could be simpler than to identify them with each other? The first objection to that translation is our observation in Chapter 3: whatever a ψυχή is, it is not part of the make-up of the living man, and its meaning is restricted to the moment of death. If it is irrelevant to identity and consciousness during his life, it cannot be right to explain its loss as the departure of his soul or ghost or spiritual core. Here we are strengthened by the lessons of the last chapter. If man lives and thinks in a way that allows no meaning to terms like flesh and spirit or body and mind, it follows that death must somehow make sense in terms of that same conception of human unity. This is already suggested in the proem passage, where the things abandoned by the ψυχαί are not corpses or bodies but the men themselves, αὐτοί. Similarly when the ψυχή of Patroclus or Hector departs it leaves behind manhood, ἀνδροτῆτα, in other words the substance of the bodily hero. When Homeric man dies he is not divided into two parts: what, then, is this other thing that leaves him at the moment of death? I will try to answer that question by beginning at the simplest level of Homeric language and working upwards, to show how the image of the flight of the ψυχή is built up on the basis of a simpler conception of what literally and visibly happens when a man breathes his last and dies.

Loss of θυμός is loss of breath and of life

We saw that θυμός is essentially breath drawn into the lungs: since to die is to breathe one's last, death is represented in plain language as the departure of θυμός. The dying man loses it, ἀπὸ θυμὸν ὄλεσσεν (I. 205, VIII. 90, 270, 358, X. 452, etc.); he falls to the ground bereft of it, θυμοῦ δευόμενος (XX. 472; sim. III. 294); it leaves, τὸν μὲν λίπε θυμός (IV. 470, etc.). Since this is the decisive sign of death, θυμός can be seen as the prize in mortal combat: when one warrior kills another he takes it from him, φίλον δ᾽ ἐξαίνυτο θυμόν (V. 155, etc.), or ἐκ θυμὸν ἕλοιτο (e.g. V. 317, 346, xvii. 236; sim. V. 673, 691, 852, xxii. 388), or θυμὸν ἀπηύρα (VI. 17, X. 495, xi. 203, etc.). More precise images confirm that just as θυμός in life is breath drawn into the lungs, so its loss is the last gasp expired by the dying man. Occasionally this is developed at length, as when Hippodamas is slain:

αὐτὰρ ὁ θυμὸν ἄϊσθε καὶ ἤρυγεν, ὡς ὅτε ταῦρος
ἤρυγεν ἑλκόμενος Ἑλικώνιον ἀμφὶ ἄνακτα
κούρων ἑλκόντων, γάνυται δέ τε τοῖς Ἐνοσίχθων,
ὣς ἄρα τόν γ᾽ ἐρυγόντα λίπ᾽ ὀστέα θυμὸς ἀγήνωρ.   (XX. 403–6)

He snorts out breath, θυμὸν ἄϊσθε, like a bellowing bull,[1] and this encapsulates the most profound loss of life. In another death the θυμός is breathed out as a stage in the coming of death rather than as a summary of the whole event:

ὁ δ᾽ ὕπτιος ἐν κονίῃσι
κάππεσεν, ἄμφω χεῖρε φίλοις ἑτάροισι πετάσσας,
θυμὸν ἀποπνείων, ὁ δ᾽ ἐπέδραμεν ὅς ῥ᾽ ἔβαλέν περ,
Πείρως, οὖτα δὲ δουρὶ παρ᾽ ὀμφαλόν, ἐκ δ᾽ ἄρα πᾶσαι
χύντο χαμαὶ χολάδες, τὸν δὲ σκότος ὄσσε κάλυψε.

(IV. 522–6; sim. XIII. 653–5)

First he falls, then he breathes out his last gasp, finally the decisive blow is struck and the darkness of death covers over his eyes. Here the dislocation of the usual sequence of events in a killing has led the poet to separate the breathing out of the θυμός from the moment of death itself, showing the meaning of the expiration in an especially tangible way.

Even without the word θυμός the final groan that signals death comes to the fore in a particularly savage killing where a warrior is gored in the pit of the stomach:

---

[1] The verb ἄϊσθε is otherwise attested only once, describing the death of a horse in battle: ὁ δ᾽ ἔβραχε θυμὸν ἀΐσθων, | κὰδ δ᾽ ἔπεσ᾽ ἐν κονίῃσι μακών, ἀπὸ δ᾽ ἔπτατο θυμός (XVI. 468–9). Here, still more clearly than in the human death, the verb must refer to violent gasping or snorting out. The form ἄϊσθον is almost certainly cognate with ἄϊον, which is used when one describes how he lost his breath and consciousness by swooning, φίλον ἄϊον ἦτορ (XV. 252; see below, p. 139). However, the nature of the semantic link is doubtful. Chantraine (s.v. *ἀΐω) regards ἄ(ϝ)ιον as the imperfect and ἄ(ϝ)ισθον the aorist of a verb *ἀϝίω, but this is not certain; Frisk (s.v. ἀΐσθων) says only that ἄϊον and ἄϊσθον are 'somehow connected', while Risch (1974: § 101) shows that the significance of such forms in -εσθ- is always difficult to pin down, since they are attested in some verbs for the present tense and in others for the aorist. It is an obvious likelihood that both ἄϊον and ἄϊσθον are tied to ἄ(ϝ)ημι, with something like the same sense 'blow, gasp, breathe out', though *LfgrE* (s.v. ἄϊσθον) considers this 'possible only.' See also Janko at XV. 252.

ὁ δ' ἑσπόμενος περὶ δουρὶ
ἤσπαιρ' ὡς ὅτε βοῦς, τόν τ' οὔρεσι βουκόλοι ἄνδρες
ἰλλάσιν οὐκ ἐθέλοντα βίηι δήσαντες ἄγουσιν,
ὡς ὁ τυπεὶς ἤσπαιρε μίνυνθά περ, οὔ τι μάλα δήν,
ὄφρα οἱ ἐκ χροὸς ἔγχος ἀνεσπάσατ' ἐγγύθεν ἐλθὼν
ἥρως Μηριόνης, τὸν δὲ σκότος ὄσσε κάλυψε.   (XIII. 570–5)

The dying man groans, ἤσπαιρε, and that is tantamount to death itself: what is crucial is not the entity called θυμός but the fact of the groan. Compare a further death from a similar blow, where the gasp is again the decisive sign that shows that the warrior has died:[2]

[sc. δόρυ] μέσηι δ' ἐν γαστέρι πῆξεν,
αὐτὰρ ὁ ἀσθμαίνων εὐεργέος ἔκπεσε δίφρου,
ἵππους δ' Ἀντίλοχος, μεγαθύμου Νέστορος υἱός,
ἐξέλασε.   (XIII. 398–401; cf. V. 585–6, XXI. 181–2)

The expiration of breath is part of the observable behaviour of the dying man, but it is also the manifestation of the loss of life in the deepest sense. Correspondingly, the meaning of the loss of θυμός is not limited by the gasp or groan itself: certain passages show that with the gasp life is taken from the vital depths of the man, from his limbs or his bones. In the passage noticed above, as Hippodamas groans out his life it comes not merely from his lungs but deeper, from his bones, τόν γ' ἐρυγόντα λίπ' ὀστέα θυμὸς ἀγήνωρ (XX. 406). Often the θυμός is said to have come from the bones, λίπε δ' ὀστέα θυμός (XII. 386, XVI. 743; iii. 455, xii. 414; sim. xi. 221, see Ch. 6, pp. 203–5), or from the limbs, ὦκα δὲ θυμὸς | ὤιχετ' ἀπὸ μελέων (XIII. 671–2, XVI. 606–7; sim. xi. 200–1). Similarly when Nestor imagines one wishing for death he speaks of breath departing from the limbs and going to Hades, θυμὸν ἀπὸ μελέων δῦναι δόμον Ἄϊδος εἴσω (VII. 131). Since the limbs, μέλεα, are the seat of vitality and strength,[3] these lines imply that when breath is lost as θυμός this is the extinction of bodily vitality as a whole—

[2] On the groan which signals the moment of death in combat see also Friedrich (1956, 14–15) apropos of ἀσθμαίνων in v. 585.

[3] Although μέλεα are simply the limbs, they seem to be specifically the inner seat of strength and vigour. A hero's limbs are filled with strength and courage, πλῆσθεν δ' ἄρα οἱ μέλε' ἐντὸς | ἀλκῆς καὶ σθένεος (XVII. 211–12; cf. xviii. 70, and see also Ch. 4, pp. 111–13 on ἲς/ἶνες).

something deeper than what we nowadays might understand by the visible realities of the dying gasp.

Loss of ψυχή is likewise loss of breath

If to lose θυμός is to gasp out the last breath, what does it mean to lose ψυχή? Already (Ch. 3, pp. 56–8) we have observed Achilles' vivid image of the ψυχή that cannot return once it has crossed over the barrier of the teeth, ἐπεὶ ἄρ κεν ἀμείψεται ἕρκος ὀδόντων (IX. 409). For him, clearly, it is something that leaves the mouth: when he risks his life he is ψυχὴν παραβαλλόμενος (IX. 322), casting it about time and again as he almost loses his last breath (Ch. 3, p. 56 n. 3). Similarly when Patroclus or Hector dies, the ψυχή departs ἐκ ῥεθέων (XVI. 856 = XXII. 362). ῥέθεα is a rare word, but in early Aeolic and in the Attic tragedians, ῥέθος in the singular means 'face',[4] and there is no reason to think that Homer uses the word in a different sense. This is corroborated by the only other Homeric attestation, where Priam predicts what will happen to him after the enemy have taken his life,

$$\text{ἐπεί κέ τις ὀξέϊ χαλκῶι}$$
$$\text{τύψας ἠὲ βαλὼν } \underline{\text{ῥεθέων ἐκ}} \text{ θυμὸν ἕληται.   (XXII. 67–8)}$$

From our study of θυμός it will be clear that unless ῥεθέων ἐκ means the same as ἐκ μελέων—which there is no reason to believe[5]—the likelihood is that Priam is describing the

---

[4] See Soph. *Ant.* 529 and Eur. *HF* 1205, both in lyrics. The word is also attested in a fragment of Sappho (22. 3 L–P), though this is less clear: later lines refer clearly to a girl's beauty, but the immediate context of ῥέθος is missing. Otherwise the ancient evidence is scholarly. Schol. A and bT at XXII. 68 (cf. also A at XVI. 856, bT at XXII. 362) say that ῥέθος is the Aeolic equivalent of πρόσωπον, citing the compound ῥεθομαλίδας—suggestive of Sappho, though no source is given—as equivalent to εὐπροσώπους, and they also cite Dionysius Thrax for the view that the ψυχαί of Patroclus and Hector leave through the mouth. Frisk (1966: 291–4) holds that ῥέθος has a semantic range extending from 'face' to 'appearance' to 'bodily member(s)', from *Gesicht* to *Gestalt*. This is speculative, and is prompted by the unnecessary desire to make ῥέθεα exactly equivalent to μέλεα. (For etymological suggestions, all guesswork, see Frisk s.v.)

[5] An unnecessarily Analytic solution is proposed by Leumann (1950), 218–22, and Snell (1953), 10–12 (cf. also Regenbogen (1948), 13–14; also Janko at XVI. 856.). They hold that ἐκ ῥεθέων means 'from the face' or 'from the mouth'

departure of breath from his mouth. The use of plural as 'mouth, lips' and singular as 'face' is paralleled by Irish *béol* and Latin *os*, so there is no semantic difficulty.

Whatever is happening when Patroclus' or Hector's ψυχή flies to Hades, it is rooted in the same source and at the same moment as the departure of θυμός. Thus it is that the loss of the two things can be co-ordinated: Antinous prophesies that Odysseus' bow will deprive many men of these two things, πολλούς . . . κεκαδήσει | θυμοῦ καὶ ψυχῆς (xxi. 153–4, 170–1), and likewise Diomedes strips Trojans' armour after killing them, θυμοῦ καὶ ψυχῆς κεκαδών (XI. 334). This suggests that in death the meanings of these two words are very close to each other, with no decisive dividing line between them. We can easily show that the bulk of references to the departure of ψυχή exactly reproduce the pattern that we observed for that of θυμός.

First, in the simplest sense to die is to lose this thing. Men who have been killed in battle are ψυχὰς ὀλέσαντες (XIII. 763 = XXIV. 168); a spear-thrust in the gullet is aimed at the place where the kill will be swiftest, ἵνα τε ψυχῆς ὤκιστος ὄλεθρος (XXII. 325);[6] Eumaeus believes his master is now dead, ψυχὴ δὲ λέλοιπεν (xiv. 134); a pig is slaughtered, τὸν δ' ἔλιπε ψυχή (xiv. 426; cf. v. 696, see below, pp. 152–3 with n. 41); and Odysseus wonders whether to merely knock an opponent down or to kill him outright: μερμήριξε . . . | ἢ ἐλάσει' ὥς μιν ψυχὴ λίποι αὖθι πεσόντα (xviii. 90–1). Secondly, in a slightly more complex image the killer takes his victim's ψυχή. Odysseus tells his followers to slaughter all the lewd servant-girls, εἰς ὅ κε πασέων | ψυχὰς ἐξαφέλησθε (xxii. 443–4). Hector says that he will respect the dead Achilles if he succeeds in killing him, σὴν

at XVI. 856 = XXII. 362, with ψυχή imagined as breath, but that ῥεθέων ἐκ at XXII. 68 means 'from the limbs', that line being the work of a late poet who did not fully understand the epic language. (On the general question of interpolation in the passage, see Richardson's conservative note at XXII. 66–76.) The argument of Snell and Leumann depends on the view that θυμός cannot be lost as breath, which throughout this study we have found good reason to reject.

[6] Compare: τὸν δ' αὖ κορυθαίολος Ἕκτωρ | αὐερύοντα παρ' ὦμον, ὅθι κληῒς ἀπόεργει | αὐχένα τε στῆθός τε, μάλιστά τε καίριόν ἐστι, | τῆι ῥ' ἐπὶ οἷ μεμαῶτα βάλεν λίθωι ὀκριόεντι (VIII. 324–7). Much the same part of the body is identified as the best place, μάλιστα . . . καίριον, for a mortal blow.

δὲ ψυχὴν ἀφέλωμαι (XXII. 257). Addressing the dead Hector in her lamentation, Hecuba recalls what Achilles did after killing him, σεῦ . . . ἐπεὶ ἐξέλετο ψυχὴν ταναήκεϊ χαλκῶι (XXIV. 754). Together, the two groups of passages recall the usual pattern for the loss of θυμός: to die is to lose it, to kill is to win it from the foe, and since victory is the foe's death it becomes a sign of the prize for which they struggle. All this suggests that in essence the loss of ψυχή is the same event as the loss of θυμός, the sudden expiration of the last breath.

A fascinating sidelight is thrown on this matter by two difficult passages where ψυχή escapes directly from the chest when it is pierced by the enemy's weapon. Patroclus hurls his weapon into Sarpedon's breast, ἔνθ᾽ ἄρα τε φρένες ἔρχαται ἀμφ᾽ ἀδινὸν κῆρ (XVI. 481); after the kill, he pulls out his spear and the φρένες slip out of the wound, bringing the ψυχή with them:

> ὁ δὲ λὰξ ἐν στήθεσι βαίνων
> ἐκ χροὸς ἕλκε δόρυ, προτὶ δὲ φρένες αὐτῶι ἔποντο,
> <u>τοῖο δ᾽ ἅμα ψυχήν τε καὶ ἔγχεος ἐξέρυσ᾽ αἰχμήν.</u>   (XVI. 503–5)

The last line emerges as a striking, but not an extravagant, image if we see the ψυχή as air hissing out of the punctured lung.[7] In the second example ψυχή rushes out when a mortal blow is struck to the flank:

> Ἀτρεΐδης δ᾽ ἄρ᾽ ἔπειθ᾽ Ὑπερήνορα, ποιμένα λαῶν,
> οὖτα κατὰ λαπάρην, διὰ δ᾽ ἔντερα χαλκὸς ἄφυσσε
> δηιώσας, <u>ψυχὴ δὲ κατ᾽ οὐταμένην ὠτειλὴν</u>
> <u>ἔσσυτ᾽ ἐπειγομένη,</u> τὸν δὲ σκότος ὄσσε κάλυψε.   (XIV. 516–19)

Some scholars have cited this passage for the theory that ψυχή can be blood, here pouring out of the gash.[8] It is just possible that this could be the meaning, in rather the same way as μένος can be blood within the breast as well as breath drawn into it (see Ch. 4, pp. 90–2); however, since λαπάρη is the hollow under the ribs, it makes better sense to see ψυχή in this passage as breath, imagined as if released suddenly when the breast is

---

[7] This is the suggestion of Janko ad loc.: 'The neat zeugma of 505 is apt: the soul is imagined as breath which escapes through the wound.' Compare the idea that a spear-thrust in the windpipe is the *swiftest* loss of the dying gasp, ψυχῆς ὤκιστος ὄλεθρος (XXII. 325).

[8] See Böhme (1929), 23; Warden (1971), 97; Claus (1981), 61.

rent open from below.[9] The key words ἔσσυτ᾽ ἐπειγομένη are at
least as well suited to rushing breath as to oozing blood.[10] The
idea of the breath hissing out of the wound is paralleled by the
case of a man whose heart is transfixed by a spear:

$$δόρυ \; δ᾽ \; \underline{ἐν \; κραδίηι} \; ἐπεπήγει,$$
$$ἥ \; ῥά \; οἱ \; ἀσπαίρουσα \; καὶ \; οὐρίαχον \; πελέμιζεν$$
$$ἔγχεος. \quad (XIII. \; 442-4)$$

When the spear sticks in the apparatus of his breast it releases
the breath in it and makes the butt-end of the spear quiver. I do
not know whether it is anatomically possible for breath to hiss
out so violently when the body is pierced by a blade, but the
close parallel between these passages suggests that Homer can
envisage this as another version of the loss of breath that
symbolizes death.

---

[9] For λαπάρη as 'flank' see III. 359 = VII. 253, and esp. XXII. 307, where a
sword in its scabbard lies ὑπὸ λαπάρην.

[10] A close look is needed at both the words ἔσσυτ᾽ ἐπειγομένη to establish that
the phrase is better suited to breath than to blood. (*a*) σεύω and compounds are
very common for all kinds of rapid and violent motion, including not only the
rushing of air or wind (e.g. vi. 20; see Caswell (1990), 53–5), and correspondingly the impulsive motion of θυμός in acts of will (I. 173, VI. 361, IX. 398,
etc.), but also the spurting of blood from wounds (v. 208, XI. 458, XXI. 167);
this means that the verb on its own does not prove the point either way. (*b*)
The action denoted by ἐπείγω is that of forcing or impelling by pressure,
either concrete or abstract. Thus, a stone weighs down a man, ἄχθος ἐπείγει
(XII. 452); a vessel full of water is made to seethe, ἐπειγόμενος πυρὶ πολλῶι
(XXI. 362); a warrior is forced back by a hail of missiles, ἐπείγετο γὰρ βελέεσσι
(v. 622 = XIII. 511); and necessity compels men to a certain course of action,
ἀναγκαίη γὰρ ἐπείγει (VI. 85; xix. 73) or πόνος . . . ἔπειγε (xi. 54). Note, however,
that ἐπείγω is not often used of spurting liquid, but occurs many times for
rushing air or wind. Water bursts onto a ship when the gale rushes on it,
ὁππότ᾽ ἐπείγηι | ἲς ἀνέμου (xv. 382–3); wheat is separated from chaff under the
force of the winds, ἐπειγομένων ἀνέμων (v. 501); a ship arrives swiftly in port
because of the the wind, ἔπειγε γὰρ οὖρος ἀπήμων (xii. 167) or ἐπειγομένη Διὸς
οὔρωι (xv. 297); a ship is smashed when it is beaten upon by tempest,
ἐπειγομένην ἀνέμωι καὶ κύματι πηγῶι (xxiii. 235). Although the last example
combines wind and water, the other instances cited show that ἐπείγω is
especially appropriate for rushing air; and given that there is no Homeric
parallel for its application to blood, it is simple and economical to accept that
the ψυχή here is most likely to be air, exactly as at XVI. 505.

The loss of ψυχή can be its annihilation

This loss of breath is a visible, sublunary phenomenon, and on the face of it this suggests that the departure of ψυχή need not of itself imply its flight to the Hades of myth. This suspicion is bolstered by the appearance of ψυχή in doublet expressions where two nouns are paired in such a way that they almost amount to a unity in their context. Consider the formula τοῦ δ' αὖθι λύθη ψυχή τε μένος τε (v. 296 = VIII. 123 = 315), narrating a death: since μένος cannot survive death, the pairing suggests that what is referred to here is not a flight to Hades but the disappearance and extinction of the final breath. It is dissipated, λύθη, just as elsewhere death is its destruction, ψυχῆς . . . ὄλεθρος (XXII. 325), and those who die are ψυχὰς ὀλέσαντες (XIII. 763 = XXIV. 168). The implication is the same when Hera looks to the prospect of Sarpedon's death, ἐπὴν δὴ τόν γε λίπηι ψυχή τε καὶ αἰών (XVI. 453): αἰών slips away into nothing at death (see Ch. 4, pp. 113–15; Ch. 6, pp. 160–1), so that unless there is a harsh zeugma here the plain sense seems to be that in a single moment ψυχή τε καὶ αἰών will be annihilated.[11] Here and in the phrases τὸν δ' ἔλιπε ψυχή (xiv. 426; sim. xviii. 90–1) and ψυχὴ δὲ λέλοιπεν (xiv. 134) the verb may mean that the breath has vanished or been lost for ever, not that it has flown to another world—just as the words ἐπεὶ λίπον ἰοὶ . . . ἄνακτα (xxii. 119) mean that the king's arrows have been used up and no more remain, and to say νῦν δ' ἤδη πάντα λέλοιπεν (xiv. 213) is to say that good fortune has passed away and disappeared for ever.

So far, these passages suggest rather than prove that ψυχή can be imagined as vanishing into nothing: but that interpretation is irresistible when we face Odysseus' words as he crows over Polyphemus with the wish that he could kill him outright:

αἲ γὰρ δὴ ψυχῆς τε καὶ αἰῶνός σε δυναίμην
εὖνιν ποιήσας πέμψαι δόμον Ἄϊδος εἴσω.   (ix. 523–4)

He would like to send him to Hades *bereft* of ψυχή and αἰών: unless the craftiest of Homeric speakers is misusing his own

---

[11] Notice Euripides' strange re-evocation of this phrase, ἀπέπνευσεν αἰῶνα (fr. 801 N), 'he breathed out his life's essence' in death.

vocabulary—which is very unlikely[12]—these words imply that it is possible for Homeric man to be imagined as losing his ψυχή at death and then going to Hades in bodily form. Our investigation of that strand of thought belongs elsewhere, but for the present this passage will stand as the most direct proof that the loss of ψυχή can sometimes be no more than the loss of the tangible and mortal substance of the last breath that is elsewhere called θυμός. ἦτορ is sometimes found instead of θυμός in this context (e.g. XI. 115, XXI. 201, XXIV. 50),[13] and in most contexts ψυχή may simply be a variant of the same kind. Compare the words in which Nestor talks hyperbolically of Peleus' wish to die of shame, and expresses it by imagining a θυμός rather than a ψυχή descending to Hades:[14]

> τοὺς νῦν εἰ πτώσσοντας ὑφ᾽ Ἕκτορι πάντας ἀκοῦσαι,
> πολλά κεν ἀθανάτοισι φίλας ἀνὰ χεῖρας ἀείραι,
> θυμὸν ἀπὸ μελέων δῦναι δόμον Ἄϊδος εἴσω. (VII. 129–31)[15]

This suggests again that in certain circumstances Homer can flatly ignore the conception that the ψυχή is what makes the descent to the nether world. The flight of the ψυχή to Hades begins to look less like a fixed canon of Homeric belief about man, and more like an occasional elaboration on the basis of that simpler motif of the loss of breath.

---

[12] C. Sourvinou-Inwood has suggested (in conversation) that Odysseus here, being rash and angry, has combined two formula-patterns to produce a vaunt which is self-contradictory according to Homer's own lights. But it is not characteristic of Homeric rhetoric for sense to break down: an impassioned speech may be more extended or complex than in narrative language, or it may be less dependent on formulae, but there is no evidence that Homer makes his characters speak incoherently for the sake of effect. (S. West suggests as a possible exception the rather garbled sequence of ideas in Telemachus' speech at ii. 70–9; there, however, there is nothing approaching absurdity or contradiction, but only pathos: note the audience's reaction, ll. 80–3).

[13] Also in swoons: xv. 252; xxiv. 345.

[14] Otto (1923: 44) explains this passage on the grounds that θυμός here is used in the sense of 'life', so that it is not literal: a weaselish explanation.

[15] Compare Laertes' allusion to loss of breath in death, θυμὸν ἀπὸ μελέων φθίσθαι (xv. 354).

θυμός can be lost temporarily by swooning

If the loss of breath is the loss of consciousness and life, it should not be surprising that the phenomenon of swooning is rendered in exactly the same way.[16] The most detailed description of this experience comes in the course of the battle by the ships in the *Iliad*, when Hector is wounded, loses consciousness, and then recovers.[17] Ajax flings a boulder at him, it strikes him on the breast and knocks him to the ground (XIV. 409–21), and as his comrades carry him away from the field he is gasping heavily, βαρέα στενάχοντα (432); when they douse him with water he regains his breath and looks around him, ἀμπνύνθη καὶ ἀνέδρακεν ὀφθαλμοῖσιν (436); then he collapses again and swoons, τὼ δέ οἱ ὄσσε | νὺξ ἐκάλυψε μέλαινα (438–9) because the blow is still overcoming the breath of his consciousness, βέλος δ' ἔτι θυμὸν ἐδάμνα (438–9). When he recalls this later he will specify that he had breathed out this consciousness, φίλον ἄϊον ἦτορ (XV. 252), just as in the deaths where the closely related verb ἄϊσθον denoted the corresponding event, θυμὸν ἄϊσθε καὶ ἤρυγεν (XX. 403, XVI. 468).[18] Then Zeus looks down on him as he lies gasping and vomiting blood:

> Ἕκτορα δ' ἐν πεδίωι ἴδε κείμενον, ἀμφὶ δ' ἑταῖροι
> ἥαθ', ὁ δ' ἀργαλέωι ἔχετ' ἄσθματι κῆρ ἀπινύσσων,
> αἷμ' ἐμέων. (XV. 9–11)

Whether or not κῆρ ἀπινύσσων means 'unable to catch his breath', as I have proposed elsewhere,[19] the sequence of events is clear: he is groaning and gasping, by losing his

---

[16] It could be argued that the resemblance between swooning and death is due simply to the paucity of words and expressions in Homer's vocabulary: for example Kirk says at v. 696 that the descriptions of swoons in the *Iliad* 'draw in different ways on a formular terminology primarily designed for describing death'. But this cannot be right, if only because several of the expressions used (e.g. ἀπὸ δὲ ψυχὴν ἐκάπυσσε) bear no resemblance to the formulae that we actually see Homer using for death. I believe Homer has the words to say exactly what he means.

[17] On the realism of this passage see Friedrich (1956), 35–6.

[18] If ἄϊον is related to ἄϊσθον and ἄημι, it refers directly to breathing out: see n. 1 above.

[19] M. J. Clarke, "πινύσκω and its Cognates: a Problem in Simonides, fr. 508" (*Glotta*, forthcoming), including some material repeated here.

breath he has lost consciousness, and the one experience implies the other. This is further confirmed when Zeus says that he is going to send Apollo to help Hector back to battle: he will again breathe vigour into him, αὖτις δ' ἐμπνεύσῃσι μένος, so that he will forget the pains that trouble him in the organs of his breast, αἵ μιν τείρουσι κατὰ φρένας (xv. 60–1). Indeed, when Apollo finds him he is gathering new consciousness, νέον δ' ἐσαγείρετο θυμόν (xv. 240), in other words breathing normally.

This is not the only example where the temporary loss of consciousness is defined as departure of breath. When Ajax is hard-pressed and exhausted in the midst of foes he has difficulty breathing and cannot inhale, αἰεὶ δ' ἀργαλέωι ἔχετ' ἄσθματι . . . οὐδέ πηι εἶχεν | ἀμπνεῦσαι (xvi. 109–11); when Menelaus recovers from the shock and pain of a wound his breath is gathered back into his breast, ἄψορρόν οἱ θυμὸς ἐνὶ στήθεσσιν ἀγέρθη (iv. 152); and Hector recovers from a sudden swoon by inhaling, ἄμπνυτο (xi. 356–60). When Odysseus arrives at Scheria he is breathless and speechless with exhaustion, ἄπνευστος καὶ ἄναυδος (v. 456), by the time he has swum to the shore, but he recovers his breath: ἄμπνυτο καὶ ἐς φρένα θυμὸς ἀγέρθη (v. 458), and later he recalls how he lay on the river-bank whooping up air, ἐκ δ' ἔπεσον θυμηγερέων (vii. 283).[20]

ψυχή is gasped out, θυμός is breathed back in

All this shows that the loss of breath can indicate temporary loss of consciousness as well as death. For us, the significant part is that in some scenes of swooning this gasp is called ψυχή at the moment it is exhaled.[21] When Andromache sees her husband dead, darkness covers over her eyes and she collapses:

---

[20] For θυμηγερέων here as corresponding to θυμὸς ἀγέρθη, see Leumann (1950), 116–17, with n. 83.

[21] On ψυχή in swoons, cf. Bickel (1926), 52–8; Böhme (1929), 97–102; Onians (1951), 44–6. These passages are usefully collected and discussed by Nehring (1947), who uses a rather complex etymological argument to draw out the connection between the expiration of breath as ψυχή and the corresponding drawing in of breath as θυμός (or equivalents) in positive mental activity. I find the details of Nehring's chain of reasoning impenetrable but his argument seems to correspond broadly to what is advanced here.

τὴν δὲ κατ᾽ ὀφθαλμῶν ἐρεβεννὴ νὺξ ἐκάλυψεν,
ἤριπε δ᾽ ἐξοπίσω, ἀπὸ δὲ ψυχὴν ἐκάπυσσε.   (XXII. 466–7)

Here when she loses consciousness she releases ψυχή: the verb ἐκάπυσσε is difficult, but if it is cognate with the noun καπνός— which seems irresistible—it must mean that Andromache emits the ψυχή as an evanescent puff of breath.[22] When she recovers and inhales, what is gathered back into her lungs is called θυμός:

ἡ δ᾽ ἐπεὶ οὖν ἄμπνυτο καὶ ἐς φρένα θυμὸς ἀγέρθη . . .   (XXII. 475)[23]

There is a further parallel in the last book of the *Odyssey*, when old Laertes recognizes his son. His knees and his breath are loosed and he collapses:

ὣς φάτο, τοῦ δ᾽ αὐτοῦ λύτο γούνατα καὶ φίλον ἦτορ,
σήματ᾽ ἀναγνόντος τά οἱ ἔμπεδα πέφραδ᾽ Ὀδυσσεύς,
ἀμφὶ δὲ παιδὶ φίλωι βάλε πήχεε, τὸν δὲ ποτὶ οἷ
εἷλεν ἀποψύχοντα πολύτλας δῖος Ὀδυσσεύς.   (xxiv. 345–8)

It is reasonable to accept that the participle ἀποψύχοντα refers to the gasping out of ψυχή;[24] and the exact match with the swoon of Andromache becomes clear as Homer describes his return to consciousness:

[22] Apart from the evidence of κεκαφηότα discussed in the next note, there is startling if unconfirmable corroboration of this in an intriguing series of glosses in Hesychius: κάπυς· πνεῦμα; κάπος· ψυχή, πνεῦμα; ἐγκαπύει· ἐμπνεῖ; κέκηφε· τέθνηκεν. All of these words are otherwise lost, and life is too short to wonder where they came from; but they suggest that various reflexes of this same root were applied to different aspects of the process of breathing out and dying.

[23] Here and in the following pages I print ἄμπνυτο, ἀμπνύνθη, etc. where the Oxford text has ἔμπνυτο, ἐμπνύνθη. There is good evidence that the forms in ἐμ- stem from an emendation imposed on the tradition for external reasons by Aristarchus (see scholia at v. 697, XIV. 436, XXII. 475, v. 458; and for the MS authority for the forms in ἀμ- see Allen's critical apparatus throughout). Nehring (1947: 109) suggests reasons why later Greek usage may have led Aristarchus to make the change. Naturally there cannot be much difference in meaning between the two forms, and the point is not worth labouring here; however, since ἀναπνέω and the noun ἀνάπνευσις are used in several unimpeachable passages for the regaining of breath in rest after toil (e.g. XI. 382, 800, XVI. 42, 302, XIX. 227, XXI. 534), it makes good sense to read the same verb for the virtually identical act of regaining consciousness after a swoon.

[24] See also Nehring (1947), 107.

αὐτὰρ ἐπεί ῥ᾽ ἄμπνυτο καὶ ἐς φρένα θυμὸς ἀγέρθη,
ἐξαῦτις μύθοισιν ἀμειβόμενος προσέειπε . . . (xxiv. 349–50)

What he breathed out was ψυχή, but when he recovers consciousness and he breathes in it is θυμός that is gathered into his breast. A third, less clear example of this aspect of ψυχή comes when Sarpedon is wounded and briefly loses consciousness:

τὸν δ᾽ ἔλιπε ψυχή, κατὰ δ᾽ ὀφθαλμῶν κέχυτ᾽ ἀχλύς,
αὖτις δ᾽ ἀμπνύνθη, περὶ δὲ πνοιὴ Βορέαο
ζώγρει ἐπιπνείουσα κακῶς κεκαφηότα θυμόν. (v. 696–8)

First he gasps out ψυχή; then he inhales again, ἀμπνύνθη, and he is revived[25] by the wind, which blows the breath of consciousness into him while he is still weakened or dissipated in respect of θυμός. Again the breath lost is called ψυχή. It is noteworthy that κεκαφηότα seems to be an intransitive perfect form of the same verb as ἐκάπυσσεν in Andromache's swoon:[26] just as she gasped out her ψυχή when she collapsed, so he is revived when he is in a dissipated state in respect of his breath.[27] κεκαφηότα

---

[25] In other contexts this verb ζωγρέω is used for taking live prisoners in battle (VI. 46 = XI. 131, X. 378). Comparing ζωιάγρια, which denotes a weregild or the value of one's life (XVIII. 407, viii. 462), it is a safe surmise that the wind is giving air to Sarpedon and thus preserving life in him (see Jouanna (1987), 209 n. 17; also Ruesche (1930), 37–41; and on the link between ζωγρέω and ζωιάγρια see both Frisk and Chantraine s.v., and *LfgrE* s.v.).

[26] The aspiration in this participle is difficult but not impossible: see Sihler (1995), § 517; Risch (1974) § 121; and n. 27 below. Nehring (1947: 113–16) holds that κεκαφηότα is unconnected with ἐκάπυσσε, partly because he finds it difficult to explain the perfect tense of the participle. He translates κεκαφηότα as 'enfeebled', and takes θυμόν in both instances as an accusative of respect. Thus both Sarpedon and Odysseus would be 'weak in respect of the θυμός' when affected in good and bad ways respectively. (For criticism of his argument see Harrison (1960), 69 n. 38). In general terms, Nehring's argument is weakened by the similarity between Andromache's experience and those of Sarpedon and Odysseus. From their form, the two words beg to be assigned to a single verb, and both are used in connection with swooning and gasping; given all this, it would be a remarkable coincidence if they were unconnected.

[27] It is difficult to be precise here, because κεκαφηότα is very difficult. In function it must be substantive, standing in place of Sarpedon's name. If we take θυμόν as direct object after κεκαφηότα, with the supporting evidence of ἐκάπυσσεν we can translate 'the wind revived Sarpedon by blowing on him when in a state of having exhaled his θυμός'. This interpretation is supported

occurs once elsewhere in the same way. Odysseus, panting and exhausted on the shore of Scheria, is afraid that exposure to the frost and dew of night and the cold dawn wind will overcome him:

μή μ' ἄμυδις στίβη τε κακὴ καὶ θῆλυς ἐέρση
ἐξ ὀλιγηπελίης δαμάσηι <u>κεκαφηότα θυμόν</u>,
αὔρη δ' ἐκ ποταμοῦ ψυχρὴ πνέει ἠῶθι πρό.   (v. 467–9)

If we take κεκαφηότα in the same way as in Sarpedon's case, Odysseus is saying that he may be overcome by the dew and frost when he is exhausted by the weakened state of his breath.

The rendering of swoons offers us the first step towards our final understanding of ψυχή. When breath exhaled is ψυχή and breath regained is θυμός, the kinship as well as the contrast between the two words is revealed. In their simplest senses θυμός is breath either drawn in or lost, ψυχή is solely breath lost and dissipated and destroyed. It follows that the two words are liable to be extended metonymically in different ways. ψυχή is associated with life and consciousness only to the extent that it is a sign of their extinction; θυμός, on the other hand, stands not only for that but also for life held and enjoyed, because it is literally warm—it is the vitality that is sucked into the lungs and surges, θύνει, as it engenders the vigour of the body. But we must look further before we can succeed in our eventual aim, to see how the flying ψυχαί of Patroclus and Hector emerge from this pattern of imagery and translate the ψυχή lost at death into the ψυχή which will live in Hades. Treating etymology with due caution, we can learn something more from the Homeric meanings of words closely cognate with ψυχή.

by Hesychius, who glosses κεκαφηότα as ἐκπεπνευκότα, but it raises its own problems. First, the same expired breath will be called ψυχή and θυμός in successive lines, which is unusual at the very least. Secondly (and more decisively), κεκαφηότα ought to be intransitive in meaning, since that is the pattern of all perfects of its type (see Hainsworth at v. 468, with Sihler's discussion (1995: § 517)). If this objection holds good, the only alternative is to take θυμόν as an accusative of respect: 'the wind revived Sarpedon, blowing on him when he was κεκαφηότα in respect of θυμός'—in other words, when he was still dissipated and emptied of what ought to have been filling his breast.

ψυχή, ψυχρός, ψύχω *refer to coldness, breath, and blowing*

Coldness, breath, and blowing are the common ground of the small group of words that share the stem ψυχ-.[28] The simple verb ψύχω appears when Athena deflects a flying missile with a breath or gust, πνοιῆι . . . ἧκα μάλα ψύξασα (XX. 439–40); the adjective ψυχρός refers to such coldness as that of water, metal, snow, or wind;[29] while the noun ψῦχος, in its one Homeric attestation, denotes the coldness of air or wind (x. 555).[30] The verbs ἀποψύχειν and ἀναψύχειν are more difficult, and repay close examination.

We have already seen that when Laertes collapses and loses consciousness he is ἀποψύχοντα (xxiv. 348): on the close analogy of the noun ψυχή in swoons, the action here must be that of gasping out breath. The same verb stands in the middle or passive for what happens to sweaty men when they rest exhausted after toil, ἱδρῶ ἀπεψύχοντο (XI. 621, XXII. 2), and similarly ἱδρῶ ἀποψυχθείς (XXI. 561). They cool down 'in respect of the sweat', in other words their temperature drops as the

---

[28] The problems of the nouns and verbs in ψυχ- are discussed by Benveniste (1932a; followed by Chantraine s.v.). Benveniste holds that ψύχω 'blow', cognate with ψυχή, is quite unconnected with ψύχω 'make cold', and that the apparent confluence is mere homonymy. This seems artificial, since (as I try to show here) there is no sharp distinction of this kind in Homer's use of these verbs; even if it is historically true that two similar-sounding roots are involved, so many of our instances combine coldness with blowing that we cannot separate the two in the language as used by our author; so that even if Benveniste is right about the prehistory of the words, it is evident at the very least that the two identical stems have led to an assocation of meaning in Homeric practice. Frisk (s.v. ψυχή) holds that ψυχή and ψύχω are cognate, and discusses parallels in other IE languages for the link between blowing and coldness. Jouanna (1987: 206–16) argues in full detail that both compound verbs can be derived from the notion of the blowing of breath or wind, with the secondary association of the coldness resulting from such blowing. Jouanna argues through an important comparison with the language of the Hippocratic corpus, showing that the distinction between blowing and coldness across ψυχή, ψύχω, ψυχρός, and cognates is a post-Homeric development.

[29] Note esp. the cold wind of the dark hour before dawn, αὔρη . . . ψυχρὴ πνέει ἠῶθι πρό (v. 469).

[30] Elpenor, having had too much to drink, goes up to the palace roof to sleep because he wants coolness, ψύχεος ἱμείρων (x. 552–5). Fresh air in particular is evidently what he is after.

sweat dries off.[31] The connection with coolness is clearest when a breeze is responsible:

> τοὶ δ' ἱδρῶ ἀπεψύχοντο χιτώνων
> στάντε ποτὶ πνοιὴν παρὰ θῖν' ἁλός. (xi. 621–2)

They cool down, ἀπεψύχοντο, by facing towards the cooling breeze. In these instances of ἀποψύχειν, the word takes its meaning either from making cool or from blowing or simultaneously from both.

The evidence of ἀναψύχειν corroborates this. The simplest instance is in Proteus' account of the delights of Elysium:[32]

> ἀλλ' αἰεὶ Ζεφύροιο λιγὺ πνείοντος ἀήτας
> Ὠκεανὸς ἀνίησιν ἀναψύχειν ἀνθρώπους. (iv. 567–8)

Ocean sends up breezes to bring coolness to men: the verb refers to the cooling effects of the sea breeze, in much the same way as in the passages cited for ἀποψύχεσθαι. The link between the two verbs is closer still when Athena finds Diomedes tending his wound as he rests away from the combat,

> ἕλκος ἀναψύχοντα, τό μιν βάλε Πάνδαρος ἰῶι.
> ἱδρὼς γάρ μιν ἔτειρεν ὑπὸ πλατέος τελαμῶνος
> ἀσπίδος εὐκύκλου· τῶι τείρετο, κάμνε δὲ χεῖρα,
> ἂν δ' ἴσχων τελαμῶνα κελαινεφὲς αἷμ' ἀπομόργνυ. (v. 795–8)

The word ἀναψύχοντα describes him as cooling off the wound by exposing it to the cool air. Somewhat similar is a description of warriors refreshing themselves by washing in the sea:

> αὐτοὶ δ' ἱδρῶ πολλὸν ἀπονίζοντο θαλάσσηι
> ἐσβάντες κνήμας τε ἰδὲ λόφον ἀμφί τε μηρούς.
> αὐτὰρ ἐπεί σφιν κῦμα θαλάσσης ἱδρῶ πολλὸν
> νίψεν ἀπὸ χρωτὸς καὶ ἀνέψυχθεν φίλον ἦτορ,
> ἔς ῥ' ἀσαμίνθους βάντες ἐϋξέστας λούσαντο. (x. 572–6)

---

[31] See Jouanna (1987), 206–8.

[32] On this I follow Jouanna (1987), 218–19. G. Nagy (1979: 167 § 28, n. 2) has used this passage to support the ambitious theory that Elysium and the Isles of the Blest were places where heroes were reanimated after death and passed to immortality. Nagy's theory (1979: 165–8, 208; 1990a: 85–121) depends on the view that θυμός and ψυχή are interchangeable both as breath expired and as breath inhaled (see esp. 1990a: 90–2); this seems to me not to be justified by the Homeric evidence. On Nagy's methodology in this essay see also Ch. 1 n. 12, Ch. 2 n. 29.

Here, it seems, by bathing they wipe off the sweat and cool themselves in respect of their breath, named here as ἦτορ.

To understand the link between these and the remaining instance of ἀναψύχειν, we must first observe that there is a close connection in each of these passages between sweating and gasping, two manifestations of exhaustion which happen not to be connected in our modern view of human physiology. The clearest indication of the meaning of this link is in a passage where Ajax, hard-pressed in battle, is forced to fall feebly back:

> αἰεὶ δ' ἀργαλέωι ἔχετ' ἄσθματι, κὰδ δέ οἱ ἱδρὼς
> πάντοθεν ἐκ μελέων πολὺς ἔρρεεν, οὐδέ πηι εἶχεν
> ἀμπνεῦσαι. (XVI. 109–11)

He is unable to draw in the breath which would bring vigour, and sweat runs along his limbs, just as Diomedes was afflicted, τείρετο, by sweat in one of the passages already quoted (v. 795–8). We find the same combination when Hector recovers after being knocked unconscious by Ajax' boulder, as described above (p. 139). He is now sitting up, no longer sweating and no longer gasping:

> . . . ἥμενον, οὐδ' ἔτι κεῖτο, νέον δ' ἐσαγείρετο θυμόν,
> ἀμφὶ ἓ γιγνώσκων ἑτάρους, ἀτὰρ ἆσθμα καὶ ἱδρὼς
> παύετ', ἐπεί μιν ἔγειρε Διὸς νόος αἰγιόχοιο. (XV. 240–2).

This connection is the key to understanding the remaining attestation of ἀναψύχειν. The Achaeans have fallen back exhausted to rest by the ships, and Poseidon rouses them:

> τόφρα δὲ τοὺς ὄπιθεν γαιήοχος ὦρσεν Ἀχαιούς,
> οἳ παρὰ νηυσὶ θοῆισιν ἀνέψυχον φίλον ἦτορ.
> τῶν ῥ' ἅμα τ' ἀργαλέωι καμάτωι φίλα γυῖα λέλυντο
> καί σφιν ἄχος κατὰ θυμὸν ἐγίγνετο. (XIII. 83–6)

Here again the action of ἀναψύχειν is connected with physical exhaustion and trouble in the limbs. It could be argued that the warriors are regaining their breath as they rest, making ἀναψύχω here a virtual synonym of ἀναπνέω; but when we note the pairing of the imperfects ἀνέψυχον and ἐγίγνετο, it makes better sense that both should refer to the warriors' exhausted state *before* Poseidon roused them. Their limbs were loosed and enfeebled, just as the warriors in the other passages were afflicted by sweat; there was trouble in their θυμός, and they were gasping out their breath, ἀνέψυχον ἦτορ, just as in the passages where Hector gasped out his breath, φίλον ἄϊον ἦτορ (XV. 252, n. 18 above), and Ajax was unable to draw breath, οὐδέ πηι εἶχεν | ἀμπνεῦσαι (XVI. 110–11).[33]

In these ways, the ranges of meaning of ἀποψύχειν and ἀναψύχειν come close to convergence. Together with the simpler ψύχω, ψῦχος, and ψυχρός they each draw on a different aspect of the same nexus of ideas associating coolness with blowing or gasping. In view of this connection, we can begin to define ψυχή as a gasp of expired breath that is cold, vaporous, and insubstantial. This helps to explain why the last breath could be described both as θυμός and as ψυχή: the first word refers to the warm, vital quality of what has been extinguished by death, the second refers to the cold evanescent quality of death and extinction itself. It makes sense in the same way that in swoons the expired breath could be ψυχή, cold and lifeless, but the inhaled breath of returning life and consciousness was always given the warmth, vigour, and vitality of θυμός.

ψυχή *has two senses in two narrative contexts*

We are now ready to return to the problem that ψυχή comes to the fore in different ways in two different environments, at the moment of death in the visible world and in the shadowy afterlife in Hades. At the beginning of this chapter we observed that there was a question mark over the relationship between these two senses of ψυχή, and that it was not easy to set them alongside each other and try to merge them. In particular the relationship between the ψυχή and the man himself is quite different in the two settings where the word comes to the fore. The ψυχή exhaled at death is an empty gasp of air, lost and

---

[33] It might be objected that this interpretation necessitates taking ἀνέψυχον φίλον ἦτορ (XIII. 84) as 'they gasped out their breath' while taking ἀνέψυχθεν φίλον ἦτορ (X. 575) as 'they cooled down in respect of their breath'. Despite the formal similarity between the two phrases, the fact that the verb is active in one and passive in the other makes it plausible that the two should be drawing on different aspects of the semantic range of the verb, just as ἀποψύχειν can refer in the active to swooning (xxiv. 348) and in the middle or passive to becoming cool (XI. 621, XXI. 561, XXII. 2).

invisible once it is breathed out, but in Hades the ψυχή is a shade or phantom or image, εἴδωλον, of the man which resembles him in appearance but lacks his substance. Implicitly there is a gap between the two identities of ψυχή on the two planes of the world. On the basis of our analysis of the other members of this family of words we can now surmise that the essence of the word's definition is not what a ψυχή is but how it acts. The ψυχή lost in death is vaporous, cold, and lifeless, diametrically opposed to the warm and vigorous θυμός (or ἀϋτμή) which man had inhaled and taken vigour from during his life; and in similar fashion the ψυχή that lives in Hades is something empty of vigour, flitting without strength or substance, partaking of the cold nothingness of drifting air. The dead in Hades are like shadows and dreams, σκιῆι εἴκελον ἢ καὶ ὀνείρωι (xi. 207); they drift around as shadows, σκιαὶ ἀΐσσουσιν (x. 495); Anticleia's wraith describes how it hovers about like a dream, ἠΰτ' ὄνειρος ἀποπταμένη πεπότηται (xi. 222), as it flies away, ἔπτατο (xi. 207–8), from Odysseus' grasp;[34] likewise Agamemnon's ghost stretches out to embrace him with flitting motion, πιτνάς (from πίτνημι, xi. 392; see Ch. 6 n. 75); and Patroclus' wandering wraith disappears off to Hades like a wisp of drifting smoke, ἠΰτε καπνὸς | ὤιχετο (XXIII. 100–1). The dead are without μένος, νεκύων ἀμενηνὰ κάρηνα (x. 521, xi. 29, etc.); and they lack the vigour of bodily strength, οὐ γὰρ . . . ἔτ' ἦν ἲς ἔμπεδος οὐδέ τι κῖκυς (xi. 393). It is this lack of life, strength and substance, expressed in their flitting movement, that gives them the same name as is the cold breath of death.

The image of the flying ψυχή yokes the two together

In this light the lines that narrate the deaths of Patroclus and Hector take on a new significance:

> ψυχὴ δ' ἐκ ῥεθέων πταμένη Ἀϊδόσδε βεβήκει,
> ὃν πότμον γοόωσα, λιποῦσ' ἀνδροτῆτα καὶ ἥβην.
> (XVI. 856–7 = XXII. 362–3)

When the two great heroes breathe their last we go momentarily beyond the normal patterns of Homeric lore. In any other

---

[34] For this interpretation see below, pp. 202–5.

narration of a death, at this point the θυμός or the ψυχή would be lost, expired, and dissipated: but here the cold breath of death takes wing, emerging suddenly in a mythical shape out of the visible realities of the battlefield, and it flies off to become one of the wraiths that live out the shadowy afterlife in Hades. In effect the dying gasp takes on a new life of its own when Homer yokes together the two senses of the word ψυχή and the two settings in which those senses have their place.

It must be emphasized that this image is unique in forging this link so clearly and vividly in the narrative. Across Homer there are only a few other references to the descent of the ψυχή to Hades, and all are oblique and allusive, tending to appear either in high-flown rhetorical imagery or in passages which look along the broad course of the action of the poem. Perhaps the closest approach to the directness of Patroclus' and Hector's deaths is in the proem of the *Iliad*, where Homer looks along the story of the Wrath which sent many ψυχαί to Hades,

> πολλὰς δ' ἰφθίμους ψυχὰς Ἄϊδι προΐαψεν
> ἡρώων, (I. 3–4)

and similarly in Nestor's elaborate rhetoric when he begins a speech of persuasion at a council of war:

> πολλοὶ γὰρ τεθνᾶσι κάρη κομόωντες Ἀχαιοί,
> τῶν νῦν αἷμα κελαινὸν ἐΰρροον ἀμφὶ Σκάμανδρον
> ἐσκέδασ' ὀξὺς Ἄρης, ψυχαὶ δ' Ἀϊδόσδε κατῆλθον. (VII. 328–30)

When he speaks in the grand style (ὑφαίνειν ἤρχετο μῆτιν, VII. 324) he articulates an image of cosmological depth which is akin to the poet's evocation of the sweep of the action of the whole poem. Similar in its rhetorical sweep is the conceit by which a warrior boasts that his foe's death will give victory to himself and a new wraith to the lord of the dead:

> σοὶ δ' ἐγὼ ἐνθάδε φημὶ φόνον καὶ κῆρα μέλαιναν
> ἤματι τῶιδ' ἔσεσθαι, ἐμῶι δ' ὑπὸ δουρὶ δαμέντα
> εὖχος ἐμοὶ δώσειν, ψυχὴν δ' Ἄϊδι κλυτοπώλωι.
>
> (XI. 443–5; sim. V. 654, XVI. 625)

The image depends for its effect on its extravagance, drawing up the specious contrast between giving a boast to the victor and a new wraith to the ranks of the dead in Hades' realm.[35] The ψυχή of this speech belongs squarely in the mythical Hades and does not articulate the separation of the wraith from the corpse at death.

Still more heightened and mythopoeic is the startling image in one of Theoclymenus' prophecies in the *Odyssey*, where he sees the wraiths of the suitors already going down to the Underworld:

> εἰδώλων δὲ πλέον πρόθυρον, πλείη δὲ καὶ αὐλή,
> ἱεμένων ἔρεβόσδε ὑπὸ ζόφον, ἠέλιος δὲ
> οὐρανοῦ ἐξαπόλωλε, κακὴ δ' ἐπιδέδρομεν ἀχλύς. (xx. 355–7)

He calls them empty images, εἴδωλα, synonymous in Hades with ψυχαί. With his supernaturally heightened vision, the prophet looks beyond the visible world into the unseen realm of the dead.[36] The same sudden switch is made by the post-Homeric author of the Second Nekuia (see Ch. 6, App. p. 227) when he launches into his narrative with Hermes leading the wraiths of the suitors on their journey to Hades:

> Ἑρμῆς δὲ ψυχὰς Κυλλήνιος ἐξεκαλεῖτο
> ἀνδρῶν μνηστήρων· ἔχε δὲ ῥάβδον μετὰ χερσὶ
> καλὴν χρυσείην, τῆι τ' ἀνδρῶν ὄμματα θέλγει
> ὧν ἐθέλει. (xxiv. 1–4)

The scene transfers itself to the mythical plane with violent abruptness, and the gap between the visible fact of death and the new identity of the flitting wraiths remains unbridged. The deaths of Patroclus and Hector are unique precisely because they bridge that gap in a single inclusive image, collapsing the mythical and non-mythical meanings of the word into a complex new unity.

Homer offers only one other reference to the descent of the ψυχή, and it is particularly instructive. The night before Odysseus' expedition to Hades, Elpenor gets drunk and falls off a roof and dies:

---

[35] Cf. Warden (1971: 97), calling this ψυχή formula 'a literary jeu d'esprit'. The idea is extended by Pindar with the image of 'paying' a ψυχή to Hades, ψυχὰν Ἀίδαι τελέων (*Isth.* 1. 68).

[36] On the fantastic tone of this vision, see Russo ad loc., with Dodds (1951), 70.

ἀλλὰ καταντικρὺ τέγεος πέσεν, ἐκ δέ οἱ αὐχὴν
ἀστραγάλων ἐάγη, ψυχὴ δ' Ἀϊδόσδε κατῆλθεν.   (x. 559–60)

This is the only place in straightforward narrative where it is said that someone's ψυχή went down to Hades, and the exception proves the rule: the image is deployed in order to prepare for Odysseus' meeting with Elpenor's wraith on the threshold of Hades seventy-odd lines later.[37] The pattern remains that in the narration of death Homer does not normally bridge the gap between the world in which the man dies and the mythological Underworld in which (for example) the narrative pattern of a *katabasis* would place him after his death.

The image of flight to Hades emerges from that of lost breath

In short, in this last group of passages the outcome of death is the entry of the wraith, ψυχή, into the mythological land of the dead, but it is not closely identified with the last gasp of the dying man. In this way the image remains vague and the juxtaposition harsh: across the whole Homeric corpus the transition of ψυχή from the world of the living to that of the dead is realized only in the deaths of Patroclus and Hector. I have suggested that this construct is complex, sophisticated, even creative. This needs to be qualified. Since the lines are repeated exactly in the two deaths, it is likely that they are not an isolated invention, and as such they should not be seen as anti-traditional; on the other hand this need not mean that they are a mere formulaic fossil. I emphasize this because ἀνδροτῆτα violates the metre, and was formerly pointed to as evidence that the whole pair of lines was a fossil preserved from an earlier stage of the epic language.[38] However, the same word ἀνδροτῆτα occurs elsewhere (XXIV. 6) with the same effect on the scansion, and it is best seen as a development in the course of post-Homeric transmission.[39] In view of this,

---

[37] For this reading see Warden (1971), 96–7.

[38] See Leumann (1950), 221. The variant λιποῦσ' ἀδροτῆτα is almost certainly a scholarly invention to repair the rhythm; see Latacz (1965: 66) on the probable origin of the variant in the period before the familiar spelling was fixed.

[39] See esp. Latacz (1965); Tichy (1981). Along with XXIV. 6 there is a similar

there is no good reason to consider the couplet as divorced from the mainstream of Homer's image-making. A closer examination will suggest something more of how it is built up from humbler materials.

The pivotal word is πταμένη. The flying ψυχή has often been compared to classical vase-paintings in which the soul is actually depicted as a bird, but there are no grounds to impose so sharp an image on the Homeric scene; the image on the vases is at least as likely to look back to a reading of Homer.[40] Closer to home, we have already seen that the movement of the ψυχή looks to that of the mythical wraith in Hades, whose characteristic movement is strengthless airy flight. In our image the departing ψυχή already takes on the identity and attributes of a wraith that will dwell in Hades. But there is a further clue to show that the image remains rooted in the world of the battlefield, and that it takes shape from a more mundane rendering of the emission of breath from the dying man. The clue can easily go unnoticed, because it is found only in the deaths of animals. A horse is struck in the shoulder and killed:

$$\text{ὁ δ' ἔβραχε θυμὸν ἀΐσθων,}$$
$$\text{κὰδ δ' ἔπεσ' ἐν κονίηισι μακών, } \underline{\text{ἀπὸ δ' ἔπτατο θυμός.}} \quad \text{(XVI. 468–9)}$$

As he groans out his breath he falls in the dust with a cry, and his θυμός goes flying away. The same words ἀπὸ δ' ἔπτατο θυμός also appear when Odysseus kills a stag (x. 163) and a boar (xix. 454), and when a dove is transfixed by an arrow its breath flies away in the same way, ὠκὺς δ' ἐκ μελέων θυμὸς πτάτο (XXIII. 880). No convincing explanation has hitherto been offered for these strange images of animals' deaths,[41] but in

---

metrical problem with another compound of ἀνδρ-, in the formulaic line Μηριόνης τ' ἀτάλαντος Ἐνυαλίωι ἀνδρειφόντηι (II. 651, etc.), where the transmitted text can be scanned only with an extremely harsh synizesis. The evidence, then, is that the syllabic ṛ of *anṛt- was still a reality in Homeric scansion (see also Ruijgh (1971), 862–3, West (1988), 156–7, and Janko (1992) 11).

[40] See Ch. 1, p. 6.

[41] It has been argued that in these passages Homer has adapted a formula designed for a human death, using θυμός in place of ψυχή because animals do not have souls (Warden (1971), 95 n. 1; Claus (1981), 62, with n. 8). This is weak for several reasons. First, Homer is elsewhere quite happy to narrate the

the more elaborate passage the words ἔβραχε and μακών suggest a simple answer: the dying animals are bellowing or (in the case of the dove) squawking more violently than men would do, so that the θυμός is gasped out with more force than in the case of a normal human death, and on that account it is described as flying. In their small way, these passages suggest that the vivid elaboration of the loss of ψυχή emerges from the idea that the hero yields up his last breath with a mighty cry. This suggestion is corroborated by Homer's description of the warrior who groans out his last breath like a bellowing bull, ὡς ἄρα τόν γ' ἐρυγόντα λίπ' ὀστέα θυμὸς ἀγήνωρ (XX. 403–6).[42] If the flight of the ψυχή takes off in this way from the violence of the hero's last cry, then it is very firmly grounded in the imagery and even the vocabulary of the gasping out of breath.

A similar strain of imagery seems to be at work in the familiar idea of winged words, as in the line καί μιν φωνήσας ἔπεα πτερόεντα προσηύδα (I. 201, II. 7, etc.). Presumably this is to be understood straightforwardly in terms of the flight of a bird or of an arrow:[43] the suggestion is that words which

death of a pig as τὸν δ' ἔλιπε ψυχή (xiv. 426), just like a human death. (Rahn (1953: 449) uses 'life' as a gloss to explain ψυχή in the pig's death, but this is merely a stopgap.) Secondly, even if Homer composes by fitting formulae together like a poor joiner, which I am unwilling to believe, still it does not make sense that he should have had to tailor a ψυχή formula to suit the narration of an animal's death, because there would already have been plenty of formulae available where the unproblematic word θυμός was used in the first place. Thirdly, even if this were done it would be surprising if the formula thus adapted were *ψυχὴ πτάτο, which is unattested among the hundreds of deaths in the two epics.

[42] Compare the words used when a man's jaw is smashed open by a spear, so that the θυμός is released with special speed and violence: τὸν βάλ' ὑπὸ γναθμοῖο καὶ οὔατος, ὦκα δὲ θυμὸς | ὦιχετ' ἀπὸ μελέων, στυγερὸς δ' ἄρα μιν σκότος εἷλεν (XIII. 671–2 = XVI. 606–7).

[43] Arrows are perhaps more likely, since the adjective is elsewhere used of them (IV. 117, V. 171, XVI. 773, XX. 68) but not of birds, and in real life the function of the feathers on an arrow is to guide it straight to the target (see esp. Thomson (1936); Latacz (1968), 27–31; S. West at i. 122; but cf. Vivante (1975), who prefers birds). Since this is in some sense the function of feathers on a bird as well as on an arrow, there is perhaps no watertight answer: the point is the poetic meaning, not the definition of the *tertium comparationis*. It does not seem useful to claim that ἔπεα πτερόεντα is an empty formulaic fossil, as M. Parry argued (1971 [1937]). The more important question is whether all talk, or only talk of a certain kind, is described by this adjective. Since Parry's

communicate successfully are ἔπεα πτερόεντα, feathered and thus flying straight to the mark: they will be contrasted implicitly with those that are vain and empty and fit to be forgotten, which are lost in the wind:

> ἔπος δ' εἴ πέρ τι βέβακται
> δεινόν, ἄφαρ τὸ φέροιεν ἀναρπάξασαι ἄελλαι.   (viii. 408–9)

Similarly ineffectual talk is like a puff of wind, ἀνεμώλια (IV. 355; IV. 837 = xi. 464),[44] and apparently a word which is ineffectual and fails to communicate is wingless, ἄπτερος μῦθος.[45] Just as

time, several studies have argued that only certain types of utterance are πτερόεντα, but there is no agreement as to the necessary characteristic. Calhoun (1935) tries to pin the formula to expressions of extreme emotion; Vivante (1975: 5) emphasizes not the speaker's emotions but the spontaneity of the utterance itself, 'unsolicited by the necessities of dialogue'; Latacz (1968: 31) argues that the key is the loudness of the speaker's voice. In practice, of course, these three aspects of effective communication may all be involved. Most recently, S. West suggests that the adjective refers not to any one species of utterance but to the 'essential characteristic' of talk: 'Any word, once uttered, is πτερόεν' (at i. 122). Compare Durante (1968a), 245–7. A final decision is impossible without a firm view on the meaning of ἄπτερος μῦθος, but unfortunately it is impossible to tell whether a wingless word is an unspoken one or an unheeded one (see n. 45 below).

[44] The adjective ἀνεμώλιος is used in the same way of a bow which has proved useless (v. 216, XXI. 474), and of deities who fail to protect their favourites (xx. 123).

[45] Here it is impossible to be precise. The wingless word appears only in the formula τῆι δ' ἄπτερος ἔπλετο μῦθος (xvii. 57 = xix. 29 = xxi. 386 = xxii. 398), which occurs in each attestation after the end of a commanding speech addressed by a man to a woman. In each case the subsequent events indicate that she obeyed the command. The questions are (a) whether the ἀ- is privative (< *n̥-) or intensive (< *sm̥-); (b) whether the μῦθος in question is the speech which has just ended, or alternatively a further speech which the woman does not utter. Of the four possible meanings, two make sense: either 'His words were winged (i.e. effective) for her (since she obeyed)', or 'a wingless (unspoken) word came to her (but she remained silent)'. Latacz (1968) argues acutely for the latter. However, ἀπτερέως occurs in the Hesiodic corpus in a rather different context: Tyndareus asks Helen's suitors to swear to come to her future husband's aid if she is ravished, and they comply, τοὶ δ' ἀπτερέως ἐπίθοντο (fr. 204. 84 M–W). If ἀπτερέως here approximates to 'swiftly' or 'willingly' (see also Parmenides, fr. 288. 17 KRS), this suggests that the ἀ- is intensive. See esp. Russo at xvii. 57. Without committing ourselves here, we can at least quote ἄπτερος . . . μῦθος, regardless of its sense, as a further indication that ἔπεα πτερόεντα is not an isolated fossil but a

winged words are those that do not vanish into the air, so the ψυχή which is flying, πταμένη, is imagined as going directly to Hades to become a wraith, in contrast with the usual image by which the ψυχή is lost and dissipated when the dying man's last breath vanishes into the air.

To fly as a bird, then, is to go straight to one's goal. The flight of the ψυχή is a leap from the world of mortals to that of Hades, to a different plane of the universe. As such the idea of the winged ψυχή finds a further parallel in the bird-imagery that Homer deploys when gods move between their own, higher world and that of mortals.[46] It is revealing that this is sometimes articulated as metamorphosis, sometimes only as simile, sometimes as something indeterminate between the two, For example, we seem to be given only a simile when Hera and Athena go down to battle with the gait or flight of doves, αἱ δὲ βάτην τρήρωσι πελειάσιν ἴθμαθ' ὁμοῖαι (V. 778). At the opposite extreme, when Apollo and Athena vanish from the battlefield and sit at the top of a tree in the semblance of vultures, ὄρνισιν ἐοικότες αἰγυπιοῖσι (VII. 59), the scene would be grotesque if they have not actually changed into the shapes of

living image with reflexes elsewhere in the Homeric repertoire: so that it is reasonable to take πτερόεντα as actively highlighting the fact that the words in question travel from speaker to listener, just as those who listen seriously to something are said to receive or accept it, δεχώμεθα μῦθον (XX. 271). This is all that we need establish to justify comparing winged words with the flying ψυχή. (For further bibliography see S. West and Russo, locc. cit.). That Sophocles understood ἄπτερος as 'wingless' is suggested when his Electra says that if she ceased her lamentation she would be 'holding back the wings of her groans', ἴσχουσα πτέρυγας ὀξυτόνων γόων (*El.* 242–3); but compare ἄπτερος φάτις in Aeschylus (*Ag.* 276), which works better in the opposite way (cf. Fraenkel ad loc.).

[46] See Dirlmeier (1967), Bannert (1978), and Erbse (1980), each with full collections of examples, and cf. Bushnell (1982). Dirlmeier maintains that each of the bird-images can be read as a simile rather than a metamorphosis, while Bannert and Erbse show that this forces the evidence. Note also the curious passage in which Poseidon disappears like an ἴρηξ ὠκύπτερος (XIII. 62) and Ajax Oïleus says that he has recognized the vanishing god by the 'traces', ἴχνια (71), of his feet and legs, as if he had glimpsed him momentarily as a bird (cf. Janko ad loc.). At iii. 371–2 the words φήνηι εἰδομένη seem definitely to indicate a metamorphosis, as S. West points out ad loc. In other examples the status of the image is less decisively defined, as XIX. 350–1; i. 319–20, v. 51–4, 333–53.

the birds.[47] More common is a vaguer association between moving deity and bird, as when Apollo descends from Ida to the battlefield:

βῆ δὲ κατ' Ἰδαίων ὀρέων, ἴρηκι ἐοικὼς
ὠκέϊ φασσοφόνωι, ὅς τ' ὤκιστος πετεηνῶν.   (XV. 237–8)

The god flies like a bird when he moves from one plane of the world to another, just as the ψυχή takes wing when it descends to Hades. The variation in shape and clarity between different versions of the image shows that the connection between birdlike flight and movement from one world to another is a symbol that can be brought to birth under different forms at different times. The flight of the ψυχή belongs at some undetermined place on that sliding scale.

In this way, when the ψυχή flies to Hades Homer builds up a uniquely complex articulation of what it means to breathe one's last, but the image takes its shape from the materials available in the simpler forms of Homeric language. I hope that the evidence has been enough to show that this picture should not prescribe our interpretation of what is happening each and every time a dying man breathes out his ψυχή. The loss of the last breath is a visible phenomenon, a tangible sign of death and not of itself an eschatological transformation. The man who gasps out that last breath is the man we sketched in Chapter 4, the indivisible bodily unity for whom the tangible stuff of blood, bones, and organs is the sole source of his human identity. If the flight of the ψυχή is a creative image rather than a fixed schematic belief, how are we to understand the process by which Homeric man dies and enters the Underworld? This is the question to which we will now turn.

---

[47] For other examples see esp. XIV. 286–91; XXII. 239–40.

6

The Corpse and the Afterlife

The corpse has lost vitality but still holds the dead man's identity

The prospect of an afterlife poses the problem of human identity anew. When darkness has fallen on a man's sight, how does he continue to exist? What has happened to his identity, to his 'I', and how does that 'I' transfer itself to the undiscovered country beyond death? We have seen much evidence that in the mortal world Homeric man is an undivided unity for whom the loss of the last breath is merely one of the visible signals of death; and I have argued that the image of the flight of the ψυχή to Hades[1] is rare and esoteric and emerges only in special circumstances from the abiding sense of human unity. With this in mind we turn to the corpse. In a sense a corpse is mere clay, κωφὴ γαῖα; but only vaguely and rarely is it so identified.[2] My argument suggests that after losing the last

---

[1] In this discussion I use the word 'Hades' both for the personal god and the place. In later Greek both these senses are common, but in Homer Ἀΐδης almost always refers to the person, along with the variant Ἀϊδωνεύς (V. 190, XX. 61). There is an exception in a speech of Achilles, εἰς ὅ κεν αὐτὸς ἐγὼν Ἀΐδι κεύθωμαι (XXIII. 244). The genitive in phrases like εἰς Ἀΐδαο, 'to [the house] of Hades', is odd but not unparalleled in our author: compare Διὸς ἔνδον (XX. 13) for 'inside the house of Zeus', εἰς Αἰγύπτοιο, διιπετέος ποταμοῖο (iv. 581) for 'into the river . . .', and ἐς πατρός (ii. 195) for 'to the father's house'. Nilsson (1967: 455), holds that Hades was originally the place, with its lord later personified; on this argument, Persephone would have begun as the sole Underworld deity, a theory that might explain why she is more to the fore than Hades himself in the Nekuia (see x. 494, 509, xi. 213, 217, 226, 386, 635). It has been argued that two separate words are involved, one originally standing for the place and the other for the person (see Thieme (1968), 137–8).

[2] When Achilles is mistreating the dead Hector, Apollo describes him as dishonouring dumb earth, κωφὴν . . . γαῖαν ἀεικίζει μενεαίνων (XXIV. 54). Unless this means that Achilles' savagery is scandalizing Gaia herself, it must refer to the corpse as 'earth'. The line is curious, since elsewhere in Apollo's speech

breath Homeric man will still be himself, that his 'I' will cling to his body and be one with it. In fact this is implied even when the flight of the ψυχή is pictured: in the proem of the *Iliad* the ψυχαί leave behind the heroes themselves, αὐτούς (I. 4), and likewise Patroclus' or Hector's ψυχή abandons not a lump of flesh but the substance of his manhood, ἀνδροτῆτα (XVI. 857 = XXII. 362).

However, the compelling evidence on this point is in the way Homer talks of the thing that modern English calls a dead body. As we will see, it is implied overwhelmingly often that the dead man's identity is still tied to his physical substance. This is borne out on the simplest level by the word νέκυς/νεκρός,[3] Homer's usual label for a dead man. This word differs crucially from modern words like 'corpse', because it goes with the nominative rather than the genitive of the noun denoting the person who has died: a νεκύς/νεκρός is not the corpse *of* someone, rather it is unambiguously identified with him. (In the length of the Homeric poems there is a single exception to this rule, which will be discussed in its place—pp. 162–3 below). Those who lie on the battlefield are not men's mortal remains but 'men who have died', νεκροὺς κατατεθνηῶτας.[4] Consistently νέκυς/νεκρός stands in apposition with the proper name:[5]

and throughout the episode the emphasis is on the fact that the corpse is Hector himself, and as such deserving of human respect (on these points see Macleod's penetrating note ad loc., with parallels in later literature). The only Homeric parallel is in a speech where Menelaus rails against the other Achaeans for refusing to face Hector in a duel: he wishes that they will become earth and water as they sit there, ἀλλ' ὑμεῖς μὲν πάντες ὕδωρ καὶ γαῖα γένοισθε (VII. 99). However, it seems that this passage refers not to death but to the idea of people being transformed into inanimate objects after a misdeed: compare the Niobe story, λαοὺς δὲ λίθους ποίησε Κρονίων (XXIV. 611), with other non-Homeric testimony noted by Richardson ad loc.; also the transformation into stone of a snake (II. 319) and the Phaeacian ship (xiii. 163).

[3] νέκυς and νεκρός are fully synonymous, presumably interchanged *metri gratia*: see e.g. IV. 492–3, XVII. 734–5, where the two are used in successive lines of the same dead man. In addition νεκάς is attested once, ἐν αἰνῇσιν νεκάδεσσιν (V. 886), perhaps collective: 'among the heaps of dead men' (thus Kirk ad loc.). See also n. 32 below.

[4] Some ambiguous cases: the genitive in XVII. 362, νεκροὶ ὁμοῦ Τρώων καὶ ὑπερμενέων ἐπικούρων, is naturally to be read as 'corpses from among the Trojans' (cf. XVIII. 540, more clearly thus); the genitive in XVII. 240, νέκυος . . . Πατρόκλοιο, is in apposition with his name (see Edwards ad loc.).

[*See opposite page for n. 5*]

κεῖται πὰρ νήεσσι νέκυς ἄκλαυτος ἄθαπτος
Πάτροκλος . . . (XXII. 386–7)

Patroclus *is* the νέκυς. Similarly Elpenor:

δὴ τότ' ἐγὼν ἑτάρους προΐειν ἐς δώματα Κίρκης
οἰσέμεναι νεκρὸν Ἐλπήνορα τεθνηῶτα. (xii. 9–10)

The gods care for Hector although he is now a νέκυς, a dead man:

ὥς τοι κήδονται μάκαρες θεοὶ υἷος ἑῆος
καὶ νέκυός περ ἐόντος. (XXIV. 422–3; sim. XXIV. 35)

In its simple way this suggests that after death the man continues to be precisely equated with the stuff of his body: the processes of thought and consciousness have ceased to happen, but the thing we call a man can still be seen and touched.

Obviously, however, that is not the full story. νέκυς/νεκρός in apposition is not simply analogous to a noun like ἥρως, Διὸς υἱός, ἀνήρ, since it often replaces a proper name already given:

κεῖται Πάτροκλος, νέκυος δὲ δὴ ἀμφιμάχονται
γυμνοῦ. (XVIII. 20–1)

νέκυς here is more than an equivalent for Πάτροκλος: rather it qualifies, almost glosses, the blunt statement in the first two words: Patroclus lies dead, the living warriors fight over a naked corpse. Compare a brief narration of Oenomaus' death:

ὁ δ' ἐν κονίῃσι πεσὼν ἕλε γαῖαν ἀγοστῶι.
Ἰδομενεὺς δ' ἐκ μὲν νέκυος δολιχόσκιον ἔγχος
ἐσπάσατ'. (XIII. 508–10; sim. XVI. 319–21)

If this is more than an accidental effect of formulaic composition, the shift from proper name to 'corpse' perhaps suggests that on dying the man passes into a new state of altered or diminished identity. However, in the course of long passages in which a particular corpse is prominent—for example, during the struggle over the dead Patroclus—the proper name and νέκυς/νεκρός are freely interchanged from line to line, and there

---

[5] Leumann (1950: 195) classes this as a secondary word, 'νέκυς as adjective', which is artificial, even if the suffix of νεκρός implies that that word began its life as an adjective (Sihler (1995), § 569. 2).

is no decisive distinction between the man and the body. This implies that the visible corpse and the bearer of the proper name are identical, and it encourages us to seek more elaborate evidence that in a fundamental sense the 'I' of the dead man resides with the corpse.

To die is to waste away enfeebled

A further pointer in this direction comes with the verbs φθί(ν)ω, φθινύθω, and compounds, which can often be translated 'die' but also refer to certain other kinds of loss and disappearance. When something φθινύθει or φθίεται it is reduced or enfeebled, wasted away rather than destroyed outright:[6] so that these verbs can refer to the gradual diminution of the stock of a household (i. 250 = xvi. 127, xiv. 95) or provisions as they are consumed (iv. 363, xii. 329). The verbs are especially appropriate to the gradual enfeeblement of a living person: for example as Laertes grieves unceasingly and starves himself the flesh wastes away from his bones:

> οὔ πώ μίν φασιν φαγέμεν καὶ πιέμεν αὔτως,
> οὐδ' ἐπὶ ἔργα ἰδεῖν, ἀλλὰ στοναχῆι τε γόωι τε
> ἧσται ὀδυρόμενος, φθινύθει δ' ἀμφ' ὀστεόφι χρώς.   (xvi. 143–5)

Similarly a bereaved woman's cheeks are ravaged by grieving, τῆς δ' ἐλεεινοτάτωι ἄχεϊ φθινύθουσι παρειαί (viii. 530). This decay can be psychological: when Achilles sulks he dwindles away in his mental substance, φθινύθεσκε φίλον κῆρ (I. 491) or φρένας ἔφθιεν (XVIII. 446); the Trojans' long-toiling allies waste away, θυμὸν ἀποφθινύθουσι (XVI. 540); and when Odysseus lingers with Circe his men's fretting affects him in the same way, μευ φθινύθουσι φίλον κῆρ | . . . ὀδυρόμενοι (x. 485–6). When the same verbs are applied to death the implication is that the one who dies, φθίεται, is worn down or diminished in stature, almost like the waxing and waning of the moon, μηνῶν φθινόντων (x. 470; sim. xiv. 162 = xix. 307, xix. 153 = xxiv. 143; cf. xi. 183 = xiii. 338 = xvi. 39),[7] and by the same token he has not decisively ceased to exist or to be himself.

---

[6] See Chantraine's subtle gloss, s.v.

[7] The Sanskrit cognate *kṣi-* is also applied to the waning of the moon (Leumann (1950), 212 n. 4, cited by Chantraine s.v.; also Sihler (1995)

Among the living, the loss of vitality through misery or exhaustion is sometimes specified as the diminution of αἰών, the oozing bodily fluid which embodies lively vigour (see Ch. 4, pp. 113–14). When Odysseus weeps this essence seeps out of him, κατείβετο γλυκὺς αἰών (v. 152), and Hermes urges him to take courage lest it should waste away, μηδέ τοι αἰὼν | φθινέτω (v. 160–1). In the same way when Penelope pines for her husband she hopes that her vitality and beauty will not ebb away,

ἵνα μηκέτ᾽ ὀδυρομένη κατὰ θυμὸν
αἰῶνα φθινύθω. (xviii. 203–4; cf. θυμὸν | τῆκε, xix. 263–4)

This is very similar to one way that Homer refers to the more decisive loss of αἰών that is death, ἐπὴν δὴ τόν γε λίπηι ψυχή τε καὶ αἰών (xvi. 453; sim. v. 685). When Andromache sees Hector dead, she interprets the change that has come over him as the destruction of this vital essence: ἆνερ, ἀπ᾽ αἰῶνος νέος ὤλεο (xxiv. 725; sim. xxii. 58); and when Achilles fears that the unburied Patroclus will suffer decay and corruption, he says that it has been destroyed, ἐκ δ᾽ αἰὼν πέφαται (xix. 27, perfect from θείνω; see Ch. 4 n. 130). What has been lost is an essence of life that is moist, flowing, glistening: so that conversely when the gods protect the dead Hector from corruption he looks dewy-fresh, ἐερσήεις (xxiv. 419, 757).[8] When Achilles uses the verb πέφαται, the perfect form suggests that this loss of αἰών is progressive, continuing after death with the decay and putrefaction of the corpse. The close verbal correspondences suggest that wastage during life is akin to wastage after death, implying again that death is seen as loss of lively vigour rather than as annihilation.

When is the corpse distinguished from the dead man?

If we have been right up to now, the sense that the dead man is the corpse must march alongside the sense that he has departed

§235. 1c; and see R. Schmitt (1967), p. 162 n. 971g), so it is a fair guess that such diminution is fundamental to the meaning carried by the root.

[8] On the relation between dew, tears, and other bodily fluids in early Greek thought see my 'Rain, Dew and the Lilied Voice of the Grasshopper' (forthcoming).

to the afterlife. The ambiguity is neatly summed up when Achilles embraces the dead Patroclus:

> τοῖσι δὲ Πηλεΐδης ἁδινοῦ ἐξῆρχε γόοιο,
> χεῖρας ἐπ᾽ ἀνδροφόνους θέμενος στήθεσσιν ἑταίρου·
> "χαῖρέ μοι, ὦ Πάτροκλε, καὶ εἰν Ἀΐδαο δόμοισιν". (XXIII. 17-19)

In one sense Achilles' friend lies stretched before him; in another sense he is already in Hades. When the man can no longer be seen in fleshly form, as after burial or decomposition, the unity between him and his body can no longer be sustained, and the dead man continues as himself only if his identity is pinned on the survivor in the mythical Hades. So it is that when Achilles has reduced Patroclus to bone and ash and holds the remains in his arms, he no longer addresses the man himself but calls on the ghost which visited him in his sleep:

> οἶνον ἀφυσσόμενος χαμάδις χέε, δεῦε δὲ γαῖαν,
> ψυχὴν κικλήσκων Πατροκλῆος δειλοῖο.
> ὡς δὲ πατὴρ οὗ παιδὸς ὀδύρεται ὀστέα καίων,
> νυμφίου, ὅς τε θανὼν δειλοὺς ἀκάχησε τοκῆας,
> ὡς Ἀχιλεὺς ἑτάροιο ὀδύρετο ὀστέα καίων. (XXIII. 220-4)

The mortal remains are no longer recognizable as a man, so they have ceased to be regarded as one: the 'I' of the dead man is now firmly assigned to the mythical Underworld (see also xxiv. 63-79, discussed below, pp. 226-7). In this context we can make sense of the one passage which contradicts our rule about the identity of the νέκυς/νεκρός with the self. Achilles is allowing the dead Hector to rot, and the gods quarrel over the scandal:

> ἐννῆμαρ δὴ νεῖκος ἐν ἀθανάτοισιν ὄρωρεν
> Ἕκτορος ἀμφὶ νέκυι καὶ Ἀχιλλῆϊ πτολιπόρθωι. (XXIV. 107-8)

If the line is not corrupt,[9] it is significant that the expression 'the corpse *of* Hector' appears in the context of Achilles' savage maltreatment of it. Since Hector is straightforwardly identified with the corpse throughout the rest of the same episode (e.g. at XXIV. 76, 115, 116, 118, 136, 151, 180), we need not make much

---

[9] The line could easily be emended to harmonize with the usual pattern: Ἕκτορί τ᾽ ἀμφὶ νέκυι καὶ Ἀχιλλῆϊ πτολιπόρθωι. It seems wiser, however, to suppose that the word may have shifted towards the pattern regularly followed by σῶμα.

of this one exception to our rule about the construction with
νέκυς/νεκρός; but it is a reasonable guess that the poet comes
closer to distinguishing the dead man from the corpse because
the context brings the prospect of its decomposition to the fore.

This suggestion brings us to σῶμα, the other (and much
rarer) word translated as 'corpse'.[10] σῶμα differs from νέκυς/
νεκρός in that it always puts the name of the person in the
genitive, implying a different perspective—the σῶμα of someone is not quite the same thing as the man himself. Most
instances are in contexts where the corpse has been, or is liable
to be, abandoned or mistreated. Just as the words Ἕκτορος ἀμφὶ
νέκυι were used when the body was rotting, so corpses afloat at
sea are σώματα φωτῶν (xii. 67–8); the mutilated carcasses which
Achilles burns with Patroclus are δρατὰ σώματα (XXIII. 169);
and in lion similes the carcass devoured by the beast is a σῶμα
(III. 23, XVIII. 161). Finally, Hector uses the word before his
duel with Ajax and when he is on his knees before Achilles,
asking that his corpse be handed over to his family for burial:

> σῶμα δὲ οἴκαδ' ἐμὸν δόμεναι πάλιν, ὄφρα πυρός με
> Τρῶες καὶ Τρώων ἄλοχοι λελάχωσι θανόντα.

(VII. 78–9 = XXII. 342–3)

Note that in the next clause of the sentence Hector uses με to
refer to himself after death. We saw that immediately after
death a man is sometimes referred to as νέκυς/νεκρός in a way
that suggests a loss or diminution of his identity. The passage
just quoted closely resembles one such instance, again in the
context of Hector's plea that he be returned to his people after
death:

> ἀλλ' ἐπεὶ ἄρ κέ σε συλήσω κλυτὰ τεύχε᾽, Ἀχιλλεῦ,
> νεκρὸν Ἀχαιοῖσιν δώσω πάλιν· ὣς δὲ σὺ ῥέζειν.   (XXII. 258–9)

Strictly speaking, νεκρόν is to be taken in apposition with σε; yet
it seems that here νεκρός, like σῶμα in the previous instance, is
not quite so comfortably identified with the person in question.

The plot thickens when we find that the remaining instances
of σῶμα occur in narratives set inside Hades. Odysseus meets

---

[10] On the question of whether a σῶμα can also be a living body see Ch. 4,
pp. 116–17; Epilogue, pp. 315–19.

the shade of Elpenor and remembers that the corpse had been left in Circe's palace without being given a funeral:

οὐ γάρ πω ἐτέθαπτο ὑπὸ χθονὸς εὐρυοδείης·
σῶμα γὰρ ἐν Κίρκης μεγάρωι κατελείπομεν ἡμεῖς
ἄκλαυτον καὶ ἄθαπτον . . . (xi. 52–4)

Similarly in the Second Nekuia (whether or not it is Homeric— see Appendix below) the shade of Amphimedon explains that his and the other suitors' corpses are lying untended and unburied:

ὡς ἡμεῖς, Ἀγάμεμνον, ἀπωλόμεθ', ὧν ἔτι καὶ νῦν
σώματ' ἀκηδέα κεῖται ἐνὶ μεγάροις Ὀδυσῆος·
οὐ γάρ πω ἴσασι φίλοι κατὰ δώμαθ' ἑκάστου,
οἵ κ' ἀπονίψαντες μέλανα βρότον ἐξ ὠτειλέων
κατθέμενοι γοάοιεν. (xxiv. 186–90)

In both cases the situation is extraordinary, because we are forced to visualize the corpse lying in the mortal world at the same time as the survivor in the mythical afterlife. The juxtaposition prompts a contrast between the two senses in which the dead man exists, so that the corpse is referred to under a name which implies that this lump of clay is something other than the man himself.

Combining the evidence from νέκυς/νεκρός with that from σῶμα, we conclude that the corpse remains fully identified with the dead man except in certain examples of two extraordinary situations: first, where it is in danger of decomposition or is being dishonoured and treated as dead meat; and second, when the shade of a dead man in the Underworld enters the scene in a way that prompts a contrast between him and the corpse that remains in the world of mortals. The lesson is that the dead man is himself in two senses, which belong on different planes of the universe and on different levels of language. The situations where the word σῶμα appears are those in which the bodily manifestation of the man exists but proves inadequate on its own, either because it has ceased to resemble him or because it is directly juxtaposed with the speaking and moving survivor in the Underworld. Clearly those situations are exceptional and untypical: in the normal course of narrative and allusion nothing happens to bring the two versions of the dead man face to face with one another.

Mutilation of the corpse is mutilation of the man

This evidence from verbal scraps needs to be corroborated on the larger scale of ideas and beliefs. It is telling that mutilation after death is seen as something inflicted on the man himself rather than on what we might call his remains. Witness the way Priam juxtaposes his fear of death itself with his fear of what will happen afterwards:

> αὐτὸν δ' ἂν πύματόν με κύνες πρώτηισι θύρηισιν
> ὠμησταὶ ἐρύουσιν, ἐπεί κέ τις ὀξέϊ χαλκῶι
> τύψας ἠὲ βαλὼν ῥεθέων ἐκ θυμὸν ἕληται. (XXII. 66–8)

The dogs will rend the man himself, and by mutilating him they will dishonour or abase him, αἰσχύνωσι (XXII. 75): Priam does not distinguish himself from the dead flesh that will be ruined, and its suffering is his own. Presumably the corpse would not be thought to actually feel pain after death, but its equation with the dead man adds immediacy and intensity to the fear that it will be tormented.[11] The same principle informs Zeus' care for the physical preservation of the dead Sarpedon (XVI. 666–83), and Apollo's for Hector:

> τοῖο δ' Ἀπόλλων
> πᾶσαν ἀεικείην ἄπεχε χροῒ φῶτ' ἐλεαίρων
> καὶ τεθνηότα περ. (XXIV. 18–20)

Hector is the corpse, and Apollo's personal bond with him continues although he is dead. This helps to explain why there is no sign in Homer of the fear of pollution from touching the dead, as is common in later Greek belief:[12] because personal and social identity persist in the corpse, it is not a strange uncanny thing as it might be in a culture for which the essence of the man has fled from the body and left something taboo or unwholesome behind it.

[11] Argued by Wilamowitz (1931), 304–6. Compare also the later Greek references to the practice of cutting off the hands, feet, and other extremities of a corpse in order (apparently) to prevent the dead man from returning to exact vengeance (see Garvie at Aesch. *Cho.* 439, with further refs.).

[12] Parker (1983), 66–70; and cf. Garland (1985), 38–47.

Hades is beyond the darkness of death

How, then, are we to analyse the process by which the first manifestation of the 'I' is replaced by the other—the process, in other words, in which the corpse becomes translated into an inhabitant of Hades? Later sources often answer that question in terms of the personal figure of Death or another guiding divinity. In Euripides' *Alcestis*, for example, Thanatos in person escorts the dead down to Hades,[13] and in the Second Nekuia Hermes plays the same role as guide of the suitors' ghosts (xxiv. 1–14). But in all his allusions to death Homer never gives this role to Thanatos[14] or Hermes: the only suggestion in this direction is a single passage where Odysseus in a lying story says that the death-divinities called Keres brought his father to Hades,

> ἀλλ' ἦ τοι τὸν κῆρες ἔβαν θανάτοιο φέρουσαι
> εἰς Ἀΐδαο δόμους.   (xiv. 207–8; cf. II. 302, 834 = XI. 332)

Elsewhere, however, the assault by the unseen divinities of death is an end in itself,[15] culminating in the descent of darkness on the sight (see Ch. 7 below), and Homer says nothing of its link with what comes after. It is easy to see why this is so. The experience of death from the sufferer's point of view is distinct from the descent to Hades because the two events belong in distinct and irreconcilable paths of thought. One's capture by Thanatos or another death-bringing divinity is the end of the life that was spent in the mortal world, but the descent to Hades is a transition out of that environment and into a mythical world beyond.[16] Darkness—ζόφος, ἀχλύς,

[13] See esp. Eur. *Alc.* 23–7, 47, 259–72. Possibly this role is already reflected in the layout of Hesiod's Hades, where Death's house is deep in Tartarus (*Theog.* 758–9), but Homer suggests nothing in this direction.

[14] Observe that when Apollo hands the dead Sarpedon over to Thanatos and his brother Sleep, they bring him not to Hades but to Lycia for his funeral: πέμπε δέ μιν πομποῖσιν ἅμα κραιπνοῖσι φέρεσθαι, | Ὕπνωι καὶ Θανάτωι διδυμάοσιν, οἵ ῥά μιν ὦκα | κάτθεσαν ἐν Λυκίης εὐρείης πίονι δήμωι (XVI. 681–3).

[15] When one is overcome by κήρ in death and subsequently goes to Hades, κηρὶ δαμεὶς Ἀϊδόσδε βεβήκει (iii. 410 = vi. 11), the two happenings remain distinct: compare (e.g.) ὃς τάχα Πηλείωνι δαμεὶς Ἀϊδόσδε κάτεισι (XX. 294).

[16] Cf. Wilamowitz (1931), 313–16. Thieme (1952: 134) points out that Hades is the god of the dead but not of the event of death itself: he is not 'Todesgott' but 'Totengott'.

σκότος, νύξ—is the only thing common to both sides of the divide: the mist that falls on the sight in death is a negation, like night itself, νύκτα . . . ὀρφναίην (ix. 143, etc.),[17] and likewise Hades is shrouded in darkness, ζόφος or ἔρεβος, from which its landscape dimly emerges (see e.g. xv. 191, xxi. 56, xxiii. 51, with xi. 57, 155, xx. 356).[18] But any image of the undiscovered country must take shape despite that murk and not because of it, so that there is no point of contact between these two areas of lore. To descend to Hades is to pass through the no man's land of darkness into an imagined landscape beyond it, just as Odysseus must pass through the darkness of the Cimmerians' country[19] before he can reach the entrance to the land of the dead:

---

[17] ὀρφναῖος is a puzzling word. In Homer it occurs only in the formula νύκτα δι' ὀρφναίην (x. 83 = x. 386, x. 276, ix. 143), where the adjective seems to refer to darkness: note especially the sequence τις θεὸς ἡγεμόνευε | νύκτα δι' ὀρφναίην, οὐδὲ προὐφαίνετ' ἰδέσθαι (ix. 143–4), where the last three words look as if they explain ὀρφναίην. The noun ὄρφνη as 'night' is not found before Theognis (1077, etc.). It is hard not to suspect that there is some connection with the words ὀρφανή (xx. 68) and ὀρφανικός (vi. 432, xi. 394, xxiii. 490), referring to orphaned children. Both Chantraine and Frisk (s.v.) deny that the words are cognate, but the similarity in sense and in form is striking: we might guess that night is ὀρφναίη because it is the time when the world is bereft of light. T. Meissner points out to me that the alternation between forms in ὀρφν- and ὀρφαν- can be explained easily in terms of the Sievers–Egerton law (Sihler (1995), § 178–80).

[18] Here it would be interesting to know whether Ἀΐδης is in origin 'the one who is not seen' or 'the lord of those who are not seen', ά-privative with the root *ϝιδ-, 'see'. This is vigorously argued by Beekes (1998); but the only Homeric corroboration is the passage in which Athena makes herself invisible to Ares by wearing the cap of Hades, Ἄϊδος κυνέη (v. 845; cf. the same cap worn by Perseus in the Hesiodic *Shield of Heracles*, 226–7). This mysterious motif would be easier to understand if Ἄϊδος κυνέη were translated 'the cap of not being seen' (cf. Kirk ad loc.). However, this must remain speculative (cf. R. Schmitt (1967), 50–1); and we cannot be certain either that this is the original meaning of the word Ἀΐδης or that Homer understands it in such a way. See also *LfgrE* s.v., suggesting *ά-ϝιδ- among several possible etymologies, all speculative; and cf. Wackernagel (1953: 765–9), arguing instead that Ἀΐδης is cognate with αἶα, as 'the place under the earth'.

[19] On Cimmerian darkness see Heubeck (1963), and Karl (1967), 95–106, with further refs. On the basis of later glosses and apparently cognate words Heubeck argues that Κιμμέριοι is a 'speaking name', identifying them as the people of misty darkness.

ἡ [sc. ναῦς] δ' ἐς πείραθ' ἵκανε βαθυρρόου Ὠκεανοῖο.
ἔνθα δὲ Κιμμερίων ἀνδρῶν δῆμός τε πόλις τε,
ἠέρι καὶ νεφέληι κεκαλυμμένοι, οὐδέ ποτ' αὐτοὺς
Ἥλιος φαέθων καταδέρκεται ἀκτίνεσσιν,
οὔθ' ὁπότ' ἂν στείχηισι πρὸς οὐρανὸν ἀστερόεντα,
οὔθ' ὅτ' ἂν ἂψ ἐπὶ γαῖαν ἀπ' οὐρανόθεν προτράπηται,
ἀλλ' ἐπὶ νὺξ ὀλοὴ τέταται δειλοῖσι βροτοῖσιν.   (xi. 13–19)

To travel to Hades is to pass through people shrouded in dark mist, with night stretched across them. When the dead man is to take up his new role in the new world beyond the grave, he must make the same leap into the darkness, across the ζόφος of death and into the ἔρεβος of Hades.[20]

Allusion to the descent to Hades in rhetorical and synoptic style

If we decline to read everything in terms of the flying ψυχαί of Patroclus and Hector, it is noticeable that the journey to Hades is referred to much more in allusion than in narrative. It is usually in speeches that we hear of it: Homer's people speak of Hades when they look to death as a prospect in the future or a memory of the past, as an element in the scheme of things rather than an easily apprehended event. The image appears in the heightened language of threats and vaunts (v. 654 = XI. 445 = XVI. 625, v. 646, VI. 487, XIII. 415, XIV. 457; ix. 524), of lamentation (XXII. 389, 482), and of fear or foreboding of death (XX. 294, 336, XXII. 52, 425); when a character wishes death on another (III. 322, VI. 284)

[20] Starting from different premises in a discussion of symbolic oppositions in general, Austin (1975: 90–108, esp. 97–8 (see also Heubeck at xi. 14–19, and cf. Thalmann (1984), 1–2)) analyses the darkness of Hades in terms of the darkness which Homer imagines as lying at the edges of the world: ζόφος is in some sense associated with the west, as being the region where the sun sets (see esp. XII. 239–40; ix. 25–6, x. 190, xii. 81, xiii. 240–1). Similarly ζόφος and ζέφυρος embody grades of the same root (see *LfgrE* s.v. ζέφυρος). It may be important that the sun goes down to ζόφος when it sets, thus identifying its downward journey as parallel with that of the dead to Hades: note especially Helios' threat to leave the upper world and shine among the dead, δύσομαι εἰς Ἀίδαο καὶ ἐν νεκύεσσι φαείνω (xii. 383). On the whole, however, it seems that the link between darkness and the west is more important for the symbolic geography of Odysseus' journey via Cimmeria than for the symbolism of death in general.

or desires to die himself out of shame or misery (VII. 131, XXIV. 246); where one recalls a death in the past (VI. 422, VII. 330; xiv. 207–8) or asks whether a third party has already died (xv. 350, iv. 834 = xx. 208 = xxiv. 264); also, indeed, where one remembers the earlier prospect of a death which did not come to pass (V. 190, XV. 251–2), or denies that he will himself die (VI. 487; x. 174–5). In speech-language the journey to the land of the dead emerges in contexts where the literal and mundane is insufficient and language becomes rhetorical, pathetic, or synoptic.

In this light the handful of instances in the poet's own voice are a telling group. Three come in passages which do not narrate specific events but evoke a broad sweep of the action of war, painting a wide canvas of the action past or to come rather than detailing a single killing. Thus in the proem of the *Iliad* Homer explains that Achilles' anger sent heroes' ψυχαί to Hades,

$$\mu\upsilon\rho\acute{\iota}\text{'} Ἀχαιοῖς ἄλγε' ἔθηκε,$$
$$\pi ολλὰς \ \delta\text{'} ἰφθίμους ψυχὰς Ἄϊδι προΐαψεν$$
$$ἡρώων \ . \ . \ . \quad (\text{I. } 2\text{–}4)$$

A briefer allusion in a similar context comes at the opening of Agamemnon's *aristeia*. Zeus lets bloody rain fall because he is about to send many to their deaths,

$$οὕνεκ' ἔμελλε$$
$$\pi ολλὰς ἰφθίμους κεφαλὰς \underline{Ἄϊδι προϊάψειν} \quad (\text{XI. } 54\text{–}5)$$

Here again, death is seen as descent to Hades when the poet looks along the sweep of future action, so that the deeper pathos of war comes to the fore. The third instance emerges equally subtly from the poet's commentary on the pathos of death in battle. When Lycaon is about to be mown down by Achilles, Homer pauses to recall that after only twelve days of liberty he is facing the same foe as in a previous encounter, this time with the certainty that he will be denied mercy and killed:

$$ἕνδεκα \ \delta\text{'} ἤματα θυμὸν ἐτέρπετο οἷσι φίλοισιν$$
$$ἐλθὼν ἐκ Λήμνοιο, δυωδεκάτηι δέ μιν αὖτις$$
$$χερσὶν Ἀχιλλῆος θεὸς ἔμβαλεν, \underline{ὅς μιν ἔμελλε}$$
$$\underline{πέμψειν εἰς Ἀΐδαο} καὶ οὐκ ἐθέλοντα νέεσθαι. \quad (\text{XXI. } 45\text{–}8)$$

These examples of the prospect of descent to Hades have their counterpart in a few instances where death is already a *fait accompli*. Thus when Agamemnon slays the sons of Antenor, the narration concludes with a mythical flourish:

> ἔνθ' Ἀντήνορος υἷες ὑπ' Ἀτρείδηι βασιλῆϊ
> πότμον ἀναπλήσαντες ἔδυν δόμον Ἄϊδος εἴσω.   (XI. 262–3)

The lines round off the episode and sum up its tragedy: they set the killings against the background of the full sweep of the brothers' short lives, working in the same way as the reminiscence which Homer draws in a little earlier in the episode to point up the pathos of the death of the first of the brothers:

> ὣς ὁ μὲν αὖθι πεσὼν κοιμήσατο χάλκεον ὕπνον
> οἰκτρός, ἀπὸ μνηστῆς ἀλόχου, ἀστοῖσιν ἀρήγων,
> κουριδίης, ἧς οὔ τι χάριν ἴδε, πολλὰ δ' ἔδωκε.   (XI. 241–3)

Elsewhere the narrative of two brothers' deaths is rounded off in the same way, setting the tragedy of their journey to Hades against the background of their home and ancestry:

> ὣς τὼ μὲν δοιοῖσι κασιγνήτοισι δαμέντε
> βήτην εἰς ἔρεβος, Σαρπηδόνος ἐσθλοὶ ἑταῖροι,
> υἷες ἀκοντισταὶ Ἀμισωδάρου, ὅς ῥα Χίμαιραν
> θρέψεν ἀμαιμακέτην, πολέσιν κακὸν ἀνθρώποισιν.   (XVI. 326–9)

All this suggests that the image of the descent to Hades marks out the full solemnity of death. It is perhaps for the same reason that it is the usual image when Homer or one of his characters alludes to a death in the distant past: ἀλλ' ὁ μὲν ἤδη κηρὶ δαμεὶς Ἄϊδόσδε βεβήκει (iii. 410 = vi. 11; sim. xiv. 207–8). In all these examples the image expresses something that is more than literal or tangible: it does not simply state that the man died but draws out the deeper meaning of mortality, *sub specie aeternitatis*.

Mutilation by birds and beasts is alluded to in the same way as Hades

In this light the image of descent makes for a good analogy with a different area of image-making, the theme of the mutilation of the corpse by dogs and vultures.[21] In the straight narrative this

[*See opposite page for n. 21*]

never actually happens,[22] but it is alluded to in the same kinds of contexts as is the journey to Hades.[23] The closest Homer comes to narrating a mutilation is when Achilles threatens to let the dead Hector be defiled by the dogs (XXIII. 182–3), but the gods go on to ensure that he does not do so (XXIII. 185–7, XXIV. 406–15). Throughout the *Iliad* the image is common when a future prospect is alluded to in the poet's voice (XVII. 125–7, 272–3) or in a speech (VIII. 379–80, XI. 817–18, XIII. 233, XVII. 153, 241, 558, XVIII. 283, XXII. 42–3, 88–9, 339); similarly when a warrior boasts of the woe he causes to his victims (XI. 394–5), and when one threatens to let another be mangled after he has slain him (II. 392–3, XI. 453–4, XIII. 831–2, XV. 351, XVI. 836, XXII. 335–6, 348–54). The fear of it appears in lamentations for a loved one (XXII. 508–9, XXIV. 211–12) or in anticipation of the speaker's own death (XXII. 66–7, 74–6). When the image is found in Homer's voice, it is in contexts similar to those which we observed for Hades. Witness again the proem of the *Iliad*, where Achilles' Wrath sent many ψυχαί to Hades and left the dead heroes to be seized by the beasts,

αὐτοὺς δὲ ἑλώρια τεῦχε κύνεσσιν
οἰωνοῖσί τε πᾶσι. (I. 4–5)

It is in the overview of the action that this allusive image-making reaches its height,[24] as in a rhetorical flourish when the advent of the vultures points up the tragedy of a series of deaths inflicted by Agamemnon in his *aristeia*:

ὣς ἄρ' ὑπ' Ἀτρεΐδηι Ἀγαμέμνονι πῖπτε κάρηνα
Τρώων φευγόντων, πολλοὶ δ' ἐριαύχενες ἵπποι
κείν' ὄχεα κροτάλιζον ἀνὰ πτολέμοιο γεφύρας,
ἡνιόχους ποθέοντες ἀμύμονας, οἱ δ' ἐπὶ γαίηι
κείατο, γύπεσσιν πολὺ φίλτεροι ἢ ἀλόχοισιν. (XI. 158–62)[25]

[21] The most complete study of the theme is Segal (1971): for my argument here, cf. esp. his pp. 9–17. Pagliaro (1956) makes many perceptive observations about the mutilation motif in the proem of the *Iliad* (see nn. 23, 24 below).

[22] Note, however, that Homer once describes the fish of the sea as nibbling on the flesh of a man who has died in the water (XXI. 203–4). It is difficult to tell how closely this strange image is associated with the system which we are studying here.

[23] Pagliaro (1956), 31–2; followed by Redfield (1979), 101.

[24] See Pagliaro (1956: 33), on this image as heroic rhetoric in the poet's voice.

[*See p. 172 for n. 25*]

This closely resembles the way that the image of descent to Hades rounded off the narration of the deaths of the sons of Antenor (XI. 262–3, p. 170 above). It is a fair guess that the mutilation of the dead is too gruesome and disturbing to break the calm surface of the Homeric narrative, and that for this reason it can be threatened more freely than it can be effected.[26] Perhaps it is in some analogous way that the descent to Hades is so remote, so strange, or so terrifying that it can be alluded to more easily than it can be narrated.[27] Since the descent removes the dead man from the mortal plane and gives him his new identity in Hades, it raises two problems. It juxtaposes the sublunary world with the mythological Underworld, prompting the question of the exact relationship between the two; and it effects the transition from one version of human identity to another, from the mortal man of flesh and bone to the mythical survivor in the world beyond. This transition is fraught with both poetic and conceptual difficulties.

The descent of ψυχή emerges from the descent of κεφαλή

The transition to Hades can be expressed along two paths of expression. On the simpler path the dead man breathes his last and dies and by the same token goes to Hades; on the more complex path the ψυχή escapes to make the descent. The latter, I have argued, is a special articulation which emerges in heightened narrative contexts, while elsewhere Homer clings to the principle that man lives and dies as an undivided bodily whole. The deaths of Patroclus and Hector are unique in using the myth of the flying ψυχή in straight narrative to effect the

[25] Cf. XI. 395, the same combination of images in a speech.

[26] In the *Odyssey*, Nestor recalls that Aegisthus was thrown to the dogs and vultures (iii. 259–61). It is revealing that in this, a very rare instance of a character saying unambiguously that a dead man was treated in this way, the victim is guilty of the most savage and inhuman of crimes: 'Nestor's hypothesis is a measure of the enormity of Aegisthus' offence' (S. West ad loc.). Proclus' summary of the *Little Iliad* records that Menelaus mutilated the dead Paris in the same spirit (see Davies (1989), 65–6).

[27] Here it could be objected that we are dealing not with a Homeric concept but with the Homeric aesthetic; but the aesthetic itself is crucial to the articulation of the concept, and if we separate the two we will lose sight of the logic of Homer's world-view.

transition to the world past the darkness of death: there the gap
is bridged not by alluding to Hades in high rhetorical language
but by narrating a higher kind of event, where the hero's dying
breath sprouts wings and the forms of mythical imagination are
separated off for a moment into the shapes of a mythical view of
the world. The motif objectifies the transition from one plane
of the universe to the other, and so it expresses the journey
after death in terms of complex cosmology—in other words, it
provides a single image to pin down the relationship between
the man who dies and the man, or remnant of a man, who will
eke out a shadowy existence in Hades. We have seen that the
man who loses that last breath is an indivisible bodily unity;
and with a further line of questioning we will see how closely
the idea of the descending ψυχή is rooted in the conception that
that unity is what makes the journey to Hades.

We noted that alongside the flying ψυχή of Patroclus and
Hector there stood a few other passages which alluded to the
descent of the ψυχή in a less direct way. The first is in the
proem of the *Iliad*, where the plan of the whole Wrath is
sketched. The warriors themselves die but their ψυχαί go down
to Hades:

> [sc. μῆνις] πολλὰς δ᾽ ἰφθίμους ψυχὰς Ἄιδι προΐαψεν
> ἡρώων, αὐτοὺς δὲ ἑλώρια τεῦχε κύνεσσιν
> οἰωνοῖσί τε πᾶσι, Διὸς δ᾽ ἐτελείετο βουλή . . . (I. 3–5)

Just as Homer deploys the image when he looks along the
whole sweep of the *Iliad*, so Nestor re-creates it more briefly
when he reviews the action of a day's fighting:

> πολλοὶ γὰρ τεθνᾶσι κάρη κομόωντες Ἀχαιοί,
> τῶν νῦν αἷμα κελαινὸν ἐύρροον ἀμφὶ Σκάμανδρον
> ἐσκέδασ᾽ ὀξὺς Ἄρης, ψυχαὶ δ᾽ Ἄϊδόσδε κατῆλθον. (VII. 328–30)

The ψυχαί have departed from the dead men and left behind
their bodily substance, identified in one instance as the men
themselves, αὐτούς, and represented in the other by their spilt
blood. A parallel passage will show how closely this pair of
images are built on the conception that the bodily man makes
the descent. When Agamemnon's *aristeia* is beginning and
Homer looks along the coming action he tells us that Zeus is
about to send many valiant men to Hades:

ἐν δὲ κυδοιμὸν
ὦρσε κακὸν Κρονίδης, κατὰ δ᾽ ὑψόθεν ἧκεν ἐέρσας
αἵματι μυδαλέας ἐξ αἰθέρος, οὕνεκ᾽ ἔμελλε
πολλὰς ἰφθίμους κεφαλὰς Ἄϊδι προϊάψειν. (XI. 52–5)

The last line is identical with the one we have seen in the proem, with the all-important difference that κεφαλαί rather than ψυχαί make the descent.[28] κεφαλή with the genitive is a common metonymy for the whole of a man, sometimes but not always connoting the essence of his life or his mortality.[29] Whatever ancient beliefs about the head may lie in the background,[30] it is clear that the κεφαλαί of this passage are the dead

[28] Compare also the Hesiodic *Catalogue*, fr. 204. 118 M–W, π]ολλὰς Ἄιδηι κεφαλὰς ἀπὸ χαλκὸν ἰάψ[ει]ν. Although the immediate context is fragmentary and the reconstruction of the future infinitive ἰάψειν is not certain, from the context it seems that the line refers to Zeus' plans for the Trojan War; so that the image of κεφαλαί descending to Hades appears in a context closely similar to that of XI. 52–5. Cf. also v. 190, VI. 487.

[29] Among the connotations of κεφαλή three broad aspects can be distinguished: (a) Sometimes it is co-ordinated with other names which are expressed without periphrasis, so that the specifying of κεφαλή perhaps does no more than to add solemnity. Addressing Zeus, Hera swears by Earth, Sky, Styx, and Zeus himself, σή θ᾽ ἱερὴ κεφαλή (XV. 36–9); Theoclymenus beseeches Telemachus in the names of sacred things and of his own self and his companions, ὑπὲρ θυέων καὶ δαίμονος, αὐτὰρ ἔπειτα | σῆς τ᾽ αὐτοῦ κεφαλῆς καὶ ἑταίρων (XV. 261–2); Telemachus says that the lewd servant girls heaped insults on him and his mother, ἐμῆι κεφαλῆι . . . μητέρι θ᾽ ἡμετέρηι (XXII. 463–4). (b) Sometimes it suggests affection for the person referred to. Agamemnon addresses Teucer as φίλη κεφαλή, Τελαμώνιε, κοίρανε λαῶν (VIII. 281); after Patroclus' death Achilles refers to Hector as φίλης κεφαλῆς ὀλετῆρα (XVIII. 114); he says that he honoured Patroclus as much as his own self, περὶ πάντων τῖον ἑταίρων, | ἶσον ἐμῆι κεφαλῆι (XVIII. 81–2), and he addresses the wraith as ἠθείη κεφαλή (XXIII. 94); Penelope speaks of her longing for Odysseus, τοίην γὰρ κεφαλὴν ποθέω μεμνημένη αἰεί | ἀνδρός (i. 343–4). (c) Sometimes it implies a reference to mortality. Ajax is afraid that he and Menelaus will be killed, ἐμῆι κεφαλῆι περιδείδια, μή τι πάθησι, | καὶ σῆι (XVII. 242–3); Menelaus imagines the men of Troy giving recompense by their own deaths and those of their families, σὺν σφῆισιν κεφαλῆισι, γυναιξί τε καὶ τεκέεσσιν (IV. 162); the ransom which Priam will provide for the dead Hector is Ἑκτορέης κεφαλῆς ἀπερείσι᾽ ἄποινα (XXIV. 276, 579); Odysseus alludes to the tragedy of Ajax' death, τοίην γὰρ κεφαλὴν . . . γαῖα κατέσχεν,| Αἴανθ᾽ (xi. 549–50). Compare also the periphrasis with κάρη or κάρηνον (see below, n. 38).

[30] Apart from A. Nussbaum's comparative-linguistic analysis of κάρη, κάρηνον, and cognates (1986), Onians (1951: 95–117) offers the only substantial study known to me of the earliest Greek ideas about the head. Onians's basic

men themselves: their bodily substance is what goes down to Hades, as in the standard pattern that we have observed in other allusive or rhetorical passages. The plot thickens when we add some scraps of information from the scholiasts.[31] First, Apollonius read κεφαλάς instead of ψυχάς in the proem passage. If his version was otherwise identical to ours, Homer would be made to say that κεφαλαί were sent to Hades while they themselves, αὐτοί, became the prey of the beasts: but since the periphrasis with κεφαλάς also stands for the men as a whole, this opposition would not make sense. The problem is solved if Apollonius' version also omitted lines 4–5, which according to further scholia were athetized by Zenodotus. We would then be left with a shorter text,

$$\mathring{\eta} \; \mu\nu\rho\acute{\iota}' \; \overset{}{A}\chi\alpha\iota o\hat{\iota}\varsigma \; \overset{}{\alpha}\lambda\gamma\epsilon' \; \overset{}{\epsilon}\theta\eta\kappa\epsilon,$$
$$\underline{\pi o\lambda\lambda\grave{\alpha}\varsigma \; \delta' \; \mathring{\iota}\phi\theta\acute{\iota}\mu o\nu\varsigma \; \kappa\epsilon\phi\alpha\lambda\grave{\alpha}\varsigma \; \overset{}{A}\ddot{\iota}\delta\iota \; \pi\rho o\ddot{\iota}\alpha\psi\epsilon\nu,}$$
$$\underline{\mathring{\epsilon}\xi \; o\hat{\upsilon} \; \delta\grave{\eta} \; \tau\grave{\alpha} \; \pi\rho\hat{\omega}\tau\alpha \; \delta\iota\alpha\sigma\tau\acute{\eta}\tau\eta\nu \; \mathring{\epsilon}\rho\acute{\iota}\sigma\alpha\nu\tau\epsilon \; \kappa.\tau.\lambda.}$$

The bald fact that ancient scholars preferred a short version to a longer one need not mean that the κεφαλάς version is more likely to be Homeric.[32] It could be argued that in Agamemnon's *aristeia* it is simply a truncated version of a familiar

argument is that the head is the seat of the ψυχή and is hence the seat of the essence of life itself. The Homeric evidence for this is of two kinds, neither fully satisfactory. First, Homer refers to several customs implying that the head is powerful, notably the decapitation of slain enemies and the significance attached to sneezing as a form of involuntary prophesying (Telemachus at xvii. 541–50). This certainly suggests that at an earlier stage of the tradition the head was in some sense spiritually important, but the survival of the customs in Homer must not be taken as the survival of specific beliefs. Onians's second piece of evidence is the similarity of certain ψυχή formulae to κεφαλή formulae in contexts of life at risk or life lost (cf. Warden (1969), 153–4). Only very hard Parryism would allow this as proof that the two words are identical or almost identical in meaning.

[31] Schol. bT on I. 3 says that Apollonius read κεφαλάς, and schol. A that "κακῶς τίνες μεταγράφουσι κεφαλάς"; schol. bT and A on VII. 330 are also aware of the reading κεφαλάς in I. 3. Schol. A on I. 4 says that Zenodotus athetized I. 4–5, but does not give a reason. The implications of these scholia are discussed in Pagliaro's study of the proem (1956: 21–36), and more briefly by Redfield (1979).

[32] It is hard to know what to make of the tradition that in the Cyclic epics the word νεκάς was used where ψυχή might have been expected (*Nosti*, fr. 12 Bernabé).

image of ψυχαί descending, and that the ancient editors mistakenly altered the proem in order to harmonize it with that
passage or to enable themselves to cut out the (supposedly)
uncharacteristic reference to the mutilation of corpses by birds
and beasts.[33] However, the logic of the words themselves
suggests that the version with κεφαλάς represents the Homeric
norm and the ψυχάς image is an exceptional creation.[34] Though
ἴφθιμος is a difficult word it refers consistently to strength and
vitality, to much the same qualities as those which we saw
embodied by the noun ἴς, vigorous mobile strength or its
embodiment in muscles and sinews (see Ch. 4, pp. 111–13).[35]
It is possible that the adjective is actually built on that noun.
A similarity, at least, between being ἴφθιμος and having good
ἴς is suggested when the adjective is used of warriors displaying their physical strength in attack, and still more closely
when ἴφθιμος is used of rivers (XVII. 749; cf. ἴς ποταμοῖο,
XXI. 356), Athena's shoulders (XVIII. 204; cf. ἴς in xi. 393–4),
and also the heads of cattle, ἴφθιμα κάρηνα (XXIII. 260; cf. ἴς at
XVII. 521–2).[36] ψυχή, on the other hand, is always weak,

[33] Suggested by Pagliaro (1956).

[34] See Pagliaro (1956), 21–3; Redfield (1979), 101–3.

[35] ἴφθιμος refers to strength, principally such strength as is borne out in
effective action. When it is used as an epithet with the names of men or women
it is hard to pin down the sense, but a few instances make it clear that what is
in question is physical power and vigour (see esp. VIII. 143–4, XII. 410–11,
XVI. 620–1, XX. 356–7; xvi. 89, 243–4). Studies of the word (principally
Warden (1969), Athanassakis (1971)) have produced theories which make
its problems seem more complex than the evidence warrants. Except for
ἰφθίμους ψυχάς (on which see my argument here), there is only one problem in
the word's usage: it is usually translatable as 'strong' or 'mighty', but as an
epithet it is used as often of women as of men. It is plain that Homeric women
are not especially weak or dainty, and that strength in a broad sense is borne
out in the bodily vitality of a woman as much as in the brute force of the male
warrior (see A. A. Parry (1973), 23 n. 1). If we accept this and allow for the
possibility that ἰφθίμους ψυχάς is modelled on ἰφθίμους κεφαλάς, then there is no
longer any need for such a complex definition as that proposed by Warden
(1969): 'seedy, rich, fertile, fat; virile, sexually potent; endowed with rich
soul-material, powerful, strong in a non-bodily sense; strong in a bodily
sense'.

[36] The evidence from etymology is equivocal. The first element of ἴφθιμος
obviously resembles the instrumental ἴφι from ἴς, and also recalls the adjective
ἴφιος (ἴφια μῆλα, of livestock, v. 556; xi. 108, etc.); but it is a problem that in
scansion ἴφι and ἴφιος regularly show the digamma required by *ϝίς, while

evanescent, and strengthless, whether it is identified as the cold and dissipated breath of death or as the vainly flitting shade of the dead man in Hades, so that on the face of it the combination of words in ἰφθίμους ψυχάς is odd and even contradictory: 'vigorous wisps', 'sinewy ghosts'. By contrast, ἰφθίμους κεφαλάς is typical of Homeric words associating strength with the head.[37] Thus a warrior puts his helmet onto his strong head, κρατὶ δ' ἐπ' ἰφθίμωι (III. 336 = XV. 480 = XVI. 137 = xxii. 123), and oxen are βοῶν ἴφθιμα κάρηνα (XXIII. 260; sim. IX. 407). The latter phrase occurs in a list of athletic prizes,

$$\text{λέβητάς τε τρίποδάς τε,}$$
$$\text{ἵππους θ' ἡμιόνους τε } \underline{\text{βοῶν τ' ἴφθιμα κάρηνα,}}$$

where from the parallelism it is clear that the heads stand metonymically for the oxen as a whole.[38] This provides a precise parallel with the ἰφθίμους κεφαλάς of the warriors as the bodily men descending to Hades. In terms of formulaic construction, then, it seems that in the proem the phrase ἰφθίμους ψυχάς has been built creatively on the simpler one which does not separate ψυχή from corpse but pins the journey on the κεφαλή, the undivided human being.[39]

That is not to suggest that the image of the separation of corpse from ψυχή is artificially imposed on Homeric death. To claim this would be to ignore the fact that the lines which

ἴφθιμος never does so. It is possible, if only barely so, that ἴφθιμος is cognate with ἴς but lost its digamma at the pre-Homeric stage (argued by Athannasakis (1971)). If this solution is not accepted, the etymology must remain obscure. There is no satisfactory explanation for the second element of ἴφθιμος. (For further, and more or less dubious, suggestions on the origins of ἴφθιμος see *LfgrE* s.v.; both Chantraine and Frisk conclude that the etymology is lost.)

[37] κεφαλή, κάρη, and κάρηνον are naturally synonymous for the head, and κάρηνον is cognate with κάρη (see Chantraine s.v., Frisk s.v.).

[38] The periphrasis with κάρη or κάρηνον and the genitive is found in similar contexts to that with κεφαλή. Note esp. the following in contexts of death or the threat of death: πυκνὰ καρήαθ' ὑφ' Ἕκτορι δάμνατο λαῶν (XI. 309); ὡς ἄρ' ὑπ' Ἀτρείδηι Ἀγαμέμνονι πῖπτε κάρηνα (XI. 158); τῆι ῥα μάλιστα | ἀνδρῶν πῖπτε κάρηνα (XI. 499–500); σῶι δ' αὐτοῦ κράατι τίσεις, meaning 'you will pay by your death' (xxii. 218); φάρμακον ... | ... ὅ κεν τοι κρατὸς ἀλάλκησιν κακὸν ἦμαρ (x. 287–8).

[39] Redfield (1979: 102) argues that the author of the proem adapted the formula ἰφθίμους κεφαλάς into ἰφθίμους ψυχάς in order to oppose 'the dead' going to Hades with 'the dead' mutilated by birds and beasts: "αὐτούς, then, motivates ψυχάς".

narrate the deaths of Patroclus and Hector are as Homeric as
anything could be, and that the briefer images include two
examples—Nestor's overview of the battle (VII. 330) and the
death of Elpenor before the Nekuia (x. 560)—which cannot be
shown to depend directly on simpler images of descent by the
whole person. What the evidence does suggest is that the
descent of the ψυχή is a difficult and recondite image which
remains bound up with the simpler and more pervasive
conception that the man who has died has gone by the same
token into the mythological land of the dead. It is for the same
reason that when Odysseus rails against Polyphemus and says
that he wishes he could kill him he talks of sending him to
Hades 'bereft of ψυχή and αἰών' (ix. 523–4), and when Nestor
imagines a wish to die he talks of one's θυμός going down to
Hades (VII. 131, see Ch. 5, p. 138). Because the abiding
meaning of the death-journey is the descent of the physical
man to Hades, it can be elaborated in ways that flatly ignore the
possibility of expressing it as descent by a ψυχή.

Hades is below the earth men stand on

If the bodily man, the κεφαλή, descends to Hades, where
exactly does he go? Although Odysseus finds its entrance by
sailing towards the edges of the world, it is fundamental that
Hades is directly below the earth on which mortals live,[40] as
Poseidon expounds when he recalls the division of the world
between himself and his brothers (xv. 187–93): Hades' portion
was the dark places, ζόφος (xv. 191), below the earth mirroring
Zeus' domain in the upper brightness. Poseidon's version is
unusually schematic,[41] but it is confirmed when the narrative

---

[40] For the principle that the mythical place is alternatively remotely distant
from or vertically below the world of mortals, compare Hesiod's Atlas: at one
point in the *Theogony* he is on the western edge of the world, ἐν πείρασι γαίης
(517–19), while at another he is deep in Tartarus (746–8).

[41] Burkert (1992: 90–6) holds that the scheme referred to by Poseidon has
been lifted directly from Near Eastern sources at a late stage in the
development of the epic tradition: this possibility must make us more wary
of taking it as an index of Homeric beliefs as such. However, within Homer
the scheme is not unparalleled: for example, we must visualize a strict
mirroring correspondence between Zeus above and Hades below if we are
to explain Ζεὺς καταχθόνιος as a title of the god of the nether world (IX. 457; cf.

leaps from the world of mortals to the world below: for example in the Theomachy of *Iliad* xx, when the Olympian family has suddenly materialized to join the battle before Troy, Poseidon shakes the earth in his wrath and Hades fears that his realm will be laid bare:

> ἔδεισεν δ' ὑπένερθεν ἄναξ ἐνέρων Ἀϊδωνεύς,
> δείσας δ' ἐκ θρόνου ἆλτο καὶ ἴαχε, μή οἱ ὕπερθε
> γαῖαν ἀναρρήξειε Ποσειδάων ἐνοσίχθων,
> οἰκία δὲ θνητοῖσι καὶ ἀθανάτοισι φανείη
> σμερδαλέ' εὐρώεντα . . . (xx. 61–5)

The image is startling, but there is no reason to think it at odds with Homer's understanding of the structure of the world,[42] which is no less complex than that expounded by Hesiod (see esp. II. 780–3, VIII. 13–16, 478–81, with *Theog.* 736–810, esp. 740–3).[43]

Homer's characters evoke the same idea in hyperbole when they say that it would be better to die than endure dishonour or defeat.[44] The wording varies from speech to speech, but the image clearly refers at once to dying and to being swallowed up by the earth: thus a hero ashamed at the accusation of cowardice would wish for the ground to yawn open before him, τότε μοι χάνοι εὐρεῖα χθών (IV. 182, VIII. 150);[45] the Achaeans remind each other of the mortification that would be caused by a retreat, ἀλλ' αὐτοῦ γαῖα μέλαινα | πᾶσι χάνοι (XVII. 416–17); Priam wishes that before he sees Troy sacked he may go

West at Hesiod, *WD* 465, on Zeus Chthonios as 'a chthonic counterpart of Zeus').

[42] Edwards ad loc. has a useful note comparing xx. 61–5 with Hesiod's descriptions of the Titanomachy (*Theog.* 678–86) and Zeus' battle with Typhoeus (839–43). On the verbal and thematic correspondences see also Mondi (1986), 35–6 (with n. 26), 42–4.

[43] M. L. West goes so far as to suggest (at *Theog.* 720–819) that the four-storey universe of VIII. 13–16 is invented to outdo the three-storey model of the *Theogony*. Neither here nor in West's more recent writings on the subject (1995) do I understand why he concludes that the influence must run in one direction rather than the other.

[44] For this hyperbolic desire for death compare also xvi. 103, xxiv. 435–6, the same idea but without mentioning the journey to the Underworld.

[45] Compare the wording at *h. Cer.* 16–17, when Hades himself emerges from his realm to seize Persephone: χάνε δὲ χθὼν εὐρυάγυια | Νύσιον ἂμ πεδίον τῆι ὄρουσεν ἄναξ πολυδέγμων.

down to Hades, βαίην δόμον Ἄϊδος εἴσω (XXIV. 246); and Hector, still more clearly, prays that before seeing Andromache dishonoured he should die and be covered over by a heap of earth, ἀλλά με τεθνηῶτα χυτὴ κατὰ γαῖα καλύπτοι (VI. 464; sim. VI. 411). The implication is that to go below the soil is the same thing as to go to Hades, a connection that Hector again makes under a slightly different form when he wishes Paris were dead:

> ὥς κέ οἱ αὖθι
> γαῖα χάνοι, μέγα γάρ μιν Ὀλύμπιος ἔτρεφε πῆμα
> Τρωσί τε καὶ Πριάμωι μεγαλήτορι τοῖό τε παισίν.
> εἰ κεῖνόν γε ἴδοιμι κατελθόντ' Ἄϊδος εἴσω,
> φαίην κε φρέν' ἀτέρπου ὀϊζύος ἐκλελαθέσθαι.   (VI. 281–5)

If the earth gapes to swallow him up, he will go to Hades. Similarly when men have died the earth holds them, κάτεχεν φυσίζοος αἶα (e.g. III. 243; XI. 301–4).[46] By extension, in battle one's collapse on the ground carries an ominous significance of its own: the victor brings his victim down to the soil, πέλασε χθονὶ πουλυβοτείρηι (VIII. 277 = XII. 194 = XVI. 418) and the slain descend towards and into the earth, γαῖαν ἐδύτην (VI. 19). Achilles draws out a similar image in scorn when he faces Lycaon, whom he had previously captured and released. Since the sea was not enough to restrain his foe from returning, Achilles asks whether this time the earth will be enough to do so,

> ἦ ἄρ' ὁμῶς καὶ κεῖθεν ἐλεύσεται, ἦ μιν ἐρύξει
> γῆ φυσίζοος, ἥ τε κατὰ κρατερόν περ ἐρύκει.   (XXI. 62–3)

The earth will hold him down in the very real sense that he will descend into it when he is killed.

The purpose of the funeral is social

If Hades lies directly below the world of the living, a journey into the soil will bring one to the land of the dead. Since the heaped earth that covers the dead man's grave, χυτὴ κατὰ γαῖα καλύπτει (XIV. 114), is by the same token what covers Hades, it

---

[46] On both occasions this line refers to the Dioscuri: it is impossible to tell whether the words φυσίζοος αἶα carry any special mythical or ironic significance in this context.

follows that burial is a ritualized version of the journey to the afterlife.[47] For example, Achilles wants Patroclus' bones to be kept so that they can accompany his own when he is buried in Hades, εἰς ὅ κεν αὐτὸς ἐγὼν Ἄϊδι κεύθωμαι (XXIII. 244), just as he says less explicitly that when he dies at Troy the earth will hold him, αὐτοῦ [sc. ἐμέ] γαῖα καθέξει (XVIII. 332),[48] and he will go down into it after Patroclus, σεῦ ὕστερος εἶμ᾽ ὑπὸ γαῖαν (XVIII. 333). In this sense when Achilles gives Patroclus his funeral he is sending him to Hades, ἕταρον γὰρ ἀμύμονα πέμπ᾽ Ἄϊδόσδε (XXIII. 137). Similarly, when he tells Agamemnon to send his men to gather materials for the funeral, the purpose is to provide the dead man with what it is fitting, ἐπιεικές, for him to have around him on the journey to the shadows below:[49]

> ὕλην τ᾽ ἀξέμεναι παρά τε σχεῖν ὅσσ᾽ <u>ἐπιεικὲς</u>
> νεκρὸν ἔχοντα <u>νέεσθαι ὑπὸ ζόφον ἠερόεντα</u>.   (XXIII. 50–1)

To be buried, to go below the earth, and to descend into darkness are complementary aspects of a single process.

However, this view of burial is complicated by the fact that Homer often implies that death is followed immediately by the descent, with no ritual process to mediate between the two. Andromache remembers that her brothers were all slain by

---

[47] For the corresponding principle in historically attested ritual, compare Redfield (1975: 179–86), Bremmer (1983: 89–108), and Garland (1985: 13–37), interpreting the early Greek funeral as a ritualized journey to the Underworld in several stages.

[48] For the implied reference to death in γαῖα καθέξει here, compare II. 699, XVI. 629; xi. 549, xiii. 427 = xv. 31; and see n. 46 above.

[49] There is some doubt over the sense in which Achilles thinks it fitting for beasts and Trojan captives to be slaughtered in Patroclus' funeral (XVIII. 336–7, XXIII. 22–3, 161–83). It has been argued that a memory of the custom of sending human victims to accompany the dead prince may lie behind his savage actions (see e.g. Andronikos (1968), 27–9). However, such human sacrifice is not attested elsewhere in Greek funerary tradition (see Hughes (1991), 49–56), and nothing that Achilles says suggests such a purpose; he carries out the slaughter in order to appease his own anger, σέθεν κταμένοιο χολωθείς (XVIII. 337 = XXIII. 23; on this ritual vengeance as a symbol of Achilles' savage mood, see esp. Schnapp-Gourbeillon (1982), 77–87). It remains possible that an ancient custom has been remembered in the epic tradition with its original eschatological purpose forgotten or suppressed (cf. below, n. 53).

Achilles in the sack of Thebe, and on that day they went to Hades:

> οἱ μὲν πάντες ἴωι κίον ἤματι Ἄϊδος εἴσω,
> πάντας γὰρ κατέπεφνε ποδάρκης δῖος Ἀχιλλεύς. (VI. 422–3)

This retrospective view corresponds to the prospective, as when a foe threatens Sarpedon before combat:

> οὐδέ τί σε Τρώεσσιν ὀίομαι ἄλκαρ ἔσεσθαι
> ἐλθόντ᾽ ἐκ Λυκίης, οὐδ᾽ εἰ μάλα καρτερός ἐσσι,
> ἀλλ᾽ ὑπ᾽ ἐμοὶ δμηθέντα πύλας Ἀΐδαο περήσειν. (V. 644–6)

The idea is the same when a warrior boasts that victory will give him glory and add a new wraith to the retinue of Hades: εὖχος ἐμοὶ δοίης, ψυχὴν δ᾽ Ἄϊδι κλυτοπώλωι (XVI. 625; sim. V. 654 = XI. 445). Similarly Hector remembers the moment when he had swooned and expected to die immediately, to reach the hosts of the dead and the house of Hades on that same day:

> καὶ δὴ ἔγωγ᾽ ἐφάμην νέκυας καὶ δῶμ᾽ Ἀΐδαο
> ἤματι τῶιδ᾽ ἵξεσθαι, ἐπεὶ φίλον ἄϊον ἦτορ. (XV. 251–2)

When Andromache laments over Hector, lying dead on the battlefield, she describes him as already on his way to the house of Hades:

> νῦν δὲ σὺ μὲν Ἀΐδαο δόμους ὑπὸ κεύθεσι γαίης
> ἔρχεαι. (XXII. 482–3)

Again, the sons of Antenor descend to Hades immediately when Agamemnon has slain them:

> ἔνθ᾽ Ἀντήνορος υἷες ὑπ᾽ Ἀτρεΐδηι βασιλῆϊ
> πότμον ἀναπλήσαντες ἔδυν δόμον Ἄϊδος εἴσω. (XI. 262–3)

Achilles produces an interesting example in his speech of vaunting irony over Lycaon. Remembering the previous occasion when he had him at his mercy, he remarks that the Trojans whom he was slaughtering will return to face him again:

> ὦ πόποι, ἦ μέγα θαῦμα τόδ᾽ ὀφθαλμοῖσιν ὁρῶμαι,
> ἦ μάλα δὴ Τρῶες μεγαλήτορες, οὕς περ ἔπεφνον,
> αὖτις ἀναστήσονται ὑπὸ ζόφου ἠερόεντος . . . (XXI. 54–6)

To return from death is to re-emerge from the darkness of

Hades and the darkness that falls on the dying man's sight. This raises the awkward question: if one who dies can be said to go immediately and directly to Hades, how can this be squared with the idea that he is transferred gradually to Hades in the course of his funeral? In a sense the difference is like that between a solitary meal and eating at an ordered feast: in purely existential terms the experience of death brings man from the mist that falls on the eyes to the gloomy darkness of Hades, but in terms of his continuing relationship with his peers he is transferred to a new environment in the shared celebration of the funeral.

Homer's words show that the funeral's purpose is essentially social: the dead man, like the living, expects to meet with his due from his peers, and the funeral expresses his status in relation to them.[50] Just as during his life he is given privileged reward, γέρας, because of his station or his personal worth, and just as the gods are accorded sacrifice as their γέρας from mortals (IV. 49 = XXIV. 70), so the rites accorded to the dead are their due portion of honour, γέρας θανόντων.[51] These words cover the cleaning of the corpse (xxiv. 186–90), the ritual lament (XXIII. 9; xxiv. 190, 295–6), weeping (iv. 196–8), the

---

[50] On this theme Garland (1984) has been especially useful; see also Edwards (1986).

[51] γέρας is indeterminately a privileged social position or a gift or mark of respect accorded by others. For example, a king's rights and privileges as lord of the household are collectively his γέρας (e.g. xi. 175, 184, xv. 522), and the giving of counsel and the communication of important messages is the γέρας of old men (IV. 323, IX. 422), while a reward apportioned to a warrior from the spoils of victory is itself a γέρας (I. 184–5, IX. 111, 334, etc.; sim. vii. 10, xi. 534, etc.). Taplin (1992: 60–3) discusses the institution of γέρας among Iliadic warriors, defining it as 'a communally ratified distinction' (61). Garland (1984: 6–7) defines γέρας as 'either concretely, a gift, service or reward; or abstractly, the entitlement to a gift, service or reward', and suggests that γέρας can sometimes be specifically what is accorded in virtue of intrinsic worth rather than in varying amounts according to different acts of merit (on this see also *LfgrE* s.v.). Similarly Agamemnon is described as γεραρός in appearance because of his air of kingly authority (III. 170). On the other hand, the giving of γέρας is regularly a sign of special τιμή, just as the cognate verb γεραίρω is used of the custom of presenting the best-deserving warrior with the choice portion at the feast (VII. 321). The word γέρας must be cognate with γέρων and γεραιός (see *LfgrE* and Chantraine s.v. γέρας; and note esp. the *figura etymologica* at IV. 323, IX. 422): if there is an active link between the meanings it is presumably that old age is intrinsically worthy of honour and deference.

cutting of the mourners' hair (iv. 197–8), the closing of the
dead one's eyes (xxiv. 296), and the erection of a memorial
(XVI. 456–7 = XVI. 674–5; see n. 61 below). Similarly, to honour
the dead is κτερ(ε)ίζειν (XI. 455, XVIII. 334, XXII. 336, XXIII. 646,
XXIV. 657) or ἐπὶ κτέρεα κτερεΐζειν (XXIV. 38; i. 291, ii. 222,
iii. 285): a κτέρας is a mark of respect towards one's peer, for
example the prestige given to a warrior as reward of his
prowess (X. 216, v. 311) or given to a guest by his hosts by
the award of a choice gift (XXIV. 235).[52] This duty is what
Agamemnon's shade refers to when he recalls that Clytaemnestra neglected to close his eyes and mouth when he was laid
out in death, denying him proper treatment on his way to
Hades:

> οὐδέ μοι ἔτλη, ἰόντι περ εἰς Ἀΐδαο,
> χερσὶ κατ᾽ ὀφθαλμοὺς ἑλέειν σύν τε στόμ᾽ ἐρεῖσαι.   (xi. 425–6)

The need for honourable treatment continues after death, and
it is to the visible dead man that such honour is accorded. The
complexities of the funeral are an expansion or elaboration of
the simple fact that death is descent into the earth, a social
working-out of the existential reality of passing into the soil
and into the Underworld.

Since social relationships persist after death, men can be sent
down with different degrees of prestige. For example, when
Deiphobus reacts to the death of a comrade by killing Hypse-
nor, he says that he is giving his friend a companion for his
journey:[53]

[52] These words can encompass the whole process of the funeral, and they
are not restricted to one ritual act within it (see esp. XXIII. 646, XXIV. 657).
Hoekstra (1965: 141–3) holds that the words κτέρεα κτερεΐζειν represent a relic
from practices in Mycenaean inhumation, no longer understood by Homer
and misapplied to cremation. For a more sympathetic view of the Homeric
meaning of κτέρεα κτερεΐζειν see Garland (1984), 21–2, with Mylonas
(1948), 64.

[53] As in the case of the slaughter of Trojans at Patroclus' funeral (see above,
n. 49), it is possible that this boast looks back to a custom by which human
victims were slaughtered to make up the retinue of a prince on his way to the
Underworld. This must remain doubtful, as the boast may simply be building
hyperbolically on the implications of the familiar practice of killing an
additional enemy in order to sate the desire for vengeance for the death of a
friend (see e.g. XI. 248–53, XIII. 660–72, XIV. 476–85, collected by Garland
(1984), 13, with n. 31).

οὐ μὰν αὖτ᾽ ἄτιτος κεῖτ᾽ Ἄσιος, ἀλλά ἕ φημι
<u>εἰς Ἀίδός περ ἰόντα πυλάρταο κρατεροῖο</u>
γηθήσειν κατὰ θυμόν, ἐπεί ῥά <u>οἱ ὤπασα πομπόν.</u>   (XIII. 414–16)

Although the image is exaggerated, it reflects the social reality that a retinue signifies prestige. Again, the mound and the stele are crucial because they ensure that the dead man will be remembered and continue to gain fame (VII. 86–90; iv. 584, xi. 75–6, xxiv. 80–4). It follows that the funeral of an insignificant man can be treated quite casually: the battlefield of the *Iliad* is strewn with corpses (VIII. 491 = x. 199, XI. 534, XX. 499, etc.) and Odysseus neglects Elpenor's funeral for vague reasons, ἐπεί πόνος ἄλλος ἔπειγε (xi. 54).[54] When one is maltreated after death or denied a funeral, it is a disgrace to those responsible, since they have withheld the respect that is owed by one man to another. For example, when Achilles restrained himself from dishonouring the corpse of Eetion he did so out of a sense of humane respect or reverence, σεβάσσατο γὰρ τό γε θυμῶι (VI. 417); Hector warns Achilles not to dishonour his corpse because such arrogance will be a cause of divine vengeance, θεῶν μήνιμα (XXII. 358–60; sim. xi. 73), and when Achilles lets the corpse rot Apollo says that he has lost pity and shame, ἔλεος and αἰδώς (XXIV. 44).

What of cremation? The devouring of the corpse by fire[55] is the most striking part of the funeral[56] (see esp. VII. 421–32,

---

[54] Garland (1984), 7–10; cf. Büchner (1937), 105–7, Reinhardt (1948), 132–4.

[55] For the image of 'devouring' consider πάντας πῦρ ἐσθίει and Ἕκτορα ... | πυρὶ δαπτέμεν (XXIII. 182–3).

[56] This chapter does not concern itself with whatever historical realities may lie behind Homer's literary evocation of funerary custom. A close similarity has been observed between the details of the funerals of Patroclus and Hector and those of the royal funerary rituals prescribed in Hittite texts from Bogazköy (see Gurney (1952), 164–9; Otten (1958); Christmann-Franck (1971); Steiner (1971)), but this cannot be used as proof that similar eschatological beliefs are involved. Similarly, our discussion of the relationship between corpse and wraith in the present chapter could be read in the light of the fact that Mycenaean burials are mostly inhumations and those of the early Archaic period are mostly cremations (for a detailed survey see Andronikos (1968)). But the relationship between real-life belief and practice and the created world-view of the epic must remain mysterious, and such speculations will not be pursued here. It is perhaps because of the symbolic importance which the choice between cremation and inhumation has acquired

XXIII. 154–261, XXIV. 784–800; xii. 8–15, xxiv. 63–84), and for the modern reader it might seem sensible to associate the smoke of the burning body with the escape to Hades of the wraith,[57] whose movement is likened in a different context to that of smoke, ἠΰτε καπνὸς | ὤιχετο (XXIII. 100–1). But the Homeric realities are different. Note that the verb θάπτω refers to the whole process of committing the corpse to the earth, not specifically to the burning.[58] Cremation is only one part of the long process of the funeral, and there is nothing to suggest that it is the decisive event that transfers the dead man to the Underworld or (still less) that it releases a wraith from the corpse. Rather, its purpose is social in the same way as that of the funeral as a whole, and allusions to cremation bear this out: a man expects that the mourners will give him his due portion of fire, πυρός με | λελάχωσι (VII. 79–80 = XXII. 342–3; sim. XV. 349–50, XXIII. 76),[59] and dead men are to be shown courtesy through fire, πυρὸς μειλισσέμεν [sc. νέκυας] (VII. 410).[60] Crema-

in Christian eschatology that it has been all too easy for scholars to over-emphasize the importance of cremation in Homeric death-belief. For the argument that cremation symbolizes the decisive banishment of the dead to a powerless afterlife, see for example Rohde (1925), ch. 1 *passim*; Nilsson (1967), 174–8, and cf. Schnaufer (1970), 58–63; and for warnings against inferring death-beliefs from the practice of cremation, see Andronikos (1968), 129; Bremmer (1983), 72.

[57] See e.g. Rohde (1925), 21; Bickel (1926), 87–95.

[58] For this as the meaning of θάπτω, note esp. οὐ γάρ πω ἐτέθαπτο ὑπὸ χθονός (xi. 52), which implies that the action of the verb is the installation of the dead man in the tomb. The reference to burial *qua* burial is equally precise when Scamander threatens to throw up a mound of earth over Achilles, boasting hyperbolically that the Achaeans will not need to raise an artificial mound over him: αὐτοῦ οἱ καὶ σῆμα τετεύξεται, οὐδέ τί μιν χρεὼ | ἔσται τυμβοχόης, ὅτε μιν θάπτωσιν Ἀχαιοί (XXI. 322–3). This accords well with the etymology of θάπτω and τάφος, since they are cognate with τάφρος, 'ditch' or 'trench' (for this point see Chantraine s.v.).

[59] Compare kindred uses of λαγχάνω: λάχομεν γέρας (IV. 49 = XXIV. 70); λαχόντα . . . ληΐδος αἶσαν (XVIII. 327; sim. v. 40 = xiii. 138); ἔλαχον κτερέων (v. 311); τιμὴν . . . λελόγχασιν (xi. 304).

[60] This seems the best interpretation of πυρὸς μειλισσέμεν, a difficult expression. In other contexts the rare verb μειλίσσω (elsewhere only at iii. 96 = iv. 326) and the commoner adjective μειλίχ(ι)ος (IV. 256, VI. 343; vi. 143, x. 173, etc.) refer almost always to speech, and characterize it as gentle or courteous or occasionally even wheedling; similarly Ajax rallies the Achaeans by telling them hyperbolically that their salvation lies in action as opposed to slack inactivity, μειλιχίηι πολέμοιο (XV. 741; for this interpretation

tion is not intended to let some spiritual part of man escape in smoke; rather, it preserves the identification of the visible body with the 'I' of the dead man—to die is to go to Hades, and to be cremated in the course of the funeral is to be sent there with due dignity. Although there is no sign in the *Iliad* or *Odyssey* of the possibility of inhumation,[61] it is interesting that the Cyclic *Little Iliad* told the story that Agamemnon had Ajax disposed of by inhumation with the express purpose of humiliating and dishonouring him after death.[62]

This view of cremation must influence our reading of the extraordinary passage in which the ghost of Patroclus appears to Achilles and begs that his funeral be carried out at once. When the ghost tells Achilles that after the cremation he will no longer return to haunt him,

$$\text{οὐ γὰρ ἔτ' αὖτις}$$
$$\text{νίσομαι ἐξ Ἀΐδαο, ἐπήν με πυρὸς λελάχητε ... (XXIII. 75–6)}$$

he says that when he has been treated fittingly, 'been given his due share of fire', he will have no need to visit Achilles again,

see Janko ad loc., comparing Hes. *Theog.* 206). Again, titbits thrown to dogs to please them are μειλίγματα θυμοῦ (x. 217).

[61] An exception has sometimes been claimed in the verb ταρχύω. This occurs in two contexts in Homer, and in both it refers in some way to the treatment of a corpse after death: Sarpedon's kin will erect a memorial for him, ταρχύσουσι ... τύμβωι τε στήληι τε (XVI. 456–7 = 674–5), and if Hector wins the duel with Ajax his foe's corpse will be returned so that he can be honoured as appropriate, ὄφρα ἑ ταρχύσωσι κάρη κομόωντες Ἀχαιοί | σῆμά τε οἱ χεύωσιν (VII. 85–6). Since the exact sense of ταρχύω is unclear, some have sought to link it to τάριχος, a mummy or a salted fish (see e.g. Blümel (1927); Hoekstra (1965), 142–3). If this is true, then the word might originally have referred to the practice of embalming the corpse. Others (see Nagy (1983), and Chantraine s.v.) hold that the word is a borrowing from Lycian, Luwian, or Hittite, 'something like *tarhu*, "conquering, victorious"' (Nagy), so that in the passage about Sarpedon's burial it would refer to the prospect that he will be deified by his people. The problem with both these interpretations is that each fails to fit one of the contexts in which the verb is attested: the defeated Greek warrior would hardly be deified by his burial in an enemy country, and the provision of mound and gravemarker is not what would bring about the preservation of Sarpedon's corpse. (Kirk at VII. 85 is similarly dubious.)

[62] *Little Iliad*, fr. 3 Bernabé. In the Nekuia Odysseus refers to the burial of Ajax in a way that is consistent, at least, with the story of his inhumation (xi. 549–50).

but he cannot mean that this will separate him into ash and wraith so as to render him physically incapable of returning:[63] the wraith already exists, and the being who addresses Achilles is referring to each in the first person, με. When Patroclus says that he will remain in Hades after funeral honours have been granted, this probably looks to stories in which the dead took vengeance on the living for insulting them and dishonouring their memory.[64] The same principle sheds light on Odysseus' encounter with the shade of Elpenor in the Nekuia. Elpenor asks that he be given a funeral as a mark of due respect:

> μή μ' ἄκλαυτον ἄθαπτον ἰὼν ὄπιθεν καταλείπειν,
> νοσφισθείς, μή τοί τι θεῶν μήνιμα γένωμαι,
> ἀλλά με κακκῆαι σὺν τεύχεσιν, ἄσσα μοί ἐστι,
> σῆμά τέ μοι χεῦαι πολιῆς ἐπὶ θινὶ θαλάσσης ... (xi. 72–5)

If he remains unburied his mistreatment will be a cause of divine anger, μήνιμα, because burial is what all men deserve from the their fellows (compare Hector at XXII. 358: discussed above, p. 185).[65] This point needs to be emphasized, because

---

[63] Proclus' summary of the Cyclic *Nosti* records that Achilles' ghost appeared in an attempt to warn his comrades of what lay in store on their homeward journeys. This was naturally long after his funeral, and it implies that the funeral rite did not prevent him from haunting the world of men. It is impossible to tell how close such a story is to Homeric conceptions of life after death (cf. Davies (1989), 56–7; Anderson (1997), 40; with the more general treatment of Griffin (1977)).

[64] The most startling example of this theme in Greek tradition is a story from Temesa preserved by Pausanias (6. 6. 3). Odysseus stopped there on his return from Troy, and one of his sailors raped a native woman, in punishment for which he was stoned to death. Odysseus sailed away without giving him a funeral, and later the ghost of the sailor, ὁ Ἥρως, ravaged the land and terrorized the people. On the oracle's advice they built a temple in his honour and dedicated a maiden at his pleasure once a year, which placated his anger. Eventually the valorous Euthymus fell in love with one of these women and fought the phantom for her; it was defeated and was never seen again. For further speculation about the fear of returning ghosts see esp. Rohde (1925), 13–24; Otto (1923), 11–13.

[65] The words μή τοί τι θεῶν μήνιμα γένωμαι also appear in Hector's plea to Achilles for proper treatment after death (XXII. 358). In his notes to xi. 66–78, Heubeck maintains that Elpenor's language deliberately draws on clichés of heroic culture for the sake of ironic or comic effect: 'The heroic language ... highlights the incongruity of Elpenor's claim to status: his birth, station in life, achievements, as well as the manner of his death, are all profoundly

many of the commentators have assumed that the passage reflects a complex doctrine about the effects of cremation on the dead man. Since Elpenor is the first of the dead to approach Odysseus, it has been argued[66] that because he has not been cremated he is in a liminal state between life and afterlife, not yet fully a wraith[67] and hence forced to wander at the entrance of Hades. Nothing in the text suggests that. Elpenor is a ψυχή (xi. 51, etc.) or εἴδωλον (xi. 83) like the others, and it is nowhere implied that he is at some intermediate stage of admission to the afterlife. When Odysseus says that he was the first wraith to come up to him from Hades, the lines

$$\pi\rho\dot{\omega}\tau\eta\ \delta\dot{\epsilon}\ \psi\upsilon\chi\dot{\eta}\ \text{'}E\lambda\pi\dot{\eta}\nuο\rho\sigma\varsigma\ \mathring{\eta}\lambda\theta\epsilon\nu\ \dot{\epsilon}\tau\alpha\acute{\iota}\rho\sigma\upsilon\cdot$$
$$\sigma\mathring{\upsilon}\ \gamma\acute{\alpha}\rho\ \pi\omega\ \dot{\epsilon}\tau\acute{\epsilon}\theta\alpha\pi\tau\sigma\ \mathring{\upsilon}\pi\dot{\sigma}\ \chi\theta\sigma\nu\dot{\sigma}\varsigma\ \epsilon\mathring{\upsilon}\rho\upsilon\sigma\delta\epsilon\acute{\iota}\eta\varsigma\quad\text{(xi. 51-2)}$$

mean simply that the urgency of his request for proper and dignified treatment, γέρας θανόντων, is what makes him stand forward first from the throng who have emerged out of the gloom (xi. 36–41): there is no implication that within Hades he is somehow different in status from the main population of the dead. When he speaks to Odysseus, his request for burial does not mention anything about its effect on his life in Hades (xi. 72–8), and the issue in the meeting is the code of mutual respect which gives every funeral its meaning.

unheroic'. It is impossible to disprove this, but there is no necessary reason to accept it; although Elpenor in life was a feeble person (see esp. x. 552–3), it can be argued that the solemnity of the present scene in Hades, with the untimeliness of his death and the pathos of his suffering, give him a new dignity which makes a higher style appropriate (cf. also Focke (1943), 212).

[66] See Bremmer (1983), 89–90, and Heubeck at xi. 51–4.

[67] This argument about Elpenor's status depends largely on the fact that he speaks to Odysseus without drinking the sacrificial blood: the scholarly explanation would be that he is not fully a wraith because he has not yet been reduced in substance by being burnt. The answer is not far to seek: since Odysseus himself at this point does not understand that the blood is what enables the wraiths to think and speak (Tiresias' explanation comes later, at xi. 147–9), it is hard to believe that Homer's audience understood the ritual so well that they would have appreciated an unstated principle which exempted the unburied dead from that requirement. As we will see later in this chapter (below, pp. 193, 216–17), Elpenor is not the only wraith for whom the poet ignores the requirement of drinking the blood; and given the shifting character of the death-lore of the whole Nekuia, there is no good reason to invent doctrinal subtleties to explain such minor inconsistencies as this.

νέκυς/νεκρός denotes both corpse and dweller in Hades

If the dead man passes into the afterlife in his bodily shape, the logical conclusion ought to be that the corpse and the dweller in Hades are the same thing: and although logic is not what we are looking for, the observable truth is surprisingly close to that suggestion. The simplest indication is that both in the mortal world and in Hades the dead are regularly called by the same name, νέκυς/νεκρός, 'corpse, dead man'. This lexical unity suggests that in some basic sense he plays his part in the same bodily form on both planes of the world: and in practice, as we will see, the careful shaping of language and story-telling prevents this from leading to absurdities.[68] Here our main source is naturally the Nekuia of the *Odyssey*, where for once the narrative brings us right down into Hades,[69] with the shorter episode where Achilles is visited in sleep by the ghost of Patroclus (XXIII. 65–107). I hope it will become clear that the two provide a single body of evidence that chimes well with the

[68] As we have noted (Ch. 2, nn. 38–40), it is central to Bickel's argument (1926) that the eschatological survivor, ψυχή, is in some sense a 'living corpse' (see esp. 6–17, 22–5). He mentions the semantic range of νέκυς to support his claim (see esp. 8–12), but he is led to odd arguments when he tries to make σῶμα equal ψυχή in meaning. Bickel believes that the language of Hades incorporates fossils preserved from different periods of death-belief; in particular, he works out the relationship between 'psyche as living corpse' and 'psyche as phantom' by assigning different images and formulae to different stages in a development towards the soul-belief familiar from Pindar (fr. 131b M). It seems throughout that Bickel is exaggerating his case as part of a polemic against Rohde (see e.g. 32–4). For reactions against Bickel's scheme see Regenbogen (1948), 6–7, with refs. A more subtle and still thought-provoking version of Bickel's line of argument is advanced by Büchner (1937: esp. 116–17), relying (perhaps vaguely) on the idea that Homer's death-mythology is affected by 'the remnant of a primitive idea'. The relationship between ψυχή and 'living corpse' is also surveyed by Schnaufer (1970: esp. 58–70), with a reconstruction of what he sees as pre-Homeric beliefs preserved in fossil form in the Nekuia (125–76).

[69] Although the Nekuia is told not by the primary narrator but by the most mendacious of Homer's heroes, I do not think anything is to be gained by declining to take it as a serious document of Homeric belief about the afterlife (see e.g. Büchner (1937: 119–22), speculating about the remoteness of the Hades of the Nekuia from 'real' death-belief; cf. also Reinhardt (1948), 52–7, 118–20). The remote is not necessarily fantastic, and the tone of the Nekuia is solemn and serious (on this see Sourvinou-Inwood (1995), 71–6).

rest of Homer's lore of the afterlife. My working hypothesis
that the Nekuia is a unity is defended separately in section 1 of
the Appendix to this chapter.

The dweller in Hades is corpse or shade

The inhabitants of Hades are seen in two ways: on the one hand
they are corpses, on the other they are wraiths, phantoms,
images. (In the latter category none of those English translations explains anything, but for brevity's sake we will use the
word 'shade', which has the advantage of being vague and
ambiguous in itself.) On the level of names the difference
between the two categories is summed up in the distinction
between νέκυς/νεκρός for the first and ψυχή and εἴδωλον for the
second, though in practice the identities run in tandem and
seem almost to jostle for supremacy from line to line and from
word to word. As νέκυς/νεκρός, the inhabitant of Hades is always
identified as the dead man proper, with the appropriate gender
and with the word νέκυς/νεκρός interchanged with the proper
name; when he is ψυχή or εἴδωλον, grammar preserves the
feminine or neuter gender and Homer speaks of the shade *of*
the dead man.[70] Observe Odysseus' first encounter in the
Nekuia. He pours a libation for all the corpses, πᾶσιν νεκύεσσι
(xi. 26) and prays to the strengthless heads of the corpses,
νεκύων ἀμενηνὰ κάρηνα (xi. 29) in their multitudes, ἔθνεα νεκρῶν
(xi. 34). But when they answer the summons they emerge not
as dead men proper but as shades:

> αἱ δ' ἀγέροντο
> ψυχαὶ ὑπὲξ ἐρέβευς νεκύων κατατεθνηώτων. (xi. 36–7).

These are literally 'wraiths of dead corpses'; but immediately
the image shifts:

> νύμφαι τ' ἠΐθεοί τε πολύτλητοί τε γέροντες
> παρθενικαί τ' ἀταλαὶ νεοπενθέα θυμὸν ἔχουσαι,
> πολλοὶ δ' οὐτάμενοι χαλκήρεσιν ἐγχείῃσιν,
> ἄνδρες ἀρηΐφατοι βεβροτωμένα τεύχε' ἔχοντες. (38–41)

Now they are the people themselves—girls, youths, old men,
children, and warriors. Note especially that the warriors bear

[70] Cf. Jahn (1987), 37.

Death and the Afterlife

the wounds by which they killed: they have the physical appearance that was theirs *after* death, because each is the bodily substance of the man who died in the mortal world. This gives new weight to the image of the house of Hades as rotting or putrefying, εὐρώεντα (xx. 65; x. 512, xxiii. 322, xxiv. 10): those who dwell there are not distinguished from the people who died, and they can be seen as decomposing flesh.[71] Here lies the logic of the fact that they are called 'corpse':

> τίπτ' αὖτ', ὦ δύστηνε, λιπὼν φάος Ἠελίοιο,
> ἤλυθες, ὄφρα ἴδηι νέκυας καὶ ἀτερπέα χῶρον;
>
> (xi. 93–4; sim. xv. 251)

A single sentence can slip from one articulation to the other. For example Achilles asks Odysseus why he has come to see the corpses, the images of worn-out men:

> πῶς ἔτλης Ἄϊδόσδε κατελθέμεν, ἔνθα τε νεκροὶ
> ἀφραδέες ναίουσι, βροτῶν εἴδωλα καμόντων; (xi. 475–6)

Similarly Odysseus describes his meeting with Tiresias:

> ἦλθε δ' ἐπὶ ψυχὴ Θηβαίου Τειρεσίαο,
> χρύσεον σκῆπτρον ἔχων, ἐμὲ δ' ἔγνω καὶ προσέειπε. (xi. 90–1)

The ψυχή of Tiresias in the first line shifts to Tiresias himself, masculine, in the second. Up to a point, this can be explained mechanically on the grounds (for example) that the appropriate formulae for describing Tiresias are all masculine anyway; but it will turn out that this shift between verbal patterns is part of a deeper ambiguity as to whether the inhabitant of Hades is the man himself or something we could call a wraith.

---

[71] The adjective εὐρώεις is found in Homer only as an epithet of the Underworld, οἰκία . . . σμερδαλέ' εὐρώεντα (xx. 64–5), Ἀΐδεω . . . δόμον εὐρώεντα (x. 512, xxiii. 322), κατ' εὐρώεντα κέλευθα (xxiv. 10), and likewise in Hesiod. Tentatively, its meaning can be inferred from later attestations of the cognate noun εὐρώς, which is found in the lyric and elegiac poets denoting rust and decay (see esp. Thgn. 452; Simon. fr. 531. 4 P; Bacchyl. fr. 4. 72 S–M). The words ὑπὸ ζόφωι εὐρώεντι in *h.Cer.* 482 closely echo ὑπὸ ζόφον ἠερόεντα (xi. 57), and this seems to have prompted the opinion in some ancient scholars that εὐρώεις refers to darkness and obscurity rather than decay. On the problem see esp. *LfgrE* s.v., glossing εὐρώεις as 'moderig'; also Aly (1914), 64–9.

To show that this ambiguity is not a matter of words alone but also of ideas and beliefs, observe the parallel question over whether or not the dead are able to think and speak for themselves. When the shade of Odysseus' mother fails to recognize him (xi. 88–9, 140–4), Tiresias explains that the dead cannot think or speak until they have drunk the blood of the sacrificial victims (xi. 146–9). Tiresias himself retains wisdom by the special favour of Persephone (xi. 90–1, and see x. 493–5), but none the less he drinks the blood before he utters his prophecy (xi. 98–9); and Anticleia, the famous women, and Agamemnon are obliged to drink it before their conversations with Odysseus can begin (xi. 153–4, 228–32, 390). Similarly, the dead are described as ἀφραδέες, foolish or heedless (xi. 476),[72] and their feebleness is borne out in another way when they cry out wordlessly, θεσπεσίηι ἰαχῆι (xi. 43) or ἠχῆι θεσπεσίηι (xi. 633) with a sound like the screeching of birds, κλαγγὴ . . . οἰωνῶν ὥς (xi. 605), just as Patroclus' wraith squeaks as it flies away to Hades, ὤιχετο τετριγυῖα (XXIII. 101; compare the bat simile in the Second Nekuia, xxiv. 5–9).[73] But elsewhere this theme is forgotten: the shades of Elpenor, Achilles, and Ajax are not said to drink the blood before they can speak normally to Odysseus, and in the latter part of the Nekuia the dead are fully in control of themselves in thought, speech, and actions alike. Just as Homer is ambivalent over whether the dead in Hades are empty images or dead men of substance, so his conception of their ability to think and speak like living men appears and disappears in different contexts.

[72] ἀφραδής is ἀ-privative with a stem built on the same root as in φράζομαι (Chantraine s.v.), which is also linked to the noun φρήν. If the basic unit of meaning is the root rather than its resultant words (a point which is admittedly doubtful) then to say that the dead are ἀφραδέες is equivalent to saying that they lack φρένες, as Achilles concludes when he finds that Patroclus' ghost lacks *physical* substance (XXIII. 104; see below, p. 209 with n. 97).

[73] Cf. Bremmer's discussion (1983: 83–9) of the 'witlessness' of the wraiths (and compare Page (1955), 21–2). The fact that the wraiths cry out does not necessarily mean that they are incapable of thought, but only that they are in anguish; and the words ἀμενηνὰ κάρηνα do not refer to intellectual feebleness, since μένος is associated not with intelligence but with bodily power and the will to vigorous action (see Ch. 4 above, esp. pp. 109–11).

The shade is defined as remnant or as counterfeit

Where does the dead man's identity, his 'I', reside in relation to this dweller in Hades? To answer that we must unravel the strands of imagery in which the survivor is something distinct from or less than the corpse that was buried. Broadly, the shade can be characterized in three ways: as a reduced remnant of the dead man, as an empty image of him, and as something that flits and wafts along on the air. These themes bear separate examination.

First, the dwellers in Hades are feeble remnants: they are νεκύων ἀμενηνὰ κάρηνα (x. 521, x. 536, xi. 29, 49), heads bereft of the μένος that is vigour of will and action. They are the καμόντες, the exhausted ones (III. 278) and they are εἴδωλα καμόντων (XXIII. 72; xi. 476, xxiv. 14), images of exhausted men. This word καμόντες is important. With the intransitive aorist one who is καμών in death is wearied and enfeebled,[74] just as κάματος in the living is tiredness and enfeeblement in the body and especially in the jointed limbs (see esp. IV. 230, V. 811, VII. 6, XIII. 85, 711, XXI. 52; i. 192, x. 363, xx. 118). The dead are worn down almost to nothing, νέκυες καταφθίμενοι (xi. 491), reduced by a lack of lively vigour that robs them not only of vitality but of strength and substance.

This concept is well illustrated in Odysseus' meeting with the shade of Agamemnon. When he stretches out his hands and is unable to touch him, his lack of substance reveals that he is a faded remnant of Agamemnon himself:

---

[74] Homeric κάμνω shows a broad range of meaning. Transitively the verb means to complete the making of something, as σκῆπτρον κάμε τεύχων (II. 101; likewise v. 735, VIII. 195, etc.); but without a direct object the emphasis shifts to cessation of an action in tiredness, so that one becomes physically weary of slaying, κάμε χεῖρας ἐναίρων (XXI. 26) and likewise one ceases to weep, κάμε δάκρυ χέουσα (XXIV. 613). The reference seems to be to tiredness alone when one about to sleep grows weary in his limbs, κάμε φαίδιμα γυῖα (XXIII. 63), and it must be in this sense that the dead are the καμόντες. For the shift from transitive to intransitive senses compare, for example, Middle English *swinken*, 'to toil', where *swinkt* can mean 'exhausted'.

κλαῖε δ' ὅ γε λιγέως, θαλερὸν κατὰ δάκρυον εἴβων,
πιτνὰς εἰς ἐμὲ χεῖρας, ὀρέξασθαι μενεαίνων,
ἀλλ' οὐ γάρ οἱ ἔτ' ἦν ἲς ἔμπεδος οὐδέ τι κῖκυς,
οἵη περ πάρος ἔσκεν ἐνὶ γναμπτοῖσι μέλεσσι.
                              (xi. 391–4; sim. *h. Ven.* 237–8)

When he stretches out his arms he is light and strengthless,
πιτνὰς . . . χεῖρας.[75] The word πάρος, 'previously', identifies this
being with the man who once lived: this is still Agamemnon,
but without the strength he had as a living man. This is borne
out by the point that he lacks ἲς and κῖκυς. ἲς, as we have seen
elsewhere (Ch. 4, pp. 111–13), is muscle and sinew or the force
of physical vigour that young men have in the prime of life;
κῖκυς here is a *hapax*, but in Homer its meaning is clear from
the adjective ἄκικυς (ix. 515, xxi. 131), referring in contempt or
shame to the weakness of a puny man. The wraith's weakness is
couched in terms very similar to those in which Nestor
describes the feebleness of his old age:

οὐ γὰρ ἐμὴ ἲς
ἔσθ' οἵη πάρος ἔσκεν ἐνὶ γναμπτοῖσι μέλεσσι.   (XI. 668–9)

The verbal correspondence suggests that the dead man has
been worn down to his present state by something akin to the
decay and reduction—φθίνειν, φθινύθειν—that the living suffer in
old age, or indeed by the more decisive loss of αἰών that comes
with death (see above, pp. 160–1). This implies that across the
divide between life and death it is the bodily substance of the
man which is reduced to the empty feebleness of the afterlife.

This marches with the distinct, even seemingly contradictory, idea that the shade is an image that resembles the dead
man in shape but lacks any physical substance. The key word is
εἴδωλον, which is freely interchanged with the other names for
the shade (see esp. XXIII. 72, 104; xi. 83, 213, 476, xx. 355).[76]

[75] Compare Homer's other two examples of this verb πιτνάω or πίτνημι,
built on the same root as πέτομαι, πετάννυμι. Hera casts a mist to drift over the
fleeing Trojans, ἠέρα δ' Ἥρη | πίτνα πρόσθε βαθεῖαν (XXI. 6–7); Hector's hair
floats behind his head as Achilles drags him along behind his chariot, ἀμφὶ δὲ
χαῖται | κυάνεαι πίτναντο (XXII. 401–2).
[76] On the disputed passage about the εἴδωλον of Heracles in Hades see
below, Appendix n. 15.

196 *Death and the Afterlife*

The heart of this word is in substitution and mimicry,[77] as is shown when it appears in other contexts. In an Iliadic battle (v. 445–53) Apollo whisks Aeneas away to safety and puts in his place a false phantom to deceive his foes:[78]

[77] Vernant (1985: 323–51; 1990: 25–34) has a theory comparing the Homeric εἴδωλον with the difficult word κολοσσός. In the passage of Aeschylus' *Agamemnon* describing Menelaus' grief at the loss of Helen, the words εὐμόρφων δὲ κολοσσῶν ἔχθεται χάρις ἀνδρί (416–17) have been taken in two ways: either the κολοσσοί are statues or pictures of Helen adorning the house, or they are images lingering in Menelaus' mind. Vernant argues for the latter, and proposes that there is an exact equivalence between κολοσσός and εἴδωλον. He holds that each word can be applied either to a phantom or to a grave-marker, both being things which serve as reminders of absent ones: 'Ils traduisent, sous des formes à des niveaux différents, l'inscription paradoxale de l'absence dans la présence' (1990: 28). However, the interpretation of κολοσσός 'sur le plan psychologique' (1985: 330) in the Aeschylus passage is not assured; and in Homer εἴδωλον is never used of a grave-marker or other concrete memorial, for which the usual word is σῆμα or τύμβος (also ἠρίον, XXIII. 126). Whatever the value of Vernant's theory for the later connotations of either word, it cannot easily be projected back onto Homer. (See Roux (1960) and Fraenkel ad loc. for the argument that Menelaus' κολοσσοί are man-made images; Benveniste (1932b) is close to Vernant, using κολοσσός to advance a theory about an Indo-European concept of image-making).

[78] Because this is the only passage in the *Iliad* where a god replaces a mortal with a phantom, some have condemned it as an interpolation. Kirk (ad loc.) is conservative, but West (1985a: 134–5), holds that both the εἴδωλον of Aeneas here and that of Heracles in the Nekuia (see Appendix, n. 15) are interpolations modelled on Stesichorus' famous story about the εἴδωλον of Helen (frs. 192–3 P). He compares III. 380–2, where Aphrodite whisks Paris away from the battle without leaving any εἴδωλον behind. But it is hard to see why the passage about Aeneas' εἴδωλον should have been interpolated in the first place, and the motif is not un-Homeric: a person is replaced by an εἴδωλον in much the same way in Penelope's dream (iv. 796–839), and the deception is similar in kind to the passages in which a god disguises himself as a mortal in order to confuse his foes: compare esp. Apollo disguised as Agenor, Ἀγήνορι πάντα ἐοικώς (XXI. 600). I see no rationale behind West's claim that the image is necessarily likely to be based on Stesichorus' Helen rather than on some more ancient floating story-pattern which Stesichorus deployed in a new context. Gods replaced people with εἴδωλα at least twice in stories preserved in the Hesiodic corpus, as West himself points out, and despite the comparatively late date of the attestations there is to be no reason to deny that the motif may go back to the earliest tradition (see Hes. fr. 23a. 17–24 M–W, Iphimede replaced by an εἴδωλον when about to be sacrificed; fr. 260, Endymion deceived by an εἴδωλον of Hera; and cf. more doubtfully fr. 358). On the question of substitute εἴδωλα in general, see most recently Crane (1988: 87–

αὐτὰρ ὁ <u>εἴδωλον</u> τεῦξ' ἀργυρότοξος Ἀπόλλων
αὐτῶι τ' Αἰνείαι ἴκελον καὶ τεύχεσι τοῖον,
ἀμφὶ δ' ἄρ' εἰδώλωι Τρῶες καὶ δῖοι Ἀχαιοὶ
δήιουν ἀλλήλων ἀμφὶ στήθεσσι βοείας . . .   (v. 449–52)

This εἴδωλον exists only as the semblance of the man.[79] The
closest analogy is with the motif of a god appearing in disguise
to distract people's attention, where he takes on the appearance, δέμας or εἶδος, of a mortal: it is in a similar way that the
εἴδωλον exists as δέμας or εἶδος alone.[80] Likewise Athena sends
an εἴδωλον to bring Penelope a message in a dream (iv. 795–
839).[81] Instead of appearing at the head of the bed herself in
mortal guise (cf. vi. 22–4),[82] she fashions this phantom to
impersonate Penelope's sister:

<u>εἴδωλον</u> ποίησε, δέμας δ' ἤϊκτο γυναικί,
Ἰφθίμηι, κούρηι μεγαλήτορος Ἰκαρίοιο.   (iv. 796–8)

It is because the shades are illusory shapes of this kind that they
are so easily confused with real people, and may even walk and
talk like them: just as the εἴδωλον of Aeneas stands on the

91), who argues against bracketing either of the disputed Homeric passages;
and on Stesichorus' Helen see also Austin (1994) with M. J. Clarke (1996).

[79] Bickel (1926: 16–17) argues that the εἴδωλον here is in fact none other
than Aeneas' 'breath-soul', available to the god because Aeneas has (presumably) breathed it out in his swoon (v. 310). It is hard not to admire the
ingenuity of this theory.

[80] εἶδος evidently provides the first element of εἴδωλον (*LfgrE* s.v.; Chantraine s.v.). On δέμας see Ch. 4, pp. 117–18.

[81] Bickel (1926: 18–21) elaborately links the εἴδωλον in this dream with
concepts of δαίμων, *mysterium tremendum*, and burgeoning soul-belief.

[82] It is difficult to tell why this dream uses the motif of the εἴδωλον rather
than making Athena herself appear in disguise in the way that she does when
she visits Nausicaa (vi. 13–41). The only available comparison is with the
dream (ii. 5–35) in which Zeus sends the personal Dream himself, οὖλος
Ὄνειρος (ii. 6, 8), to Agamemnon in the guise of Nestor. Perhaps it is because
Zeus must remain aloof from the other meddling gods of the *Iliad* that he
sends an emissary rather than descending to Agamemnon's bedside himself.
But in the *Odyssey* passage there is no reason why Athena should not come
herself, since the plot does not oblige her to be in any particular place on that
night. S. West ad loc. suggests that if Athena had come herself she would have
been unable to avoid giving Penelope news of Odysseus, while the εἴδωλον is
able to avoid a straight answer (iv. 836–7).

battlefield and fights in his likeness, so the shade of Achilles can
stride across the meadows of Hades with the hero's own gait:

ψυχὴ δὲ ποδώκεος Αἰακίδαο
φοίτα μακρὰ βιβᾶσα κατ᾽ ἀσφοδελὸν λειμῶνα.   (xi. 538–9)

The principle of substitution has a further remarkable consequence: when the phantom dweller in Hades speaks, he tends
to pin his own identity, his 'I', on his physical body rather than
his current manifestation as a shade. When the dead Elpenor
confronts Odysseus he comes forward as a shade, ψυχὴ Ἐλπήνορος (xi. 51), and in telling the story of Elpenor's own death
the first person singular and the masculine gender are used for
what he did when he was alive:

Κίρκης δ᾽ ἐν μεγάρωι καταλέγμενος οὐκ <u>ἐνόησα</u>
ἄψορρον καταβῆναι ἰὼν ἐς κλίμακα μακρήν,
ἀλλὰ καταντικρὺ τέγεος <u>πέσον</u>.   (xi. 62–4)

Here the 'I' in the wraith's mouth attaches to his bodily
substance; so that by following this thread, when he narrates
the actual death he speaks of the wraith in the third person:

ἐκ δέ μοι αὐχὴν
ἀστραγάλων ἐάγη, <u>ψυχὴ</u> δ᾽ Ἄϊδόσδε κατῆλθε.   (64–5)

Again, when he demands a funeral the 'I' of the speech is the
corpse, who must here be completely distinct from the wraith
which is speaking:

ἔνθα σ᾽ ἔπειτα, ἄναξ, κέλομαι μνήσασθαι ἐμεῖο,
μή μ᾽ ἄκλαυτον ἄθαπτον ἰὼν ὄπιθεν καταλείπειν
νοσφισθείς.   (71–2)

It is easy to see why this makes sense despite the apparent
paradox: the identity of the shade is not its own, but that of the
undivided bodily man whose appearance it represents. In due
course we will see that later in the Nekuia Odysseus' mother
speaks of 'my shade', ψυχή, in exactly the same way.

The shade's movement names it as ψυχή

How do the concepts of remnant and counterfeit exist in
harmony? Athena's dream-phantom suggests an answer. Just

as elsewhere the stuff of dreams is strengthless, ἀμενηνῶν . . . ὀνείρων (xix. 562), like the ἀμενηνὰ κάρηνα of the dead, so here the εἴδωλον is airily feeble, ἀμαυρόν (iv. 824 = 835),[83] so that it can slip into the bedroom through the slit provided for the bolt-strap, παρὰ κληῖδος ἱμάντα (iv. 802),[84] and after delivering its message it blows away into the winds:

ὣς εἰπὸν σταθμοῖο παρὰ κληῖδα λιάσθη
ἐς πνοιὰς ἀνέμων.   (iv. 838–9)

Because it exists only in appearance it can vanish into thin air. The dissipation of this εἴδωλον suggests that the common ground between remnant and counterfeit is in the shade's characteristic motion: it flits, it floats, it moves along the air without strength or substance. It is under this aspect that the word ψυχή comes into its own: just as in the mortal world this word names the strengthless gasp whose loss was death, so here it names the insubstantial wisp that lives out this shadowy semblance of a life. The shade flies like a dream or a shadow, σκιῆι εἴκελον ἢ καὶ ὀνείρωι | ἔπτατο (xi. 207–8), and the dead are shadows who flit about, σκιαὶ ἀΐσσουσιν (x. 495); similarly Anticleia's wraith moves with a fluttering motion, ἀποπταμένη πεπότηται (xi. 222); the feeble shade of Agamemnon stretches out its hands in the same way, πιτνὰς εἰς ἐμὲ χεῖρας (xi. 392); the wraith of Patroclus moves like smoke, ἠΰτε καπνὸς | ὤιχετο (XXIII. 100–1). Such movement indeterminately represents the

[83] In Homer the word ἀμαυρός is found only here, and its meaning is uncertain. There is no secure etymology. The other earliest attestation is in Hesiod, where lawless oathbreakers are punished in the second generation when their progeny is ἀμαυροτέρη (*WD* 284). There is also a Hesiodic fragment in which, apparently, the ψυχή of a dead snake is ἀμαυρωθεῖσα when it descends into the earth (fr. 204. 140–2 M–W; see Epilogue, pp. 291–2), and Sappho describes a dead person as flitting about in Hades among the dead, πεδ᾽ ἀμαύρων νεκύων (fr. 55. 4 L–P: see n. 90 below). Although it has been customary to translate ἀμαυρός as 'blind', 'dark', or similar (see e.g. LSJ s.v.), McKinlay (1957) shows exhaustively that in later and less ambiguous passages the reference is to weakness rather than darkness; in the absence of better evidence, this makes good sense in the Homeric and Hesiodic passages also. Note also that Simonides says that neither decay, εὐρώς, nor time will weaken, ἀμαυρώσει, the renown of the heroes of Thermopylae (fr. 531. 4–5 P). The association with εὐρώς recalls the Homeric Hades (see above, n. 71).

[84] See Stanford ad loc. Note also that in Nausicaa's dream Athena enters the chamber like a breath of wind, ἀνέμου ὡς πνοιή (vi. 20).

lack of substance of an empty image, or the thin enfeeblement
of the man whose substance has been worn away to nothing: as
such it suggests how a single broad conception can be borne out
along two such different strands of imagery.

The identity of the shade is indeterminate

The three identities yield place to each other in consistent ways
in the course of Achilles' encounter with Patroclus' ghost and
in many of the individual meetings that make up the Nekuia.
The pattern is simple: the dead man appears as a wafting ψυχή,
then stands still and converses in the fully convincing shape of
the man who lived, and finally as it drifts away again its
emptiness is seen again. For example, when Patroclus' ghost
first appears to Achilles we are told that it is not the man proper
but something that resembles him:

> ἦλθε δ' ἐπὶ ψυχὴ Πατροκλῆος δειλοῖο,
> πάντ' αὐτῶι μέγεθός τε καὶ ὄμματα κάλ' ἐϊκυῖα
> καὶ φωνήν, καὶ τοῖα περὶ χροῒ εἵματα ἕστο.   (XXIII. 65–7)

Patroclus himself lies dead nearby and the image mimics his
shape, 'resembling the man himself in everything'. But as the
scene proceeds the distinction becomes less clear, and the
wraith uses the first-personal pronoun both of itself and of
the dead Patroclus proper:

> καί μοι δὸς τὴν χεῖρ', ὀλοφύρομαι· οὐ γὰρ ἔτ' αὖτις
> νίσομαι ἐξ Ἀΐδαο, ἐπήν με πυρὸς λελάχητε.   (75–6)

Logically the antecedent of μοι and the subject of νίσομαι is
Patroclus manifested as the ghost, but the antecedent of με is
Patroclus the corpse. Achilles addresses the wraith as if it
were Patroclus himself, ἠθείη κεφαλή (94); and it is only when
he fails to embrace it and it disappears off to Hades that we
return to the image of the flitting and gibbering wraith:

> ψυχὴ δὲ κατὰ χθονὸς ἠΰτε καπνὸς
> ὤιχετο τετριγυῖα.   (100–1)

In other words, it is when the wraith moves that it is most
clearly identified as empty and strengthless; but when we are
drawn into the scene in which it talks and acts, the gap closes

over between the real Patroclus and the wraith that mimics his appearance.

Similarly, from the first part of the Nekuia we have already seen that hosts of the dead emerge as flitting ψυχαί but are seen as solid substantial beings when they stand still. Elpenor presents a still closer parallel with the Patroclus episode. First the ghost comes forward, πρώτη δὲ ψυχὴ Ἐλπήνορος ἦλθεν ἑταίρου (xi. 51), and is explicitly distinguished from his corpse, which Odysseus remembers having left unburied on Aeaea: σῶμα γὰρ ἐν Κίρκης μεγάρωι κατελείπομεν ἡμεῖς (xi. 53). The image then shifts to the man himself,

> τὸν μὲν ἐγὼ δάκρυσα ἰδὼν ἐλέησά τε θυμῶι,
> καί μιν φωνήσας ἔπεα πτερόεντα προσηύδων,
> "Ἐλπῆνορ, πῶς ἦλθες ὑπὸ ζόφον ἠερόεντα;" (xi. 55–7)

Odysseus describes him, speaks to him, and is addressed by him as one human being to another; but at the close of the scene it is again specified that this is an empty image, εἴδωλον:

> νῶϊ μὲν ὣς ἐπέεσσιν ἀμειβομένω στυγεροῖσιν
> ἥμεθ', ἐγὼ μὲν ἄνευθεν ἐφ' αἵματι φάσγανον ἴσχων,
> εἴδωλον δ' ἑτέρωθεν ἑταίρου πόλλ' ἀγόρευεν. (81–3)

In other words, when the wraith moves forward its flitting motion reveals its emptiness; as the scene develops its contours settle down so that it is undistinguished from the living man; as the scene closes its emptiness is revealed again.

The structural parallel between these scenes and the visit of Patroclus' wraith to Achilles lies in the fact that in both cases the dead must emerge from Hades to confront the living man. At this stage of the Nekuia Odysseus is outside Hades and close by its entrance, χριμφθεὶς πέλας (x. 516) and surrounded by the gloom of the death-world: when he summons the dead out of its darkness, ὑπὲξ ἐρέβευς (xi. 37), they either flit out from the doors or rise up, perhaps via the trench itself, from the world below the soil. (Neither here nor at the corresponding point in Circe's instructions (x. 526–9) is this made fully clear: ἔρεβος means simply darkness,[85] and perhaps the narrative reads

---

[85] Despite the conventional capital letter of the printed texts, there is good evidence for taking ἔρεβος not as a proper name but as an ordinary word for darkness in general and the darkness of death in particular. When Circe

vaguely because little but darkness is visible to the hero himself.) Just as Patroclus' wraith moved between the mortal world and Hades with the drifting movement of smoke, ἠΰτε καπνὸς | ὤιχετο (XXIII. 100–1), so the wraiths of this scene are flitting out to meet Odysseus and drifting back when at the end of each interview. Hence it is natural that they show the same progression, with the initial image of the flitting ψυχή giving way to the concrete image of the dead man proper in the course of the encounter, only to be replaced by the ψυχή as the interview ends and the dead one withdraws. The tendency is that when the shade is imagined in sharp detail it takes on a more concrete identity and is no longer distinguished from the dead man whose form a ψυχή or εἴδωλον represents.

The fullest commentary on this shifting identity is in Odysseus' meeting with the shade of his mother. When he tries to embrace her but finds that there is nothing to touch, the shade flits away from him:

> τρὶς μὲν ἐφωρμήθην, ἑλέειν τέ με θυμὸς ἀνώγει,
> τρὶς δέ μοι ἐκ χειρῶν σκιῆι εἴκελον ἢ καὶ ὀνείρωι
> ἔπτατ᾿· ἐμοὶ δ᾿ ἄχος ὀξὺ γενέσκετο κηρόθι μᾶλλον.   (xi. 206–8)

In his grief and confusion he asks why she she does not stay still, τί νύ μ᾿ οὐ μίμνεις; (210), and he wonders if Penelope has sent a false phantom instead of his mother:[86]

describes Scylla's cave as πρὸς ζόφον εἰς ἔρεβος τετραμμένον (xii. 81) she seems only to mean that it is directed at darkness and gloom, not that it is an entrance to Hades. No one place called Erebus is part of the layout of the landscape of Hades and environs visible to Odysseus in the Nekuia, and throughout Homer ἔρεβος seems to be equivalent to ζόφος as the place of darkness to which the dead descend when they go to Hades (see VIII. 368, IX. 571–2, XVI. 326–7; xx. 356). Note also the cognate adjective ἐρεβεννός, as an epithet of the night of the world (VIII. 488, etc.), the night that falls on the eyes when one loses consciousness (v. 659, etc.), and fog, ἀήρ (v. 864).

[86] The words ἦ τί μοι εἴδωλον τόδ᾿ . . . are hard to construe, but the sense seems to be that for the first time Odysseus is addressing the possibility that this is not his mother at all but a spectre: 'Mother, why do you not wait . . .? And indeed (ἦ) [if you are not my mother after all] why has Persephone sent this spectre to me . . .?' This is more effective than the alternative, 'Mother, why do you not wait . . .? Why else has Persephone sent this [your] spectre to me, [if it is only] in order to grieve me more?' In support of the former interpretation, compare other examples of ἦ introducing a question suggesting an alternative possibility, e.g. iii. 251, x. 284, xi. 160.

ἦ τί μοι εἴδωλον τόδ᾽ ἀγαυὴ Περσεφόνεια
ὄτρυν᾽, ὄφρ᾽ ἔτι μᾶλλον ὀδυρόμενος στεναχίζω;   (213–14)

Anticleia reassures him by explaining the truth about what confronts him in Hades:

οὔ τί σε Περσεφόνεια, Διὸς θυγάτηρ, ἀπαφίσκει,
ἀλλ᾽ αὕτη δίκη ἐστὶ βροτῶν, ὅτε τίς κε θάνηισιν·
οὐ γὰρ ἔτι σάρκας τε καὶ ὀστέα ἶνες ἔχουσιν,
ἀλλὰ τὰ μέν τε πυρὸς κρατερὸν μένος αἰθομένοιο
δαμνᾶι, ἐπεί κε πρῶτα λίπηι λεύκ᾽ ὀστέα θυμός,
ψυχὴ δ᾽ ἠΰτ᾽ ὄνειρος ἀποπταμένη πεπότηται.   (217–22)

This speech is difficult and repays examination. In the past it has been taken as a doctrinal summary which 'neatly summarizes the main points of Homeric belief concerning the ψυχή'.[87] On this reading Anticleia says that after death two things happen: on the one hand (μέν) the body is dissolved by the fire of cremation and on the other hand (δέ) the ψυχή flies away to Hades. Here is what I take to be the assumed translation:

Persephone, Zeus' daughter, is not deceiving you: rather, this [i.e. the following] is the way of mortals when somebody dies: the sinews no longer hold flesh and bones together, but the dominating force of blazing fire overcomes them, as soon as the θυμός leaves the white bones; but the ψυχή, slipping away like a dream, floats away [to Hades].

If this were right it would fly in the face of much of the argument in this book. First, cremation would be emphasized in a wholly uncharacteristic way: elsewhere in Homer the burning of the body is relevant only as the pivotal moment of the γέρας θανόντων, the social acknowledgement of the dead man's status, and where the ψυχή is said to escape from the dying man it does so as his last breath. Secondly, an unparalleled distinction would be set up between loss of θυμός and of ψυχή, with the θυμός leaving the bones and the ψυχή going to Hades. We have shown that at the moment of death θυμός is not sharply distinguished from ψυχή, the two names being applied to the loss of the last breath under different aspects: if so, a sudden contrast between the two would not make sense. Both

---

[87] Heubeck at xi. 217–22. For the same view see most recently Sourvinou-Inwood (1995), 59.

these objections depend on controversial arguments advanced earlier in this book, and if we depended on them alone we would be begging our own questions. The decisive pointer to an accurate reading of the lines is in two grammatical points, the force of γάρ (219) and more importantly the perfect πεπότηται (222). If Anticleia is expounding a sequence of mortals' death, cremation, and journey to Hades, the switch from present to perfect can only be explained as a very loose use of language by Homer;[88] but if we assign a perfect *meaning* to πεπότηται the speech takes on a very different aspect as a simple and direct answer to Odysseus' questions, 'Why do you not stay still to receive my embrace?' and 'Is this a false spectre?' Let me offer a revised translation:

Persephone, Zeus' daughter is not deceiving you: rather, this [i.e. what you have found by trying to embrace me] is the way of mortals when somebody dies, *since (γάρ) the sinews no longer hold flesh and bones together, but the strong force of blazing fire overcomes them as soon as the breath leaves the white bones*—the wraith, slipping away like a dream, is in a state of floating [away from you].

The burden of the whole is in the last words: strengthlessness is the state of the dead in Hades, so the ghost in front of him has been unable to make contact with his embrace. Anticleia speaks in the third person about her own shade, just as Elpenor did in the earlier passage (xi. 65); and she uses the perfect because she is describing the phantom's continued empty drifting movement when Odysseus confronts it after it has slipped away from his grasp, ἐκ χειρῶν σκιῆι εἴκελον ἢ καὶ ὀνείρωι | ἔπτατο (xi. 207–8). The γάρ shows that the sequence of ideas is digressive, in 'spiral composition',[89] moving away from the main point about the emptiness of the wraith and

---

[88] The Homeric perfect is a strictly marked form of the verb indicating a resultant state (see Ruijgh (1971), §215, 217), so that in the present passage the sequence ἐστί, ὅτε ... θάνηισιν, δαμνᾶι, ἐπεί κε λίπηι, πεπότηται would not make grammatical sense as a single sequence of events. (The use of a perfect form in place of an aorist, notably βεβήκει for ἔβη, is a rare irregularity which does not reflect on the semantics of the perfect in general.) On the Homeric semantics of the perfect middle see Wackernagel (1926), 166–71; Sihler (1995), §519. Also helpful is the acute treatment of Duhoux (1992: 406–14) on the equivalent issues in the Classical language.

[89] See Thalmann (1984), esp. ch. 1.

returning to it at the end. Far from expounding a doctrine of death, cremation, and journey to Hades, Anticleia is reassuring Odysseus that this is not a spectre sent to mock him but an example of the shadowy feebleness of all the shades.[90] It is because of this explanation that Odysseus understands what is happening a little later when the shade of Agamemnon stretches out its floating hands, πιτνὰς εἰς ἐμὲ χεῖρας,[91] but cannot touch him because it lacks the sinewy strength, ἴς and κῖκυς, that Agamemnon had in life.

The shade is an image of the undivided bodily man

This interaction of the three aspects of the survivor in Hades shows that whether he is a corpse or an image or a feeble remnant, his shape and identity are those of the bodily man who was sent down to the earth at death. This brings us back to the subtleties of the word ψυχή. When we studied Homeric death we saw that this name was given to the last breath of the dying man, which is lost and dissipated in the air; and we observed the special situations in which that breath takes wing and flies away into the unseen and to Hades. It will now be clear that the dying breath under that name should not simply be identified with the wraith in Hades: what unites the two is their flitting strengthless motion and nothing else, and the shade and the last breath relate to the substance of the dead man in distinct and unconnected ways. When the last breath is

[90] Sappho uses a compound form of this verb in a very similar sense when she tells a woman that after death she will linger in Hades, forgotten by the living: ἀλλ' ἀφάνης κἀν Ἀίδαι δόμωι | φοιτάσῃς πεδ' ἀμαύρων νεκύων ἐκπεποταμένα (fr. 55. 3–4 L–P). The context makes it clear that the woman herself is the subject of the sentence, so that the participle refers not to the departure of her ψυχή at death but to her movement as a shade *during* the afterlife. Thus Sappho is depicting the shade as an enfeebled version of the bodily being, flitting back and forth strengthlessly—when compared with the Nekuia, this articulation is midway between Homer's depictions of the shades of Anticleia and Agamemnon. (Page's rendering of ἐκπεποταμένα as 'flown from our midst' (1956: 137) is an over-translation justified neither by the context nor by the Homeric exemplar.)

[91] It is noteworthy that the verbs rendering the movement of the shade— ἔπτατο (xi. 208), ἀποπταμένη πεπότηται (xi. 222), πιτνάς (xi. 392) all embody grades of the same root *pet-. As so often, it is impossible to tell whether this link is semantically significant.

lost by the dying man, his identity remains in the substance of the corpse: thus when Patroclus or Hector dies, the flying ψυχή leaves behind manhood and youth, ἀνδροτῆτα καὶ ἥβην (XVI. 857 = XXII. 363),[92] and the ψυχαί of the proem to the *Iliad* are separated from the men themselves, αὐτοί (I. 6). But in the afterlife the shade as ψυχή relates to the dead man in a very different way, since the word refers to the wafting strengthless movement of a remnant or image in the imagined landscape of Hades. Since it is not a constituent part of the living man or of the man who died, it makes nonsense to work through the familiar categories of our own culture and picture the wraith as the spirit of man rather than his body: here as elsewhere Homer forbids us to invoke that dichotomy and forces us to understand the wraith in terms of the undivided thinking and bodily whole of the dead man.

This is well illustrated by Homer's rendering of the idea that the shades are *intellectually* weak and witless. The matter is elusive and disappears in the course of the Nekuia (see above, p. 193), but it has been mentioned beforehand by Circe in explaining that Tiresias is the only one of the dead whose wits remain to him:

> . . . μάντιος ἀλαοῦ, τοῦ τε φρένες ἔμπεδοί εἰσι·
> τῶι καὶ τεθνηῶτι νόον πόρε Περσεφόνεια
> οἴωι πεπνῦσθαι· τοὶ δὲ σκιαὶ ἀΐσσουσιν.   (X. 493–5)

Tiresias' ability to breathe in his thought, νόον . . . πεπνῦσθαι (see Ch. 4, pp. 84–6), just as a living man might do, is contrasted with the fact that the other wraiths lack substance and flit about as shadows. The fact that this opposition makes sense is enough to show that the wraiths' mental feebleness is bound up with the feebleness of their bodily movement.

The opposite side of the same coin turns up when Achilles is visited by the ghost of Patroclus. Here he reaches out to touch his friend and finds that the wraith is empty nothingness: but when he awakes and describes the experience he says that the

---

[92] It is hard to decide whether this refers to their identity as men or to their manly vitality. The latter may be better, as ἀνδροτῆτα καὶ ἥβην will then make up a single concept, as is usual with such pairs of nouns. In its other attestation, ἀνδροτής acts in the same way as part of a doublet: Πατρόκλου . . . ἀνδροτῆτά τε καὶ μένος ἠΰ (XXIV. 6). See also Ch. 5 n. 39, and above, p. 158.

wraith lacks the organs of the mental apparatus, φρένες οὐκ ἔνι
πάμπαν (XXIII. 104). This cannot simply mean that it was
without wits and intelligence, since what it told him was fully
cogent; rather, Achilles must mean that the wraith lacked the
concrete substance that a living and thinking man carries in his
breast, since only this will explain what happened when he
tried to embrace his friend (see also above, Ch. 4, pp. 74–5 with
n. 30). But his use of the word φρένες suggests that the
vocabulary of physical weakness and mental weakness are
bound up together, so that the one is expressed in words that
would be equally appropriate to the other. Taking these two
passages together, it emerges that the feebleness of the dead is
indeterminately physical and mental, and applies by the same
token to thought and bodily life. In so far as the inhabitant of
Hades is no longer identified directly with the bodily substance
of the dead man, he is a vestige or image of the flesh and blood
who went down into the world beyond the grave; and in this
sense, he continues in the afterlife to take both his appearance
and his identity from the indissoluble bodily whole which he
was in life. In every stage of this movement between different
states of life and different poetic environments, Homeric man
preserves the unity of what our modern languages encourage us
to divide into body and soul.

These articulations are irreconcilable: the question is a problem

Corpse, εἴδωλον, ψυχή: is it possible to fit these three identities
into a single simple conception of the afterlife? One avenue of
escape would be to take Homer's Hades as an artificial
amalgam made up by combining formulae framed in different
periods under different conceptions of life after death, in much
the same way that (for example) the names of weapons or the
description of manœuvres in battle might be shown to be culled
from different epochs of warfare and perhaps not fully understood by the poet.[93] In particular, the pattern that we have
observed in the meetings of the Nekuia and the episode of
Patroclus' ghost can be explained away in terms of the

[93] An approach of this kind is taken in the carefully constructed study of
Homeric death by Christiane Sourvinou-Inwood (see Ch. 1 n. 64).

mechanics of formulaic composition: the formulae for the
invocation and withdrawal of the dead specify ψυχαί, while
the encounters themselves revert to formulae framed for a
meeting between two living men. However, to do this would
be to ignore the subtlety with which the two concepts are
merged in Homeric practice. Since the image slides from νέκυς/
νεκρός to ψυχή and back again between individual words and
formulae, no dividing line can be set: so that we can expect the
combined strands of imagery to make up a coherent whole in a
way that we would not expect (for example) from a table of
Homeric weapons extrapolated from different contexts by a
modern scholar. This means that nothing would be gained by
trying to isolate the Hades of the νέκυς/νεκρός and the Hades of
the ψυχή as two separable elements in an amalgam of heterogeneous fossil formulae. For the mythology of Hades as for the
language of the corpse and the funeral, the ambivalence itself
must provide the key to understanding what the afterlife
means.[94]

Vitally, the problem of reconciling the concepts is as real
for Homer's characters as it is for us. When the ghost comes
to Achilles he is confused by its resemblance to the real
Patroclus and addresses it as if it were the man himself,
ἠθείη κεφαλή (XXIII. 94), but after they talk the illusion
breaks down when Achilles reaches out and finds that there
is nothing to touch:

> ὣς ἄρα φωνήσας ὠρέξατο χερσὶ φίλῃσιν,
> οὐδ' ἔλαβε· ψυχὴ δὲ κατὰ χθονὸς ἠΰτε καπνὸς
> ᾤχετο τετριγυῖα· ταφὼν δ' ἀνόρουσεν Ἀχιλλεὺς
> χερσί τε συμπλατάγησεν, ἔπος τ' ὀλοφυδνὸν ἔειπεν . . .

> (XXIII. 99–102)

It is when he tries to throw his arms around his friend that he
confronts the wraith's emptiness, and he cries out about the
experience to those who lie around him on the beach:

---

[94] Cf. for example Vermeule (1979: ch. 1 *passim* and 42) for the assumption
that it was a 'natural confusion' of the early Greeks' true eschatological beliefs
when they identified the dead man in the Underworld with the dead man who
had been buried. I do not know what the word 'confusion' means here.

"ὦ πόποι, ἦ ῥά τίς ἐστι καὶ εἰν Ἀΐδαο δόμοισι
ψυχὴ καὶ εἴδωλον, ἀτὰρ φρένες οὐκ ἔνι πάμπαν·
παννυχίη γάρ μοι Πατροκλῆος δειλοῖο
ψυχὴ ἐφεστήκει γοόωσά τε μυρομένη τε,
καί μοι ἕκαστ᾽ ἐπέτελλεν, ἔϊκτο δὲ θέσκελον αὐτῶι."   (103–7)

When ὦ πόποι begins a speech the speaker is very often reacting to something newly noticed or newly understood.[95] Achilles is amazed because what he encountered was not Patroclus but something identical in appearance: it is new and confusing to him to find that what lives in Hades is a wraith and an empty image[96] without the φρένες that give bodily and mental substance to a living man.[97] As he tries to find words for something obscure and difficult, he expresses a single concept by coordinating two nouns of allied but distinct meaning. Achilles has tried to reach out to touch the loved one and has been confused and dismayed to find that he has been with a mere spectre: previously, then, he had not fully grasped what the

[95] Examples from the *Iliad* of ὦ πόποι in a reaction to something newly noticed or understood: II. 272, 337, VIII. 352, XIII. 99 = XV. 286 = XX. 344 = XXI. 54, XVII. 171, 629, XX. 293, XXII. 168, 297, 373. The exclamation seems also to stand for dismay (e.g. I. 254 = VII. 124), grief (e.g. XVIII. 324), irritation (e.g. II. 157, XXI. 420), and may be heavily ironic (e.g. XVI. 745). Its range in the *Odyssey* is similar.

[96] In XXIII. 103, substantive τι is well attested as a *varia lectio* for adjectival τις. With τις, as in Allen's text, the meaning will be, 'There is some ψυχή and εἴδωλον [sc. replacing the substance of man] even in Hades, but it lacks φρένες'. With τι, two meanings are possible: either (*a*) with τι as the predicate of the sentence, 'The ψυχή and εἴδωλον is something [sc. that has existence] even in Hades, but it lacks φρένες', or (*b*) with ψυχὴ καὶ εἴδωλον as epexegetic of τι, 'There is something in Hades, a ψυχή and εἴδωλον, but it lacks φρένες'. There is hardly any difference of meaning between the version with τις and version (*b*) with τι, and for our argument here there is no need to choose between them. Version (*a*) with τι does not commend itself, because the καί—'even in Hades'—seems to imply that a ψυχὴ καὶ εἴδωλον also exists in living men, which is not Homeric. Richardson ad loc. prefers τι on the grounds that τις 'goes rather awkwardly with ψυχὴ καὶ εἴδωλον'.

[97] Much has been written on φρένες in 104 (see Richardson ad loc., with discussion of scholia and refs. to modern treatments; and cf. Schnaufer (1970), 73–9), since the wraith's lack of physical substance ought not to lead Achilles to think it has no mind or wits. Following the argument that in mental life φρένες are identified with the lungs and the breast in general (Ch. 4, *passim*, esp. p. 74) it is easy to understand Achilles as saying that there was no substance to the breast which he had reached out to embrace.

shades of the dead actually are.[98] The episode confronts him for
the first time with the nature of survival in the afterlife. That
meaning is difficult, obscure, almost inexpressible: from which
it follows *a fortiori* that the particular definition of the shade
which is revealed to him there should not be be assumed in
advance whenever Homer's characters—or, by the same token,
the poet himself—talk of the world beyond the grave.

Similarly, when Anticleia explains the nature of the shade to
Odysseus she speaks as if she were revealing something new,
something which Odysseus had not known or had not understood. The nearest verbal parallel to the introductory part of
that passage (xi. 217–19) is in *Odyssey* xix, where the unseen
Athena holds a lamp over Odysseus and Telemachus, and the
son is amazed to find that the hall has become preternaturally
bright. He suspects that some god must be present, but his
father silences him:

> σίγα καὶ κατὰ σὸν νόον ἴσχανε μηδ᾽ ἐρέεινε·
> αὕτη τοι δίκη ἐστὶ θεῶν, οἳ Ὄλυμπον ἔχουσιν.   (xix. 42–3)

The δίκη θεῶν here is something strange and hidden which the
stripling does not understand.[99] Anticleia's δίκη βροτῶν, it
seems, is still more esoteric: she is revealing something which

---

[98] This has been noticed before, but with different priorities in mind: first
by Wilamowitz (1931), 371. Claus (1981: 98) remarks on Achilles' speech after
his dream that 'What is remarkable about these lines is not that they explain
the particular nature of the shade but that they show a *need* to explain and
define'. Dodds (1951) sees both passages in terms of growing Hellenic
rationalism, and takes them as a novel doctrine relayed by the epic poets,
distinguishing the strengthless eschatological survivor from the corpse and
thus countering the primitive fear of the dead: 'To have formulated that
distinction with precision and clarity and to have disentangled the ghost from
the corpse is, of course, the achievement of the Homeric poets. There are
passages in the poems [sc. xxiii. 103–7; xi. 216–24] which suggest that they
were proud of the achievement and fully conscious of its novelty and
importance. They had, indeed, a right to be proud: for there is no domain
where clear thinking encounters stronger resistance than when we think about
death' (136–7).

[99] Of course this point should not be pressed too far. δίκη with the genitive
is used several times of customs and usages which are not at all mysterious, the
normal behaviour of a particular social group (iv. 691, xiv. 59–60, xviii. 275).
However, it is only in the two passages quoted here that one character explains
such a thing to another who is ignorant of it.

even πολύμητις Ὀδυσσεύς has been unable to grasp: and she tells
him to explain it to his wife:

> ἀλλὰ φόωσδε τάχιστα λιλαίεο· ταῦτα δὲ πάντα
> ἴσθ᾽, ἵνα καὶ μετόπισθε τεῆι εἴπησθα γυναικί.   (xi. 223–4)

Something novel and esoteric has been revealed, something
which will advance Odysseus' understanding of death beyond
what ordinary mortals know.[100]

Patterns of the relation between shade and corpse

This sense of darkness and confusion provides the cornerstone
of our final interpretation. The survivor of death is in some
sense a corpse and in some sense a flitting wraith, but the
relation between those articulations is not clearly determined.
The indeterminacy is part and parcel of the ambiguity that
surrounds the nature of death itself: what lies beyond the
darkness is in some sense the grave and in some sense the
house of Hades, and narrative and image-making about death
normally proceed as if the two were collapsed into each other.

This marriage is expressed most fully in Achilles' interview
with the ghost of Patroclus. Before the dream Achilles has
embraced the dead Patroclus in the form of the corpse, but has
addressed him as if he is already in Hades (XXIII. 17–19), and
the wraith is able to appear although the man himself, the αὐτός
whom it resembles, is lying dead near by—so that after its
disappearance Achilles and his companions spend the night
gathered around the dead Patroclus himself, ἀμφὶ νέκυν ἐλεεινόν
(XXIII. 110). When the wraith instructs Achilles to carry out the
funeral the two manifestations of the dead man merge into each
other:

> θάπτε με ὅττι τάχιστα, πύλας Ἀΐδαο περήσω.   (XXIII. 71)

The two half-line membra juxtapose two renderings of a single
event: in the world of mortals he will be given his burial, so that
by the same token he will pass into the mythological Hades,

---

[100] πάντα here must refer specifically to the nature of the wraith, as it is the
only thing she has told him which Penelope would not already know. Lines
xi. 223–4 are used by Page (1955: 46–7) in support of his theory that in the
original *Odyssey* the Nekuia was a story told by Odysseus to Penelope.

πύλας Ἀΐδαο περήσω.[101] The logic of the command implies that the entry of the corpse into the earth and the entry of the dead man into Hades are two parallel ways of looking at the same process of going down into the earth and staying in the nether world. By receiving his funeral Patroclus will be able to enter Hades proper: in other words he will be decisively separated from the society of the living and integrated into that of the dead. The correspondence becomes more subtle when the wraith says that the other shades of the dead are refusing to let him join them because he has not been duly honoured with the γέρας θανόντων:

> τῆλέ με εἴργουσι ψυχαί, εἴδωλα καμόντων,
> οὐδέ μέ πω μίσγεσθαι ὑπὲρ ποταμοῖο ἐῶσιν,
> ἀλλ' αὔτως ἀλάλημαι ἀν' εὐρυπυλὲς Ἀΐδος δῶ.   (XXIII. 72–4)

He has not been properly committed to the earth in his bodily form, so he cannot integrate among the shades of the dead: in other words, his plight on the plane of the mythological Underworld is the reflex of what has happened, or failed to happen, in the world visible to the living. The topographical details here are precise: he is now wandering along by the broad entrance, ἀν' εὐρυπυλὲς Ἀΐδος δῶ;[102] in burial he will pass through the doors of the tomb and the gates of Hades, and after doing so he will cross the river into the heart of Hades and stay there.[103] There is a direct correspondence between what will happen on the two planes, and the distinction between them is not between events but between avenues of expression, the

[101] For the image cf. esp. v. 646, where the hero boasts that his foe will be killed, ὑπ' ἐμοὶ δμηθέντα πύλας Ἀΐδαο περήσειν.

[102] In his note on this line, Richardson mentions an 'apparent inconsistency' between this line and XXIII. 71, where Patroclus implies that he has not yet passed through the gates. There is no inconsistency if we take ἀνά with accusative as referring to motion *along the edge of* Hades: the wraith will then be hovering up and down the entrance by broad gates, ἀν' εὐρυπυλὲς . . . δῶ. This sense of ἀνά is paralleled (for example) in the Epipolesis, when Agamemnon strides up and down by the line of warriors, ἀνὰ οὐλαμὸν ἀνδρῶν (IV. 251).

[103] It seems that these details of gates and rivers are fixed in Homer's traditional death-lore, and they correspond closely enough to the more detailed layout set forth in the *Odyssey* (see esp. x. 508–15; the Nekuia itself is less clear) and in Hesiod's *Theogony* (see esp. 736–45, 807–10).

mythical and the non-mythical, which the are set alongside each other in the scene of a wraith's visit to the world of the living. In terms of the everyday world of visible experience, Patroclus is the corpse that is to be buried; in terms of the unseen mythological world, he belongs beyond the darkness in Hades. In this way, the logic of Patroclus' situation and his pleas illustrates that what lies beyond death is *simultaneously* the grave and the mythical Hades. These twin patterns of language and imagery take shape in the rendering of a single process of burial and entry into the afterlife throughout which the 'I' of the dead man is tied to the substance of his body.

Although here a single narrative manages to juxtapose the two articulations of the journey, it is clear that a gulf still yawns between them. In particular, as we have seen, there is no single or satisfactory explanation of how the dead man as a corpse relates to the dead man as a wraith or image. That problem is posed but not answered by the few images which portray the dead man already reduced to a shade when he makes the journey of death: for example when Theoclymenus with a prophet's foresight sees the phantoms of the doomed suitors descending into the darkness:

εἰδώλων δὲ πλέον πρόθυρον, πλείη δὲ καὶ αὐλή,
ἱεμένων ἔρεβόσδε ὑπὸ ζόφον. (xx. 355–6)

He sees the bodily suitors already translated to the false images that will represent their bodily shape in the hereafter. The sudden mythical vision fits the heightened perception granted to seers: but he says nothing to explain how the one manifestation of their identity will translate into the other, and the two patterns of story-telling and image-making remain distinct and unreconciled. There is the same violent juxtaposition in the post-Homeric Second Nekuia, where the scene in Odysseus' hall abruptly switches to the unseen journey of the suitors' wraiths down to Hades, guided by Hermes and squeaking like bats:

Ἑρμῆς δὲ ψυχὰς Κυλλήνιος ἐξεκαλεῖτο
ἀνδρῶν μνηστήρων· ἔχε δὲ ῥάβδον μετὰ χερσὶ
καλὴν χρυσείην, τῆι τ᾽ ἀνδρῶν ὄμματα θέλγει
ὧν ἐθέλει, τοὺς δ᾽ αὖτε καὶ ὑπνώοντας ἐγείρει·
τῆι ῥ᾽ ἄγε κινήσας, ταὶ δὲ τρίζουσαι ἕποντο. (xxiv. 1–5)

Whoever shaped this passage, it poses the problem of afterlife beliefs in the most vivid possible way. Hermes as divine guide translates the suitors and the narrative itself into the unseen world of myth, but without explaining how their identity in that world relates to their identity in the world in which they had lived and died.

Here lies the creative importance of the image of the flying ψυχή articulated in the deaths of Patroclus and Hector. The pivot on which the image turns is the word ψυχή itself. In very different senses, ψυχή is the *vox propria* both for the wraith in the Hades and for the last gasp of the dying man; by identifying the ψυχή simultaneously as both, these lines purport to explain how the dead man of flesh and blood crosses the gulf to become a wraith in the Hades of myth. In this way, the flying ψυχή becomes a vehicle for co-ordinating two departments of the Homeric world-view. By separating the dead man into two things, a lifeless corpse and an immortal wraith, these images bring to birth a scheme of human identity which seems (with hindsight) to be little less than a dichotomy of body and soul. If our overall analysis of the language and lore of death has been correct, then this concept is anything but typical, and it must be seen as a product rather than a corner-stone of the Homeric view of man. Here lies our final difficulty. If the flight of the ψυχή does not constitute Homeric belief *qua* belief, it is nevertheless deeply serious and cannot be called poetic fantasy. How, then, are we to make sense of it, and how are we to incorporate it into our overall analysis of the Homeric view of man? That question cannot be answered by sweeping statements about 'the primitive mind' or 'parataxis' or 'polyvalency' or 'tolerance of contradiction' or 'asyndetic multiplicity'.[104] All these are merely labels for our own inability to fully understand the Homeric realities in terms of their own structure and their own logic. If we are right in identifying several different Homeric answers to the question 'What happens to a man at death?', and if we are right in privileging the simple one which

---

[104] This line of argument goes back to the speculations of Lévy-Bruhl (see Perry (1937); Notopoulos (1949)) and continues to rear its head in classical scholarship: see especially the measured discussion of C. J. Rowe (1983). The phrase 'asyndetic multiplicity' I owe to H. J. Versnel (paper as yet unpublished).

sends the corpse to Hades over the complex one which translates the dying breath into the wraith in the afterlife, then we ought to be able to show that this multiplicity is structured in a meaningful way. In other words, we must show that it constitutes a system which is ordered and not chaotic. To do this we will take a backward step and observe other systems of mythical image-making which inform Homer's rendering of death.

APPENDIX

1. *The unity of the Nekuia*

The Nekuia succumbs readily to interpretations in the Analyst tradition, based on the belief that Book xi as we have it represents an Homeric original which has been added to and meddled with so as to form an artificial and confused whole. If that is the case the non-Homeric part of the book ought to be left out of account in a study of the present kind. In this chapter I have treated the Nekuia as an integrated unity, and this must now be defended.

Analyst dissection of the Nekuia has been justified in three ways. The successive episodes seem awkwardly joined and can easily be cut up into separate units. Although this carries little weight on its own, it chimes with two deeper problems. First, in the course of Odysseus' account there is a change of perspective: at the beginning he seems to be standing outside the gates of Hades and calling up the shades from within, but later on he is moving around inside in the landscape where they live out the afterlife. Since we begin with an account of conjuration of spirits (*nekuomanteion*) but end up with a journey through the Underworld (*katabasis*) it easy to attribute the first part to Homer and the second to someone else. Secondly, there is a major inconsistency as to the nature of the afterlife. Circe has told Odysseus that Tiresias is the only one of the dead whose power of thought remains intact (x. 493–5), and the shades of Anticleia and Agamemnon are unable to speak to him or even recognize him until they have drunk the blood which he has offered in the sacrifice at the beginning of the *nekuomanteion* (see Tiresias at xi. 146–9, with 153–4, 390); but from what Homer tells us it seems that Elpenor and the dead of the later episodes do not need to drink the blood before they can think and talk as living men would do.

Once the Nekuia is resolved into *nekuomanteion* and *katabasis* it is easy to posit a separate origin for each of the two parts. Odysseus' tour of Hades can be explained as modelled on the *katabasis* of Heracles, which is referred to several times in the *Iliad* (VIII. 367–9; also, more ambiguously, V. 395–404, with XI. 690–3) and might have been the subject of a pre-Homeric epic poem. Because the scene in which Patroclus' ghost visits Achilles (XXIII. 65–107) follows a similar pattern of events and imagery to the individual meetings in the *nekuomanteion*, it is easy to guess that both draw on a traditional narrative type in which the dead emerge from Hades to confront the living. In particular, the Patroclus episode has so much in common with the Mesopotamian story of the visit of Enkidu's ghost to Gilgamesh[1] that it is tempting to suppose that the two belong to a widely spread story-type of this kind. It is possible that the consultation of Tiresias owes something to the lore of oracles of the dead,[2] whether practised in Greece or known from abroad, and the burgeoning hero-cults of the eighth century may well have involved ritual conjurations from the Underworld.[3] It makes sense

[1] See *The Epic of Gilgamesh*, Tablet xii, in Dalley (1991), with (e.g.) Germain (1954), 329–70; Kirk (1970), 108; (1974), 260; Burkert (1992), 65–73.

[2] See Huxley (1958), arguing that the imagery of the *nekuomanteion* was originally associated with the Thesprotian oracle of the dead; on the Thesprotian connection, compare Merkelbach (1951), 220–30; and on the general question of the influence of the lore of oracles of the dead on the shaping of the Nekuia, see esp. Germain (1954), 371–81; Crane (1988), 93–6. Page (1955: 24–5), argues on internal grounds that the consultation of Tiresias was originally set in an oracle of the dead. In Greece, attestations of such oracles are mostly late; the earliest are Herodotus' story (5. 92η) of Periander of Corinth using the Thesprotian oracle to consult the shade of his wife Melissa, and the episode in Aeschylus' *Persae* (598–852) in which Atossa calls up the ghost of Darius. There can be no direct evidence that such lore is on Homer's horizon; for eastern exemplars see Loretz (1993).

[3] On the question of the antiquity of hero-cult see esp. Coldstream (1976) and Snodgrass (1982). Coldstream holds that hero-cult developed mostly after *c*.650 BC, partly in response to the growing popularity of Homeric epic, while Snodgrass regards the developments of epic and of cult as parallel manifestations of the same cultural movement. Midway between them Patzek (1992: 162–77) argues that the Homeric lore of heroic burials draws on contemporary hero-cult of the 8th cent. but also influenced subsequent developments in cultic practice. (See also Seaford (1994), 180–90.) However that may be, there is no evidence that early hero-cult involved invocation of the wraiths of the dead, or that such rituals are reflected in the Nekuia. The drinking of the sacrificial blood by Homer's shades suggests a link with practices in later hero-cult (see e.g. Soph. *OC* 621–3), but that implies nothing about associated beliefs. (Cf. also Pulleyn (1997), 121–2.)

that the dead called up in necromancy should be seen as wispy and insubstantial images, while the dead during a journey into Hades itself are more substantial and more in control of their shadowy existence. This might also explain why the drinking of the sacrificial blood is remembered in some of Odysseus' meetings and forgotten in others, since that offering belongs in the story-pattern of a necromantic ritual rather than a journey inside the land of the dead.

Together, these ambiguities provide the Analyst with much licence, and an endless variety of solutions has been proposed.[4] Most believe that the uncontaminated Homeric *Odyssey* included a visit to Hades to consult Tiresias, while opinions vary as to whether the meetings with Anticleia and Elpenor are fully Homeric.[5] The Catalogue of

---

[4] It has not been possible to respond to the Analysts in full detail here; the most useful surveys have been those by Heubeck in the Oxford *Commentary* and by Lesky (1967), 125–6. On the problems noticed by the scholiasts, many of which coincide with those raised by Analysts, see esp. Petzl (1969), pt.i *passim*. I felt compelled to adopt a basically Unitarian approach after studying the most often cited Analyst treatments, those of Merkelbach (1951) and Page (1955) (see detailed discussion below). For Unitarian defences see esp. Büchner (1937), esp. 104, 119–22; Reinhardt (1948), 52–144; Erbse (1972), 23–33. Erbse builds his argument on the fact that it is strictly unnecessary for Odysseus to consult Tiresias in order to find out about his homecoming, since what the sage tells him about Thrinacia is substantially repeated by Circe later on (xii. 127–41); this encourages the supposition that the consultation of Tiresias is a peg on which to hang the other meetings, each of which Erbse justifies both as examples of Homeric compositional technique and in terms of their relevance to the overall themes of the *Odyssey*. Lesky (1967: 125–6) is more cautious, arguing that the confusion between *nekuomanteion* and *katabasis* is Homeric, but proposing also that there are major post-Homeric interpolations; Kirk (1962: 236–40) offers a similar argument. Among more recent studies the most useful has been the strongly Unitarian reading by Crane (1988: 87–108), emphasizing the overall cohesion which Homer has imposed on elements drawn from separate traditions of *nekuomanteion* and *katabasis*, and accepting as Homeric even the doubtful εἴδωλον passage in Odysseus' meeting with Heracles (see below, n. 15).

[5] Merkelbach (1951: 186–8) accepts all three on grounds of poetic excellence. Page (1955) accepts the Tiresias scene (24–5) and the Anticleia scene, but has an odd view on Elpenor (44–6): he holds that in the original Nekuia Odysseus did not know that Elpenor had died, and that the two lines in which he refers to this (xi. 54, 58) have been added by whoever adapted the Nekuia to fit its present position. The added lines he describes as 'two of the silliest in Greek epic' (46). For Unitarian defences of the Elpenor scene see Büchner (1937), 105–7; Reinhardt (1948), 132–4; and Heubeck ad loc. From an Analyst point of view, the principal problem with the story of Elpenor is that it is not immediately obvious why Homer should have told the story of the death of this insignificant character and his appearance in Hades: consequently it is

Women (225–327) is easily excised,[6] though Odysseus' meetings with
Agamemnon (387–466), Achilles (467–540), and Ajax (541–65) re-
semble the earlier encounters too closely to be cut so easily.[7] Finally,
it is easy to bracket the scene known as the *Hadesschau*, in which
Odysseus describes the spectacle of Minos, the famous sinners, and
Heracles (568–626).[8] Analysts generally hold that the Catalogue of
Women was fitted in from a source akin to what survives as the
Hesiodic *Ehoiai*,[9] and that the latter part of the Nekuia draws on a
(hypothetical) poem of the *katabasis* of Heracles.[10]

The central objection to all this is not on details but on a single
point of principle. By assuming that the Nekuia is cobbled together
from earlier poems, and by transferring the blame for the difficulties
from Homer to a further poet or hack for whose existence there is no
real external evidence, the Analysts succeed only in explaining a
complex problem through models which are themselves still more
complex. Take for example the schemes reached in the two most
influential full Analyst treatments, those of R. Merkelbach[11] and D. L.
Page.[12] Merkelbach holds that two epics, a Homecoming of Odysseus

tempting to suppose that the story was added or adjusted to strengthen the
link between the Nekuia and the rest of Odysseus' story. Crane (1988: 95–6)
holds that the story is an integral part of the Nekuia, and suggests that it looks
back to a more ancient tradition whereby the consultation of the dead had to
be preceded by the sacrifice of a human victim. His only evidence for this is
based on much later lore of necromancy (see Servius at *Aen*. 6. 107), but the
possibility remains that some such story-pattern has survived in our *Odyssey*
with its original sacral meaning suppressed or forgotten.

[6] e.g. Merkelbach (1951), 188–90; Page (1955), 36–9. The Catalogue of
Women is defended by Erbse (1972: 27–8), who links its themes to those of
Odysseus' meeting with his own mother. Since catalogue poems seem to have
been part of the epic tradition since the earliest times (West (1985*a*), esp. 3–
11) I see no reason to reject the possibility that Homer inserted one at this
point in the Nekuia, much as with the Catalogue of Ships in the *Iliad*.

[7] Merkelbach (1951) accepts these meetings, though at this stage the
panorama seems already to have broadened into something like the
Hadesschau (note esp. xi. 388–9, 539).

[8] Merkelbach (1951), 191; Page (1955), 25.

[9] See Merkelbach (1951), 188–90.

[10] First suggested by von der Mühll (1938), 8; the fullest recent treatment is
by Crane (1988), 102–88. N. Robertson (1980) reconstructs an archaic epic of
Heracles in detail, but does not define its relation to Homer; Erbse (1972: 31–
3), believes that Heracles' *katabasis* lies behind Homer's Nekuia, but he
suggests that the source may not have been in the epic verse tradition. See
also Kirk on v. 396–7 for possible sources of the Heracles legend as mentioned
in Homer.

[11] (1951), 185–91.   [12] (1955), 21–51.

('A') and a Telemachy ('T') were combined into our present poem by an inferior poet, the *Bearbeiter* ('B'). He assigns the meetings with Tiresias, Elpenor, Anticleia, and Odysseus' comrades from the Trojan War to A, and gives everything else (up to xi. 636) to B. This judgement is made partly on stylistic grounds and partly because of the topographical details introduced in the *Hadesschau*.[13] Page, on the other hand, would have it that Odysseus' visit to Hades was originally told in an independent poem where Odysseus narrated the story to Penelope (note xi. 223–4, comparing xxiii. 322–5), and that in the original *Odyssey* Circe herself gave Odysseus the information which in ours is imparted by Tiresias (cf. xii. 127–41). The Catalogue and the scene of Minos and the famous dead will have been added by another meddler again. Both these hypotheses seem more difficult and problematic than the problem they address, which is simply that for the modern reader the Homeric Hades is dark and confusing and emerges only dimly from the gloom. Why should it have seemed clearer and brighter to Homer? Applying Occam's razor, it is simple and economical to take it that the ambiguities and inconsistencies may already have been inherent in the tradition inherited by Homer: in which case the blame should be directed less at the poem itself than at the over-systematized minds of scholars.

In this light it is particularly easy to answer the problem that the nature of the afterlife is different at different parts of the book. Given that Odysseus and Achilles are confused and uncertain about the nature of the shades of the dead when they confront them (above, Ch. 6, pp. 208–11), it makes sense that *Homer*'s sense of what happens after death should be no less doubtful, shaped by a complex set of ideas and traditions which will come together full of ambiguities and unresolved contradictions. A more real stumbling-block is put before us by the claim that two narratives have been conflated, one an oracular consultation of the dead and the other a journey through Hades itself. It is undeniable that there is a change of perspective in the course of the book; but we can answer that this may be because Homer himself is drawing on several different narrative traditions, not because someone else has added heterogeneous bits and pieces to a smaller and smoother Homeric original. If we can show that the change of perspective is itself characteristically Homeric, then the resulting shifts of focus will deserve to be seen as part of the overall shaping of Homeric death-lore. In fact, the shift between types of narrative will emerge as a larger-scale version of the ambiguity between 'corpse' and 'shade' which we have seen infecting the way

[13] Merkelbach (1951), see esp. 191.

Homer and his characters perceive the dead as individuals. It is this point that will occupy us now.

The essence of the move from *nekuomanteion* to *katabasis* is that we begin outside Hades looking into the darkness from which the shades emerge, then we are drawn into Hades and are moving around its landscape.[14] The movement is towards increasing clarity, depth and resolution. So described, it follows the same pattern as the shift of focus discernible on a smaller scale within each of the earlier episodes: just as the landscape gains in clarity and immediacy as the narration progresses, so within each of the earlier meetings the shadowy wraith gains clarity and concreteness and begins to be treated as if it were the dead man himself. The Analysts credit some or all of these meetings to the authentic voice of Homer; consequently, they provide clear evidence that the large-scale shift is a characteristic effect of the Homeric depiction of the afterlife.

Let us plot this in more detail. We have observed (above, pp. 200–2) that in the episode of Patroclus' ghost and the earlier meetings of the Nekuia, the image of the afterlife survivor shifts from shade to corpse and back again according to a consistent pattern: the flitting emptiness of the shade is revealed as it flits forward, then as it stands and speaks the image resolves into that of the dead man proper, and finally it is often revealed again as a wraith or empty image as it flits back into Hades and the scene ends. The meetings with Anticleia and Tiresias repeat the pattern that we observed for the first throng of shades and for Elpenor. Tiresias comes to Odysseus as a wraith, ἦλθε δ' ἐπὶ ψυχὴ Θηβαίου Τειρεσίαο (xi. 90), but is treated as the seer himself until he withdraws back into Hades,

> ὣς φαμένη ψυχὴ μὲν ἔβη δόμον Ἄϊδος εἴσω
> Τειρεσίαο ἄνακτος, ἐπεὶ κατὰ θέσφατ' ἔλεξεν.   (xi. 150)

Similarly Anticleia is a ψυχή when she appears first, but the description immediately settles down into treating her as the woman herself:

> ἦλθε δ' ἐπὶ ψυχὴ μητρὸς κατατεθνηυίης,
> Αὐτολύκου θυγάτηρ μεγαλήτορος Ἀντίκλεια.   (xi. 84–5)

Odysseus describes her as μητρὸς . . . ψυχὴ κατατεθνηυίης (xi. 141) when he asks Tiresias how to deal with her. During the conversation she is

---

[14] Page (1955: 27) describes the shift as 'careless and awkward composition'. For the view that this shift may reflect the ambiguities of a single composer, see Büchner (1937), esp. 104, 111–15; Reinhardt (1948), 136–44; also Erbse (1972: 33), who emphasizes the diversity already inherent in Homer's inheritance.

again imagined as the woman herself, until he attempts to embrace her, μητρὸς ἐμῆς ψυχὴν ἑλέειν κατατεθνηυίης (xi. 205), and she is revealed as empty nothingness, after which the scene ends with the start of the Catalogue of Women (xi. 225).

In Odysseus' meetings with the women Homer says nothing to acknowledge that they are shades rather than people of flesh and blood: for the Analysts, then, the Catalogue is artificially drawn into a poem where it does not belong. However, the concreteness of the women can be seen equally well as part of the gradually increasing resolution of the overall picture of Hades, and the difference between this and the earlier scenes is one of degree rather than kind. There is a close parallel with the meetings of the *nekuomanteion* when Odysseus picks up his tale after Alcinous' interruption and the women are scattered aside by Persephone:

$$\psi υχὰς\ μὲν\ ἀπεσκέδασ᾽\ ἄλλυδις\ ἄλληι$$
$$ἁγνὴ\ Περσεφόνεια\ γυναικῶν\ θηλυτεράων\ .\ .\ .\ \ \ (xi.\ 385–6)$$

Here as before the sudden movement of the dead ones is what reveals their emptiness as shades. Even deep in the *katabasis* Homer does not entirely rid himself of the picture of flitting wraiths emerging from Hades to meet Odysseus, and the image of the dead moving and thinking exactly like living men continues to alternate with the image that they are shadowy and strengthless. For example Odysseus' meeting with Agamemnon (387–466) follows a very similar pattern to that with Anticleia. He flits up to Odysseus as a shade,

$$ἦλθε\ δ᾽\ ἐπὶ\ ψυχὴ\ Ἀγαμέμνονος\ Ἀτρεΐδαο,$$
$$ἀχνυμένη\ .\ .\ .\ \ \ (387–8)$$

but the image shifts to that of the man himself:

$$ἔγνω\ δ᾽\ αἶψ᾽\ ἐμὲ\ κεῖνος,\ ἐπεὶ\ πίεν\ αἷμα\ κελαινόν,$$
$$κλαῖε\ δ᾽\ ὅ\ γε\ λιγέως.\ \ \ (390–1)$$

He stretches out to touch Odysseus, but has not enough strength and substance to reach him. They then converse as man to man, and when Agamemnon narrates his own death he uses the first-personal pronoun of his corpse, just as Patroclus and Elpenor had done, telling how Clytaemnestra dishonoured him when he was on his way to Hades:

$$οὐδέ\ μοι\ ἔτλη,\ ἰόντι\ περ\ εἰς\ Ἀΐδαο,$$
$$χερσὶ\ κατ᾽\ ὀφθαλμοὺς\ ἑλέειν\ σύν\ τε\ στόμ᾽\ ἐρεῖσαι.\ \ \ (425–6)$$

He continues as Agamemnon himself until the end of the episode, but he does not withdraw back into the gloom: the shift of focus towards the interior of Hades has begun, and at the close of the scene Agamemnon and Odysseus remain standing together, ἕσταμεν ἀχνύμενοι (466). When they are joined by the shade of Achilles (467–540), it continues to be a ψυχή and feminine in gender until the speeches themselves, when the articulation shifts as usual to νέκυς/νεκρός: Odysseus describes him as ruler over the dead, μέγα κρατέεις νεκύεσσιν (xi. 485), and Achilles reminds him of the horrors of rule over πᾶσιν νεκύεσσι καταφθιμένοισιν (491). When the meeting ends Achilles is again a wraith, but he strides across the now visible landscape of Hades with none of the feebleness of the earlier ψυχαί:

> ψυχὴ δὲ ποδώκεος Αἰακίδαο
> φοίτα μακρὰ βιβᾶσα κατ' ἀσφοδελὸν λειμῶνα,
> γηθοσύνη ὅ οἱ υἱὸν ἔφην ἀριδείκετον εἶναι. (538–40)

The meeting with Ajax shows a variant on the same pattern. He begins as an angry wraith, ψυχὴ κεχολωμένη (xi. 543–4) among the crowd who are now thronged around Odysseus, but the image shifts to that of the dead man himself when Odysseus recalls their quarrel and Ajax' death:

> ὡς δὴ μὴ ὄφελον νικᾶν τοιῶιδ' ἐπ' ἀέθλωι·
> τοίην γὰρ κεφαλὴν ἕνεκ' αὐτῶν γαῖα κατέσχεν,
> Αἴανθ', ὃς περὶ μὲν εἶδος, περὶ δ' ἔργα τέτυκτο
> τῶν ἄλλων Δαναῶν μετ' ἀμύμονα Πηλείωνα.
> τὸν μὲν ἐγὼν ἐπέεσσι προσηύδων μειλιχίοισιν . . . (548–52)

The picture is fixed in this way until he flits away into the darkness as a wraith:

> ὁ δέ μ' οὐδὲν ἀμείβετο, βῆ δὲ μετ' ἄλλας
> ψυχὰς εἰς ἔρεβος νεκύων κατατεθνηώτων. (563–4)

At this point Odysseus pushes further into Hades in the hope of seeing more wraiths, ψυχὰς . . . κατατεθνηώτων (xi. 567).

It is now that the overall panorama achieves clear contours. The beings that he sees are described as dead men proper (νέκυσσιν, 569), and they are doing just the kind of things that the insubstantial wraiths of the earlier scenes were incapable of: the idea of ghostly weakness has been superseded altogether when Minos gives judgement, Orion hunts, Tityus' liver is pecked by the vulture, Tantalus stands in the river reaching for food, and Sisyphus pushes his boulder up the hill (568–600). Odysseus' meeting with Heracles is especially revealing here. Odysseus is inside Hades, with the dead (νεκύων, 605) surrounding him in crowds, and the being he meets must be Heracles himself rather than a shade. That impression is strengthened rather

than the reverse by the disputed passage which explains that this
Heracles is not the hero himself but a phantom, εἴδωλον:

> τὸν δὲ μετ' εἰσενόησα βίην Ἡρακλείην,
> εἴδωλον· αὐτὸς δὲ μετ' ἀθανάτοισι θεοῖσι
> τέρπεται ἐν θαλίῃς καὶ ἔχει καλλίσφυρον Ἥβην,
> παῖδα Διὸς μεγάλοιο καὶ Ἥρης χρυσοπεδίλου. (601–4)

This is not an εἴδωλον in the sense that the wraith of a dead man is an
εἴδωλον or ψυχή: the motif of a false image is used to explain how
Heracles can be in Hades and on Olympus at the same time, in just
the same way that Aeneas in the *Iliad* is replaced by an εἴδωλον when
Apollo whisks him out of the battlefield to safety (v. 449–53; see
above, pp. 196–7).[15] If Heracles were already identified as a wraith in

[15] No great weight can be placed on xi. 602–4, since very many ancient and
modern scholars have condemned them as an interpolation (for ancient
opinions analysed, see Petzl (1969), 28–36). The scholia are unusually precise
in ascribing the lines to Onomacritus (cf. Hdt. 7. 6. 3), but it is likely that this
is a late guess rather than a genuine tradition (Petzl (1969), 35, with further
refs.). The main reasons which the scholiasts give to justify the excision are (*a*)
that the apotheosis of Heracles is foreign to Homeric mythology, and (*b*) that
this is the only place where Homer mentions him as matched with Hebe. But
although this is the only place where Homer specifically says that Heracles
went to Olympus, he does refer to similar stories elsewhere: Calypso says that
she wanted to make Odysseus immortal (see v. 136, vii. 257, xxiii. 336), while
Ino (v. 333–5), Ganymede (v. 265–6, xx. 232–5), Clitus (xv. 250–1), and
Tithonus (v. 1 etc.) are all mortals who have been elevated to the society of the
gods. The Cyclic *Thebaid* contained an interesting variant on this pattern in
the story that Athena cancelled her offer of immortality to Tydeus because of
his savagery towards a dead enemy (see fr. 9 Bernabé, with Davies (1989), 27–
8). The parallel of Tithonus shows that Heracles' marriage follows a pattern
which is not foreign to Homeric mythology: Tithonus is a translated mortal
married to the deity of a natural phenomenon, Dawn, just as Heracles is
married to Youth. In principle there seems to be nothing especially 'late'
about the story: in the *Iliad*, Hebe ministers to the gods (IV. 2–3, v. 722, 905),
and the story of her marriage to Heracles is certainly as old as Hesiod (*Theog.*
950–5). Scholiasts on the *Odyssey* passage object to the marriage of Hebe to
Heracles on the grounds that in the *Iliad* her duties include washing the gods,
which they hold to be the duty of a παρθένος rather than a married woman; but
there seems to be no fast rule about this, since (for example) Helen describes
washing Odysseus in Troy (iv. 252), at a time when she had left maidenhood
far behind. (On the whole problem see Petzl (1969), 32–4.) There would be
better grounds for suspecting the passage if it could be proved that the idea of
explaining someone's presence in two places by means of the concept of an
εἴδωλον was an invention of the post-Homeric period, but on the evidence
there is no good reason to believe that this is the case (see Ch. 6 n. 78). In the
Hesiodic *Catalogue of Women*, the story that an εἴδωλον was substituted for

virtue of being one of the dead, it would not make sense to say that he is a substitute εἴδωλον standing in for the Olympian Heracles: hence the passage implies that what was expected here in Hades scene was the man himself, the man of flesh and blood.[16] After Heracles withdraws Odysseus continues as if he were among the dead themselves, surrounded by hosts of corpses, ἔθνεα . . . μυρία νεκρῶν (xi. 632); and he withdraws at last because he fears that Persephone will send out the Gorgon's head (633–5), just as in his meeting with Anticleia he had feared that Persephone had sent a false εἴδωλον to deceive him (xi. 213–14).

In this way the deepening of perspective in the course of the book is bound up with the shift of emphasis observable within each of the earlier meetings. When the dead man rises up from Hades, he moves as a wraith and his lack of substance is remembered, but when the conversation between him and Odysseus gets under way he gains enough vividness and substance to be treated as a being of flesh and blood; correspondingly, as Odysseus' story grows in length it grows in vividness and clarity, with the mythological contours of Hades emerging ever more from the gloom, so that eventually he is moving among the dead within their realm. But even under that influence the shift of focus is one of degree rather than of kind, and the image of the flitting wraith does not wholly disappear until close to the end of the whole. In other words, on every level the Nekuia is shot through with ambiguities which belong as much in Homer's inheritance of narrative patterns as in his hoard of words and formulae. Just as two conceptions of the dead man's nature jostle

Iphimede (= Iphigenia) at her sacrifice seems to have been introduced in exactly the same verbal pattern as in the Heracles passage (Hes. fr. 23a. 17–24 M–W, with supplements); but since the date of the Hesiodic *Catalogue* itself can only be guessed at, this does not help to decide whether the Heracles passage is typical of the earliest mythical patterns. It is easy to see how an interpolator *might* have inserted these lines as an answer to objections prompted by knowledge of the story of Heracles' ascent to Olympus, but it remains equally possible that Homer is himself seeking to reconcile that tradition with stories in which Heracles descended to the Underworld after his death. It is worth comparing the passage which explains that the Dioscuri alternate daily between life and death (xi. 301–4), against which another passage simply says that they are dead and below the earth (iii. 243–4). This stands as another example of an unusual device being used to account for the presence of a person in both the upper and the lower world. The most recent full discussion of the Heracles passage is by Crane (1988: 87–91), arguing that it is Homeric.

[16] *Pace* Pötscher (1965: 208–10), who assumes that this εἴδωλον is identified in the normal way as the afterlife survivor of the dead Heracles.

with each other in the language of the Nekuia, so the imagery of *nekuomanteion* vies with that of *katabasis* in the poet's basic concept of what is going on. There is no escaping this ambivalence between two story-patterns and two vying aspects of the afterlife, and the overall change of focus in the later episodes of the book is directly paralleled by the change of focus that characterizes each encounter in the earlier section. Since that section is definitely attributed to Homer, it is evident that the large-scale shift reflects a characteristic aspect of Homer's conception of the afterlife. This ought to strengthen the case for trying to understand the Nekuia as a complex unity.

2. *The authenticity of the Second Nekuia*

At various points in this study, our references to Homer have included passages from the Second Nekuia (xxiv. 1–204), which it is particularly easy to regard as an interpolation.[17] However, all those references have been to words and images which are paralleled at least once elsewhere in the two epics, so that none of our arguments has had to depend solely on a passage from this episode. This means that there has been no pressing need for us to decide whether or not to accept it as Homeric; consequently, this is not the place to discuss whether excision is justified by its most striking oddities[18]—the peremptory way in which the suitors' *katabasis* is narrated at this

[17] The question of the authenticity of the Second Nekuia must be distinguished from the general question mark that hangs over everything after xxiii. 296, the τέλος or πέρας fixed by Aristarchus and Aristophanes. The single continuous story-line of the main narrative after xxiii. 296 makes it reasonable to take it as a whole when deciding whether or not to include it as Homeric; but within that narrative the Second Nekuia hangs so loosely on its context, and involves such a cluster of special difficulties, that it is marked out as a separate problem. If it is an interpolation, its origin will be separate from and later than that of any part of the main narrative from xxiii. 296 to the end of xxiv. An approach of this kind may have been taken by the greatest Alexandrian scholars themselves, since those who fixed the 'conclusion' (in whatever sense) at xxiii. 296 seem also to have condemned the Second Nekuia in a separate act of criticism (compare scholia at xxiii. 296 with scholia at xxiv. 1).

[18] For complete surveys of the ancient opinions on these and more trivial problems of the Second Nekuia, see Petzl (1969), pt. ii *passim*, and Garbrah (1977); and see also Page (1955), 116–24. Arguments in favour of accepting the episode as Homeric are advanced by Thornton (1970), 4–10; Erbse (1972), 231–6; Wender (1978), 19–44; and by Heubeck in his introduction to xxiv in vol. 3 of the Oxford *Commentary*. The fullest recent study is that of Sourvinou-Inwood (1995: 94–106), who denies that it is Homeric, mostly because of the direct narration of the descent in the poet's own voice.

point, the anomaly of making the wraiths of Achilles and Agamemnon meet for the first time ten years after Agamemnon's death (xxiv. 24–97), the various difficulties of Agamemnon's account of the funeral of Achilles (36–97), the irrelevance of the two heroes' conversation to the themes of the *Odyssey*, the slips in Amphimedon's account of the suitors' downfall (121–202), the unusually otiose repetitions when he retells the story of Penelope's loom (126–48; see ii. 93–110, xix. 139–62), and the *non sequitur* when Agamemnon responds to Amphimedon, his own ξεῖνος (xxiv. 114), not by blaming or consoling him but by launching into general remarks about Penelope's virtues (192–202). But it will be useful to compare the death-lore of the Second Nekuia point by point with the death-lore which we know to be Homeric, gauging the extent to which it differs from the norm.

(i) *The concept of survival in the afterlife.* The dead of the Second Nekuia are always referred to as ψυχαί, never as νέκυες/νεκροί, and the feminine gender is kept up quite consistently (note esp. ψυχή in xxiv. 14–23, 35, 105, 120, 191) except in the wording of the conversations themselves, when the wraith is naturally treated as if he were the dead man himself. This pattern closely resembles that which Homer follows in the *katabasis* section of Odysseus' Nekuia, which is also the part closest to the Second Nekuia in subject-matter. Some lines are identical (note esp. xxiv. 20–2 = xi. 387–9), though this proves nothing in itself. However, one slight departure from the Homeric norm appears in Amphimedon's speech to Agamemnon. After telling of Odysseus' vengeance he ends with the words

> ὣς ἡμεῖς, Ἀγάμεμνον, ἀπωλόμεθ', ὧν ἔτι καὶ νῦν
> σώματ' ἀκηδέα κεῖται ἐνὶ μεγάροις Ὀδυσῆος. (xxiv. 186–7)

We have seen in Chapter 6 that in speeches by wraiths the usual pattern is that 'I' is used indiscriminately of the wraith itself and of the corpse, making no firm distinction between these two manifestations of the dead man's identity: Amphimedon's speech is unique in the way he distinguishes the suitors themselves, as wraiths, from their σώματα. In this way, Amphimedon's words come exceptionally close to articulating a body–soul dichotomy, and might therefore reflect a post-Homeric development in death-lore. However, there is only a small difference between this use of σῶμα and that found in Odysseus' account of the wraith of Elpenor (xi. 51–4), so that the usage cannot definitely be considered un-Homeric.

(ii) *The concept of the funeral.* When the wraith of Agamemnon tells the wraith of Achilles about the latter's funeral (xxiv. 36–97), he speaks exactly in the pattern which we have sketched throughout this chapter: the corpse of Achilles is identified with the Achilles whom Agamemnon addresses, σε (xxiv. 43–6, 58, 63, 65, 71) until he is burned, after which the bones are distinguished from the dead man proper (72–9).

(iii) *The mythical imagery of the wraiths' descent to Hades.* Ancient scholars were worried by the fact that the suitors' wraiths go down to Hades while still unburied;[19] but this need not be a problem, since we have seen that it is in fact the normal pattern in *Iliad* and *Odyssey* alike that the ψυχή's arrival in Hades is a direct consequence of death and is not mediated by the funerary ritual. The scholiasts were also troubled by details of the topography which do not correspond to what Odysseus mentions in his own journey, notably the rock Leucas (xxiv. 11),[20] but this is hardly a serious problem: there is no reason to think the topography of Hades was sharply fixed in Homer's own tradition, and in any case Odysseus' route was hardly the usual one taken by the dead. Much more unusual is the way in which the descent of the suitors is narrated. Hermes summons forth the wraiths, ἐξεκαλεῖτο (xxiv. 1), and they follow him down dank pathways, κατ' εὐρώεντα κέλευθα (10), into the subterranean realms, gibbering and squeaking like bats. The imagery of the bat simile does seem to draw on aspects of Homer's image of the ψυχή, but in its visual precision is unlike anything in Odysseus' Nekuia or in the *Iliad*: this suggests strongly that the poet of the Second Nekuia is drawing on the more baroque image of the ψυχή actually taking on the form of a bird (see Ch. 1, p. 5). The appearance of Hermes as guide of the dead is not directly attested elsewhere in Homer,[21] and the episode takes the narrative into the world of Hades and the wraiths with unparalleled abruptness. The switch from the image of dead men as corpses to that of dead men as wraiths is almost violent: no device is used to smooth the transition from one plane to the other and to explain how the dead men in Odysseus' hall have given rise to the wraiths now making their way to the Underworld.[22]

[19] Schol. at xxiv. 1 ff., xxiii. 71, xxiv. 187; and see Petzl (1969), 51–3.
[20] Schol. at xxiv. 1; and see Petzl (1969), 54–5.
[21] Schol. at xxiv. 1, xxiv. 362; and see Petzl (1969), 47–9. The nearest Homeric analogy for the role of Hermes as guide of the dead is a distant one, the passage in Odysseus' Nekuia where Heracles says that Hermes and Athena sent or escorted him, ἔπεμψεν, on his journey to Hades (xi. 626; and cf. also *h. Merc.* 572).
[22] See Sourvinou-Inwood (1995), 103–6.

This is enough to suggest that the composer of this passage is following a different (perhaps cruder, perhaps later) pattern of myth-making from those followed by whoever articulated the image of the flying ψυχαί of Patroclus and Hector and the complexities of the journey of Odysseus to Hades. It is a fair guess that the composer of the Second Nekuia was inspired by the image of wraiths going down to Hades which Theoclymenus built up in his fantastic vision,

$$εἰδώλων \ δὲ \ πλέον \ πρόθυρον, \ πλείη \ δὲ \ καὶ \ αὐλή,$$
$$ἱεμένων \ ἔρεβόσδε \ ὑπὸ \ ζόφον \ . \ . \ . \quad (xx. \ 355–6)$$

and simply re-created the heightened imagery of the prophet's vision on the level of the primary narrative. It is because Homeric narrative proper tends not to effect the transition to the mythical world of the wraiths with such glib ease that the image of the flight of the ψυχή plays the elusive role which we have followed throughout this study. At the same time, it must be acknowledged that apart from the role of Hermes there is nothing in the mythical motifs of the journey which seriously contradicts the Homeric view of the journey to the Under-world and the life which the wraiths lead there: so that any decision to distinguish that mythology from the Homeric norm must stand or fall on different grounds. Hence it may be best not to commit ourselves either way, if only because there is no good reason for expecting uniformity in death-mythology.[23] If one were to accept the Second Nekuia as Homeric, then its importance for this study would be as an articulation which prompts but does not answer the question 'How does the dead man as corpse relate to the dead man as dweller in Hades?': in other words, it thrusts forward the problem to which a solution is provided by the complex image of the flying ψυχή in the deaths of Patroclus and Hector.

[23] Cf. Wender (1978), 37–44, and Heubeck on xxiv. 1–4.

PART IV

The Shaping of Myth

7

The Personalities of Death

How does the visible world relate to the mythical?

We have shown that ψυχή is simply and literally the dying man's last gasp, released from his mouth and lost in the cold moment of death. But when the ψυχή of Patroclus or Hector flies to Hades, its identity is suddenly transformed: it gibbers, it squeaks, it flies to Hades to join the wraiths of the dead. This wisp of breath becomes part of the unseen, imagined, mythical world, the world that the gods inhabit and only the Muses can see; yet none the less its meaning remains rooted in the everyday, non-mythical phenomenon of the dying man's last gasp. How are we to understand the relationship between the two articulations, between the ψυχή that disappears into nothing and the ψυχή that soars away to another plane of the universe?

The divinities of death

In this chapter I will seek an answer by looking at another pattern of image-making in Homeric death. In one sense death is a visible, sublunary event—a man's limbs are loosed, he falls to the ground, darkness envelops his sight. But in another sense death is the business of divine beings who approach and seize him when he dies. The most prominent of these is Θάνατος, Death, along with Μοῖρα, 'Portion', and the beings called Κήρ, whose name feebly translates as 'Fate' or 'Doom'. The crucial fact about these beings is that each of their names also belongs in plain unvarnished language without any reference to the things of myth. θάνατος is the nominal reflex of the root of θνήισκω, while μοῖρα can denote simply sharing or assignment (x. 253; iv. 97, etc.), and κήρ is probably from the same root as κείρω, 'I cut'—death is what is cut out or apportioned to mortal man.[1] To cope with each of these nouns in a given context we have to choose between the mythical sense or the colourless, everyday sense, with nothing but common sense and sensitivity to guide us. Thus these words offer a similar problem to that posed by ψυχή: the single word has both a mythical and a non-mythical meaning, and doubt hangs over the relationship between them. It would be no solution to try to prise the two levels apart as if they belonged in different provinces of thought and imagination, and we will see that the Homeric realities demand a more radical approach: the meaning of these divine personalities is rooted in the simple or non-mythical experience of dying, and they emerge from that experience in fluid and supple ways.

Let us begin with θάνατος. Once we abandon the convention of printing a capital letter to distinguish θάνατος, death, from Θάνατος, the so-called god *of* death, we see the word sliding between the two extremes.[2] The divinity named Death, as it were the Grim Reaper, has a fully-fledged identity of his own among the other gods,[3] though in Homer he emerges into the

[1] On μοῖρα as 'portion' see esp. Pötscher (1960); also Dietrich (1965), 61; Erbse (1986), 274–9; and on κήρ and κείρω see *LfgrE* s.v. with A. Nussbaum (1986), 66–9. On this group of etymologies see also Dietrich (1965), 249–73.

[2] The fullest source for the personality of Thanatos is the first scene of Euripides' *Alcestis*, where he appears as a character. It has been needlessly argued that this version of Thanatos comes from the conventions of popular fable rather than from a literary tradition still current in the late 5th cent. (see de Ruyt (1932); Garland (1985), 56–9; and A. M. Dale's edition, pp. xx–xxi and on lines 24–6). For Homeric purposes, the problems of the personal Death are discussed by A. Lesky in *RE* vA(1), s.v. 'Thanatos', 1246–51; Vermeule (1979), 37–41, 145–7; and briefly by Erbse (1986), 22–3. Lesky points out that with the Homeric θάνατος it is impossible as well as misguided to try to separate poetic invention from reflections of genuine religious belief, and correspondingly that the personal figure is deeply rooted in the semantics of the word θάνατος itself. Vermeule (1979) notes the explicit personification in the Sarpedon story and its reflexes elsewhere, but is inclined to minimize its importance: 'Death is a negative, a cessation of life, but not a physical enemy' (37), and 'The elemental form of θάνατος in the *Iliad* is not as dangerous agent but as dark colour' (39). Vermeule's argument loses force if one accepts that there is no reason to give precedence to the 'elemental' form over the personal.

[3] The word 'god' or 'divinity' obviously begs questions here, but there is no alternative. Some would deny Thanatos the name of a god on the grounds that he had no cult (see e.g. Wilamowitz (1931), 315, followed by Dietrich (1965), 88, and cf. 59). This view is unnecessarily limiting, since it assumes that the

light of day only at Sarpedon's death.[4] Here Zeus commands
Apollo to hand the dead hero over to Death and his brother
Sleep, so that they can carry him back to his Lycian home for
burial:

> αὐτὰρ ἐπὴν δὴ τόν γε λίπηι ψυχή τε καὶ αἰών,
> πέμπειν μιν Θάνατόν τε φέρειν καὶ νήδυμον Ὕπνον,
> εἰς ὅ κε δὴ Λυκίης εὐρείης δῆμον ἵκωνται,
> ἔνθα ἑ ταρχύσουσι κασίγνητοί τε ἔται τε
> τύμβωι καὶ στήληι. (XVI. 453–7)

Homer does not say what Death does when he arrives (XVI. 667–
83), nor is it clear whether Sarpedon's experience is unlike that
of other mortals when they die.[5] Hesiod gives us a still more
vivid image of the personal Thanatos:

> τοῦ δὲ σιδηρέη μὲν κραδίη, χάλκεον δέ οἱ ἦτορ
> νηλεὲς ἐν στήθεσσιν, ἔχει δ' ὃν πρῶτα λάβηισιν
> <u>ἀνθρώπων</u>, ἐχθρὸς δὲ καὶ ἀθανάτοισι θεοῖσιν. (*Theog.* 764–6)

The key word is λάβηισιν: this unseen agent seizes or snatches
the dying man. What does that mean? Since here we see
Thanatos in the same precise and detailed contours as we
would see any other god, we must ask whether that picture

poetic tradition about godhead is trivial wherever it does not coincide with the
practice of worship, and a fragment of Aeschylus' *Niobe* is enough to counter
it: μόνος θεῶν γὰρ Θάνατος οὐ δώρων ἐρᾶι (fr. 161. 1 N). He receives no cult but
he remains a god, albeit a peculiar one. It remains possible to argue that such
evocations are purely speculative or rhetorical, like Aeschylus' τὸ δ' εὐτυχεῖν, |
τόδ' ἐν βροτοῖς θεός τε καὶ θεοῦ πλέον (*Cho.* 59–60) or Euripides' θεὸς γὰρ καὶ τὸ
γιγνώσκειν φίλους (*Hel.* 560); but the richness of the Homeric evocation of
Thanatos shows that his personal identity is intensely real.

[4] There is some evidence that Thanatos appeared in person elsewhere in
early epic. It is possible that in the *Aethiopis* Sleep and Death carried
Memnon away in just the manner that they carry Sarpedon in the *Iliad*.
(See Schoeck (1961: 8), drawing on the evidence of vase-paintings and
including this among many parallels claimed between the episodes of
Memnon and Sarpedon; but cf. also J. Pley in *RE* xv(1), s.v. 'Memnon',
642, for the suggestion that he was carried away by wind-spirits. Davies (1989:
57–8) is more sceptical as to whether this occurred in the *Aethiopis* at all.) It is
also possible that the stories of κατάβασις and conflicts with Hades by Heracles
(esp. v. 395–400) and Sisyphus (Thgn. 702–12; Alc. fr. 38A L–P) existed from
the earliest times in versions where they fought Thanatos himself.

[5] Possibly the special part of Sarpedon's experience is merely that the joint
presence of both Sleep and Death makes his end especially gentle.

should be projected back onto the θάνατος of ordinary epic language. How does this snatching or seizing relate to the visible fact that the dying man falls to the ground and loses consciousness?

A different species of the same question is prompted by κήρ. That word often translates easily enough as 'fate' or 'death', but it also names a female deity or monster who roams the battlefield and seizes victims; and as we will see in detail below, in rhetorical and allusive language the death that hunts and captures the dying man is identified as κήρ almost as often as θάνατος. Only once in Homer do we find her explicitly articulated, among the strange beings who infest the battle scene on the Shield of Achilles:[6]

> ἐν δ’ Ἔρις, ἐν δὲ Κυδοιμὸς ὁμίλεον, ἐν δ’ ὀλοὴ Κήρ,
> ἄλλον ζωὸν ἔχουσα νεούτατον, ἄλλον ἄουτον,
> ἄλλον τεθνηῶτα κατὰ μόθον ἕλκε ποδοῖιν.
> εἷμα δ’ ἔχ’ ἀμφ’ ὤμοισι δαφοινεὸν αἵματι φωτῶν.
> ὡμίλευν δ’ ὥς τε ζωοὶ βροτοὶ ἠδ’ ἐμάχοντο,
> νεκρούς τ’ ἀλλήλων ἔρυον κατατεθνηῶτας.   (XVIII. 535–40)

Who is this figure who drags the dead and dying across the plain? Is she present on every Homeric battlefield, or is she

---

[6] Of this scene lines 535–8 also appear (with ἐθύνεον for ὁμίλεον in 535) in the Hesiodic *Shield of Heracles* (156–9), and inevitably each has been condemned as an interpolation from the other text (Solmsen (1965); Lynn-George (1978); cf. also Lamberton (1988), 141–4). Here we need only answer the claim that the *Iliad* version is interpolated from the *Shield of Heracles* (Lynn-George (1978)). The main argument is the aesthetic one, that these macabre and gory death-demons are foreign to the style of the *Iliad*: for example Dietrich (1965: 245) describes the κήρ of the Shield of Achilles as 'poetic fancy' that 'lacks reality'. Certainly there is no artistic representation described in Homer which is quite so baroque as this one; but that is equally true of the Shield of Achilles as a whole. In favour of accepting the passage as Homeric, we can argue (a) that the behaviour of κήρ on the Shield is consistent with κήρ in allusive language throughout Homer (see esp. II. 302, II. 834 = XI. 332; xiv. 207; and below, pp. 243–50); (b) that the depiction of κήρ, Ἔρις, and Κυδοιμός is not un-Homeric in character, since Homer regularly includes such personified agents among the images on armour; (c) that in the Shield of Achilles itself there is a parallel for the appearance of divine figures who would not normally be visible to mortals, since in the siege scene an army is led by Ares and Athena, ὥς τε θεώ περ | ἀμφὶς ἀριζήλω (XVIII. 518–19). In effect, the only serious reason that could be adduced for excising the passage is that it is more detailed than any other Homeric description of images on armour.

simply an exuberant poetic invention in the Shield? Faced with
this array of forms, it would be all too easy to divorce the literal
from the figurative, or ordinary language from 'Religion', so as
to assume either that the personal beings are whimsical one-off
inventions or that they are walking unseen over each and every
battlefield. Neither of those alternatives does justice to the
facts, because across the full range of Homeric poetry the
divinities' presence is evoked in endlessly varying degrees of
clarity. As we will see, the plainest and simplest evocation of
death is in the straight narration of events in the poet's own
voice. Sharper lines emerge in rhetoric and allusion, both when
the poet draws out the meaning of past and future deaths and
when Homer's characters put the idea of death into words;[7] and
at times the narrative itself rises to a higher plane, on which we
find ourselves fully translated out of the world of mortals and
into one where these divinities act like any other personal god.
Along this sliding scale the mythical world is latent, emerging
and receding from scene to scene or even from word to word,
but as it does so it follows a strict visual logic of its own.

Sleep has a fluid personality

Before facing θάνατος and κήρ head-on, it will be helpful to
glance at Sleep, ὕπνος or Ὕπνος, where the pattern is similar
but the evidence is easier to digest at a glance. Sleep sometimes
has the full identity of a personal deity.[8] He is the brother of
Death (see XIV. 231), both of them are sons of Night (as in Hes.
Theog. 212, 756–9),[9] and Zeus sends him along with Death in

[7] This distinction between the lean language of the narrative and the higher
language of rhetoric will be justified empirically, and it does not depend on
any theoretical model. That said, de Jong (1987) has been useful on the
distinction between the voice of the poet, that is the 'primary narrator-
focalizer', and the utterances or viewpoints of other characters; but I have
not found her model of the narratological 'accordion' (see esp. 31–6) to be
directly applicable to the shaping of Homeric death. See also Griffin (1986);
and on pathos in Homeric language see Griffin (1980), ch. 4.

[8] On the use of the words 'god' or 'deity' here, cf. above, n. 3. In later times
Sleep had a cult at Troezen, shared with the Muses (Paus. 2. 31. 2; see also
Jones (1949)), and artistic depictions of Sleep seem to have been numerous
(e.g. Paus. 2. 10. 12, 5. 18. 1).

[9] Hesiod apparently includes Sleep and Death among the brood produced

attendance on the dead Sarpedon (XVI. 454, 667–83). He comes still more to the fore in the story of the Deception of Zeus, where at Hera's entreaty he uses his powers to put Zeus to sleep. Here he talks and intrigues and travels as any personal god might do (XIV. 230–91, 352–62), and he recalls being involved in a previous quarrel among the Olympians, during Heracles' return from Troy (XIV. 249–62).[10] The crux is that even where there is no obvious hint of a personality, Homeric sleep is described not as a state but as an agent. Sleep arrives to a person, ἱκάνει (I. 610, X. 96; ix. 333, etc.) or ἐπήλυθε (iv. 793, etc.); it seizes him, αἱρεῖ (X. 192–3, ix. 372–3, etc.), μάρπτει (XXIII. 62, XXIV. 679, etc.), ἔχει (II. 2, X. 4, etc.); the sleeper has been overcome by it, δεδμημένος (X. 2, XXIV. 678; vii. 318, etc.); when he awakes it releases him, ἀνῆκεν (II. 34, vii. 289, etc.). When a god puts someone to sleep he pours it over the eyes, χεύει (XIV. 164–5, ii. 395,

by Night on her own, without male seed (*Theog.* 211–25). Also, at *Theog.* 758–66 Hesiod gives Death and Sleep adjoining houses in the deeps of the earth, mirroring the family and conceptual kinship in spatial terms. There is good reason to think that Homer too recognizes Night as their mother: note XIV. 258–61, where Sleep recounts the occasion when he was protected by Night from the anger of Zeus, and compare Night's identity as δμήτειρα θεῶν . . . καὶ ἀνδρῶν (XIV. 259) with that of Sleep as ἄναξ πάντων τε θεῶν πάντων τ' ἀνθρώπων (XIV. 233; and cf. XXIV. 4–5, ix. 372–3). A complex reconstruction of the family and conceptual relationships of Night and her children is presented by Ramnoux (1959). Fränkel (1960: 319–20) analyses Hesiod's account and holds that it represents independent proto-philosophical thinking rather than a naïve tradition about anthropomorphic deities. To support this, he points out that the children produced by Night on her own are all dark and evil things, while the children fathered on her by Erebus are Day and Bright Air, Ἡμέρη and Αἰθήρ (*Theog.* 116–25). In this way, he argues, in Hesiod's mythical discourse sexual generation symbolizes the coming-to-be of vital self-moving things.

[10] The inevitable question has been posed: Is Sleep's reference to the earlier incident invented by the poet of the *Iliad*, or is Sleep's appearance in the Deception story modelled on the corresponding episode in a pre-Homeric epic of Heracles? (See Kullmann (1956), 30; Braswell (1971), 22; Erbse (1986), 18–23; Janko at XIV. 259–61.) No answer is possible, since each detail of the Heracles epic in question can only be reconstructed on the basis of references in the *Iliad* and *Odyssey*, and each such detail can equally be dismissed as *ad hoc* mythological innovation by Homer. The same goes for the appearance of Sleep as an actor in the story of Heracles' fight with Alcyoneus, which is directly attested only in later sources but might go back to the same ancient Heracles epic (see Kullmann, loc. cit.).

xii. 338, etc.).[11] Sleep falls on the eyelids and sits there, ἐπὶ βλεφάροισιν ἔπιπτεν (ii. 398, etc.) and ἐπὶ βλεφάροισιν ἐφίζανε (x. 26; sim. x. 91–2); and it constrains or immobilizes the sleeper as it envelops his sight, ἐπέδησε φίλα βλέφαρ' ἀμφικαλύψας (xxiii. 17). All of this is consistent with the action of a personal agent, even if that is not articulated on the surface of the words.

How do we make sense of this? Geoffrey Lloyd[12] has pointed out that the key to Homeric sleep is in its very multiplicity:

None of these can be considered *the* definitive description of sleep. Each image illustrates the phenomenon under a different aspect, though each, if pressed, would seem to imply a slightly different conception of the nature of sleep . . . They should be treated as complementary rather than as alternative conceptions of the same phenomenon.[13]

We can go further. Setting the ordinary language of sleep alongside his mythical personality, we find that the conceptions are not merely complementary but indistinguishable.[14] In the everyday world sleep is πανδαμάτωρ (XXIV. 4–5; ix. 372–3), the one who conquers all; addressing the god in person, Hera calls him king over men and gods, ἄναξ πάντων τε θεῶν πάντων τ' ἀνθρώπων (XIV. 233). Just as Sleep and Death are brothers, so a particularly sound sleep resembles death, θανάτωι ἄγχιστα ἐοικώς (xiii. 80; and note a more elaborate comparison by Penelope, xviii. 201–5),[15] while death in battle is a brazen sleep, χάλκεον ὕπνον (XI. 241).[16] The link is at once between two brothers and between two adjacent phenomena.

The continuum between god and phenomenon is borne out

---

[11] Hermes also puts people to sleep with his wand (XXIV. 343–5), an alternative image which does not affect the mythical identity of Sleep proper.

[12] (1966), 201–9; for a later discussion of the same topic see Lloyd (1987), 175–6. The question is inseparable from that of metaphor in general: see Lloyd (1990), 14–38, and Ch. 4 above, pp. 107–9.

[13] Lloyd (1966), 202.

[14] This is pointed out briefly by Jolles in *RE* ix(1), s.v. 'Hypnos'.

[15] Cf. Alc. fr. 3. 61–2 P, with Vermeule (1979), 145–7.

[16] On this striking image see Moulton (1979), 284. It occurs in one of the passages in which Homer creates a pathetic effect in his own voice by using allusive language of the kind normally reserved for speeches (see Ch. 6, pp. 169–70).

perfectly in the Deception story, when Sleep describes his own actions:

> ἤτοι ἐγὼ μὲν ἔλεξα Διὸς νόον αἰγιόχοιο
> νήδυμος ἀμφιχυθείς.   (XIV. 252–3)

The Sleep who is speaking identifies himself precisely with what was poured, ἀμφιχυθείς, over Zeus' eyes: he describes his own activity with the very verb that Homer might use to say that an ordinary mortal fell asleep, τὸν ὕπνος ἔμαρπτε . . . νήδυμος ἀμφιχυθείς (XXIII. 62–3). It had originally been said simply that Hera planned to pour sleep over Zeus' eyes herself,

> τῶι δ' ὕπνον ἀπήμονά τε λιαρόν τε
> χεύηι ἐπὶ βλεφάροισιν ἰδὲ φρεσὶ πευκαλίμηισι . . .   (XIV. 164–5)

but when she asks Sleep to help her she describes it as his personal act:

> κοίμησόν μοι Ζηνὸς ὑπ' ὀφρύσιν ὄσσε φαεινώ.   (XIV. 236)

Later, the story-line forces the issue of reconciling the person with the phenomenon. Sleep hides in a tree in the shape of a bird, waiting for the time at which he is to put Zeus to sleep; Zeus then has his way with Hera and nods off, but of the actions of Sleep himself we hear only that Zeus is now overcome by him, δαμείς (XIV. 353). This done, Sleep goes off to the battlefield to converse with Poseidon, and says that he has personally enveloped Zeus in the darkness of slumber:

> ἔτι εὕδει
> Ζεύς, ἐπεὶ αὐτῶι ἐγὼ μαλακὸν περὶ κῶμ' ἐκάλυψα.   (358–9)

After delivering the message, Sleep withdraws to his work among mortals, ἐπὶ κλυτὰ φῦλ' ἀνθρώπων (361). This last detail must mean that he can be seen in personal terms when he works among ordinary mortals no less than among gods: this, perhaps, is the mythical meaning of the 'gift of sleep', ὕπνου δῶρον (VII. 482).

All of this makes good logical and verbal sense if we accept the unity underlying the endless shifts between the levels of image-making. The mythical personality of Ὕπνος takes shape only in the light of Homer's everyday means of expressing what it is to fall asleep, and correspondingly we would rob the language of its meaning if we sought to exclude that personality from the simplest rendering of what happens when someone closes his eyes. This is the principle that must inform our approach to death. We cannot split θάνατος or κήρ into two parts and call one an abstract noun and the other a personification: to understand the Homeric realities, we will need to study how individual images take shape in different ways on the shifting ground *between* those polar extremes.

The descent of darkness is the experience of death

We begin with the plain rendering of death in the narrative of the *Iliad*.[17] The examples form a miniature type-scene system,[18] and the sequence of events is rigidly fixed. The victor deals the decisive blow; a wound is inflicted as it strikes home; the victim's defeat is indicated by one or more external signs, such as falling headlong to the ground; he experiences

---

[17] If the *Odyssey* seldom figures in this section it is simply because there are not enough deaths in it to provide a good supply of examples. What evidence there is suggests close uniformity with the patterns found in the other epic. Another way of saying this is that the main group of deaths in the *Odyssey*, the slaughter of the suitors, was written as an imitation of the duels of the *Iliad* (see e.g. Fernández-Galiano (1992), 209, and throughout his notes to *Odyssey* xxii).

[18] Niens (1987) is the most detailed study of the structuring of Homeric battle scenes. Niens's approach is to define the typical combat scene as a sequence of seven structural units or 'parameters' (see pp. xiii, 259–60 for her programme), and then to collect all the possible formulaic and other expressions which are employed to fill each of the seven slots. Of these parameters, no. 7 is the event of death as treated in this chapter. Otherwise, the extensive literature on Homeric battle scenes is mostly concerned with large narrative structures rather than smaller units like those which we are trying to distinguish here. The treatment of Fenik (1968) has been especially useful, but mostly on points of principle: he addresses himself to the order of events within sequences of battle rather than to the arrangement of formulaic members in single events of such a sequence, so that he does not consider the arrangement of ideas within the line or lines which express the idea 'he died'. Again, Latacz (1977) deals only with large-scale structures. On the sequence of events in killings, there is some useful treatment by Friedrich (1956), esp. 47–83; while Marg (1942) has a briefer but very incisive survey of the patterns of narration in individual deaths. On the formal structures cf. also Létoublon (1983). The data collected in this chapter have also been checked against Garland's survey of Homeric death-language (1981).

death; and his armour is stripped.[19] Naturally the deaths of important heroes tend to be more complex, while in briefer killings the moment of death can be represented elliptically, so that ὧσε χαμᾶζε or θυμὸν ἀπηύρα or simply ἐνάριξε will be enough on its own to indicate that a minor warrior was killed;[20] but such expansion and contraction must be distinguished from the rearrangement of members in a different sequence, which is much less common.[21] If we isolate the point at which the narrative turns to the subjective experience of the victim, we will be close to the kernel of how death is imagined.[22] The key phrase usually states that the dying man loses his final breath or the essence of life, as θυμός, ψυχή, μένος, or αἰών, or that darkness descends on his sight. It is in the latter group of

[19] On typical battle scenes in general, Fenik (1968: 229) notes in conclusion that a practical distinction can be made between 'short sequences of standard elements which are arranged in a relatively fixed order' and 'larger structural outlines which extend over longer stretches of the action and allow considerable variation of detail'. Within the type-scene of the narrative slaying, elaborate deaths at crucial 'joints' in the story—Hector and Patroclus—tend to the latter of Fenik's extremes and exhibit not only the rearrangement of members but also more vivid use of mythical motifs.

[20] The pregnant associations of some of these expressions are very strong. Fenik (1968: 132) notes that γούνατα λῦεν and similar usually refer to a death rather than to a temporary discomfiture (but cf. e.g. XVIII. 31), and this accords well with the deeper association of the knees with inner vitality. On vitality and the knees see Onians (1951), 174–86; Burkert (1979), 44–5, with n. 45 and figs. 3 and 4. Gladigow (1968) proposes a link between knees and generation in terms both of ideas and of etymology (γόνυ, γίγνομαι built on the root *gen), though it is impossible to prove that in the Homeric world this is more than a linguistic fossil. See also Ch. 4 above, pp. 111–13, on vitality embodied in the flexibility of the limbs.

[21] Among the 120 or so narrative killings in which one or other expression states or implies that the vanquished hero died, there are a few (notably IV. 467–72, 501–4, 519–26, XVI. 330–4, 502–5, XX. 413–18) in which the order is dislocated: in some of these a generalized or allusive expression (e.g. λῦσε δὲ γυῖα, IV. 469; λῦσε μένος, XVI. 332) anticipates a more precise expression or follows after it, perhaps for the sake of pathos.

[22] On the sequence of events shifting from the visible sign of death to the experience of the dying man and the fall of darkness onto his eyes, see Marg (1942), 172–4; Mueller (1984), 82–9; and on this as a shift from the outer perspective to the inner, cf. also de Jong (1987), 15. The distinction between these two types is obviously a fine one, and most of the briefer killings include only one of the two. Niens (1987) does not distinguish between these two varieties of *Schlussvers*, and groups them both under her seventh 'parameter.'

images that the narration turns most closely to dying man's point of view. At this level of narration, alongside θάνατος and κήρ stand μοῖρα and a group of other nouns, notably πότμος, ὄλεθρος, and φόνος, which are closely linked to them and seem to act as their virtual synonyms. κήρ and μοῖρα differ significantly from θάνατος, since in other contexts they are also associated with the planning of the courses of a man's whole life; but when his end finally comes their character and identity are closely bound up with the figure of Death, and expressions such as κῆρες θανάτοιο or θάνατος καὶ μοῖρα κραταιή, the latter usually with a singular verb, encourage us to consider them as a close-knit group.[23] When we do this the rendering of death as descent of darkness falls into a consistent pattern.

Observe the verbal forms that this takes.[24] Night covers the eyes, τὸν δὲ κατ' ὀφθαλμῶν ἐρεβεννὴ νὺξ ἐκάλυψεν (v. 659 = XIII. 580), or gloom covers them, τὸν δὲ σκότος ὄσσε κάλυψεν (IV. 461, 503, 526, VI. 11, XIII. 575, XIV. 519, XV. 578, XVI. 316, XX. 393, 471, XXI. 181; sim. XVI. 325); death covers over the man, θάνατος δέ μιν ἀμφεκάλυψε (v. 68); the black cloud of death envelops him, θανάτου δὲ μέλαν νέφος ἀμφεκάλυψεν (XVI. 350; sim. XX. 417–18; iv. 180), or the fulfilment of death covers his eyes and nose, τέλος θανάτοιο κάλυψεν | ὀφθαλμοὺς

[23] The question of functional synonymy between these nouns has not been fully investigated. Paraskevaides (1984: 43–6) presents lists which show that many epithets are shared between these and related nouns, further suggesting close semantic association. Including the language of narrative, the principal combinations of this kind are (a) θάνατος with πότμος (II. 359, XV. 495, XX. 337; xxiv. 31), also found in the form θανεῖν καὶ πότμον ἐπισπεῖν or similar (IV. 170, VII. 52; iv. 196, and six other instances in *Odyssey*); (b) θάνατος with μοῖρα (III. 101, V. 83, and seven other instances in *Iliad* only), also found in the form μοῖρα . . . θανάτοιο (XIII. 602; ii. 100 = iii. 238, xvii. 326, etc.); (c) θάνατος with κήρ (XVI. 47, XXI. 66, 565; ii. 283 and ten other instances in *Odyssey*); also κῆρ(ες) θανάτοιο (II. 302, IX. 411, XI. 332, XII. 326, XVI. 687; xi. 171 and three more in *Odyssey*); (d) φόνος with κήρ (II. 352, III. 6, XI. 443; ii. 165 and three more in *Odyssey*). O'Nolan (1978: 25) compares doublets in general to noun-epithet formulae, in Parryist terms: 'The combination represents a double image but a single idea'. Writing on the *Odyssey* in particular, he gives some specific attention to doublets with θάνατος, κήρ, and μόρος, but he is content to assume a priori that such doublets are indeed acting as synonyms (23, etc.). See also below, n. 27.

[24] It has been useful to compare this list with the tables assembled by Garland (1981), esp. 46, and by Niens (1987), *passim*. See also Moreux (1967), 238–41.

ῥῖνάς τε (XVI. 502–3; sim. v. 553). Akin to this is the slightly different image that something is *poured* over the eyes: either a dark fog, κατὰ δ' ὀφθαλμῶν κέχυτ' ἀχλύς (XVI. 344; sim. xxii. 88), or simply death itself, ἀμφὶ δέ οἱ θάνατος χύτο θυμοραϊστής (XIII. 544, XVI. 414). Evidently this refers to the clouding of sight at the moment consciousness is lost—indeed its temporary loss in a swoon is rendered in the same way, as covering (v. 310, XI. 356, XIV. 438–9, XXII. 466) or pouring (v. 696).

So far, then, the imagery seems straightforward: the eyes lose their sight, darkness falls, and that is what it means to die. This darkness is a cloud which covers over the dying man, or it is poured over him like a liquid, perhaps blood dripping down his face, κατ' ὄσσε . . . πορφύρεος θάνατος. Clearly in these instances the darkness is purely negative and carries no hint of mythical development. But a few of the formulae in this group are less simple, because the cloud or mist or darkness is imagined as actively seizing the dying man: hateful darkness takes him, στυγερὸς δ' ἄρα μιν σκότος εἷλε (v. 47, XIII. 672 = XVI. 607); the portion of black death seizes him, κατὰ μοῖρ' ἔλαβεν μέλανος θανάτοιο (xvii. 326); dark death seizes him along his eyes, τὸν δὲ κατ' ὄσσε | ἔλλαβε πορφύρεος θάνατος καὶ μοῖρα κραταιή (v. 82–3, XVI. 333–4 = XX. 476–7). ἔλλαβε, ἔλαβεν, εἷλεν: this suggests something more like an assault by an aggressor. The ambiguity between pouring and seizing recalls what we observed in the rendering of sleep, where the personal Ὕπνος described himself as poured over Zeus' eyes: so that we seem to be coming a little closer to the actions of a personal deity in the very moment of dying.[25] But the subject of the verb of covering-over and seizing is often either a periphrasis, as τέλος θανάτοιο (v. 553, XVI. 502, XXII. 361; also in speeches, IX. 416, XI. 451),[26] or a

---

[25] The mist which falls on the sight, Ἀχλύς, is among the strange and savage personifications on the Hesiodic *Shield of Heracles* (264–70). There is no telling whether such exotica represent late decadence of the epic tradition or stem from old traditions which Homer draws on but does not usually make explicit (cf. above, n. 6).

[26] τέλος in such expressions is difficult, but makes more sense if we compare it with the pattern of Death's slow approach discernible in rhetorical language (see below, pp. 243–50). The descent of darkness on the eyes would thus be the fulfilment, τέλος, of his journey to his victim. Compare τὸν δ' ἄγε μοῖρα κακὴ θανάτοιο τέλοσδε (XIII. 602), and also the image evoked by πείρατα in ὀλέθρου πείρατα (see below, n. 52). On τέλος as fulfilment or accomplishment see

doublet with a singular verb, θάνατος καὶ μοῖρα κραταιή (v. 83 = XVI. 334, XVI. 855 = XXII. 361, XX. 477).[27] These round-about expressions naturally prevent us from fixing the image as sharply as we do when the personal Thanatos walks onto the stage at Sarpedon's death; but it remains significant that even at this lean level of language death can be rendered not only as a negative thing, a nightfall, but also as an external agent who overpowers the dying man when he is enveloped in darkness.

Death approaches and seizes the victim

In his storytelling Homer seems unwilling to linger on the moment of death: the leanness of the imagery perhaps suggests a kind of taboo or εὐφημία.[28] It is when Homer goes beyond the narrative proper that language becomes more vivid and more richly allusive: principally when characters mention the prospect of approaching death, but also when the poet himself looks along the broad sweep of past or coming events. Imagery of this kind is also occasionally found when the poet refers to death in the negative, by saying that a man was *not* killed. Here language bodies forth not only the plain fact of death but its deeper meaning, and correspondingly the mythical element comes more to the fore and death is more clearly envisaged as an assault by a mythical aggressor.[29] As in the narrative

Heubeck (1972), suggesting a complex scheme for the spatial relationships indicated by τέλος and πείρατα; also M. J. Clarke (1995*b*), 314–17.

[27] In such doublets it is impossible to tell whether separate images should be assigned to the two nouns. On the words θάνατος καὶ μοῖρα κραταιή (XVI. 853), Janko (ad loc.) remarks that 'death and fate, treated almost as synonyms, are personified by the verb'. The singular verb does not necessarily prove that Thanatos and Moira are not both present in person. Poetically, however, a doublet like θάνατος καὶ μοῖρα focuses the meaning more sharply than either noun could do on its own: this is the sort of death whose inevitability is in its nature. We might compare the passage (XVI. 849–50) in which Patroclus says that Apollo, cruel fate (μοῖρ' ὀλοή), and Euphorbus have together killed him. For μοῖρα as the partner of other deities see also esp. XVIII. 119, XIX. 87, 410. See also above, n. 23.

[28] Compare the bowdlerizing vocabulary used of the sexual act. In the narrative people simply 'lie together' or 'mingle', and it is only in the speech of his characters that Homer is willing to speak of semen dripping into a woman's womb (see Ch. 4, p. 110 with n. 124).

[*See p. 244 for n. 29*]

formulae, the pattern emerges most clearly if we concentrate less on the noun than on the verb: death's personality is emerging not in name but in actions. This means that here as before we cast our net not only on the simple θάνατος and κήρ but also on μοῖρα and a few further nouns which are never fully personified, notably ὄλεθρος, as well as doublets and periphrases such as θάνατος καὶ πότμος, θανάτοιο τέλος, θάνατος καὶ μοῖρα, κῆρες θανάτοιο.

The essence is that a man does not go to meet death, but rather it is death that comes to meet him. Presumably this is rooted in the less easily visualized idea of his approach through time,[30] but as the details emerge they are pinned on movement through space. Hector fears that fate is approaching him, νῦν αὖτέ με μοῖρα κιχάνει (XXII. 303); Odysseus warns that if the gods are vigilant the fulfilment of death is approaching Antinous, Ἀντίνοον πρὸ γάμοιο τέλος θανάτοιο κιχείη (xvii. 476; cf. IX. 416); a man can see that death-and-fate is on its way to the tryst, νῦν αὖ θάνατος καὶ μοῖρα κιχάνει (XVII. 478 = XVII. 672 = XXII. 436); similarly one warns another that sheer destruction is approaching him, ἦ μάλα δή σε κιχάνεται αἰπὺς ὄλεθρος (XI. 441). Correspondingly, when one courts disaster he is going out to meet death,[31] θανατόνδε κιόντα (XXIV. 328), and he follows after or accompanies it, θάνατον καὶ πότμον ἐπίσπηι (II. 359, XV. 495, XX. 337; xxiv. 31), πότμον ἐπίσπηι (VI. 412, XXII. 39; ii. 250, iii. 16, iv. 714, xi. 197, 372, xxii. 317 = 416, xxiv. 471), θανέειν καὶ πότμον ἐπισπεῖν (VII. 52; iv. 196, 562, v. 308, xi. 389, xii. 342, xiv. 274, xxiv. 22). When a warrior is about to die, Death is near him, ἐγγύθεν (XVIII. 133): so that when Hector dons the armour of Patroclus, Zeus pities him for

---

[29] Cf. A. Lesky in *RE* v A(1), s.v. 'Thanatos', 1249–51; Dietrich (1965), 197; Erbse (1986), 22–3.

[30] Space and time are indistinguishable here. Note the use of ὀλέθριον ἦμαρ (XIX. 294, 409, etc.), αἴσιμον ἦμαρ (XXI. 100, etc.), νηλεὲς ἦμαρ (XI. 484, 588, XIII. 514, XV. 375, XVII. 511, etc.), and ὀλέθρου πείρατα (VI. 143 = XX. 429, VII. 402, XII. 79) in expressions very like those which we collect here. For the same ambiguity compare also πρόσθ' ὁρόων θάνατον (XX. 481); θάνατος καὶ κῆδε' ὀπίσσω | ἔσσεται (IV. 270–1). A man sees the prospect of a future death and by the same token sees it approaching across the field. (On this ambiguity between space and time cf. Snell (1952), 175–85.)

[31] Compare the passage where the gods are said to call Patroclus to his death, θεοὶ θανατόνδε κάλεσσαν (XVI. 693).

the death which is now moving ever closer to him, σχεδὸν εἶσι (XVII. 201–2).[32] Correspondingly, when Telemachus reviles the suitors he threatens to release the agents of death against them, κακὰς ἐπὶ κῆρας ἰήλω (ii. 316), suggesting perhaps that he will unleash them like hounds.[33] When a warrior is in danger he hopes to flee from the assailant, εὐχόμενος θάνατόν τε φυγεῖν καὶ μῶλον Ἄρηος (II. 401; sim. I. 60, XI. 362 = XX. 449, XVI. 98, XXI. 66, 103, iv. 789, xv. 300). One in danger of death considers how to do this, ὅπως . . . θάνατον καὶ κῆρα φύγωμεν (XVII. 714; sim. ix. 61, 467, xii. 157). When Hector is being pursued by Achilles, Homer asks how he could have evaded the divinities of death without Apollo's help: πῶς δέ κεν Ἕκτωρ κῆρας ὑπεξέφυγεν θανάτοιο; (XXII. 202). Odysseus in his wrath tells a suitor that he will not escape death, τῶ οὐκ ἂν θάνατόν γε δυσηλεγέα προφύγοισθα (xxii. 325); similarly one who gets divine help would not otherwise have made his getaway from the Ker, οὐδὲ γὰρ οὐδέ κεν αὐτὸς ὑπέκφυγε κῆρα μέλαιναν (v. 22, sim. XVI. 687).

Since one who evades death escapes from these beings, ἔκφυγε κῆρα or ἔκφυγε κῆρας (iv. 502, 512, xv. 235; sim. XVIII. 117), it makes sense that he can be said to elude their grasp, ἀλεύατο κῆρα μέλαιναν (III. 360 = VII. 254, XI. 360, XIV. 462), as he runs away from peril, ἂψ δ' ἑτάρων εἰς ἔθνος ἐχάζετο κῆρ' ἀλεείνων (III. 32 = XI. 585 = XIII. 566 = XIII. 596 = XIII. 648 = XIV. 408 = XVI. 817). Those who hope to survive perils look to the same prospect, ἤ κεν ἀλευάμενοι θάνατον καὶ κῆρα φύγοιμεν (xii. 157). To avoid death is to ward off its agents, θάνατον καὶ κῆρας ἀλύξαι (XXI. 565; ii. 352 = v. 387, xvii. 547 = xix. 558, xxii. 66), similarly κακὰς ἀπὸ κῆρας ἀλύξαι (XII. 113; xxiii. 332; sim. xv. 287). The one who preserves his life is warding off the fulfilment of death, τέλος θανάτου ἀλεείνων (v. 326), or escaping from the Ker, ἀλύσκων κῆρα μέλαιναν (xxii. 363, 382; sim. xxii. 330), and a protecting god

---

[32] Some MSS read σχεδὸν ἐστί, but εἶσι is more vivid as well as being the more difficult reading from the point of view of the post-Homeric transmitter of the text (see Edwards ad loc.).

[33] An image of the same kind appears when Hector threatens that he will kill Diomedes before he can go home: he will 'give the divinity' to him, πάρος τοι δαίμονα δώσω (VIII. 166). If Thanatos or Ker is the δαίμων in question the image at least makes sense, but it remains difficult: Kirk (ad loc.) considers it 'hard to stomach'. Zenodotus emended to πότμον ἐφήσω.

fights away the Keres, κῆρας ἀμύνει (IV. 11, XII. 402), just as he might fight away visible enemies. Similarly, to save one from death at the last moment is to release him, θανάτοιο δυσηχέος ἐξαναλῦσαι (XVI. 442; also XX. 300). The image is no less vivid when Hephaestus tells Thetis that he wishes he could hide her son from his coming death when its agent arrives:

αἲ γάρ μιν θανάτοιο δυσηχέος ὧδε δυναίμην
νόσφιν ἀποκρύψαι, ὅτε μιν μόρος αἰνὸς ἱκάνοι. (XVIII. 464–5)

Although the name of the bringer of death changes even between two lines, the process which this describes is a single progress by the assailant or assailants to the victim.[34]

To die is to be met at last by these agents of death. It is such a meeting that Achilles refers to when he says that he will suffer death when the gods will it:

κῆρα δ᾽ ἐγὼ τότε δέξομαι, ὁππότε κεν δὴ
Ζεὺς ἐθέληι τελέσαι ἠδ᾽ ἀθάνατοι θεοὶ ἄλλοι. (XVIII. 115–16)

Homeric δέχομαι does not denote the kind of mental process that we refer to in woolly English expressions like 'I will accept my fate'; rather it is the physical act of awaiting or receiving a thing or a personal visitor, who is very often an enemy coming to attack one in battle (see e.g. V. 228, 238, XX. 377). Hence Achilles must mean that he is awaiting a personal encounter with the agent of death. Similarly when Odysseus is about to kill a foe he tells him that death has arrived first at the rendezvous: φθῆ σε τέλος θανάτοιο κιχήμενον, οὐδ᾽ ὑπάλυξας (XI. 451). At the fatal moment μοῖρα fastens on a dying man, καθέληισι (ii. 100 = iii. 238 = xix. 145 = xxiv. 135), overcomes him, ἐδάμασσε (xxii. 413), or pins him down, μοῖρα πέδησε (IV. 517).[35] When a man realizes that death is inevitable he knows that he will be seized, νῦν δέ με λευγαλέωι θανάτωι εἵμαρτο ἁλῶναι (XXI. 281 = v. 312; sim. xxiv. 34). But what exactly does this mean? An answer is suggested by an intriguing passage

---

[34] Μόρος, who is listed by Hesiod among the children of Night (*Theog.* 211), seems to be little more than a by-form of Moira with no special identity of his own (see Dietrich (1965), 249, 260–7, 277–8; Erbse (1986), 278–9).

[35] The same phrase is less closely identified as the moment of death at XXII. 5.

where Apollo stands by Agenor and protects him from death at Achilles' hands:

$$\pi\grave{\alpha}\rho \ \delta\acute{\epsilon} \ o\acute{\iota} \ \alpha\mathring{v}\tau\grave{o}s$$
$$\ddot{\epsilon}\sigma\tau\eta, \ \ddot{o}\pi\omega s \ \theta\alpha\nu\acute{\alpha}\tauo\iota o \ \beta\alpha\rho\epsilon\acute{\iota}\alpha s \ \chi\epsilon\hat{\iota}\rho\alpha s \ \mathring{\alpha}\lambda\acute{\alpha}\lambda\kappa o\iota.$$ (XXI. 547–8)

Allen reads $\kappa\hat{\eta}\rho\alpha s$ here, but $\chi\epsilon\hat{\iota}\rho\alpha s$ is better attested and better suits the context: Death's hands are reaching out to seize his foe.[36] I suspect that the same image is implied, even very distantly, in the narrative formula which describes the 'fulfilment of death' covering over the dying man: since a $\tau\acute{\epsilon}\lambda os$ is regularly a completion or fulfilment by encirclement, these words may mean that Death's hands seize the dying man in a lethal embrace, $\tau\acute{\epsilon}\lambda os \ \theta\alpha\nu\acute{\alpha}\tauo\iota o \ \kappa\acute{\alpha}\lambda\upsilon\psi\epsilon\nu \ | \ \grave{o}\phi\theta\alpha\lambda\muo\grave{\upsilon}s \ \acute{\rho}\hat{\iota}\nu\acute{\alpha}s \ \tau\epsilon$ (see above, n. 26).

Certain passages of exceptionally high rhetorical tone bring us still closer to the point at which a divine agent has fully materialized on the battlefield. When Patroclus is on his knees before Hector he sees with the urgency of foresight[37] that Death is close to his foe:

$$o\ddot{v} \ \theta\eta\nu \ o\mathring{v}\delta' \ \alpha\mathring{v}\tau\grave{o}s \ \delta\eta\rho\grave{o}\nu \ \beta\acute{\epsilon}\eta\iota, \ \mathring{\alpha}\lambda\lambda\acute{\alpha} \ \tauo\iota \ \ddot{\eta}\delta\eta$$
$$\ddot{\alpha}\gamma\chi\iota \ \pi\alpha\rho\acute{\epsilon}\sigma\tau\eta\kappa\epsilon\nu \ \theta\acute{\alpha}\nu\alpha\tauo s \ \kappa\alpha\grave{\iota} \ \muo\hat{\iota}\rho\alpha \ \kappa\rho\alpha\tau\alpha\iota\acute{\eta}.$$

(XVI. 852–3; sim. XXIV. 131–2, and cf.
XXIV. 28–9)

---

[36] $\chi\epsilon\hat{\iota}\rho\alpha s$ is the vulgate reading, and $\kappa\hat{\eta}\rho\alpha s$ is supported by only one surviving MS and the testimony of Eustathius. There is a similar problem at I. 97, where there is some ancient authority for the phrase $\lambdao\iota\muo\hat{\iota}o \ \beta\alpha\rho\epsilon\acute{\iota}\alpha s \ \chi\epsilon\hat{\iota}\rho\alpha s$ (see Kirk ad loc.). From our treatment throughout this chapter it will be clear that the image of Death's hands is consistent with the overall pattern but is unusually vivid for an image in the straight narrative in the poet's own voice. Richardson compares the image of the 'mighty hand of Zeus' at XV. 694–5, though its role there is to propel Hector forward rather than to seize him; the parallel is closer at Patroclus' death, when Apollo strikes him with his hand and enables Euphorbus to kill him (XVI. 791–2). Note also the picture which Helen makes of the sufferings that the warriors undergo at the hands of Ares, $\mathring{v}\pi' \ \mathring{A}\rho\eta os \ \pi\alpha\lambda\alpha\mu\acute{\alpha}\omega\nu$ (III. 128).

[37] There is something more than human in such knowledge; the same prophecy recurs word for word in Thetis' lament over the coming death of Achilles himself (XXIV. 132). Janko (at XVI. 852–4) quotes later Greek literature for the belief that men have foresight at the moment of death; there is no direct statement of this principle in Homer.

In Hector's final duel with Achilles, when Athena deserts him he recognizes that Death is now at hand:

νῦν δὲ δὴ ἐγγύθι μοι θάνατος κακός, οὐδ' ἔτ' ἄνευθεν,
οὐδ' ἀλέη·
. . . νῦν αὖτέ με μοῖρα κιχάνει.   (XXII. 300–3)

Similarly, earlier in his wild career Achilles reminds one of his victims that death is at hand for them both in this place:

ἔπι τοι καὶ ἐμοὶ θάνατος καὶ μοῖρα κραταιή.   (XXI. 110; cf. XX. 390)

Again, Tiresias prophesies to Odysseus the final advent of Death, coming across the sea to kill him:

θάνατος δέ τοι ἐξ ἁλὸς αὐτῶι
ἀβληχρὸς μάλα τοῖος ἐλεύσεται, ὅς κέ σε πέφνηι
γήραι ὕπο λιπαρῶι ἀρημένον . . .   (xi. 134–6; cf. xiii. 59–60)

Since Death will kill Odysseus, πέφνηι, he must be the agent rather than merely the experience of dying. In an unusual passage Odysseus uses the word αἶσα—normally associated with Moira in the planning of death rather than its fulfilment[38]—to name the agent of death who stood by him and his followers when they faced death at the hands of the Cicones:

τότε δή ῥα κακὴ Διὸς αἶσα παρέστη
ἡμῖν αἰνομόροισιν, ἵν' ἄλγεα πολλὰ πάθοιμεν.   (ix. 52–3)

The woes, ἄλγεα, in question are presumably the deaths of six men from each of Odysseus' ships, which follow immediately (ix. 60–1), so that Aisa seems to be fulfilling the role we have elsewhere seen given to Thanatos.

The Keres prompt a few remarkable images in rhetoric which beg to be read in the light of the scene made explicit on the Shield of Achilles, where they roam the battlefield and drag their victims hither and thither. When Sarpedon urges Glaucus to the onslaught, he reminds him that they are surrounded by κῆρες who make death inevitable:

νῦν δ' ἔμπης γὰρ κῆρες ἐφεστᾶσιν θανάτοιο
μυρίαι, ἃς οὐκ ἔστι φυγεῖν βροτὸν οὐδ' ὑπαλύξαι.   (XII. 326–7)

---

[38] On αἶσα see Dietrich (1965), esp. 249–60.

Perhaps the idea is similar when one in fear for his life is seeing death before him, πρόσθ' ὁρόων θάνατον (xx. 481). Similarly, Idomeneus says that the coward in battle expects to meet the κῆρες of his approaching death:

> ἐν δέ τέ οἱ κραδίη μεγάλα στέρνοισι πατάσσει
> κῆρας ὀϊομένωι, πάταγος δέ τε γίγνετ' ὀδόντων.
>
> (xiii. 282–3; cf. xvii. 381)

Patroclus' ghost produces a revealing image of the fulfilment of death when he tells Achilles that he cannot return to the land of the living because the κήρ of his fate gaped around him[39] with her jaws when he died:[40]

> οὐ μὲν γὰρ ζωοί γε φίλων ἀπάνευθεν ἑταίρων
> βουλὰς ἑζόμενοι βουλεύσομεν, ἀλλ' ἐμὲ μὲν κὴρ
> ἀμφέχανε στυγερή, ἥ περ λάχε γιγνόμενόν περ. (xxiii. 77–9)

By ἀμφέχανε, 'yawned', 'gaped', he must mean that the Ker opened her mouth to seize him like some monstrous beast. Several times we hear that the Keres carry dying men away, κῆρες ἔβαν θανάτοιο φέρουσαι (ii. 302; xiv. 207), just as on the Shield of Achilles they drag the corpses to and fro.

This helps to explain another rhetorical image of κῆρες. Hector, in high war-fury as he nears the pinnacle of his success against the Greeks, hopes that Zeus will enable the Achaeans to be expelled for ever from Troy:

---

[39] Although ἀμφέχανε here is a *hapax*, its sense is clear enough from Homer's use of the simple verb χαίνω, 'to gape open-mouthed': of a man (xvi. 350, 409; xii. 350), of a raging lion (xx. 168), as well as of the earth yawning open to swallow someone up (iv. 182, vi. 282, viii. 150, xvii. 417).

[40] This image is potentially misleading. We have noted elsewhere (Ch. 6, pp. 166–8) that with one exception (xiv. 207–8) Homer does not associate the agents of death with the journey to Hades. At first glance the present passage seems to be an exception, with Patroclus implying that the κήρ of death is holding him fast in Hades. For example, Richardson (ad loc.) translates 'a hateful doom *has gaped* around me' (my italics). But if this were correct, a perfect or present tense would be required; since ἀμφέχανε is aorist, it more naturally refers to a single event in past time: κήρ seized Patroclus in her jaws and he died. Thus the κήρ in question is the death which seized Patroclus on the field of battle *before* he made his way to Hades, with no connection implied between the two events. Cf. n. 63 below.

εὔχομαι ἐλπόμενος Διί τ' ἄλλοισίν τε θεοῖσιν
ἐξελάαν ἐνθένδε κύνας κηρεσσιφορήτους,
οὓς κῆρες φορέουσι μελαινάων ἐπὶ νηῶν.　(VIII. 526–8)

The last line unpacks the hard adjective κηρεσσιφορήτους,[41] and
the meaning has been taken to be that the Achaeans have been
drawn or carried by κῆρες on their murderous voyage to Troy.[42]
But such an image would be very unusual: nowhere else do
κῆρες bring about their work of slaughter by actively sending
human adversaries to make war on each other. Although the
verb φορέω can refer to carrying something as one might carry
men on a ship, it is also found in a frequentative sense, meaning
to drag or carry something hither and thither.[43] Thus we can
take the adjective as predicative: Zeus, or Hector acting on his
behalf, will set the Achaeans to flight, ἐξελάαν, to be slain and
thus to be seized and dragged away by the κῆρες of death. Since
Hector is speaking during a break in the fighting, the present
tense of the last line is part of the vividness of the prophecy:
Hector suggests that on the eve of the slaughter the Keres are
already roaming among the Achaeans in their camp beside the
ships, ἐπὶ νηῶν,[44] just as elsewhere men go to battle despite
prophecy of disaster because they are already being dragged
away, κῆρες γὰρ ἄγον μέλανος θανάτοιο (II. 834). Hector's rhetoric
is a less vivid version than what is depicted on the Shield of
Achilles, but it springs from the same underlying conception of
death.

[41] It is a reasonable guess (Zenodotus, Aristarchus, and Kirk ad loc.; on the
ancients' views of the lines see Nickau (1977), 127–8), that 528 is a post-
Homeric interpolation originating as a gloss on the difficult κηρεσσιφορήτους of
527. If this is the case it does not affect our interpretation one way or the
other, since the gloss sheds no light on the meaning of the carrying or
dragging.

[42] See L. Malten in *RE* Suppl. iv. 887; Erbse (1986), 282, with further refs.

[43] Cf. Sihler (1995), § 468. 2. The adjective φορητός is not attested elsewhere
in Homer, but given the frequentative sense of the parent verb it will describe
something as dragged about hither and thither. It is found in later verse in this
sense (see Pind. fr. 33d. 1 M).

[44] For ἐπί meaning 'close to, alongside' rather than 'on' see e.g. XVIII. 557,
XXII. 153, i. 185, ix. 140, etc., and note μελαινάων ἐπὶ νηῶν (V. 700) in the sense
'to the area beside the ships'.

The planning of fate leads to death's fulfilment

All these images are drawn out in contexts of especially intense
and dramatic emotion, where Homer's supple aesthetic allows
him to forsake the leanness of the plain narrative and rise close
to the highest level of articulation. We saw that in rhetoric and
in the leaner language of narrative the different agents of death
could not be clearly distinguished from each other. However,
when they emerge more fully into the limelight they take on
distinct individual roles and identities. In particular μοῖρα and
κήρ (along with πότμος, αἶσα, and οἶτος[45]) differ from θάνατος in
that they are responsible not only for death but also for the
planning of man's fate at his birth and its execution throughout
his life.[46] On one perspective, our words are the names of
divinities who have spun out man's fate as thread from the
moment of his birth, as Hecuba puts it when she urges Priam
to accept that it is inevitable that the dead Hector will be
mutilated:

τῶι δ' ὥς ποθι <u>Μοῖρα κραταιὴ</u>
<u>γιγνομένωι ἐπένησε λίνωι,</u> ὅτε μιν τέκον αὐτή,
ἀργίποδας κύνας ἆσαι ἑῶν ἀπάνευθε τοκήων.   (XXIV. 209–11)

We find the same image elsewhere with αἶσα (XX. 127–8) and
αἶσα . . . κλῶθές τε βαρεῖαι (VII. 196–8) instead of μοῖρα; once
again, the conception is constant even when the agents have
different names.[47] The image of spinning itself is another
example of the problem of language and myth. From the
angle of 'Religion' it could be seen as part of a complex
belief about fate and the deities responsible for it;[48] but in

---

[45] οἶτος in Homer usually but not always refers to death in particular, as the
fulfilment of one's fate: οἵ κεν δὴ κακὸν οἶτον ἀναπλήσαντες ὄλωνται
(VIII. 34 = 354 = 465). On one occasion those who have died have followed
it, ἐπέσπον (III. 134), as one might follow θάνατος or πότμος. On οἶτος see
Dietrich (1965), 272–3; Erbse (1986), 280.

[46] A full treatment of the divinities of fate would be out of place here. On
the group as a whole, the most useful studies have been those of Pötscher
(1960), Dietrich (1965), and Erbse (1986), 273–86. The main concern of these
scholars is with the relationship between the will of the gods and the divinities
of fate, which is not relevant to this study.

[47] On these passages see Erbse (1986), 278.

[48] See Dietrich (1965), 289–96. Hesiod assigns personal names and identities to three Moirai, but gives them different parentage in different passages

the most mundane Homeric language a plot or a plan is spun or woven in the thoughts, ὑφαίνειν or ῥάπτειν, so that the idea of Moira or Aisa spinning one's future fate like a thread might simply be a realization of this idea on the plane of myth.[49] In this way the spinning of fate is another example of a conception which is brought to birth at different times on different levels from the most ordinary language to the mythical shaping of personal agents.

It is difficult to be sure about the relationship between the spinning of fate and the final fulfilment of death. To die is to complete one's fate, often πότμον ἀναπλήσειν, but πότμος may also be the death to which one is being brought (e.g. XVIII. 96).[50]

(*Theog.* 218–19, 904–6). It is impossible to tell whether Homer is looking to any such precise lore about them. One of Hesiod's Moirai is called Κλωθώ, from the action of spinning itself; Homer names the spinners as αἶσα Κλῶθές τε βαρεῖαι (vii. 197).

[49] Note κακὰ ῥάψαι for Hera's scheming against the Trojans (XVIII. 367), the suitors' plots (xvi. 421–3), and the plans that led to the making of the Trojan Horse (iii. 118), together with the noun κακορραφίη in the equivalent sense (xv. 16; ii. 236, xii. 26); φόνον αἰπὺν ῥάπτομεν of the suitors' plot against Telemachus (xvi. 379); πυκινὸν δόλον . . . ὕφαινε (VI. 187), of Proetus scheming against Bellerophon; πάντας δὲ δόλους καὶ μῆτιν ὕφαινον (ix. 422), Odysseus on his stratagems against Polyphemus; μῆτιν ὕφαινον of the suitors' plots (iv. 678), and similarly ὑφαίνειν ἤρχετο μῆτιν (VII. 324 = IX. 93), introducing speeches of policy by Nestor (see also iv. 739, xiii. 303, 386); again μή τίς μοι ὑφαίνῃσιν δόλον αὖτε | ἀθανάτων (v. 356–7), Odysseus' fear of further punishment by hostile gods. It is worth comparing the spinning of plots with the story of Penelope's loom (ii. 93–110, xix. 137–56, xxiv. 128–48), which can be seen as a working-out of the same simple idea into a self-contained narrative: to make cunning plots is to weave, and Penelope's stratagem is the act of cunning *par excellence*. (On this suggestion see Russo at xix. 137, on 'her literal actions paralleling her metaphorical description'; also Heubeck at xxiv. 128–9.) Further, the verb ἐπικλώθειν is used of the gods' actions in planning or working out the experiences—usually sufferings—of mortals, especially in the *Odyssey* (see XXIV. 525; i. 17, iii. 208, iv. 208, viii. 579, xi. 139, xvi. 64, xx. 196). Can we tell whether the use of this verb implies the full image of the spinning of fate? Achilles uses the verb when he states the principle that the gods bring about suffering for mortals, ἐπεκλώσαντο θεοὶ δειλοῖσι βροτοῖσι | ζώειν ἀχνυμένοις (XXIV. 525–6), but goes on to explain this (γάρ, 527) not by extending an image of spinning but by recounting the story of the three jars from which Zeus doles out good and evil (527–51). Unless Achilles' language is oddly disjointed in this sequence of ideas, this is enough to suggest that the verb ἐπικλώθειν has not been enough in itself to prompt the image that the experiences of mortals are spun.

[50] In the case of μοῖρα, Dietrich (1965: 59–90, 194–231) argues that Moira

The gap is bridged when Moira, Ker, and others are seen neither as planning nor as killing but as drawing a man on towards death: τὸν δ' ἄγε μοῖρα κακὴ θανάτοιο τέλοσδε (XIII. 602; sim. v. 613–14). Fate draws a man to his end by launching him against an opponent who is sure to win:

Τληπόλεμον δ' Ἡρακλείδην, ἠΰν τε μέγαν τε,
ὦρσεν ἐπ' ἀντιθέωι Σαρπηδόνι μοῖρα κραταιή.   (v. 628–9)

Again, Patroclus' shade merges the two roles of the agent of fate when he says that the κήρ who seized him in death had already assigned herself to him at birth, ἥ περ λάχε γιγνόμενόν περ (XXIII. 78–9). The pattern is the same when Achilles represents the choice between life and glory as the choice to be brought to death by one κήρ rather than another:[51]

μήτηρ γάρ τέ μέ φησι θεὰ Θέτις ἀργυρόπεζα
διχθαδίας κῆρας φερέμεν θανάτοιο τέλοσδε.   (IX. 410–11)

At the scene of death the Keres seize victims and drag them away; here, in a distinct image, they draw a man *towards* his death.

The same names can be used without mythical import

It is impossible to tell whether the full complexity of the role of Keres and Moira as planners is implied every time their names emerge: and in the case of death proper the language is still more difficult to read. Even when rhetoric and allusion clothes death in shapes very close to those of fully-fledged myth, there is no telling whether the mythical agents are fully present each and every time their names are used. The imagery is fluid, immanent, alluding obliquely to something which is perhaps unknowable from Homer's point of view as well as ours. Two things in particular warn us against reading our images with too rigid a sense of personification. First, the

or the Moirai were originally goddesses of death and only later came to be associated with the planning of fate at birth (see also Erbse (1986), 274–9). On the relationship between κήρ as death and κήρ as fate, see also Nilsson (1967), 222–5.

[51] There is a similar image of twin κῆρες, one of death and one of old age, at Mimn. fr. 2. 5–7 W; cf. also *Adesp. Eleg.* 14 W, of unguessable date.

names of the different agents alternate freely, even within a
single scene, and the repertoire includes examples involving
nouns which have no known personal identity in myth, notably
ὄλεθρος[52] and φόνος. Secondly, there are some expressions with
θάνατος and κήρ which draw up images irreconcilable with the
personal ones. When Achilles accuses Agamemnon of shrink-
ing from danger in battle he says simply that the king knows
this is death, τὸ δέ τοι κὴρ εἴδεται εἶναι (I. 228). Murderous men
bring death with them, φόνον καὶ κῆρα φέροντες (II. 352, III. 6;
iv. 273), as even a fisherman's line does to his prey (XXIV. 82).
Death must be something abstract or intangible when a man
scheming against another is said to plant or establish his death,
φόνον καὶ κῆρα φυτεύει (ii. 165, xvii. 82),[53] or θάνατον καὶ κῆρ᾽
ἀραρόντε (xvi. 169; sim. xxiv. 153), or θάνατον μητίσομαι
(xv. 349). Likewise when one brings about another's death it
has been made or wrought, θάνατος καὶ μοῖρα τέτυκται (III. 101),
and a killer can boast to his victim that he will 'forge' or
'fashion' the κήρ of his death, σοὶ δ᾽ ἐγὼ ἐνθάδε φημὶ φόνον καὶ
κῆρα μέλαιναν | ἐξ ἐμέθεν τεύξεσθαι (V. 652–3; sim. xi. 409, xx. 11,
xxii. 14). Death must be no more than an abstract event in time

---

[52] ὄλεθρος carries an interesting image with it. Death is like a snare or bond
cast on the dying man, ὀλέθρου πείρατ᾽ ἐφῆπται (VII. 402, XII. 79; xxii. 33, 41),
and he walks into the snare if he risks his life in foolish audacity
(VI. 143 = XX. 429). This image is normally separate from the spatial approach
of death as an attacker, though once the two seem to combine in a new context
when Poseidon describes a peril about to be undergone by Odysseus as μέγα
πεῖραρ ὀιζύος, ἥ μιν ἱκάνει (v. 288–9). The meaning of this image of ὄλεθρος
becomes clear in the light of other uses of πεῖραρ. The most elaborate example
is when Zeus and Poseidon exercise their powers in favour of Trojans and
Greeks respectively, and the force of their influences is seen as a bond
stretched over the struggling hosts: τοὶ [sc. the two gods] δ᾽ ἔριδος κρατερῆς
καὶ ὁμοιΐου πτολέμοιο | πεῖραρ ἐπαλλάξαντες ἐπ᾽ ἀμφοτέροισι τάνυσσαν (XIII. 358–9;
cf. XIV. 389–91, with XV. 410–13). Similarly, Menelaus elsewhere says that the
gods have the power to decide who will win, νίκης πείρατ᾽ ἔχονται ἐν ἀθανάτοισι
θεοῖσιν (VII. 102). These images of binding make sense in the light of humbler
senses of πείρατα as spatial limits or boundaries—of earth (VIII. 478–9, XIV. 200,
301; iv. 563), of Ocean (xi. 13), of an island (ix. 283–4), or of a parcel of land
(XVIII. 501)—as well as literal ropes used to tie a man down (xii. 51, 162, 179).
For this analysis of ὀλέθρου πείρατα see Onians (1951: 310–42), and cf. the
more abstract analyses by Nothdurft (1978) and Heubeck (1972), which treat
more fully of certain more difficult uses of πεῖραρ in other contexts.

[53] This image seems to take off from κακὸν φυτεύειν and similar (XV. 134;
v. 340, xiv. 110, etc.). See Fernández-Galiano at xxii. 14.

when it is said to happen, θάνατον . . . γενέσθαι (XIX. 274), or
when people are saved out of it, ὑπὲκ θανάτοιο φέρονται (XV. 628;
sim. XXII. 175, iv. 753, ix. 63 = 566 = x. 134), or when its
fulfilment is appointed or ordained for a given moment,
θανάτοιο τέλος πεπρωμένον ἐστίν (III. 309; sim. XI. 443),[54] or
prophesied, θάνατον μαντεύεαι (XIX. 420), or when the gods
plan someone's death, φράσσαντ' ἀθάνατοι θάνατον καὶ κῆρα
μέλαιναν (iii. 242; sim. xxiv. 127). A monster's jaws are full of
death, πλεῖοι μέλανος θανάτοιο (xii. 92). One who knows that he
will die at Troy is εὖ εἰδὼς κῆρ' ὀλοήν (XIII. 665; sim. ii. 283). At
such times the personal identities of the agents of death must
be forgotten if the words are to make sense. This is enough to
show that it is possible for personification to be denied fully, in
rhetoric as well as in narrative, and consequently that the
mythical identities of κήρ and θάνατος are not necessarily
invoked on any given occasion when these nouns appear.

A few particularly revealing passages show that the personal
identities of Keres can be bypassed when ideas of death are
articulated along other avenues of image-making. A choice
between two κῆρες need not be imagined as two beings pulling
towards different deaths, as Achilles sees it (IX. 410–11), but
simply as two different events, as Odysseus says when he asks
his mother's shade how she died:

> τίς νύ σε κὴρ ἐδάμασσε τανηλεγέος θανάτοιο;
> ἢ δολιχὴ νοῦσος, ἢ Ἄρτεμις ἰοχέαιρα
> οἷς ἀγανοῖς βελέεσσιν ἐποιχομένη κατέπεφνεν;   (xi. 171–3)

The fact that a κήρ is potentially a personal divinity does not
obtrude on Odysseus' thought when he follows a different
thread and imagines a gentle death as the advent of Artemis.
Similarly, the familiar shapes of the Keres are irrelevant to the
famous scenes where Zeus decides the outcome of combat by
weighing Keres in the pans of a balance—once to decide the
issue of a battle (VIII. 69–74), and once to seal Hector's fate in
his final duel with Achilles (XXII. 209–13).[55] In the case of

[54] The phrase θανάτοιο αἶσα (XXIV. 428, 750) seems to refer to the temporal
moment of death, but it is hard to see how this relates to the more usual senses
of the word αἶσα.
[55] Although there are close verbal correspondences between these two
weighings, they are not identical: the first determines which of the two

Hector and Achilles, the prospects of their two deaths, δύο κῆρε τανηλεγέος θανάτοιο, are set in the balance and Hector's sinks down: this is identified with the certainty that his death is now fixed, ῥέπε δ' Ἕκτορος αἴσιμον ἦμαρ, and that already his journey to death has been set in motion, ᾤχετο δ' εἰς Ἀΐδαο.[56] In the other passage, when it is the κῆρε(ς) of the two armies that are weighed, the result is explained in more detail: the κῆρες of the Achaeans settle on the earth, ἐπὶ χθονὶ πουλοβοτείρηι | ἑζέσθην, while those of the Trojans are lifted up into the air.[57] As already suggested in Chapter 1, the logic of this image lies in the idea of uncertainty, the two prospects poised and ready to fall one way or the other. The mythical identity of κῆρες as death-goddesses is at best tangential to the image, which depends simply on the idea of two decisions or events being realized as weights in the pans of the balance. These scenes remind us more forcefully than any others that sometimes the potential for lending personality to κήρ can be bypassed entirely, even on the level of a fully-fledged mythical narrative where Zeus in person sits as steward over the battlefield.

What we have seen is an endlessly fluid relationship between

hosts will gain the upper hand in a single battle, but the second decides which of the two heroes will be killed. Note that other references to the τάλαντα of Zeus (XVI. 658, XIX. 223–4) imply that the weighing determines what is in store for the entire armies rather than for two individual opponents. Compare also the echo in ἡμῖν αἰπὺς ὄλεθρος ἐπιρρέπηι (XIV. 99), a phrase which evokes the prospect of defeat with the same verb but does not specify the scales of a balance.

[56] Thus Kirk ad loc.

[57] This reconstruction remains very doubtful, since there are problems with the text of VIII. 70–4. First the dual number is used, δύο κῆρε (70), evidently one for each of the two hosts; but then the Achaeans have plural κῆρες (73), taking a dual verb ἑζέσθην (74), with ἕζεσθεν as an ancient varia lectio. Throughout Homer κήρ seems to be used indiscriminately in singular and plural across different passages, but we have a right to expect consistency within this one image; and although Homer often tends to slip between dual and plural in the sequence of a single sentence, this is not enough to explain the shift from δύο κῆρε to two groups of several κῆρες. There is evidence that the dual number is sometimes used of two groups, or an individual and a group, rather than a pair of individuals (see II. 123–4, V. 487, VIII. 185–6, XXIII. 413, with Hainsworth at IX. 182; and Chantraine (1942), ii. 27–8), but it would strain credulity to extend this to the number 'two' itself and take the words δύο κῆρε as referring to two groups. Aristarchus athetized 73–4, but Kirk (ad loc.) prefers caution.

the forms of language and those of myth. Each word—θάνατος, κήρ, μοῖρα, αἶσα—can give birth to an endless different range of images on every level from the simpest description of visible things to the fully-fledged articulation of the unseen world of the gods. In each instance the image is a function of its context: the personal divinities are emergent, not crystallized or defined by a doctrine or a strict definition of the referents of their names, and across the planning of fate and the fulfilment of death they emerge in different ways and in different degrees of clarity.

Death comes from the arrows of Artemis and Apollo

In each of the nouns that we have observed, the scale of mythical development begins with a simple noun—θάνατος, κήρ, μοῖρα, death, cutting, portion—and builds up by progressive stages to the point at which it is separated and becomes a fully-fledged divine personality. To complete the picture, there is another pattern of death-imagery that works in the opposite direction, beginning from the identities of personal Olympian gods and receding into the vaguer shapes of rhetoric and allusion. On this pattern certain kinds of death are attributed to the archer-gods Apollo and Artemis.[58] Although nouns such as θάνατος or κήρ may refer to these deaths, the corresponding personal agents are irrelevant, and the archer-gods replace them in much the same way as Hermes the giver of sleep (XXIV. 343–4; v. 47–8, xxiv. 3–4 etc.) is substituted for Sleep, Ὕπνος, himself.

[58] The origins of this myth or motif are doubtful. Neither Apollo nor Artemis is a deity of death in any other contexts; and it is possible either that both became associated with death by archery for different reasons, or that an attribute of one of them has been transferred to the other twin. Artemis may have taken on the role because she is a huntress, or because she is associated with death in the pangs of childbirth (see e.g. Nilsson (1967), 482; Hoekstra on xv. 411): such a connection is nowhere explicit in Homer, but is perhaps suggested by XXI. 483–4. Given the complex syncretism that seems to lie behind Apollo's many aspects, it is very possible that his death-dealing role originated with oriental deities such as the Semitic Reshep (see e.g. Schretter (1974), 174–215; Burkert (1985), 145–7). On the other hand, Homer's Apollo is the patron of archery in all its uses, so that his role as the one who shoots from afar, ἑκάεργος, might have been enough to associate him with death of arrowlike swiftness.

To die from the arrows of Apollo and Artemis is to die
swiftly or peacefully or both.[59] Observe again how Odysseus
asks his mother's shade whether her death was a slow sickness
or a swift shot from Artemis' painless arrows:

> ἢ δολιχὴ νοῦσος, ἢ Ἄρτεμις ἰοχέαιρα
> οἷς ἀγανοῖς βελέεσσιν ἐποιχομένη κατέπεφνεν;   (xi. 172–3)

Again, Nestor recalls the sudden death of his helmsman as an
attack by Apollo's arrows, οἷς ἀγανοῖς βελέεσσιν (iii. 279–80), and
Eumaeus describes the sudden death of his nurse in the same
way (xv. 477–8). There is an obvious contrast between this
conception and the pattern which we have sketched for the
assault of Thanatos and his associates. They approach one
slowly and stealthily through the mounting perils of battle, or
with the growing inevitability of a fated end, but a swift or a
peaceful death comes as what an English-speaker (coinciden-
tally) might call a bolt out of the blue.

Apollo the killer steps onto the stage more fully in the
episode of the Plague in *Iliad* i, when he deals out sudden
death among the Achaeans: he goes unseen like nightfall, νυκτὶ
ἐοικώς (i. 46–7), but the arrows rattle in his quiver, and he is
present as fully and vividly as any other Olympian interfering
on the battlefield. In the same way he fights with bow and
arrows in the Theomachy (xx. 68). But in the normal course of
story-telling, shooting by the gods is found only in the
language of speeches, reminiscences, or reflections, where Homeric characters express the deeper meaning of a swift or

[59] Schretter (1974: 174–215) uses his analysis of the syncretism of Apollo
and Reshep to distinguish sharply between two types of killing by Apollo: on
the one hand the sudden death which he delivers with his κῆλα (i. 53, 383)
when he kills the Achaeans in the Plague episode, and on the other the gentle
death which comes through his ἀγανοῖς βελέεσσι (see esp. xxiv. 758–9; xi. 172–
3, xv. 409–11). Noting that Reshep is associated with fire, and that fever is
naturally imagined as burning, he associates κῆλα etymologically with the verb
καίω and the adjective κήλεος, and adduces passages (xii. 280; Hes. *Theog.*
706–8) in which thunderbolts are the κῆλα of Zeus. Similarly Schretter links
the title Smintheus (i. 39), under which Chryses invokes Apollo when he asks
him to shoot the Achaeans, with the noun σπινθαρίδες denoting the sparks or
beams of a star to which Apollo himself is being compared (*h. Ap.* 440–2; but
see also iv. 77).

peaceful death.[60] When this happens the speaker clearly does not mean that the god was present in the same open way that Apollo is present in the Plague episode: the act of Apollo or Artemis sounds like a shadowy image rather than a full epiphany. Since among the Olympians they are fully-fledged personal actors, but as bringers of death they fade back into the figurative language of allusion, the structure is the mirror image of what we observed in the case of Thanatos and Ker, who take shape in that figurative language and only emerge into the full identity of personal gods in the Shield of Achilles and the story of Sarpedon's death.

Mythical forms emerge in stories of the gods and in works of art

In saying that the relationship between the mythical and the non-mythical is fluid or ambiguous, we should not suggest that the Homeric world-picture is vague or chaotic. Rather, we have seen that the personalities of death emerge each time according to the logic of the context: suppressed in the ordinary narrative, emergent in the heightened language of rhetoric, and fully separated off in certain privileged narratives. There is clearly something special about the circumstances in which the highest level of the scale is reached. Take the examples of Sleep and Death, who reached it only in the stories of Hera's deception of

---

[60] To complete the list: apart from the three examples quoted in our text, and the Olympian quarrel where Hera mentions Artemis' role as a 'lion to women' (XXI. 482–4), the image occurs where a character wishes death on him- or herself (xviii. 202–3, xx. 61–81) or on another (XIX. 59; xvii. 251, 494); also when Hecuba says that Hector looks as peaceful as one shot by Apollo (XXIV. 758–9); in a generalized statement in the poet's voice about the easy lives and gentle deaths of the people of Syria (xv. 409–11); and when Anticleia's shade explains that she died of longing for Odysseus and was *not* shot by Artemis (xi. 198–9). We find the same formulae used in inset narratives recounting the shooting of mortals by Apollo or Artemis in the legendary past (VI. 205, 428, XXIV. 605–7; v. 123–4, vii. 64–5, viii. 227–8, xi. 324–5; possibly IX. 564). These references are ambiguous: except where Apollo and Artemis kill from some stated personal motive, such as Apollo's anger at Niobe and her children (XXIV. 605–7) or at Eurytus (viii. 227–8), it is impossible to be sure whether the gods appear in this role because elevated or allusive language is usual in such stories, or because Homer believes that the gods moved more openly among earlier generations of mortals.

Zeus and the death of Sarpedon. Both these stories are set in the cosmologically exalted world of Olympian society, when Zeus' own son meets his end and when his and Hera's sexual politics is at its most exotic.[61] Seemingly the divine loftiness of the actors at the centre of the stage is what allows these others to emerge from the shadows and join the group around the limelight.[62]

Just as these personalities emerge from the shadows in a heightened narrative of divine society, so too they can come to the fore in the visually heightened environment of a work of art. The Shield of Achilles is the best example, where the κῆρες roam to and fro in their bloody cloaks[63] along with figures like Strife and 'Battle-Confusion', Ἔρις and Κυδοιμός. The Shield of Achilles is a thing apart, but the scene has close parallels in others evoked in Homer's descriptions of works of art. Compare the aegis worn by Athena, adorned with images of other and still stranger personal agents:[64]

> . . . αἰγίδα θυσσανόεσσαν
> δεινήν, ἣν περὶ μὲν πάντηι Φόβος ἐστεφάνωται,
> ἐν δ' Ἔρις, ἐν δ' Ἀλκή, ἐν δὲ κρυόεσσα Ἰωκή,
> ἐν δέ τε Γοργείη κεφαλὴ δεινοῖο πελώρου,
> δεινή τε σμερδνή τε, Διὸς τέρας αἰγιόχοιο.   (v. 738–42)

---

[61] Cf. Erbse (1986: 34) on personifications at 'high points' of the narrative.

[62] Compare West at *Theog.* 140, on the personifications there of Βροντή, Στερόπη, and Ἄργης: 'Because there are three separate words, the unsophisticated mind thinks of three separate things.' But what kind of mind is unsophisticated?

[63] It is fascinating to compare this scene with one of the images Pausanias saw on the 7th-cent. Chest of Cypselus at Elis. In a scene of the battle of the Seven against Thebes, a monstrous κήρ was about to pounce on the doomed Polynices: τοῦ Πολυνείκους δὲ ὄπισθεν γυνὴ ἕστηκεν ὀδόντας τε ἔχουσα οὐδὲν ἡμερωτέρους θηρίου καὶ οἱ τῶν χειρῶν εἰσὶν ἐπικαμπτεῖς οἱ ὄνυχες· ἐπίγραμμα δὲ ἐπ' αὐτῆι εἶναί φησι Κῆρα, ὡς τὸν μὲν ὑπὸ τοῦ πεπρωμένου τὸν Πολυνείκην ἀπαχθέντα, Ἐτεοκλεῖ δὲ γενομένης καὶ σὺν τῶι δικαίωι τῆς τελευτῆς (Paus. 5. 19. 6). It remains possible, of course, either that the artist was inspired directly by the epic Shield, or that Pausanias' memory is contaminated by knowledge of such texts (compare, for example, the Hesiodic *Shield of Heracles* 248–57, a very similar image of κῆρες with talons; also Ap. Rhod. *Argon.* 4. 1665–7).

[64] On the personified deities depicted on the aegis and on other works of art, see Erbse (1986), 28–32.

Similarly Agamemnon's shield (XI. 36–7) bears devices not
only of the Gorgon but also of Rout and Terror, *Φόβος* and
Δεῖμος, who are not only psychological phenomena but also the
sons and attendants of Ares (see XIII. 299–300, XV. 119–20; and
cf. Hes. *Theog.* 933–6). The lesson is that Homer allows
himself to rise to baroque heights of image-making on the
level of vividness that he finds appropriate for a work of art:[65]
the forms of the artistic depiction are an extended and
sharpened version of the shapes that image-making takes on
in the rhetorical language used by Homer's characters at
moments of highest emotion. In terms of the structures of
myth-making, the visual extravagance of the figured metalwork
is on the same level as is the narrative extravagance of a story of
Olympian politics or the highest moments of drama in the
events of the mortal world.

'Everything is full of gods'

It is in this sense of unity in multiplicity that the lesson lies
for our problem of defining *ψυχή*. Just as *θάνατος* begins as
death in the simplest sense, takes on his mythical identity in
rhetorical language under shadowy suggestive forms, and
finally emerges into the light of day in a few narratives
where the action is on the plane of the gods, so *ψυχή* takes
on its meaning on different levels in different contexts. Its
structure follows exactly the pattern that we have formulated
in this chapter: in ordinary narrative the *ψυχή* is no more than
the last breath lost in the air of the battlefield, in the language
of rhetoric its potential flight to Hades is obliquely suggested,
and at two pivotal moments it is separated off as a birdlike
thing that gibbers and squeaks and flies away to join the
wraiths in the unseen Underworld. The parallel is exact
between the *ψυχή* of Patroclus' and Hector's deaths and the
Θάνατος of Sarpedon's: in both cases an ordinary word is given
an extraordinary identity, and the world of myth erupts for a
while from that of the battlefield: the winged *ψυχή*, crying out

---

[65] On the vividness of representation in the Shield of Achilles as a whole,
see for example C. H. Whitman (1958: 205) and A. S. Becker (1990).

as it flies to Hades, belongs not in the immanent imagery of poetic evocation but in the unseen and transcendent world of divinity. It is easy to see why the two places where the myth appears should be the deaths of Patroclus and Hector. These are the decisive turning-points of the causal chain which draws the action of the *Iliad* inevitably on towards the death of Achilles: Patroclus' last words prophesy the vengeance that awaits Hector at Achilles' hands (XVI. 851–4),[66] and when that doom is fulfilled Hector tells Achilles of the death that awaits him at the Scaean gate (XXII. 358–60).[67] Just as briefer images of descent to Hades belong in contexts of deepened emotional force, so here the most elaborate and most dramatic version of the myth takes shape at the two moments of cardinal significance in the progress of the story of the *Iliad*.

The crucial point in both cases is that the most elaborate articulation does not prescribe the meaning of the simpler ones. We saw that alongside the emerging personal shapes of κήρ and θάνατος there are other images where their personalities either remain unacknowledged or are altogether ignored. In exactly the same way, the last gasp of the dying man *may* be seen as flying to Hades but can also, and far more easily and often, remain seen as nothing more than a puff of air lost on the wind. In both cases the mythical element in the world of experience is ambiguous and potential, emerging into full articulation only in certain controlled moments of heightened image-making. For Homer there is a sense in which 'everything is full of gods',[68] full of the unseen mythical things that the Muse tells of: but in the interpreter's reading this principle must not be pushed beyond its proper limits: there is

---

[66] On the cardinal significance of the death of Patroclus in the causal chain, see most recently Taplin (1992), 179–85.

[67] For the causal link between the two deaths, note esp. the tenor of Thetis' anticipatory lament for her son when he rises up against Hector: αὐτίκα γάρ τοι ἔπειτα μεθ' Ἕκτορα πότμος ἑτοῖμος (XVIII. 96; see Edwards ad loc. for further refs.).

[68] Thales, fr. 91 KRS: πάντα πλήρη θεῶν εἶναι (Arist. *De an.* 411ᵃ7). As KRS point out (p. 95) this is probably a word-for-word quotation rather than a summary of Thales' idea, since the same words are recalled in Plato's *Laws*, though without Thales' name (899b). See most recently M. J. Clarke (1995b).

also a structure which limits the florescence of myth in the depiction of the world of mortals.[69] We will end our study with a broader look at this principle.

[69] The most useful essay on this problem for Greek god-names as a whole has been that by Walter Pötscher (1959*b*); see also Pötscher (1978). Pötscher shows that Homer and Hesiod's mythological language gives personal identity to qualities, intangible phenomena, and cosmic entities in a system of expression where priority cannot be assigned either to the personal or the abstract articulation ('Person', 'Bereich'). Pötscher suggests (1959*b*: 15–16) that the key to understanding the system lies in understanding the flux between the two extremes (cf. Erbse (1986), ch. 1, esp. 9–11). A similar insight is touched on by Snell (1952), 160–2.

8

Conclusion: The Dynamics of Mythical Image-Making

The suppleness of myth

In the ψυχή of the deaths of Patroclus and Hector a tangible phenomenon of mortal experience is translated into something that belongs in the unseen world of the afterlife. In the last chapter we saw that this ambiguity or shift is not unique to the problem of that particular word. If we make the personal identity of Death or Sleep parallel to the mythical form of the ψυχή which flies to Hades and lives there as a wraith, and if we make the rendering of sleep or death as mist falling on the eyes parallel to the simple identification of ψυχή as the dying man's last breath, then the words θάνατος, ὕπνος, and ψυχή will each prompt the same question: within the range of possibilities for image-making represented by a single noun, where does the mythical identity belong in the poet's view of the world?

So stated, this a case of the more general problem of explaining how the stuff of mortal experience relates to the stuff of myth. Everywhere in Homer and still more obviously in Hesiod, nouns that might nowadays be called 'abstract' are liable to take on the identities of personal gods. Witness W. Burkert on 'the special character of Greek anthropomorphism': 'Locution and ideation is structured in such a way that a complex personality emerges which has its own plastic being. This cannot be defined, but it can be known, and such knowledge can bring joy, help and salvation.'[1] In our study of ψυχή, θάνατος, and their kin we face a peculiar species of this 'plastic being' in terms of the meanings of nouns.[2] We need to

---

[1] Burkert (1985), 183. Cf. Webster (1954); Reinhardt (1960).

[2] For the principle that the individual noun is the key to the meaning of each deity, see esp. Snell (1954), followed by the other savants' useful

study the phenomenon a little more widely before we can achieve a final analysis of Homeric belief about life after death.[3]

Across the epic tradition as a whole the most instructive example of this dynamic is Hesiod's meditation on Rumour, Φήμη:

> δεινὴν δὲ βροτῶν ὑπαλεύεο φήμην·
> φήμη γάρ τε κακὴ πέλεται κούφη μὲν ἀεῖραι
> ῥεῖα μάλ', ἀργαλέη δὲ φέρειν, χαλεπὴ δ' ἀποθέσθαι.
> φήμη δ' οὔ τις πάμπαν ἀπόλλυται, ἥντινα πολλοὶ
> λαοὶ φημίξουσι· θεός νύ τίς ἐστι καὶ αὐτή. (*WD* 760–4)

As he considers the indestructible power of rumour, he builds up its contours until it is no less than an immortal goddess.[4] But even if the deification emerges spontaneously out of the argument, the structure which generates it is deeply traditional: indeed, the shaping of the personal Φήμη draws on a pattern which is further exemplified in Homer by Ὄσσα and Θέμις, words which take on the form of divine beings responsible for (or identified with) the spreading of news and instructions (see below, pp. 266–7). What is important is not the ancestry or credentials of each individual personification, but the patterns of image-making which the poet follows whenever he brings it to the fore.

discussion of Hesiod's personified Γαλήνη; also Schwabl (1955), 529; and on the creative aspects of Homer's deployment of personified nouns, see esp. Reinhardt (1960).

[3] The most recent study relevant to the main argument of this chapter is Erbse (1986), esp. 9–85; but I have found more that is helpful in the penetrating articles of W. Pötscher (1959a, 1959b, 1960, 1978) and H. Schwabl (1955). On these see also Ch. 7 n. 69. An illuminating sidelight from a neighbouring part of the world is thrown by J. Bottéro's work on language and divinity in Mesopotamian religion, where he emphasizes the one-to-one correspondence between the individual divine personality and the individual word (1987: *passim*, esp. 125 ff.). I have also learned much from S. Dalley on this and kindred themes.

[4] Wilamowitz (1931: 17–19) held that θεός took on a special meaning when it was used predicatively, to identify something as divine in a novel way. Pötscher (1959b: 4–8) has shown that this principle should not be pushed too far; and indeed in Pindar's world—if not in Hesiod's also—φήμη is a real enough goddess for her to be woken up and dragged out of bed by Poseidon (Pind. *Isthm.* 4. 37–42), just as Dawn rises from beside Tithonus.

The divine society

From the outsider's point of view there are two broad categories among Homer's countless examples of divine personalities tied to ordinary nouns. On the one hand stand parts of the furniture of the world—Οὐρανός, Γαῖα, Ὠκεανός, and so on—along with cosmological phenomena such as Νύξ, Ἠώς, or the so-called 'Seasons', Ὧραι;[5] and on the other hand stand intangible happenings in human experience—not only θάνατος, ὕπνος, and the agents of fate but also such varied things as Rumour, Ὄσσα (II. 93–4; xxiv. 413–14; cf. i. 282–3, ii. 216–17);[6] Dream, Ὄνειρος (II. 5–35); Grace or Beauty, Χάρις or the Χάριτες (v. 338, XIV. 267–76, XVIII. 382–3); Strife, Ἔρις (IV. 440–5, V. 740, XI. 3–4, 73–7, XVIII. 535, etc.);[7] the law of social organization, Θέμις (XV. 87–100, XX. 4–6; ii. 68–9);[8] Panic, Φύζα, who accompanies Phobos the groom of Ares (IX. 1–2); and Rout and Valour, Ἰωκή and Ἀλκή, depicted on Athena's aegis (v. 738–42). In practice there is no clear dividing line between these and the familiar personal gods of Olympian society. For example Ares belongs in both camps, since he is not only a major Olympian personality but also a noun translatable as 'war' or 'battle-fury' (see below, pp. 269–72); and the names of Hephaestus (II. 426; and cf. IX. 468 = XXIII. 33, XVII. 88,

---

[5] When gods come to and from Olympus the Ὧραι in person open and close the gates and look after their horses (v. 749–51 = VIII. 393–5, VIII. 433), and in the same capacity they supervise the journeyings of the gods whose movements mark the passage of time and the seasons (see XXI. 450–1, with ii. 107, x. 469, xi. 295, and esp. xxiv. 344; also Hes. *Theog.* 901–3; *WD* 75), presumably because day, night, dawn, the sun, and so on are imagined as passing in and out of Olympus on their travels (for the image cf. Hes. *Theog.* 748–57; and see also Austin (1975), 88). The elaborate role of the Ὧραι in later Greek thought, especially in Pindar's evocation of political well-being, lies beyond the scope of this book.

[6] Ὄσσα is cognate with ὄψ, roughly 'voice' (see Chantraine s.v.). Erbse (1986: 34–5) points out that the divine personality is at least hinted at in every instance of the word. See also Durante (1968a: 244), adducing a Vedic cognate.

[7] On Eris see esp. Erbse (1986), 28–9.

[8] On the non-personal meaning of θέμις in Homer (II. 73, IX. 134; iii. 45, and often), see esp. Lesky (1985), 5–17, and Pötscher (1960), 31–3. The shadowy chthonic mythology of Themis (see esp. Aesch. *Eum.* 1–7, *PV* 209–10, with Sourvinou-Inwood (1987)) is beyond the scope of this book.

xxiv. 71) and Aphrodite (xxii. 444) are sometimes used to denote the phenomena of fire and sexuality in such a way that their personal identities must be set aside. We would be missing the point if we asked of each noun whether it refers originally to a thing or a god, or whether this or that usage is literal or metaphorical: what is essential is that myth-making allows personalities of all these kinds to rub shoulders together as a single social group in a single narrative.

We have seen a startling example of this in Hera's negotiations with Sleep, where Sleep schemes and bargains with her like any other personal god (Ch. 7, pp. 236–9). Similar are such scenes as that in which Dawn arrives at Olympus from the bed she shares with the human Tithonus, bearing light to Zeus and the other gods (II. 48–9; cf. XI. 1–2 = v. 1–2, XIX. 1–2, xxiii. 241–6), or where Iris the rainbow acts as a messenger between Olympus and the world below,[9] or where Youth, Ἥβη, is a servant-girl at the feasts of the gods (IV. 2–3, v. 722–3, 905; xi. 603–4). Here the logic of story-telling allows the gods' relationships to be worked out in terms of the court and family structures of Olympian society, regardless of their

---

[9] The problem of Iris and the rainbow is nicely balanced. Iris in person frequently acts as a messenger on behalf of Zeus or another god (defined, XV. 144; see VIII. 397–432, XVIII. 165–202, etc.), and she responds to Achilles' prayer for wind by visiting the Winds' cave in person to give them instructions (XXIII. 194–213). She also acts as a charioteer and maidservant for Aphrodite returning from the battlefield to Olympus (v. 365–9), and twice she takes on the guise of a mortal in order to transmit a message from a god (II. 790–5, III. 121–40). It is easy to see an analogy, if no more, between the rainbow stretching from heaven to earth and the messenger passing between the gods' world and that of mortals. But the connection is in fact more intimate than that. Iris' epithets (πόδας ὠκέα, ταχεῖα, ἀελλόπος, χρυσόπτερος, ποδήνεμος) are appropriate to the personification of a rainbow, and she descends with instantaneous speed (see the similes at XV. 170–2, XXIV. 77–83; and note also Hes. *Theog.* 266–9, 784–6); and furthermore the two Iliadic references to rainbows in the ordinary sense represent them as bringing messages from Zeus: images on Agamemnon's armour gleam like rainbows, ἴρισσιν ἐοικότες, which Zeus sends as a sign to mortals (XI. 27–8), and Athena descends to earth like a rainbow, ἴρις, which Zeus extends as a sign of war or storm (XVII. 547–52). All this makes it impossible to draw a dividing line between the person and the phenomenon (thus Erbse (1986), 64; also Chantraine s.v., and Frisk s.v.; *LfgrE* holds that the person and the phenomenon are distinguished in Homer but not in Hesiod, which seems arbitrary). See most recently Bader (1991).

individual origins and credentials. To take a more thorny
example, in Demodocus' tale of the adultery of Ares and
Aphrodite (viii. 266–366) it is tempting to look behind their
all-too-human personalities and read the story as something
like an allegory of the union of love and strife,[10] especially if we
supply from Hesiod (*Theog.* 937) that the children of their
union were not only Phobos and Deimos but also Harmony;[11]
but to take that step is to rob the story of its organic meaning,
since as a whole it makes sense only through the social order
which makes Ares, Aphrodite, and Hephaestus live in neighbouring houses and interact with gods like Apollo, Hermes, or
Poseidon, who are never identified with phenomena or things.

This social logic is parallel to the genealogical logic which
controls Hesiod's *Theogony*,[12] where (for example) Gaia
mothers a family that includes Πόντος, the Mountains,
Themis, Memory, the Titans, and the Hundred-hander
giants (see ll. 126–53). She is mother of sea and mountains in
the sense that they arise from the physical fabric of the earth;
Themis and Memory seem to be chthonic in a more deep and
intangible sense;[13] while the Titans and the Hundred-handers

[10] There is no telling how creative or 'anti-traditional' this story is. In the
Iliad and in Hesiod, Hephaestus woos or is married to one of the Charites
(xviii. 382–3; *Theog.* 945), and many have argued that Demodocus' story is a
novel invention (see survey of secondary literature by Burkert (1960)).
However that may be, outside Homer we often find Ares' name linked with
Aphrodite's in poetry, art, and cult (see Burkert (1960), 132 n. 6; (1985), 220;
Nilsson (1967), 524; Hainsworth at viii. 267). Possibly the story of Ares' union
with Aphrodite originated because of warlike aspects of her personality which
were early abandoned on the Panhellenic level (see West at *Theog.* 933, with
refs.). Be that as it may, in later tradition the theme was understood to be the
union of polar opposites (Burkert (1985), loc. cit.), and it is suggestive that
Hesiod lists the children as Phobos, Deimos, and Harmonia (*Theog.* 933–7):
the production of the first pair fits the union of two warrior deities, the
production of the third fits the union of war and love. Might Harmony have
been added by or before Hesiod in an attempt to reinterpet an old story?

[11] Note also Aesch. *Sept.* 135–42, referring to Harmony's marriage to
Cadmus.

[12] On the genealogical logic see esp. Schwabl (1955); Stokes (1962); Lloyd
(1975).

[13] West at *Theog.* 135 says that Themis and Memory are included among
the children of Gaia 'merely because of their antiquity': this is perhaps less
than the whole truth about Themis (see above, n. 8), but no other explanation
suggests itself for Memory being one of this family.

are anthropomorphic (or monstrous) beings, so that Gaia must be their mother only in the sense that a human mother might bear children. The unifying factor is the genealogical grammar of Hesiod's exposition, which expresses all these kinds of relationship in terms of the same family structure. In the same way Homer's stories are controlled and moulded by the social structures of Olympian life, and their meaning cannot be translated onto another level of exposition.

Ares and war

A contradiction lies implicit in the way each such deity is to be understood. Here a case in point is Ares, who is sometimes identified with the fury of battle as a whole but can also intervene on the battlefield to fight on behalf of one or other host of warriors.[14] At one end of its range, the word ἄρης/Ἄρης evokes no image of a personal deity. For example, enemies carry war with them, φέρον πολύδακρυν ἄρηα (III. 132, VIII. 516, etc.); warriors longing for battle are ἐσσύμενοι . . . ἄρηος (XIII. 630) or ἐπειγόμενοι . . . ἄρηος (XIX. 142, 189); to join battle is ἄρηα συνάγειν (II. 381 = XIX. 275, etc.) or ἄρηϊ κρίνεσθαι (XVIII. 209; XVI. 269, etc.); to fight is μαχέσασθαι ἄρηϊ (XVII. 490, and cf. XX. 50).[15] The same name stands for what enters Hector when he becomes filled with battle-fury, δῦ δέ μιν ἄρης | δεινὸς ἐνυάλιος (XVII. 210–11),[16] and a wound inflicted by a single blow is itself a manifestation of ἄρης:

---

[14] Erbse (1986: 166–8) shows that the noun ἄρης/Ἄρης moves between phenomenon and personal god in the same way as nouns like ἄτη. See also Pötscher (1959a), arguing that the two identities of ἄρης/Ἄρης are inextricably fused. Less satisfactory are Burkert (1985: 169–70), who describes Ares as 'apparently originally an abstract noun meaning throng of battle, war', and Nilsson (1967: 518–19), who is content to explain the complexities of the noun in terms of metonymy.

[15] By the same token the famous οἶδα δ' ἐνὶ σταδίηι δηΐωι μέλπεσθαι Ἄρηϊ/ἄρηϊ (VII. 241) could refer either to performing a war-dance in Ares' honour or to leaping nimbly about in hand-to-hand combat, depending on how we understand the verb.

[16] Despite the title ἐνυάλιος here, it seems best not to see this image in personal terms, since it would be an extraordinary and (in Homer) unparalleled idea for a personal god to enter a man in this way. Compare κρατερὴ δέ ἑ λύσσα δέδυκεν (IX. 239), also of Hector, and see n. 18 below.

βάλε δουρὶ
αἰδοίων τε μεσηγὺ καὶ ὀμφαλοῦ, ἔνθα μάλιστα
γίγνετ' ἄρης ἀλεγεινὸς ὀϊζυροῖσι βροτοῖσιν. (XIII. 567–9)

It follows that the personal Ares represents the frenzy of the whole action of battle from the point of view of both parties, raging amok like fire (see esp. xv. 605–6).[17] Thus Hector hopes to kill Achilles because the struggle is evenly matched, ξυνὸς Ἐνυάλιος καί τε κτανέοντα κατέκτα (XVIII. 309);[18] similarly, struggling hosts divide the fury of war between them, μένος Ἄρηος δατέονται (XVIII. 264); to join battle is to rouse Ares up, Ἄρηα ἐγείρειν (II. 440, IV. 352, etc.); Odysseus remembers Neoptolemus' skill when all was confusion in battle, ἐπιμὶξ δέ τε μαίνεται Ἄρης (xi. 537); Helen weaves a picture of the toils which both Trojans and Achaeans underwent at Ares' hands, οὓς ἔθεν εἵνεκ' ἔπασχον ὑπ' Ἄρηος παλαμάων (III. 128). When a weapon misses its mark it is Ares who takes away its force, ἀφίει μένος ὄβριμος Ἄρης (XIII. 444 = XVI. 613 = XVII. 529); he spills the blood of those who die in battle, τῶν νῦν αἷμα κελαινὸν . . . | ἐσκέδασ' ὀξὺς Ἄρης (VII. 329–30), and their blood sates his thirst, αἵματος ἆσαι Ἄρηα (v. 289 = xx. 78 = XXII. 267); he is the ultimate cause of Sarpedon's death at the hands of Patroclus, τὸν δ' ὑπὸ Πατρόκλωι δάμασ' ἔγχεϊ χάλκεος Ἄρης (XVI. 543), or those of Priam's sons at the hands of Achilles, τῶν μὲν πολλῶν θοῦρος Ἄρης ὑπὸ γούνατ' ἔλυσεν (XXIV. 498).

The problem of definition looms when Ares in person enters the battle to fight on one side rather than the other—for example, when he joins the fray on the Trojan side in *Iliad* IV (439–45). After a spate of fighting, Athena leads him away to sit inactive on the sidelines (see v. 35–7, 355–63), which enables the Achaeans to gain the upper hand, Τρῶας δ' ἔκλιναν Δαναοί (37); but later Ares returns to the fray and gives new prowess to

---

[17] On Ares' association with the most savage aspect of battle see Vian (1968: 54–6), arguing that for Homer he represents a memory of the ferocity of primitive warfare. Similarly Janko (at XIII. 301–3) suggests that Ares may be associated with Thrace (XIII. 298–303; viii. 361; and see Nilsson (1967), 517–18) not because he was a foreign import but because deities who personify unruly forces tend to be regarded as originating beyond Greek lands.

[18] Ἐνυάλιος is a title of Ares and no more: see XVII. 210–11, and also XIII. 519, where a son of Ares is called υἱὸς Ἐνυαλίοιο. The relationship between Ares and the female Enyo (v. 333, 592; also Hes. *Theog.* 273) remains mysterious.

his favourites.[19] Encouraging them first with a speech made in the guise of Acamas (461–70), he runs alongside Hector in human shape, βροτῶι ἀνδρὶ ἐοικώς (604), as they advance against Diomedes:

> Ἄρης δ᾽ ἐν παλάμηισι πελώριον ἔγχος ἐνώμα,
> φοίτα δ᾽ ἄλλοτε μὲν πρόσθ᾽ Ἕκτορος, ἄλλοτ᾽ ὄπισθε.

(594–5; cf. v. 508)

At one point Ares kills a man himself: Diomedes then faces him in single combat and wounds him (v. 846–63), forcing him to ascend back to Olympus to be healed. In this episode he is a personal actor like any other god interfering on the battlefield, and his influence on the action is limited to what he brings about in his personal form. This means that he can no longer be globally identified with war or warlike fury as he was in the first group of passages we observed. The snag is that when Diomedes fights this personal Ares, the mortal warrior exemplifies the quality or mood or type of behaviour which is called ἄρης. This is more than an idle academic paradox, because when he wounds the god and makes him cry out in pain, a single sentence manages to invoke the two extremes of image-making represented by the name:

> ὁ δ᾽ ἔβραχε χάλκεος Ἄρης,
> ὅσσον τ᾽ ἐννεάχιλοι ἐπίαχον ἢ δεκάχιλοι
> ἀνέρες ἐν πολέμωι ἔριδα ξυνάγοντες ἄρηος.

(v. 859–61; cf. XIV. 148–51)

Ares in person cries out as men do when they clash in the strife of ἄρης.[20] The two identities seem to jostle with each other: the mythical and non-mythical levels no longer run in tandem, and

---

[19] The opposition between Ares and Athena in this episode and in the Theomachy (xx. 33–48, xxi. 391–414) can be seen as a conflict between the savagery represented by Ares and the more sober and disciplined combat represented by Athena: see Erbse (1986), 156–66.

[20] It is just possible that this could be translated as 'leading in Eris, daughter of Ares', just as horses described as φόβον Ἄρηος φορεούσας (II. 767) might be imagined as bringing the son of Ares into battle in person in a chariot (see Kirk ad loc., and compare XIII. 298–300, XV. 119–20). However, Eris is elsewhere the sister of Ares rather than his daughter (IV. 440–1; and another genealogy in Hes. *Theog.* 225), so that it seems better to read the present image without personification.

the flow of story-telling can only bypass the gap which yawns
between them.

Helios and Scamander

This problem is posed still more starkly by deities that personify parts of the physical world: when these beings move as
personal actors they retain their non-mythical identity as
things that would be visible to ordinary mortals. For example,
if we think in English of the 'sun-god', Helios, remembering
his role in Olympian stories and the human shape of his
children Circe and Aeëtes (see x. 135–9), it seems easy to
imagine him as a man-shaped figure drawing the sun behind
him, perhaps on a chariot or in a bowl; but it is clear from
Homeric practice that this being is precisely identified with the
sun which shines in the sky.[21] When he acts in the narrative
his importance is that he sees what is going on in the world below,
touching all things with the beams of sight which are his rays,
καταδέρκεται ἀκτίνεσσιν (xi. 16).[22] In the Adultery of Ares and
Aphrodite he spies for the cuckolded Hephaestus (see viii. 270–
1, 302),[23] and in the story of the slaughter of his own cattle he
tells Zeus of the pleasure with which he used to look down on
them in his daily journey,[24]

[21] Distinguish Dawn, who rides in a chariot drawn by horses called
Lampos and Phaethon (xxiii. 246). In the Cyclic *Titanomachy* Helios had a
chariot led by horses with similar names (fr. 7 Bernabé), and the sun was also
imagined as being held in a bowl or cup (fr. 8 Bernabé; compare Stesich., esp.
fr. 185 P).

[22] Vision is imagined as rays (ἀκτῖνες, αὐγαί) emanating from the eyes, not as
images entering them: see Janko at XIII. 837, with further refs. In the
Thrinacian story, news of the slaughter of the cattle is brought to Helios by
his daughter Λαμπετίη τανύπεπλος (xii. 375), and it is tempting to guess that
she and her sister Φαέθουσα (see xii. 131–3) might be personifications of the
rays themselves.

[23] Compare *Homeric Hymn to Demeter* 24–9, 59–89, where Helios as the
spy, σκοπός (62), of gods and men sees and hears things that other deities do
not notice. Richardson at 24–6 cites instances of this role of the sun in later
Greek literature, as well as parallels in other traditions.

[24] One wonders whether the image of the evening-time when the sun goes
down *towards* the unyoking of cattle, ἦμος δ' ἠέλιος μετενίσετο βουλυτόνδε
(XVI. 779 = ix. 58), might not refer to him unyoking his own personal oxen
in Thrinacia, as in the *Odyssey*, or in some other western place (cf. Hoekstra at
xii. 260–402, with Herodotus 9. 93).

$$\mathring{\eta}\iota\sigma\iota\nu\ \dot{\epsilon}\gamma\acute{\omega}\ \gamma\epsilon$$
$$\chi\alpha\acute{\iota}\rho\epsilon\sigma\kappa o\nu\ \mu\grave{\epsilon}\nu\ \dot{\iota}\grave{\omega}\nu\ \epsilon\grave{\iota}s\ o\mathring{\nu}\rho\alpha\nu\grave{o}\nu\ \dot{\alpha}\sigma\tau\epsilon\rho\acute{o}\epsilon\nu\tau\alpha,$$
$$\mathring{\eta}\delta'\ \acute{o}\pi\acute{o}\tau'\ \mathring{\alpha}\psi\ \dot{\epsilon}\pi\grave{\iota}\ \gamma\alpha\hat{\iota}\alpha\nu\ \dot{\alpha}\pi'\ o\mathring{\nu}\rho\alpha\nu\acute{o}\theta\epsilon\nu\ \pi\rho o\tau\rho\alpha\pi o\acute{\iota}\mu\eta\nu. \quad \text{(xii. 379–81)}$$

Similarly, when Agamemnon calls on the gods to witness a pledge he includes Helios who sees and hears all things, $\ddot{o}s\ \pi\acute{\alpha}\nu\tau'$ $\dot{\epsilon}\phi o\rho\hat{\alpha}\iota s\ \kappa\alpha\grave{\iota}\ \pi\acute{\alpha}\nu\tau'\ \dot{\epsilon}\pi\alpha\kappa o\acute{\nu}\epsilon\iota s$ (III. 277; also xii. 323); and Zeus tells Hera that when they lie with each other under a mist not even the sun will be able to see them:

$$o\mathring{\nu}\delta'\ \mathring{\alpha}\nu\ \nu\hat{\omega}\ddot{\iota}\ \delta\iota\alpha\delta\rho\acute{\alpha}\kappa o\iota\ \ddot{}\!H\dot{\epsilon}\lambda\iota\acute{o}s\ \pi\epsilon\rho,$$
$$o\mathring{\nu}\ \tau\epsilon\ \kappa\alpha\grave{\iota}\ \dot{o}\xi\acute{\nu}\tau\alpha\tau o\nu\ \pi\acute{\epsilon}\lambda\epsilon\tau\alpha\iota\ \phi\acute{\alpha}os\ \epsilon\grave{\iota}\sigma o\rho\acute{\alpha}\alpha\sigma\theta\alpha\iota. \quad \text{(XIV. 344–5)}$$

Again, when Helios threatens to descend to Hades he implies that it is he himself who glows when the sun shines,

$$\delta\acute{\nu}\sigma o\mu\alpha\iota\ \epsilon\grave{\iota}s\ \ddot{}\!A\ddot{\iota}\delta\alpha o\ \kappa\alpha\grave{\iota}\ \dot{\epsilon}\nu\ \nu\epsilon\kappa\acute{\nu}\epsilon\sigma\sigma\iota\ \underline{\phi\alpha\epsilon\acute{\iota}\nu\omega} \quad \text{(xii. 383)}$$

and Zeus responds in the same way,

$$\mu\epsilon\tau'\ \dot{\alpha}\theta\alpha\nu\acute{\alpha}\tau o\iota\sigma\iota\ \underline{\phi\acute{\alpha}\epsilon\iota\nu\epsilon}$$
$$\kappa\alpha\grave{\iota}\ \theta\nu\eta\tauo\hat{\iota}\sigma\iota\nu\ \beta\rho o\tauo\hat{\iota}\sigma\iota\nu\ \dot{\epsilon}\pi\grave{\iota}\ \zeta\epsilon\acute{\iota}\delta\omega\rho o\nu\ \mathring{\alpha}\rho o\nu\rho\alpha\nu. \quad \text{(xii. 385–6)}$$

Somehow this being who talks and wills is also the round thing that men see in the sky. Occasionally the two articulations of the sun's nature are juxtaposed in rapid succession, as when Hera orders the sun to go down so that the world will be darkened:[25]

$$\underline{\ddot{}\!H\dot{\epsilon}\lambda\iota o\nu}\ \delta'\ \dot{\alpha}\kappa\acute{\alpha}\mu\alpha\nu\tau\alpha\ \beta o\hat{\omega}\pi\iota s\ \pi\acute{o}\tau\nu\iota\alpha\ \ddot{}\!H\rho\eta$$
$$\pi\acute{\epsilon}\mu\psi\epsilon\nu\ \dot{\epsilon}\pi'\ \dot{}\!\Omega\kappa\epsilon\alpha\nuo\hat{\iota}o\ \rho o\grave{\alpha}s\ \underline{\dot{\alpha}\acute{\epsilon}\kappa o\nu\tau\alpha}\ \nu\acute{\epsilon}\epsilon\sigma\theta\alpha\iota\cdot$$
$$\underline{\ddot{}\!H\dot{\epsilon}\lambda\iota os}\ \mu\grave{\epsilon}\nu\ \mathring{\epsilon}\delta\nu,\ \pi\alpha\acute{\nu}\sigma\alpha\nu\tauo\ \delta\grave{\epsilon}\ \delta\hat{\iota}o\iota\ \dot{}\!A\chi\alpha\iotao\grave{\iota}$$
$$\phi\nu\lambda\acute{o}\pi\iota\delta os\ \kappa\rho\alpha\tau\epsilon\rho\hat{\eta}s\ \kappa\alpha\grave{\iota}\ \dot{o}\mu o\acute{\iota}o\nu\ \pio\lambda\acute{\epsilon}\mu o\iota o. \quad \text{(XVIII. 239–42)}$$

Here the mythical and the non-mythical rub shoulders. On the level of the divine society, Helios sulkily ($\dot{\alpha}\acute{\epsilon}\kappa o\nu\tau\alpha$, 240) obeys Hera's command, loath to disturb the ordered sequence of his journey, while on the level of mortal experience the sun simply and visibly sinks below the horizon.[26] The range of

---

[25] Compare Athena delaying Eos in person in order to prolong the night (xxiii. 242–6).

[26] Erbse (1986: 45–8) compares the sun's overtly personal truculence in the Thrinacian story (xii. 374–88) with the more subtle hint of personification in the $\dot{\alpha}\acute{\epsilon}\kappa o\nu\tau\alpha$ of the present passage, and suggests (p. 47) that the latter shows the 'pure Homeric spirit'. It could equally be said that the personality of

articulations represented by the word ἠέλιος makes up a supple
unity, and the poet glides from one level to the other.[27]

A revealing example of the same dynamic is offered by the
river Scamander. Scamander is the son of Zeus (XXI. 2),[28] and
we hear of his priest (v. 77–8; cf. XXI. 130–2) and glimpse him
battling among the other gods in the Theomachy (XX. 40, 73–
4); while rivers in general are accorded cult (XXIII. 141–51),
called on to witness oaths (III. 278), included among those
called to council by Zeus (XX. 7), and remembered as fathers of
human children (e.g. v. 544–5, XVI. 173–8).[29] None the less, in
the usual course of the narrative nothing happens to disturb
our understanding of Scamander as a visible and inanimate
feature of the Trojan plain; and he emerges into full personal
prominence only through a strange development of the story-
line in Achilles' final onslaught on the Trojans.[30] When the
hero drives his foes into the river it becomes clogged with
corpses and bursts its banks, and at this point Homer gives a
hint of Scamander's personality:

> ἐν δ' ἔπεσον μεγάλωι πατάγωι, βράχε δ' αἰπὰ ῥέεθρα,
> ὄχθαι δ' ἀμφὶ περὶ μεγάλ' ἴαχον· οἱ δ' ἀλαλητῶι
> ἔννεον ἔνθα καὶ ἔνθα, ἑλισσόμενοι περὶ δίνας. (XXI. 9–11)

The tormented river groans and roars as if with its own
personal voice. Over his next victim Achilles boasts that

Helios emerges to the appropriate extent in each case, since the slaughter of
his cattle naturally involves his emotions in a more intimate way.

[27] Compare the combination of anthropomorphic and non-anthropo-
morphic images in a single sentence narrating the dawn, ἠὼς μὲν κροκόπεπλος
ἐκίδνατο πᾶσαν ἐπ' αἶαν (VIII. 1 = XXIV. 695).

[28] Compare Hes. *Theog.* 337–45, where Scamander is one of the rivers born
of Tethys and Oceanus. The cosmogonic role of this couple appears
occasionally in Homer (see XIV. 201 = 302, 246, with Janko at XIV. 200–7),
but seems mostly to be bypassed in favour of the Olympian scheme.

[29] Note the story of Tyro (xi. 238–53), a mortal woman who fell in love with
a river and dallied by his banks, enabling Poseidon to disguise himself as the
river (τῶι . . . εἰσάμενος, xi. 241) in order to have his way with her. Tyro's
passion was apparently inspired by the river's beauty, πολὺ κάλλιστος ποταμῶν
(xi. 239): in the world of Homer's anthropomorphism there is no reason why
such attraction should not be sexual.

[30] On Scamander's personality see also Elliger (1975), 71–3. Elsewhere I
have included the present discussion of the river-god in a study of early Greek
approaches to landscape (M. J. Clarke (1997)).

Scamander will be unable to protect the Trojans despite all the sacrifices offered him in the past (XXI. 130–2), and at this the river becomes enraged:

> ὣς ἄρ᾽ ἔφη, ποταμὸς δὲ χολώσατο κηρόθι μᾶλλον,
> ὥρμηνεν δ᾽ ἀνὰ θυμὸν ὅπως παύσειε πόνοιο
> δῖον Ἀχιλλῆα, Τρώεσσι δὲ λοιγὸν ἀλάλκοι.   (XXI. 136–8)

From now on, Scamander's behaviour is fully that of a personal god. Achilles slays Asteropaeus, who is himself the son of a river, and declares that he has the victory because one sprung from a river will never be a match for the descendant of his own great-grandfather, Zeus (184–99). So Scamander bursts into anger, and addresses Achilles in human guise:

> καί νύ κ᾽ ἔτι πλέονας κτάνε Παίονας ὠκὺς Ἀχιλλεύς,
> εἰ μὴ χωσάμενος προσέφη ποταμὸς βαθυδίνης,
> ἀνέρι εἰσάμενος, βαθέης δ᾽ ἐκ φθέγξατο δίνης . . .   (211–13)

The familiar pattern of a god disguising himself in human form, ἀνέρι εἰσάμενος (compare e.g. XIII. 216, XVI. 716, XVII. 73; i. 105) explains how the river can manifest his personal identity when he speaks. These two words pin down the visual image, and yoke together the mythical and non-mythical identities of the river in a way that goes beyond anything that we could find in Homer's evocation of Helios. Crucially, however, the anthropomorphic image is forgotten as soon as it is articulated, and when Scamander returns to the onslaught he is again precisely identified with the physical substance of the water:

> ὁ δ᾽ ἐπέσσυτο οἴδματι θύων,
> πάντα δ᾽ ὄρινε ῥέεθρα κυκώμενος, ὦσε δὲ νεκροὺς
> πολλούς, οἵ ῥα κατ᾽ αὐτὸν ἅλις ἔσαν, οὓς κτάν᾽ Ἀχιλλεύς·
> τοὺς ἔκβαλλε θύραζε, μεμυκὼς ἠΰτε ταῦρος,
> χέρσονδε· ζωοὺς δὲ σάω κατὰ καλὰ ῥέεθρα,
> κρύπτων ἐν δίνῃσι βαθείῃσιν μεγάλῃσι.
> δεινὸν δ᾽ ἀμφ᾽ Ἀχιλῆα κυκώμενον ἵστατο κῦμα,
> ὤθει δ᾽ ἐν σάκεϊ πίπτων ῥόος.   (XXI. 234–41)

The rushing river-water and the raging river-god are one. The same unity is preserved to the end of the battle and during Scamander's ensuing conflict with Hephaestus (note esp. 248–9, 268–71, 305–7, 324–7, 356–8). For a moment, the words ἀνέρι εἰσάμενος seemed to crystallize the relationship between

the two levels: but the personality of Scamander was not fixed
by this anthropomorphic shape, and as the narrative proceeds it
remains inseparably identified with the river itself.[31] Compare
the words with which Odysseus addresses the river of Scheria
when he swims into its estuary from the sea:

> αἰδοῖος μέν τ' ἐστὶ καὶ ἀθανάτοισι θεοῖσιν
> ἀνδρῶν ὅς τις ἵκηται ἀλώμενος, ὡς καὶ ἐγὼ νῦν
> σόν τε ῥόον σά τε γούναθ' ἱκάνω πολλὰ μογήσας.   (v. 447–9)

The swimmer spreads abroad his arms as he moves through the
outpouring water, and the river itself is also the god: so that his
action is precisely that of seizing its knees in the gesture of
supplication. Neither the image which fixes the river as an
anthropomorphic god, nor the image which denies it personality of any kind, has any binding force over the overall
definition of what it is to be a river.

The supple identity of ψυχή

We are now ready for a last look at ψυχή. Let us recapitulate the
burden of our earlier chapters. Normally ψυχή is the dying
man's last gasp, lost on the air like any puff of air, but in certain
controlled circumstances it takes on a mythical identity and
flies away to Hades like a bird. We saw that Homeric death-lore
overall does not take shape in terms of that mythical version of
ψυχή, and instead sends the dead man to Hades in bodily form:
and we needed to justify the claim that the mythical articulation of ψυχή does not prescribe the essential meaning of the

---

[31] Nagy (1992a: 325) compares Achilles' fight with Scamander with
Archilochus' lost version of Heracles' fight with the river Acheloüs over
Deianira. Archilochus made the river take the form of a bull (fr. 287
W = schol. at XXI. 237), and Homer describes Scamander bellowing like a
bull, μεμυκὼς ἠΰτε ταῦρος (XXI. 237), while continuing to fight in his own shape.
Sophocles refers to a version—possibly Archilochus' own—in which Acheloüs
changed shape in Protean fashion, one of his guises being that of a bull (*Trach.*
9–23). Nagy argues that Homer knows but avoids making explicit the
tradition that fighting rivers take the shape of bulls. On the other hand, it
may be that Homer's version and Archilochus' represent two different
responses to a traditional association of ideas: both in Homer and historically,
bulls were the beasts usually sacrificed to rivers (see XXI. 131, with Nilsson
(1967), 238).

word. The examples gathered in this chapter show that a system of unity in multiplicity characterizes the overall place of myth in Homer's depiction of the world. The words ἀνέρι εἰσάμενος do not prescribe the identity of Scamander the river-god; the anthropomorphic form of Helios does not affect his status as the glowing disc in the sky; Ares is indeterminately a phenomenon of the mortal world and a divine personality. It is because these articulations take shape through a logic of creativity, rather than of terms, that the identity of Ares, Helios, or Scamander can clothe itself in different forms in the course of a single movement of poetry without absurdity or contradiction. If we accept that, it follows that the variable identity of ψυχή is typical of words of its kind.

The double plane of causation

This leaves us with one final question hanging over the Homeric view of what it means to die. We suggested that the journey into the grave is a mythical version of the journey to Hades: the two articulations are normally collapsed into each other, so that when Patroclus' shade begs for a funeral he can see the prospect simultaneously as descent into the earth and personal integration among the inhabitants of Hades (Ch. 6, pp. 211–13). Here the claim for unity in multiplicity was made on the level of fully-fledged cosmology rather than the word-meanings, and as such it requires separate justification.

There is a pointer towards such justification in one of the passages we have observed already in this chapter. The intervention of Ares on Hector's side in *Iliad* IV (above, pp. 270–1) can be seen as a projection onto the mythical plane of a sudden rush of battle-fury inside Hector himself: and as such it is an example of the 'double plane' of causation, the system which allows Homer to explain sudden thoughts and emotions both as independent human psychology and as the intervention of personal deities.[32] The crux is that the two planes exist in

---

[32] Very many studies of this problem exist, the most recent being A. Schmitt (1990), pt. 1. For me the most useful monograph has been Lesky (1961); also helpful have been Dodds (1951), 1–18; Schwabl (1954); Kullmann (1956); Erbse (1984); Edwards (1987), 131–8; and Janko (1992), 3–4. The term 'over-determination' (Dodds, Schwabl) is unfortunate because

harmony, and the god's intervention need not imply that the mortal man is less than fully responsible for his actions.[33] This is borne out most simply when a single sentence juxtaposes the two levels, as when Phemius attributes his poetic skills both to himself and to the inspiration from the god:[34]

αὐτοδίδακτος δ' εἰμί, θεὸς δέ μοι ἐν φρεσὶν οἴμας
παντοίας ἐνέφυσεν. (xxii. 347–8; cf. esp. viii. 44–5)

He is simultaneously self-taught and instructed by a divine teacher. The principle is the same when Diomedes says that Achilles will eventually respond to divine prompting and the urge of his θυμός,

τότε δ' αὖτε μαχήσεται, ὁππότε κέν μιν
θυμὸς ἐνὶ στήθεσσιν ἀνώγηι καὶ θεὸς ὄρσηι . . . (IX. 702–3)

or when Odysseus tells Eurycleia to be quiet despite the thing which she herself has discovered and the idea which a god has placed in her breast:

ἀλλ' ἐπεὶ ἐφράσθης καί τοι θεὸς ἔμβαλε θυμῶι,
σίγα. (xix. 485–6)

Here the divine and human levels of causation are co-ordinated, not contrasted, and the two levels of image-making run parallel. In the same way, a character can represent a single decision or movement of thought as originating indeterminately from within man or from divine prompting, as when Phoenix warns Achilles not to be led into error:[35]

ἀλλὰ σὺ μή μοι ταῦτα νόει φρεσί, μηδέ σε δαίμων
ἐνταῦθα τρέψειε, φίλος. (IX. 600–1)

it suggests that the Homeric view of motivation should be seen as a single system or doctrine (cf. Adkins (1960), 10–17, for such an approach). Otherwise the most dangerous temptation is to see the so-called *Götterapparat* as an ornamental device: 'The poet weaves his fabric from the threads of rational human action, and the supernatural is an embroidery or appliqué of ornamental design' (Calhoun (1937); cf. Chantraine (1954), 61, and Willcock (1970)).

[33] On this principle see esp. Lesky (1961), 22–32.
[34] On the united work of the two levels of poetic inspiration, see also Murray (1981).
[35] Lesky (1961), 32–40.

Phoenix is not distinguishing two separate routes by which Achilles might err, but referring to a single psychological event under its mythical and non-mythical aspects.[36] Either version would suffice on its own, and the two together are opposite sides of the same coin (compare e.g. v. 251–6).

The same principle also operates over longer stretches of story-telling. For example, there is no contradiction when an artefact is described as the work of Hephaestus or Apollo in one passage and as the work of a human craftsman in another;[37] and a god can move among men in the guise of a specific person without forcing us to ask what has happened to the mortal himself at that time.[38] In each case the mythical and non-mythical levels run on their own separate paths, and the need to reconcile the two does not arise.

So stated, this pattern corresponds on the larger scale to the semantic pattern which allows a single word to have both a mythical and a non-mythical identity at one and the same time. In both cases the stuff of myth is latent in the furniture of the world and the events of mortal experience, and the poet's control over the ebb and flow of image-making allows him to move without contradiction from one type of rendering to the other. Crucially, however, where motivation is concerned it is also possible for Homer to draw a contrast between the divine and human levels, denying that a thought or emotion was of human origin and assigning it solely to the gods.[39] Among very

[36] See Lesky (1961), 23. There are many such instances in which it is difficult or impossible to tell whether a real bifurcation of alternatives is in question (for doubtful instances see e.g. iv. 712–13, xiv. 178–9).

[37] Willcock (1970) cites the example of Pandarus' bow, which is once described as a gift of Apollo (II. 827) and once as the work of a craftsman who made it from the horns of an ibex which Pandarus himself had shot (IV. 105–11). For kindred examples of gifts of the gods which can also be seen as ordinary human acquisitions or skills learnt by mortal wit, see Lesky (1961), 30–1.

[38] Willcock (1970) uses the example of Iris addressing the Trojan assembly in the guise of Poulydamas (II. 786–806). The *Odyssey* shows one curious example of this principle being played upon self-consciously, when one of the Ithacans is puzzled by the contradiction between Athena's behaviour in the guise of Mentor and the things that he knows the real Mentor has been doing (iv. 653–6).

[39] Lesky (1961), 38–44.

many examples in both epics, the case of ἄτη will suffice as an illustration.[40]

Like the other individual nouns that we have studied in this chapter, ἄτη exists on two levels: at one extreme it denotes the ruin which results from the folly of mortals,[41] and at the other extreme it is a divine being whom Zeus (or occasionally another god: see iv. 261–2, xv. 233–4) releases in order to drive men to that same ruin. Phoenix builds up the contours of this personal Ate when he warns Achilles of the consequences of pride:[42]

> ἡ δ' Ἄτη σθεναρή τε καὶ ἀρτίπος, οὕνεκα πάσας
> πολλὸν ὑπεκπροθέει, φθάνει δέ τε πᾶσαν ἐπ' αἶαν
> βλάπτουσ' ἀνθρώπους. (IX. 505–7)

Coming as it does in a speech of stern admonition, this image of Ate as a personal agent cannot imply that her personal presence makes Achilles any less blameworthy for what will ensue: once again, the world of mortals and the world of divinity are one and the same. However, there is a crucial difference between Homer's evocation of ἄτη and the pattern which we have observed in other nouns. In certain circumstances Ate is treated as a divinity specifically in order to argue that the folly in question did *not* originate with the mortal agent. Agamemnon subtly exploits this when he admits that he erred by alienating Achilles. First, when his peers are gathered around him in private he admits that the folly was his own, ἐμὰς ἄτας (IX. 115; cf. I. 412 = XVI. 274), and he co-ordinates the two levels of causation by saying that the fault lay both in his own φρένες and in the favour which Zeus showed to Achilles:

---

[40] On Homeric ἄτη see Stallmach (1968); Lloyd-Jones (1971), ch. 1; Doyle (1984), 7–22; Erbse (1986), 11–15.

[41] For ἄτη used without a hint of its mythical identity, see e.g. VI. 356, VIII. 237, X. 391, XXIV. 28; xxi. 302. It is cognate with the verb ἀάω (see *LfgrE* s.v. for the philology) and seems to be associated closely with it in sense, since the two words are often linked by *figura etymologica* (VIII. 237, XIX. 91, 129, 136–7; xxi. 295–302).

[42] On the (possible) creative originality of Phoenix' image of Ate and the Supplications, who are daughters of Zeus, see Doyle (1984), 7–22; Erbse (1986), 11–15; and Hainsworth at IX. 505–12.

ἀασάμην, οὐδ' αὐτὸς ἀναίνομαι. ἀντί νυ πολλῶν
λαῶν ἐστιν ἀνὴρ ὅν τε Ζεὺς κῆρι φιλήσηι,
ὡς νῦν τοῦτον ἔτεισε, δάμασσε δὲ λαὸν Ἀχαιῶν.
ἀλλ' ἐπεὶ <u>ἀασάμην φρεσὶ λευγαλέηισι πιθήσας,</u>
ἂψ ἐθέλω ἀρέσαι δόμεναί τ' ἀπερείσι' ἄποινα.   (IX. 116–20)

However, when the final reconciliation takes place and Agamemnon addresses the assembled host he shifts the cause
squarely onto the divine level and denies that he himself
deserves the blame:[43]

ἐγὼ δ' οὐκ αἴτιός εἰμι,
ἀλλὰ Ζεὺς καὶ Μοῖρα καὶ ἠεροφοῖτις Ἐρινύς,
οἵ τέ μοι εἰν ἀγορῆι φρεσὶν <u>ἔμβαλον ἄγριον ἄτην.</u>   (XIX. 86–8)

Moving onto the plane of fully mythical narrative, he tells how
Zeus himself was subject to Ate until he expelled her in person
from Olympus and sent her to plague mortals. Agamemnon
ends his speech in almost the same words as those which he
used in the earlier meeting with the elders, but with the change
that he identifies his ἄτη as a force from outside:

οὐ δυνάμην λελαθέσθ' Ἄτης, ἧι πρῶτον ἀάσθην.
ἀλλ' ἐπεὶ <u>ἀασάμην καί μευ φρένας ἐξέλετο Ζεύς,</u>
ἂψ ἐθέλω ἀρέσαι δόμεναί τ' ἀπερείσι' ἄποινα.   (136–8)

When Agamemnon defied Achilles he was subject to a deity
whom even the king of the gods was once powerless to resist.
Throughout this speech he presses home a rhetorical point by
exploiting the fluid possibilities contained in the word ἄτη.[44]

[43] Lesky's analysis of this passage (1961: 39–42) is revised by Erbse (1986:
11–15), who argues that Agamemnon uses the story of Ate expelled from
Olympus not to shift blame from himself to the deity, but rather to defend
himself on the grounds that not even Zeus is proof against her influence when
she is near by. Taplin (1992: 203–12) argues that the words ἐγὼ δ' οὐκ αἴτιός
εἰμι ought to imply in themselves that Agamemnon owes Achilles no
reparation, so that they do not square with the rest of what Agamemnon is
saying and doing: his speech involves 'a blatant *non sequitur*' (209) and 'his
blaming of the gods is clearly special pleading' (208). I do not know who is
right: we might be able to decide if we knew what Achilles means when he
refers obliquely to Agamemnon's speech with the verb κλοτοπεύειν (XIX. 149),
but this *hapax* baffles the learned.

[44] Notice the verbal parallel in Achilles' speech to the Embassy, ἐρρέτω—ἐκ
γάρ εὖ φρένας εἵλετο μητίετα Ζεύς (IX. 377), where the image cannot imply any
diminution of Agamemnon's guilt (cf. also VI. 234, XVII. 469–70, XVIII. 311,

That is not to say that Agamemnon is simply lying or dissimulating when he draws out such one-sided images. If this were the case, Achilles could not concur in the way that he does in the final ritual of reconciliation:[45]

$$Ζεῦ πάτερ, ἦ μεγάλας ἄτας ἄνδρεσσι διδοῖσθα·$$
$$οὐκ ἂν δή ποτε θυμὸν ἐνὶ στήθεσσιν ἐμοῖσιν$$
$$Ἀτρεΐδης ὤρινε διαμπερές, οὐδέ κε κούρην$$
$$ἦγεν ἐμεῦ ἀέκοντος ἀμήχανος· ἀλλά ποθι Ζεὺς$$
$$ἤθελ' Ἀχαιοῖσιν θάνατον πολέεσσι γενέσθαι.   (XIX. 270–4)$$

In the wider context of the Wrath as a whole, Achilles' words suggest not only that it is possible for what has happened to be explained in several alternative ways, but also that each of the levels of explanation remains fully valid on its own. Priam does something similar when he tells Helen that she is not responsible for the war because it is the work of the gods:[46]

$$οὔ τί μοι αἰτίη ἐσσί, θεοί νύ μοι αἴτιοί εἰσιν,$$
$$οἵ μοι ἐφώρμησαν πόλεμον πολύδακρυν Ἀχαιῶν.   (III. 164–5)$$

It would also have been possible to attribute the elopement either to her and Paris' folly or indeterminately to them and the gods together (cf. e.g. VI. 355–8, XIII. 620–39; IV. 145–6), but in these special rhetorical circumstances Priam produces a special image, explicitly contrasting the divine level with the human.[47] What he says takes its meaning—and its generosity—from the way it emerges from a much wider range of possibilities for image-making.

The double plane of death

In this way, the picture which emerges is that the shifting perspectives in shifting contexts are all valid in their own ways: there is no single definition of the relationship between human and divine agency, and the system makes sense only if we

where the same image of φρένες taken away by a god appears in less grave contexts).

[45] Compare Zeus' complaint that mortals blame the gods for their own follies (i. 32–4).

[46] Lesky (1961), 39–40.

[47] On this passage see Taplin (1992), 96–103: 'Putting *all* the blame on the gods is, in effect, an attempt to reduce the double motivation to single' (100).

consider it in its full breadth and complexity.[48] This begs to be compared with the principle that what lies beyond death is *simultaneously* a journey to the darkness of the grave and a journey to the darkness of Hades. The two levels are yoked together in Patroclus' plea that he be buried and by the same token allowed to pass fully into Hades:

θάπτε με ὅττι τάχιστα, πύλας Ἀΐδαο περήσω.   (XXIII. 71)

Structurally, this corresponds exactly to the pattern in expressions like Phemius' αὐτοδίδακτός εἰμι . . ., 'I am self-taught *and* inspired by the god'. When his mythical integration into Hades and the non-mythical process of burial are juxtaposed in a single sentence they are exactly co-ordinated, the one implying the other without challenge or ambiguity. The same path is followed in a slightly different way by the shade of Elpenor, when he asks to be given a funeral and refers to his physical substance indeterminately as 'himself' (xi. 72–4); and throughout the shaping of death-lore this supple unity enables death to be expressed on either level or on both at once.

However, we saw that this correspondence between the two aspects of the journey of death is replaced by a complex bifurcation in the deaths of Patroclus and Hector, because here the poet articulates a contrast between the corpse which remains in the mortal world and the ψυχή which flies off to the unseen world of Hades. Just as in Agamemnon's description of his own ἄτη, Homer exploits the semantic complexities of a single noun to separate something off from the world of mortal experience and assign it to the world of myth. In both cases the complex articulation makes sense only as a development on the basis of the simpler ones which lie behind it, and no one image is a more significant part of the Homeric realities than another. Crucially, it is the complex articulation which seems to answer best to a modern Western view of the world. Just as a view of human motivation which attributes some things to divine influence and others to human folly is appealing to modern ideas about religious modes of thought, so the myth of the flying ψυχή looks at first sight like proof of a doctrine of the

---

[48] On the point that the elements of the system are complementary rather than mutually contradictory, see Lesky (1961), 42.

soul. In its Homeric context, however, each is only one among many possible workings-out of a larger nexus of images and creative patterns: and it is the whole of this nexus, rather then any one of its products, which makes sense in the Homeric world-picture.

It is in this way that the image of the flying ψυχή emerges from, but does not govern or supersede, the shifting patterns of Homer's conception of the dead man's journey to Hades. The sources of image-making are fixed in his traditional repertoire, and the range of possibilities for their articulation is fixed by the traditional techniques of composition, so that an overall unity underlies the poet's movement along different paths of song[49] to produce different images and myths. If we accept this point we can appreciate the authentically Homeric character of the flying ψυχή without letting it mislead us into believing that Homer sees man and his identity in the dualistic way that such things might be seen in our own age. In this way we can conclude both by confirming our original hypothesis and by accepting Homer's lore of man and ψυχή in its full variety. In the words of another maker of subtle images, the myth is saved and is not lost: οὕτως οὖν ὁ μῦθος ἐσώθη καὶ οὐκ ἀπώλετο.[50]

---

[49] On song as a road or path (οἶμος, οἴμη) see esp. xxii. 347, *h. Merc.* 451, with Thalmann (1984: 123–5), and the wider gleanings of Becker (1937), Durante (1968*a*, 1968*b*).

[50] Pl. *Resp.* 621b7.

EPILOGUE

Flesh and Spirit in Language and Lore after Homer

Our reconstruction of Homeric ideas has rested on the observable meanings of certain words, above all ψυχή and the nouns of the θυμός family. The policy has been to treat the semantic range of each word as the index to a significant cultural unity: in effect the word's meaning became the map of a province of the Homeric world picture. But it might be objected that a poet or any user of language is the master and not the slave of the words he uses. However deeply Homer is rooted in his *Kunstsprache*, or however clearly he expresses the tradition embodied by the Muse, still it is impossible to prove that the categories of his vocabulary correspond exactly to the concepts and beliefs that shape his view of man. Consider M. L. West's dismissal of arguments relying on the point that Homer (unlike Hesiod) never applies the word σῶμα to a living body rather than a corpse:

[σῶμα is used] in Homer only of the dead body . . ., the living body being represented by μέλεα, γυῖα, and where appropriate by δέμας 'build', χρώς 'skin'. Much has been made of this by B. Snell [see our Ch. 4, pp. 115–19] . . . who argues that Homer has no conception of the body as a physical unity . . . Etymology throws no light on the original sense, but if it had been 'corpse' its application to the living body could never have come about. Of Homer I should say that he simply did not have occasion to refer to any person's live body as a *lump*, just as he did not have occasion (as Hesiod does in *WD* 515) to refer to the ῥινός of a live animal. He had other words for the body as a visual object (δέμας, εἶδος), as a repository for energy and strength (μέλεα, γυῖα), etc.; σῶμα encroached upon their territory in later Greek, as ψυχή did upon that of the Homeric θυμός.[1]

---

[1] West at Hes. *WD* 540.

West's argument can be criticized in detail—for example, it is hard to see how a poet who could name the body as a unit would 'simply not have occasion' to use that word anywhere in thousands of lines describing such things as hand-to-hand combat: but the fact remains that the sceptic can pour cold water on any attempt to use words as an index of ideas. For ψυχή in particular we have been dogged by two questions: Does the semantic range of this word bear directly on Homer's conception of what happens when a man breathes his last? And does the fact that ψυχή and the θυμός family come to the fore in different contexts, overlapping only at the moment of the last breath, indicate that the locus of mental life is distinct from anything that passes into the afterlife?

This is a case of one of the most awkward questions in sociolinguistics, the question which dogs any claim that the norms of a language can prescribe the beliefs and conceptual schemes of its speech-community.[2] If a native American language has a peculiar and untranslatable tense-system, does that tell us something about its speakers' conception of time? If the Inuit had a hundred different words for snow, would it mean that they interpret the sight of a white Christmas in a different way from you and me?[3] If the Nuer people speak of twin children as if they were birds and vice versa, does this bear witness to a deep interactive structure in their understanding of what both those things mean?[4] It seems that among academic linguists it is no longer respectable to claim that languages in general have this prescriptive power,[5] and I can do no more

---

[2] Among linguists the label 'Sapir–Whorf hypothesis' sticks to most versions of this claim (see esp. Sapir (1921), Whorf (1956)). In practice, modern assessments of the hypothesis seems to centre primarily on the prescriptive power of syntactic structures and only secondarily on the meanings of words. Colour terms and kinship terms are the examples most often chosen, and I have not found any serious discussion of the cultural power of the category of words in which I place ψυχή—that is, the class of nouns which (a) lack concrete referents and (b) are important in the expression of serious traditional beliefs. This is not the place to argue out my hunch that in any language such nouns may have an especially insidious power to prescribe the categories of thought.

[3] On the history of this enduring myth see Pullum (1991), ch. 1.

[4] Evans-Pritchard (1956), 128–33.

[5] See e.g. Hudson (1980), 103–5; Pinker (1994), 59–64, comparing the essays in Hoijer (1954) and Penn (1972).

here than suggest that the language of Homeric epic may be a special case. A general appeal can be made to the arguments advanced in Chapter 1, where I suggested that Homeric language and ideas are bound together in an especially intimate way because of the power and antiquity of the poetic tradition which simultaneously prescribes both words and world-picture. However, in this epilogue I will try to advance a further, more down-to-earth argument for the cultural significance of ψυχή. We will see that in Greek of the period immediately *after* Homer the word has a very different character, with a range of meaning which serves to associate mental life with life after death in a way that has no parallel in the early epic. Moreover, it will emerge that this semantic change exactly matches religious and cultural innovations that are attested for the same historical period. The evidence for both lingistic and cultural change will bolster the suspicion that the word ψυχή answers to significant concepts in the conceptual world of its users, both for Homer and for others who wielded Greek with authority in the period after the fixing of the Homeric text.

The concept of the soul

It is plain at a glance that concepts of body and soul were firmly fixed in Greek culture by the Classical period, that is the late fifth and fourth centuries. At this time intellectuals' assumptions about the structure of man can seem closer to those of our own age than to those of Homer. To Plato, for example, it is obvious that the soul is a reality, whatever its true nature may be: it is a constant which underlies his different versions of the struggle between body and spirit, mortal and immortal in human life.[6] Even the sceptics in the *Phaedo* do not question

[6] The changes in Plato's definition of the soul and its relation with the body are traced by T. M. Robinson (1970). The most important ambiguity in the earlier dialogues is that in some the required mastery is that of the soul over the body (*Phaedo*, for example) while in others it is that of the superior part of the soul over the base parts (as *Phaedrus*, *Republic*). The mediation of the dichotomy in later dialogues, notably the *Timaeus* and the *Laws*, says more about the development of Plato's own thinking than about his intellectual background, and it need not concern us here. The *Laws* offers a very useful definition of the ψυχή as that which is self-moving and consequently divine (*Laws* 891e–896e).

the presupposition that if there is an afterlife the survivor beyond the grave will be the same as the ψυχή which had existed in the living man; and the struggle to become 'master of myself' makes sense only if the body is distinguishable from the soul, the non-bodily core which is to achieve that mastery.[7] The ψυχή in turn shades into 'myself', so that the thinking mind and the immortal spirit are identified with each other and distanced by the same token from the periphery of the body.[8] How, then, do we bridge the gulf between Homer and the fourth-century thinker? It is possible (if no more) that the new concept was injected into Greek culture through the influence of a single well-defined intellectual movement: perhaps as a result of the growth of new doctrines of soul among the Ionian philosophers, perhaps because of the dissemination of esoteric doctrines associated with Orphic or Pythagorean teachings. As we turn to the evidence for those doctrines it will be impossible to prove that they represent currents of thought that were strong enough to mould the Greek language; but they will at least give us some insight into ideas that seemed new and distinctive in their time.

Among the Presocratic philosophers, ψυχή and later νόος take on an increasingly significant role both in human psychology and the macrocosm. The major innovators seem to have been Anaximenes and Heraclitus for ψυχή and Anaxagoras for νόος. Apparently Anaximenes took ψυχή to embody the essence of self-propelled motion in the same way as the air which imbues the universe itself: οἷον ἡ ψυχή, φησίν, ἡ ἡμετέρα ἀὴρ οὖσα συγκρατεῖ ἡμᾶς, καὶ ὅλον τὸν κόσμον πνεῦμα καὶ ἀὴρ περιέχει (fr. 160 KRS).[9] If this is to make sense, he must be seeing the ψυχή

---

[7] See Ingenkamp (1975), 51–61; also cf. Lovibond (1991: 50), emphasizing what she sees as the novelty of Socrates' emphasis on the moral role of ψυχή, 'the *début* of a world-historic idea: that of the *centred* or *integrated subject*' (50). On Socratic and Platonic concepts of ψυχή, see also Claus (1981), 156–80; and on their Presocratic antecedents, see Wright (1990).

[8] On this point see esp. Havelock (1972), 9: 'To conceive of self-dialectic as an operation of primary importance to a person's welfare and then to imagine it as proceeding inside the ghost was to assert implicitly that the essence of life was introspective thought'.

[9] As KRS point out ad loc., the wording of this passage is probably not Anaximenes' own; so that it cannot be absolutely guaranteed that ψυχή was the word on which he hung this doctrine.

as the active foundation of life rather than merely as something released when it ends. Heraclitus clearly regarded the ψυχή as central to human nature,[10] though it is harder to say whether he explicitly formulated a dichotomy between body and soul;[11] but, however that may be, his ψυχή must be far away from the Homeric conception if he can imagine it as having hidden depths: ψυχῆς πείρατα ἰὼν οὐκ ἂν εὕροιο, πᾶσαν ἐπιπορευόμενος ὁδόν· οὕτω βαθὺν λόγον ἔχει (fr. 232 KRS). This image stands alongside others in which (if the wording is his own) Heraclitus seems to regard the ψυχή in a less mysterious sense as the core of human identity: men who trust in their senses too much have barbarous ψυχαί (B 107 D–K), drunkenness makes the ψυχή wet (fr. 231 KRS; cf. 229), and a dry ψυχή is wisest (fr. 230 KRS). A man's ψυχή is the centre of his consciousness, and this links it to divinity: the mysterious words ἦθος ἀνθρώπωι δαίμων (fr. 247 KRS) seem to mean either that man's personality is divine, or conversely that what men call δαίμων is no more than the essence (or product?) of the human character.[12] Either way, for Heraclitus as for Anaximenes there is an autonomous spirit in man which somehow partakes of divinity.

The evidence about the Pythagoreans and the exponents of

[10] See esp. frs. 229–32 KRS. On ψυχή in Heraclitus see M. C. Nussbaum (1972); Barnes (1979), i. 61; Kahn (1979), 249; Schofield (1991); Dilcher (1995), ch. 5. Both Nussbaum (1–14) and Schofield (21–7) propose that Heraclitus is emphasizing the positive role of the ψυχή in life as an explicit counterblast against the Homeric conception. Nussbaum further maintains (153–8) that Heraclitus attacks the Homeric assumption that the corpse, rather than the ψυχή, is the true 'I' of the dead person: here the evidence is fr. 229 and the intriguing apophthegm that 'corpses deserve to be thrown away more than dung', νέκυες κοπρίων ἐκβλητότεροι (B 96 D–K). Schofield (27–34) opposes this emphasis. More difficult is the question of the cosmic role of ψυχαί: see KRS pp. 203–5.

[11] See esp. Schofield (1991), 13–15. The best candidate for an explicit formulation of a body-soul model would be the remarkable fragment (B 67a D–K) according to which Heraclitus is supposed to have compared the soul in the body to a spider at the centre of its web. As the fragment is in Latin and at several removes from the original, using the word *anima*, we cannot be sure that ψυχή was the word originally used; and it is not certain that the account of Heraclitus' doctrine is genuine anyway (compare Kranz (1938), who accepts it fully, with the doubts of Marcovich (1967: 577)). The fragment is again discussed and argued from by M. C. Nussbaum (1972: 6–8), and in detail by Dilcher (1995), 82–4.

[12] KRS ad loc. suggest the latter. Cf. fr. 78 D–K.

Orphic wisdom points in the same direction, although the paucity of the evidence makes it less than certain that in pre-Classical times they drew on a clearly framed concept of the soul.[13] The fragments of the first part of the Derveni papyrus, dated about 300 BC, seem to refer to a doctrine that souls, ψυχαί, depart to Hades and become spirits of the Underworld named as δαίμονες or Ἐρινύες;[14] and in principle it is hard to see how any doctrine of transmigration and reincarnation could have been articulated without a clear notion of a spirit separable from the body.[15] However, the earliest direct evidence for Orphic doctrine dates from the late fifth and fourth centuries, and there is no telling when such doctrines were first made explicit.[16] The sense of body and soul that was summed up in tags like 'body is tomb', σῶμα σῆμα (see esp. Pl. *Crat.* 400c; *Grg.* 493a1–3) and 'body is garment of soul', σῶμα χιτὼν

[13] For Pythagorean soul-doctrine considered as a novel invention, see Jaeger (1947), 83–9. Burkert (1972: 133–5) does not commit himself: 'To what extent does the doctrine [of metempsychosis] imply clearly formulated beliefs, and how important was the word ψυχή? Was there present at its beginning the significant semantic innovation whereby the soul was regarded as the complete coalescence of life-soul and consciousness—a world away from the Homeric conception—or is "soul" primarily a mysterious, meta-empirical self, independent of consciousness, as some important witnesses seem to indicate? . . . It is only too easy for the modern scholar, from the vantage point of his own rationalistic and systematic activities, to suppose that at the beginning there was a unified, carefully worked out, and firmly defined theory.' (Cf. Burkert (1985), 300.)

[14] On the fragments of cols. III and IV of the Derveni papyrus, see esp. Tsantsanoglou (1997), and on its origins see esp. Janko (1997).

[15] For the transmigrating soul as ψυχή see Xenophanes, fr. 7a. 4 W (on which see also Regenbogen (1948), 22), and cf. Hdt. 2. 123, Ion B 4 D–K; also Claus (1981), 111–21. For the transmigrating soul as δαίμων see Empedocles, frs. 401, 407 KRS, comparing Heraclitus' ἦθος ἀνθρώπωι δαίμων (fr. 247 KRS).

[16] It is impossible to do more than speculate about the gold tablet from Hipponium (*c.*465 BC; see below, n. 53) which contains instructions about the journey of the dead man's ψυχή into Hades for reincarnation, and describes the activity of the souls waiting in Hades with the line ἔνθα κατερχόμεναι ψυχαὶ νεκύων ψύχονται. Here the *figura etymologica* apparently equates the movement of the ψυχαί with the strengthless movement of wind. (See Ch. 5, pp. 144–7 on the link with strengthless blowing in verbs in ψυχ-.) Calvert Watkins (in a seminar discussion at Cambridge (England), May (1994)) has suggested a translation based on a different part of the semantic range of the verb: 'The souls of the dead chill themselves out.' In the absence of clearer evidence no firm answer is possible.

ψυχῆς,[17] is not necessarily as old as was claimed by the later proponents of such wisdom. The minimal fact remains that in the form current in Plato's day it was part of the basis of Orphic and Pythagorean doctrine that man has an immortal or spiritual part and a mortal or bodily part. Apparently Philolaus represented this as an inheritance from ancient lore:

μαρτυρέονται δὲ καὶ οἱ παλαιοὶ θεολόγοι τε καὶ μάντιες ὡς διά τινας τιμωρίας
ἁ ψυχὰ τῶι σώματι συνέζευκται καὶ καθάπερ ἐν σάματι τούτωι τέθαπται.

(B 14 D–K; cf. frs. 450–5 KRS)

If the soul is 'yoked to' the body and 'buried in' the body in such a way that one's moral and intellectual life will be tied to the same soul's fate in the afterlife, it must follow that the mental 'I' and the survivor of death are a single entity, begging to be called the soul of man.

One enigmatic fragment of the Hesiodic *Catalogue of Women*—of uncertain date, but probably earlier than 500 BC[18]—offers a final shred of evidence for a doctrine in which ψυχή is the carrier of human identity in a cycle of resurrection and rebirth. Part of Zeus' plan for the Trojan War was ostensibly to bring about the deaths of heroes, πρ[ό]φασιν μὲν ὀλέσθαι | ψυχὰς ἡμιθέω[ν (fr. 204. 99–100 M–W), but to translate them afterwards to new life in the Isles of the Blest (lines 102–4). In the Homeric variant on this myth, which appears when Proteus prophesies Menelaus' future (iv. 561–5; compare also Hes. *WD* 167–73), the journey to new life is made by the bodily hero who will simply avoid death altogether and be removed to Elysium.[19] The poet of the *Catalogue* seems to have articulated a very different version, in which the ψυχαί of the heroes depart from their bodies and carry their identity into their new state of

---

[17] On σῶμα χιτὼν ψυχῆς see Zuntz (1971), 205, 405–6. The Orphic poem *The Robe* seems to have presented the relationship of soul to body in terms of the interstices of air in a net: see West (1983: 10), quoting Pl. *Ti.* 78b ff. The authenticity of the fragment of Philolaus quoted here has been severely doubted (see Huffman (1993), 404–6).

[18] West (1985a: 130–7) suggests a date as low as 'between 580 and 520' for the *Catalogue*, while Janko (1982: 221–5) argues from the diction that the poem is closely linked, at least, to Hesiod proper.

[19] The mythology of Elysium is complex and doubtful and cannot be discussed in full here: see esp. Burkert (1961); Sourvinou-Inwood (1995), 32–56; Beekes (1998).

immortality. Gaps in the papyrus make the connection of ideas difficult to follow, but it seems that the poet first describes the grim weather that gripped the earth after Zeus' decision to cause the Trojan War, and then moves on to tell of a snake (ἄτριχος, l. 129, a kenning), which descends into underground darkness and is destroyed by the weapons of Zeus:

> ἀλλά μιν ὑβριστήν τε καὶ [ἄγριον
> κῆλα Διὸς δαμνᾶι φὴ λυ.[
> ψυχὴ τοῦ [γ'] οἴη καταλείπε[ται
> ἢ δ' ἀμφ' αὐτόχυτον θαλαμ[
> ἠβαιήν ελ.(.)ειρα κατὰ χθ[ονός
> εἶσιν ἀμαυρωθεῖσ[.]ποθε[
> κεῖται δεχ[

(fr. 204. 137–143 M–W)

M. L. West has made the ingenious suggestion[20] that the passage expressed an analogy between the fate of the heroes and the life cycle of the snake: the heroes die but are restored by Zeus to their blessed afterlife, just as the snake descends into the earth and is miraculously restored to life when it sloughs off its skin and re-emerges. Since the lines are incomplete and the fragment breaks off before the end of the account of the snake, West's suggestion remains unproven. If he is right, the words ψυχὴ τοῦ [γ'] οἴη καταλείπε[ται imply that the ψυχή of the snake survives apart from its body and passes on to give life to its new incarnation; and the echo of the earlier words πρ[ό]φασιν μὲν ὀλέσθαι | ψυχὰς ἡμιθέω[ν (ll. 99–100) suggests that that process is presented as an exact parallel to what happens to the ψυχαί of the heroes translated by Zeus. Again, the fragmentary word ἀμαυρωθεῖσ[.] (whose stem at least is clearly legible) recalls the Homeric εἴδωλον ἀμαυρόν (iv. 824, 835), and further suggests that what happens to the snake is seen in terms of the separation of wraith from body.[21]

---

[20] (1985*a*), 120. See also his earlier article (1961) with further discussion of the connection of ideas in the earlier parts of the fragment and a number of more ambitious supplements which are not printed in the Oxford text.

[21] More cannot be said of this; but the theory is worth comparing with the suggestions of Nagy (1979: 174–210; cf. 1990*a*: 85–121) and Crane (1988: ch. 1 and *passim*) about other traditions in early epic concerning the revival of heroes in the Isles of the Blest.

Here, then, an account of death and reincarnation seems to be held together by the notion that human identity can be held and transmitted in the form of a disembodied soul. On similar lines it has sometimes been suggested that an explicit dichotomy between body and soul was first prompted by accounts of trance and ecstasy like those that have been studied among shamans in modern Asia.[22] Mystical journeys and *katabaseis* were made by Orpheus and Pythagoras as well as by other sages more loosely connected with them—Aristeas, Abaris, and the Thracian Salmoxis[23]—and since shamans' journeys can be described in terms of the soul standing outside the body, it is an easy inference that our Greeks might have explained their travels in the same way. The notion of a man 'standing outside himself' seems to involve at least an implicit distinction between the body and the true or spiritual self that makes the journey. However, it is worth mentioning that in the modern Asian traditions the shaman's journey can be narrated and explained without necessarily invoking such a distinction: when the shaman recounts his journey in mythical form his people simply turn a blind eye on the fact that his visible body has been lying on the floor all the time;[24] and in fact the early

[22] Dodds (1951), 135–78; Burkert (1972), 120–65; Bolton (1962), 142–75, on Aristeas; also, West (1983: 3–7, 39–67) connects the stories of Orpheus, and other early poets with the shamanism theory. On the general question of Near Eastern sages and shamans on the fringes of the Aegean world of the Dark Age, see Burkert (1992), 41–87.

[23] On Aristeas see Hdt. 4. 13–14; on Abaris, Hdt. 4. 36; and on Salmoxis, Hdt. 4. 94–6.

[24] See Eliade (1964): the journeys of Eliade's Asian shamans seem to be regarded within their own culture as utterances of a special kind where the distinction between the visible world of the onlookers and the inner experience of the shaman can be explained (if at all) in various ways without invoking a distinction between body and soul. He may be re-enacting celestial journeys which were common to all in the mythological past (see esp. 143–4, 171); or the modern shaman may be regarded as a decadent who makes his journey only symbolically, while his forebears could ascend to heaven or descend to the Underworld literally (see esp. 130, 250). The 'I' of the shaman remains undifferentiated (*passim*, but for a particularly clear example see the account by an Altaic shaman, 190–7), and no need arises to face the problem of reconciling his account with what was seen of his visible body, since it is implicit throughout his account of his journey that he is acting and speaking on the mythopoeic level: 'Only [the shamans] transform a theological concept into a concrete mystical experience . . . What for the rest of the community

Greek evidence teaches a somewhat similar lesson. For example, in the earliest surviving account of the journey of Aristeas (Hdt. 4. 13–14) there is nothing to suggest that a soul separated itself from the bodily man. Aristeas falls down dead in a fuller's shop in Proconnesus, and when his relatives go to the shop to fetch the corpse it has disappeared. In the mean time he embarks on his mystical journey, appearing along the way in Cyzicus, and eventually makes his way to the mythical lands in the East. The disappearance of the *corpse* implies that the traveller is the undivided bodily man.[25] In this way, there can be no certainty that such tales prompted the invention of a new concept of soul to explain how the journey takes place.

Given all these doubts, it turns out that in surviving Greek the earliest unmistakable statements that the human body contains a soul are made by Pindar, in passages which almost certainly betray the influence of Orphic teaching or some kindred body of doctrine. The most striking testimony is the fragment in which he distinguishes the mortal body, σῶμα, from the immortal wraith, αἰῶνος εἴδωλον, which dwells in it (fr. 131b M). Further passages set forth the idea that life, death, and afterlife are a journey of the soul through stages of corruption and purification (*Ol*. 2. 56–80; frs. 129, 130, 133, 137). However, before we examine these texts we will be able to show that the dualism exhibited there is anticipated in less obvious ways by a semantic development undergone by the word ψυχή in the post-Homeric period, a development that is clearly visible in earlier and less exalted poetry than Pindar's. Throughout the literature of this period ψυχή stands not only for life threatened by death, as in Homer, but also for the centre of thought, consciousness, and identity.[26] In the follow-

remains a cosmological ideogram, for the shamans . . . becomes a mystical itinerary' (265).

[25] Hindsight can make later accounts misleading. For example, *Suda*, s.v. Ἀριστέας (= fr. 3 Bernabé) describes the sage's experience as a journey by his ψυχή.

[26] In literary terms selfhood and identity raise special problems in lyric and elegy, where the first personal pronoun may correspond to the persona of the inspired poet, that of the ordinary man, or (in the case of choral lyric) those of the members of the chorus themselves. The question is especially urgent for Pindar: see Bremer (1990) and, in particular, Lefkowitz (1991). Lefkowitz

ing pages we will observe the new shape of ψυχή by surveying
the attestations of our word in lyric and elegiac verse up to and
including Pindar's time, a corpus that can conveniently be
referred to as the poetry of the Archaic period.[27] If the evidence
is convincing, it will suggest that the range of meaning of ψυχή
in this period corresponds in miniature to the ideas of the soul
that were writ large in esoteric religious belief and philosophical doctrine at the same stage of Greek history.[28]

(1–71) distinguishes three stances—the chorus as 'I', the inspired poet as 'I',
and Pindar the man as 'I'—and argues that in the Epinicians the chorus is
never the 'I'. In later chapters (pp. 111–46) she goes some way to break down
the distinction between the personal identity of the poet and his masks as
inspired teacher or seer (see esp. 114). See also Burnett (1983), 1–7 and *passim*,
and Jarcho (1990); and on the corresponding problems of Archilochus' stance
as an iambic poet see West (1974), 1–39, esp. 25–8. The history of interpretations of the lyric 'I' is sketched by Slings (1990*b*); cf. also Tsagarakis (1977).

[27] Pindar provides a convenient if arbitrary cut-off point; I have been
content to exclude all poets whose date of birth or floruit is more than a few
years later than his, so that (for example) I include Bacchylides but not Ion or
Melanippides. On chronological grounds Aeschylus might also have been
included, but I have excluded dramatic poetry, since the decisive change in
the semantic range of ψυχή can be traced fully through poetry produced in the
more antiquated genres. By 'Theognis' is meant everything that makes up the
Theognidean *sylloge*: although there may be some material here from as late as
the early 5th cent., the style and language of the whole is homogeneous, and
the political tone of the parts attributable to Theognis himself suggests a date
as high as the 630s (see West (1974), 65–71). 'Simonides' likewise covers the
whole corpus of poems ascribed to him in antiquity. Although some of the
elegiac epitaphs from the Persian War were probably ascribed to him long
after they were composed (see Page in the preface to PEG), it is reasonable to
suppose that all or most are contemporary and thus date from Simonides'
time, so that the question of authorship need not affect us here.

[28] The most influential post-war study of this problem has been Regenbogen (1948, esp. 22–8), developing his view of the Homeric ψυχή as '*sine qua
non* aller körperlichen, geistigen und emotionalen Regungen' (defined, 20)
and emphasizing the Homeric roots of the Archaic usages. As I have
disagreed with Regenbogen's definition of the Homeric ψυχή (see Ch. 2,
pp. 46–7), I will differ correspondingly on the Archaic material; but many of
his observations on individual fragments have proved very useful in preparing
this chapter. Ingenkamp (1975) draws mostly on the philosophers but also
includes material from the Archaic poets, and proposes a semantic development of ψυχή from 'life-carrier' (Regenbogen's *sine qua non*) to Plato's concept
of the unified 'inner self.' Claus (1981) has a useful survey of the post-
Homeric ψυχή, including the 5th-cent. tragedians and prose writers (69–91),
and shows that their ψυχή is a mental agent still more clearly than for the

ψυχή as life lost or threatened

We saw that the Homeric ψυχή is fundamentally the cold breath whose loss is a sign of death. Among the Archaic poets a few instances survive in which this simplest meaning is active. In a sixth-century epitaph the dying man's breath is lost, ψυχὴ ὄλετ' ἐ[ν δαΐ] (47H), and in a lyric fragment Simonides describes a dying child as breathing it out, γλυκεῖαν . . . ψυχὰν ἀποπνέοντα (fr. 553 P). Extending the symbolic importance of the lost breath, one of Simonides' epitaphs speaks for the patriots who rescued Greece with their ψυχαί, by dying:

> Ἑλλάδα πᾶσαν
> ταῖς αὐτῶν ψυχαῖς κείμεθα ῥυσάμενοι.   (12 PEG)

Again, Theognis will be a lifeless corpse after losing this thing:

> δηρὸν γὰρ ἔνερθεν
> γῆς ὀλέσας ψυχὴν κείσομαι ὥστε λίθος
> ἄφθογγος.   (567–9)

Here when the poet looks beyond his own death he makes 'I' correspond to the dead matter of his corpse (cf. Thgn. 877–8, also 1070a–b). If we compare this with Homeric patterns the question arises: when the poet compares his corpse to lifeless stone, is it implicit that he thinks of the departed ψυχή as the thing that had animated the living man and given him his identity? In the same way when Simonides calls the child's lost breath 'sweet' is he assimilating it to the sweet essence, γλυκὺς αἰών (Ch. 4, pp. 113–14; and cf. Ch. 5 n. 11), that courses in the body of a living person?

When we asked the equivalent question of Homer we were able to answer in the negative, and consequently to deny that he gives man a single spiritual core for life, death, and afterlife. The Archaic poets will demand a different answer, an answer best approached by first observing how they differ

Archaic poets; his analysis of the Archaic poets' usage (92–102) has a helpful collection of examples but reaches odd conclusions (see above, Ch. 2, n. 37). Briefer surveys, assuming a simple semantic change under Orphic or philosophical influence, include Böhme (1929: 108–9); Simon (1978: 47–77), making an interesting contrast between Homeric and Platonic ψυχή in psychoanalytic terms; also Padel (1992: 31–3).

from Homer when they make ψυχή stand not for life lost but for life *liable to be* lost. We saw in Chapter 3 that Homer's ψυχή does not figure in this way without an open or implied threat of death, as when one who risks death casts his breath before him at hazard: the warrior in battle is tossing it around, ψυχὴν παραβαλλόμενος (IX. 322), and pirates abroad are proffering it to the sea, ψυχὰς παρθέμενοι (iii. 74 = ix. 255). In the same way, when Tyrtaeus' ideal warrior remains in the battle-line he is risking the loss of his life's breath, ψυχὴν καὶ θυμὸν τλήμονα παρθέμενος (fr. 12. 18 W). However, he and other Archaic poets push this imagery further when they identify ψυχή not only with life threatened but with life held and preserved, even in contexts where no risk is implied. It is at this point in the semantic range of ψυχή that the decisive difference from Homer appears. Archilochus in a stray phrase talks of men in peril at sea who hold onto their lives, ψυχὰς ἔχοντες κυμάτων ἐν ἀγκάλαις (fr. 213 W),[29] and similarly Solon describes a sea-going merchant as one who has no 'thrift' for his breath, φειδωλὴν ψυχῆς οὐδεμίαν θέμενος (fr. 13. 46 W): when he risks death at sea he takes no care to keep the life in his body. Likewise Theognis speaks of thoughts, φροντίδες, which are pondering how to gain a livelihood, μυρόμεναι ψυχῆς εἵνεκα καὶ βιότου (729–30). If ψυχή here is breath it is also life—life that is defended, held, and actively enjoyed by living men.

This sense of ψυχή takes on special significance in military ethics. Tyrtaeus bids men fight without sparing their lives, ψυχέων μηκέτι φειδόμενοι (fr. 10. 14 W); and he goes further when he describes how the brave man holds his life cheap:

> ἰθὺς δ' ἐς προμάχους ἀσπίδ' ἀνὴρ ἐχέτω,
> ἐχθρὴν μὲν ψυχὴν θέμενος, θανάτου δὲ μελαίνας
> κῆρας ⟨ὁμῶς⟩ αὐγαῖς ἠελίοιο φίλας.   (fr. 11. 4–5)

To make an enemy of the ψυχή is to welcome a glorious death, and to protect it is to turn inward to self-preservation: regard

---

[29] The source for the fragment is the scholiast on Ar. *Frogs* 704, who glosses Archilochus' line as ὄντες ἐν πολλοῖς κινδύνοις. Aristophanes' line is a parody of this. A comparable image appears in a similar context in one of the few surviving lines of Aristeas' epic poem, again describing the perilous life of sailors: ὄμματ' ἐν ἄστροισι, ψυχὴν δ' ἐνὶ πόντωι ἔχουσιν (fr. 11. 4 Bernabé). The meaning must be that they keep their eyes on the stars while risking their lives at sea.

for one's ψυχή becomes equivalent to selfishness.[30] The Spartan patriotic ideal glorifies self-sacrifice in a way that goes beyond the ethics of the *Iliad*; and the fact that the image of κῆρες is hyperbolic suggests that Tyrtaeus may be consciously exaggerating or perverting the Homeric imagery.[31] Similarly, when he exhorts men to battle he sets the brave warrior's expanding θυμός against the coward's love of his ψυχή:

> ἀλλὰ μέγαν ποιεῖσθε καὶ ἄλκιμον ἐν φρεσὶ θυμόν,
> μηδὲ φιλοψυχεῖτ᾽ ἀνδράσι μαρνάμενοι.   (fr. 10. 17–18)

Here θυμός and ψυχή stand for two contrasting parts or aspects of conscious life: θυμός is the will to violent action, but ψυχή is life enjoyed and reflected upon.[32] This sense of ψυχή has no parallel in Homer, even in the introspective images of ψυχή built up by Achilles in his speeches to the Embassy. Observe, however, that Tyrtaeus' sense of ψυχή finds an Homeric parallel in an expression involving θυμός: Diomedes describes those who shirk battle as θυμῶι ἦρα φέροντες (XIV. 132), showing love or favour to the stuff in their breasts as they seek to keep themselves alive.[33] Tyrtaeus' evocation of the warrior's spiritual anatomy suggests that he is thinking through a new and non-Homeric structure of selfhood, even when he echoes Homer's images deliberately.

---

[30] For this distinctive role of ψυχή in Tyrtaeus, see Snell (1969), 11–13.

[31] This is not the place to argue out the relative chronology of Tyrtaeus and Homer. M. L. West has recently asserted (1995) that Homer imitates Tyrtaeus, reversing the received opinion of most scholars; my answer here is only that Tyrtaeus' use of ψυχή chimes exactly with that of other poets conventionally given a lower date than the Homeric epics. It remains possible that the difference is between earlier and later genres and registers rather than earlier and later poets.

[32] See Dihle (1982), 10.

[33] ἦρα is a difficult word. In Homer it seems to mean something like 'help', possibly suggesting affection as well (see esp. I. 572, 578, comparing iii. 164, xvi. 375, xviii. 56; and note the cognate adjective ἐρίηρος). To appreciate Tyrtaeus' reminiscence of Homer, it is worth noting that Bacchylides uses ἦρα in the sense 'for the sake of', like Homeric χάριν (Bacchyl. 11. 20–1, cited by Russo at xviii. 56); if Tyrtaeus understands ἦρα as exactly equivalent in meaning to χάριν, then in the passages quoted here his reminiscence of Diomedes' words will be all the closer.

ψυχή as the centre of emotion, passion, audacity

So far we have seen ψυχή creeping away from its Homeric starting-point in the last dying gasp of breath, and moving towards the point where 'life' looks like a possible translation. The life that is liable to be lost shades into the life that is preserved, and thus into the life that is enjoyed, so that vitality and consciousness are drawn into our word's province. Simonides urges one to give pleasure to the ψυχή throughout his life:

βιότου ποτὶ τέρμα
ψυχῆι τῶν ἀγαθῶν τλῆθι χαριζόμενος.   (20. 11–12 W)

There is a similar turn of phrase in an Eritrean mariner's epitaph of the same period:

ἐνθάδε Φίλων κεῖται· τόνδε κατὰ γαῖ' ἐκάλυψεν,
ναυτίλον, ὃς ψυχῆι παῦρα δέδωκ' ἀγαθά.   (76 H)

If the sailor's poverty meant that he gave few good things to his ψυχή, it must have been the focus of pleasure and happiness.[34] With a further short step in this direction it makes sense that the ψυχή is the seat of sexual passion. Anacreon says that his beloved boy controls it like a charioteer, driving him with reins:

τῆς ἐμῆς
ψυχῆς ἡνιοχεύεις . . .   (fr. 360. 3–4 P)

Likewise Archilochus in his longing is bereft of ψυχή, perhaps literally breathless:

δύστηνος ἔγκειμαι πόθωι,
ἄψυχος.   (fr. 193. 1–2 W)

Conversely, Theognis sees grief as a gnawing of the ψυχή:

ἐμοὶ μέγα πένθος ὄρωρεν
καὶ δάκνομαι ψυχήν, καὶ δίχα θυμὸν ἔχω.   (909–10)

His ψυχή suffers in the way that the mental stuff of Homeric man suffers when an experience bites into it: as when Hector is insulted, δάκε δὲ φρένας Ἕκτορι μῦθος (v. 493).[35] In this light, it

---

[34] On the ψυχή of this epitaph see esp. Dihle (1982), 12; Claus (1981), 96–100.

[35] Compare also Alc. fr. 117(b) 34–5 L–P, which seems to mention a ψυχή in connection with tears, but is too fragmentary to be interpreted.

is not surprising that the passion of the patriotic warrior can itself be localized in the ψυχή: Simonides says (if the line is genuine) that the heroes of the Persian Wars died in obedience to its daring will, εὐτόλμωι ψυχῆς λήματι πειθόμενοι (15 PEG). Now a problem seems to loom if we turn from these to our earlier examples where Tyrtaeus bade the brave man hate his ψυχή. In one sense to die bravely is to follow the ψυχή as source of passion, while in another sense it is to hate it as a symbol of the cowardly desire to preserve life. Of course the contradiction only appears when the lexicographer tries to frame a definition: the basis of both images is that the ψυχή is the centre of man's life, with associations which are by turns existential and emotional.

ψυχή as the essence of man

So much for the prospect of death, and for passion and emotion. The Archaic ψυχή is also the core of moral life and the focus of reflection and self-awareness. Theognis declares that there is nothing slavish in his character, οὐδ' ἐν ἐμῆι ψυχῆι δούλιον οὐδὲν ἔνι (530; cf. Heraclitus, B 107 D–K); Bacchylides describes the daughters of Proetus going to the temple with girlish nature or character, παρθενίαι . . . ψυχᾶι (11. 47–8); Hipponax threatens that if his demands are not met he will 'give the groan-filled ψυχή to evil,' to let it be destroyed or made miserable:

> κακοῖσι δώσω τὴν πολύστονον ψυχήν,
> ἢν μὴ ἀποπέμψηις ὡς τάχιστά μοι κριθέων
> μέδιμνον . . .   (fr. 39. 1–3 W)

Although there is no context and the sense is difficult,[36] ψυχή here seems to be the subjective core of life. By a further extension in the same direction, the ψυχή becomes tantamount

---

[36] On our interpretation here, cf. Regenbogen (1948), 24. This fragment seems very obscure: in particular, it is not clear whether the ψυχή in question is that of the speaker or the one addressed. If the latter is the case, Hipponax would be threatening to lay a curse on the other person if he refuses his request; and if the curse were intended to operate after death, the ψυχή would be his afterlife survivor as much as the core of his identity during life (for such a curse compare e.g. Sappho, fr. 55 L–P).

to the person as a whole. Sappho addresses someone (herself?) as ψυχὰ ἀγαπάτα (fr. 62. 8 L–P),[37] and Simonides addresses his own ψυχή in introspection:

> οὐ δύναμαι, ψυχ[ή], πεφυλαγμένος εἶναι ὁπηδός,
> χρυσῶπιν δὲ Δίκην ἄζομαι ἀχνύμενος.   (fr. 21. 1–2 W)

He cannot be the guardian of his ψυχή, he is unable to keep to the ethical ideal: ψυχή here is the seat of his moral identity.

ψυχή, then, is the essence of man: but it is also the wraith in the Underworld, for the Archaic poets no less than for Homer.[38] Here we touch on one of the central questions of our entire study. How closely do the Archaic poets identify the ψυχή of the living with the ψυχή which dwells in Hades? Do they see life, death, and afterlife as the journey of a single entity, a spirit in the living man which is separated off at death as his immortal soul? The question is prompted in a small way when Simonides complains against Disease personified:

> αἰαῖ, Νοῦσε βαρεῖα, τί δὴ ψυχαῖσι μεγαίρεις
> ἀνθρώπων ἐρατῆι πὰρ νεότητι μένειν;   (70 PEG)

If Disease grudges 'to let people's ψυχή remain in them alongside their lovely youth', how closely does it follow that he wants to send this same ψυχή to Hades?

This question again smacks of the lexicographer, and it would not be worth pursuing as speculation; but we are forced to address it by the poet's own words in the fifth Ode of Bacchylides, where the two aspects of ψυχή are brought together explicitly. During a narration of the *katabasis* of Heracles, couched in Homeric terms with the dead as ψυχαί (5. 64, 77, 83, 171) and including images borrowed from the

---

[37] This is the most likely interpretation of what is a rather slight fragment. For comparison, note the passage in which she uses ἀγαπάτα in (presumably) the same way with a proper name (fr. 132 L–P).

[38] Apart from Bacchyl. 5. 56–175, the most extensive example is Thgn. 701–12, briefly treating the *katabasis* of Sisyphus. For the language of Hades in the Archaic poets see also Sappho, fr. 55 L–P; Thgn. 243–4, 802, 906, 917, 1014, 1124; Mimn. fr. 2. 14 W; Semon. fr. 1. 13–14 W; Solon, fr. 24. 8 W; Tyrt. fr. 12. 38 W.

Homeric Nekuia,[39] the wraith of Meleager urges the hero not to shoot his arrows at the shades of the dead:

> μὴ ταὔσιον προΐει
> τραχὺν ἐκ χειρῶν ὀϊστόν
> ψυχαῖσιν ἔπι φθιμένων·
> οὔ τοι δέος. (5. 81–4)

As Meleager's wraith proceeds to tell the story of his own life and death in the world of mortals, at one point he describes how men were struck by missiles in battle and killed:

> τυφλὰ δ᾽ ἐκ χειρῶν βέλη
> ψυχαῖς ἐπὶ δυσμενέων φοι-
> τᾶι θάνατόν τε φέρει . . . (132–4)

The missiles flew at their lives, at their ψυχαί. The words closely echo those in which he had told Heracles not to shoot at the wraiths, also ψυχαί: is Bacchylides deliberately, even ironically, pointing up an identity between the spiritual core of the living men and the wraiths of the dead that he has set before the audience's eyes? The plot thickens when he goes on to describe how he found himself to be bewitched, so that he grew feeble as he drew near to death:

> μίνυθεν δέ μοι ψυχὰ γλυκεῖα·
> γνῶν δ᾽ ὀλιγοσθενέων,
> αἰαῖ· πύματον δὲ πνέων δάκρυσα τλά[μων,
> ἀγλαὰν ἥβαν προλείπων. (151–4)

μίνυθεν . . . ψυχά: his vital essence grew less or wasted away, he breathed his last, and died. Noting the words ἀγλαὰν ἥβαν προλείπων, 'leaving gleaming youth behind', we recall the departure of Patroclus' or Hector's ψυχή to Hades:

> ὃν πότμον γοόωσα, λιποῦσ᾽ ἀνδροτῆτα καὶ ἥβην.
> (XVI. 857 = XXII. 363)

The correspondence suggests that Bacchylides is directly, even consciously, recalling Homer's words:[40] but there is an all-

---

[39] On the Homeric echoes in Bacchyl. 5 see J. Stern (1967); also Lefkowitz (1969: esp. 78–83), touching on the ψυχή problem.

[40] In his note at 5. 151–4 Maehler notes that this passage echoes Hector's death, and compares Meleager ὀλιγοσθενέων, with Hector ὀλιγοδρανέων (XXII. 337).

important difference of perspective. The speaker who describes
himself as ἀγλαὰν ἥβαν προλείπων corresponds to Homer's
departing ψυχή, and that speaker is himself a shade in
Hades:⁴¹ so that a new and striking thread of ideas runs
through Meleager's speech. He implies that the ψυχή which
wasted away as he grew weaker, the 'I' which left vitality
behind, and the wraith now telling the story, are all one and
the same. If so, Bacchylides is very close to associating the
spiritual core of the living with the survivor in Hades in a single
definition of ψυχή, a definition which seems to demand that we
now use 'soul' to translate the word.

*The coalescence of ψυχή with the θυμός family in the language of
mental life*

When the Archaic poets render mental life they speak of θυμός
and its family in much the same way as Homer, with φρένες and
νόος particularly prominent as the locus of thought and
emotion.⁴² The crucial difference is that ψυχή now acts as a
fully-fledged member of the family, and it is associated with
the kind of imagery that Homer uses of the mental apparatus.
There are many examples of this among the passages already
cited. For example Tyrtaeus' life-preserving coward gives

⁴¹ The ambiguity is noted by Regenbogen (1948), 26. The feebleness of the
shades was an element of epic death-lore not easily forgotten: cf. e.g. Sappho's
curse on an enemy: ἀλλ' ἀφάνης κἀν Ἀίδα δόμωι | φοιτάσηις πεδ' ἀμαύρων νεκύων
ἐκπεποταμένα (55. 3–4 L-P). See Ch. 6 n. 90.
⁴² For full surveys of these nouns in the lyric poets, see Darcus (1979b) for
φρήν, Darcus (1980) for νόος, Darcus Sullivan (1981) for θυμός, and Claus
(1981), 48–91. It has sometimes been suggested that in the lyric poets θυμός
and its family act as mental agents (rather than functions) more forcefully than
they do for Homer: see esp. Jarcho (1968), arguing that in the Archaic poets
ψυχή and θυμός alike tend to act as independent agents; also Darcus (1979a),
172–3; Darcus Sullivan (1981), 152–3. νόος is a difficult case; Darcus argues
(1980: 43–4) that νόος is more clearly under the control of the person as such in
the Archaic poets than in Homer; this seems difficult to demonstrate, and
Darcus herself presents plenty of Archaic examples of the νόος as mental agent
(42–3). In later verse the semantic ranges of the individual members of the
θυμός-family nouns differ significantly from the Homeric pattern; this is
clearest when we compare Homer with 5th-cent. authors, for whom θυμός
(for example) tends to stand for violent passion in particular, and is associated
with thought as such less closely than are νοῦς, φρένες, and καρδία. See esp.
Claus (1981), 48–56.

favours to his ψυχή where Homer's gave favours to his θυμός (above, p. 298); Simonides addresses his ψυχή where a Homeric character would address his mental apparatus (Ch. 4, pp. 67–8); and even Heraclitus describes drink as wetting the ψυχή, just as Homer describes it as wetting the φρένες (Ch. 4, pp. 91–2). One or two passages suggest that the converse process is also under way, with the attributes of the Homeric ψυχή being applied to the θυμός group. There is a striking example from Ibycus, a stray line in which he addresses his θυμός:

$$αἰεί μ' ὦ \underline{φίλε θυμὲ} τανύπτερος ὡς ὅκα πορφυρίς ... \quad (fr. 317b\ P)^{43}$$

Although the context is lost, it seems that this is the start of an introspective address where he compared the motion of his mental apparatus to that of a spreading-winged bird. Similarly when Theognis mentions thoughts, φροντίδες, he describes them as flying on wings:[44]

$$φροντίδες ἀνθρώπων ἔλαχον, πτερὰ ποικίλ' ἔχουσαι,$$
$$μυρόμεναι ψυχῆς εἵνεκα καὶ βιότου. \quad (729–30)$$

This recalls the birdlike flying ψυχαί of Patroclus and Hector (XVI. 856 = XXII. 362) and the batlike wraiths of the Second Nekuia. Since the imagery of ψυχή is spilling over into the θυμός family, as well as the reverse, it seems that it has been drawn in as one of many merging parts or manifestations of the single core of human identity.

The coalescence is well illustrated by three passages in which Archilochus expresses the same sense of unfulfilled sexual desire. First comes the passage already cited in which he describes himself as breathless or 'soul-less' with desire, δύστηνος ἔγκειμαι πόθωι | ἄψυχος (fr. 193 W). ἄψυχος recalls the Homeric ἄθυμος for 'breathless'; but it also recalls Archilochus' turn of phrase when he says that lust has stolen the φρένες from his breast,

---

[43] Reading θυμέ for Athenaeus' οὔμε, following Page after Valckenaer. For πορφυρίς as a type of bird, see Ar. *Birds* 304, with the λαθιπορφυρίδες of Ibyc. fr. 317a P.

[44] West (1993) translates 'Man was assigned to Cares, whose wings are many-coloured . . .' More precisely, the construction seems to be 'genitive of the object aimed after': the φροντίδες are imagined as battening onto men of their own will. On the problem see also van Groningen ad loc.

πολλὴν κατ᾽ ἀχλὺν ὀμμάτων ἔχευεν,
κλέψας ἐκ στηθέων ἀπαλὰς φρένας . . .   (fr. 191. 2–3)

as well as a third fragment in which it is the speaker himself who is overcome:

ἀλλά μ᾽ ὁ λυσιμελὴς
ὦταῖρε δάμναται πόθος.   (fr. 196)

ψυχή, φρένες, and 'I' amount to the same emotional agent. Similarly when Theognis associates doubt in the one with the biting of anguish in the other, δάκνομαι ψυχὴν καὶ δίχα θυμὸν ἔχω (910), ψυχή is an integrated part of the thinking apparatus.

The evidence we have gathered teaches one decisive lesson. Where Homer's language and lore stopped far short of assimilating ψυχή as the breath lost at death into the system of mental life represented by θυμός and the kindred nouns, the Archaic poets allow all to be subsumed into a single system of psychological identity. The 'I' who thinks and feels in the mortal world is potentially identical with the 'I' which lives on in the death-world, and both in life and in death it is represented not merely by the simple ἐγώ or αὐτός but by the discrete spiritual entity now identified as ψυχή. The upshot of this is that a dictionary definition of the Archaic ψυχή would correspond closely to a modern definition of a soul: it is the emotional agent, the centre of will and introspection, and the survivor in the world of the dead. This implies that the Homeric conception of man is sundered from that of subsequent generations of Greek poets no less decisively than from that of Plato or, indeed, of those who speak and think in our own world.

The semantic range of ψυχή in Pindar

As we noted earlier, it is in a few mysterious passages of Pindar that we first see this structure of man and soul explicitly realized on the level of religious doctrine. Before turning to these it should be noted that in less marked contexts Pindar takes ψυχή as the core of man in just the same way as his lyric predecessors.[45] It is the seat of emotional life and passion, so

---

[45] See Regenbogen (1948), 25. Claus (1981: 69–91) surveys the range of ψυχή in Pindar along with the 5th-cent. dramatists and prose writers, drawing on much the same evidence as is presented here.

that one rejoices through it, ἂν περὶ ψυχὰν . . . γάθησεν (*Pyth.*
4. 122); and conversely one who is unmoved by erotic passion
in θυμός and καρδία (fr. 123. 1–6 M) carries or tosses about his
ψυχή in feebleness,

> γυναικείωι θράσει
> ψυχὰν φορεῖται πᾶσαν ὁδὸν θεραπεύων.   (fr. 123. 8–9 M)[46]

Just as ψυχή here joins the θυμός family as the centre of
emotion, so it can be the locus of moral life: the just men of
Aetna have spirits stronger or loftier than mere possessiveness,
κτεάνων ψυχὰς ἔχοντες κρέσσονας | ἄνδρες (*Nem.* 9. 32–3),
doughty men are χερσὶ καὶ ψυχᾶι δυνατοί (*Nem.* 9. 38), and it
is by or in his ψυχή that Apollo refuses to tolerate the
destruction of his child:

> οὐκέτι
> τλάσομαι ψυχᾶι γένος ἀμὸν ὀλέσσαι.   (*Pyth.* 3. 40–1)

Similarly Hiero remained steadfast in war, ἐν πολέμοισι μάχαις |
τλάμονι ψυχᾶι παρέμεινε (*Pyth.* 1. 47–8), and the young Heracles'
childish stature is belied by his unconquerable spirit, so that he
is μορφὰν βραχύς | ψυχὰν δ᾽ ἄκαμπτος (*Isthm.* 4. 71–71b). In the
inspired poet the same entity is the object of introspection. We
have already seen Simonides addressing his ψυχή (fr. 21 W,
above, p. 301); Pindar does so in a more profound context
when he stops the flow of his song and urges moderation with
due awareness of human mortality,

> γνόντα τὸ πὰρ ποδός, οἵας εἰμὲν αἴσας.
> μή, φίλα ψυχά, βίον ἀθάνατον
> σπεῦδε.   (*Pyth.* 3. 60–2)

When he turns inward his introspection engenders a kind of
σωφροσύνη by checking his aspiration to themes too extravagant
for the mortal poet.[47] The crux is that the core of the living is
also what will be lost at death and sent to Hades (e.g. *Ol.* 8. 39;
Pyth. 3. 101; *Nem.* 1. 47; *Isthm.* 1. 68); so that when Pindar

---

[46] Reading ψυχάν rather than ψυχράν, with Schneider. On the crux see
Darcus (1979a), 37 n. 23, with refs.
[47] On the 'I' of this passage and the address to the ψυχή see Lefkowitz
(1991), 32–3.

describes Clytemnaestra's murders he makes the ψυχή of Agamemnon accompany Cassandra herself:

Κασσάνδραν πολιῶι χαλκῶι σὺν Ἀγαμεμνονίαι
ψυχᾶι πόρευ' Ἀχέροντος ἀκτὰν παρ' εὔσκιον
νηλὴς γυνά. (*Pyth.* 11. 20–2)

The pairing of the proper name with the periphrasis implies that one's ψυχή is tantamount to oneself. This is neatly confirmed by two passages where Pindar uses the phrase ψυχὰν κομίξαι, to convey or dispatch a ψυχή. In the first passage (*Pyth.* 4. 159) the phrase refers to 'laying the ghost' of Phrixus, sending his hitherto restless ghost to repose in the tomb;[48] in the second (*Nem.* 8. 44), Pindar says that he cannot 'bring back the ψυχή' of a dead person, in other words he cannot bring him back to life. Since what leaves at death and goes to Hades is also what underlies consciousness, emotion, and moral life in the mortal world, it follows that if this thing came back after death it would restore the living man.

This survey of the Pindaric ψυχή prepares the way for the doctrines of dualism and personal immortality that loom large in the second *Olympian* and two further fragments that are often held to have come from dirges (*thrēnoi*). There is no way of knowing whether these texts in combination bear witness to a single body of ideas, nor is there any guarantee that they represent beliefs held by the poet himself. It is likely that the second *Olympian* refers to mysticism favoured by Pindar's Sicilian patron, while the *thrēnos* fragments probably refer to Eleusinian lore; but we can only guess at the relationship between Sicilian cults and the lore of the Athenian mysteries.[49]

[48] This is tentative. At *Pyth.* 4. 159, Pelias tells Jason that Phrixus orders them to go to Colchis and ἐὰν ψυχὰν κομίξαι together with the Golden Fleece. The scholiast took the words to mean Jason was to call up his shade from Hades; Farnell (ad loc.) thinks it means that his body is to be brought back, assuming that his ψυχή would return to remain near it, just as the shade of a hero might remain at his shrine. He is followed by Bolton (1962: 159–60) and Braswell ad loc. However, Braswell accepts that the same words at *Nem.* 8. 44 cannot be taken in the same sense, since in them 'a recall to life is implied as well'. Since Pindar does not mention the Phrixus story again in *Pyth.* 4, the words remain mysterious. On the background to the legend see D. S. Robertson (1940).

[49] On the problem of the possible combination of Eleusinian, Orphic, and Bacchic elements in Pindar, see esp. Graf (1974), 79–94.

That said, we can use the texts together as witnesses to the kind of new or esoteric lore that was current in his generation, and as examples of the ultimate development or working-out of the pervasive Archaic concept that the ψυχή is a soul or inner self.

In the second *Olympian* Pindar says that in this life the virtuous use of wealth brings blessedness and defeats care, and then turns to what lies ahead for the wealthy man:

εἰ δέ νιν [sc. τὸν πλοῦτον] ἔχων τις οἶδεν τὸ μέλλον,
ὅτι θανόντων μὲν ἐνθάδ' αὐτίκ' ἀπάλαμνοι φρένες
ποινὰς ἔτεισαν—τὰ δ' ἐν τᾷδε Διὸς ἀρχᾷ
ἀλιτρὰ κατὰ γᾶς δικάζει τις ἐχθρᾷ
λόγον φράσαις ἀνάγκᾳ.   (*Ol*. 2. 56–60)

The general sense is that when men die their feeble φρένες pay retribution, and they are punished in the Underworld for the crimes committed in the earthly realm of Zeus; but beyond that the exact meaning is obscure, perhaps deliberately so. Although the last δέ clause must refer to punishment within the land of the dead, perhaps recalling Agamemnon's reference in the *Iliad* to the punishment of oathbreakers in Hades (III. 278–9), it is hard to pin down the meaning of the ἀπάλαμνοι φρένες and the penalties which they pay.[50] Either the penalty is death itself or it is something suffered afterwards in Hades: this depends on how we understand αὐτίκα, 'immediately' or 'there-upon', and on how sharply we take the antithesis of μέν and δέ. The question is important. If Pindar is saying that men's φρένες are extinguished by death, then that is nothing strange or new; but if on the other hand he is saying that the φρένες of men are punished in Hades, then this represents a decisive difference from the Homeric conception, where the wraith is utterly different from the φρένες or θυμός of the living (see esp. XXIII. 103–4). If this is so Pindar is using φρένες rather than ψυχή to name the survivor in the afterlife, in much the same

[50] Most (e.g. Zuntz (1971), 84–7) have assumed that the φρένες pay the penalty by their punishment in the afterlife. Lloyd-Jones (1985: 252–6) takes ἐνθάδ' αὐτίκ' . . . to imply that the 'hapless minds' of men are punished when they are enfeebled by the experience of death itself. However, he goes on to associate the ποινάς of *Ol*. 2. 58 with the ποινά accepted by Persephone in fr. 133 M, so that even on his view φρένες in the former and ψυχή in the latter must be very close to each other in meaning. On the question of the ποιναί in the second *Olympian*, see also Nisetich (1989), 52–4.

way as he and his Archaic predecessors use ψυχή along with
θυμός and its kin as an integrated set of names for the spiritual
essence of the living.

The passage remains ambiguous, and nothing certain can be
made of what I have just suggested. Pindar goes on to recount
the life of the favoured dead in the Isles of the Blest, and links
success in the afterlife to moral purity maintained in the
virtuous man's ψυχή through successive mortal lives:

> ὅσοι δ' ἐτόλμασαν ἐστρὶς
> ἑκατέρωθι μείναντες ἀπὸ πάμπαν ἀδίκων ἔχειν
> ψυχάν, ἔτειλαν Διὸς ὁδὸν παρὰ Κρόνου τύρσιν.   (*Ol.* 2. 68–70)

It is clear enough that this refers to a sequence of incarnations
through which a man achieves perfection of soul and attains to
a state of full blessedness in the afterlife; but beyond that the
details of the doctrine are again difficult. Does ἑκατέρωθι refer
to a simultaneous double existence of the ψυχή in the mortal
world and the world of the dead, or does it mean that the ψυχή
which a man cultivates in each mortal life will be translated in
the same state into the Beyond?[51] In isolation the passage
cannot be fully understood; either way, however, it is clear
that the condition of men's ψυχαί in this life has repercussions
on the fate of their ψυχαί in the afterlife. The doctrine depends
on an exact identification between the core of man's identity in
the mortal world with the carrier of his identity in the world of
the dead: as such, it seems to bear directly on a well-defined
concept of an immortal soul.[52]

One of the fragments corroborates the second *Olympian* on
the point that rewards and punishments attend the passage of

---

[51] On the ambiguities of ἐστρὶς ἑκατέρωθι see McGibbon (1964). A further
fragment (94a M) included among the *Partheneia* declares that mortals will
have 'deathless days' despite bodily death, and is about to expound something
about events before birth (πρὶν γενέ[σθαι]) when it breaks off. With a few more
words here we might have much more to say about Pindar's doctrines of
reincarnation.

[52] For other Pindaric references to such a journey within the mythical
afterlife, see also frs. 129, 137 M. The details of the imagery clearly look back
to the punishment of sinners in the latter part of the Nekuia and Menelaus'
story of the Isles of the Blest (iv. 561–70); with so much Homer in the air, the
new and very un-Homeric soul-doctrine is all the more striking. On the
Homeric exemplars of the mythology of the second *Olympian*, see esp.
Nisetich (1989), 27–72 passim.

the ψυχή between the world of mortals and the world of the dead. Here it is said that Persephone exacts a penalty from the dead and sends them back as purified souls, ψυχαί, inside living people:

> οἶσι δὲ Φερσεφόνα ποινὰν παλαιοῦ πένθεος
> δέξεται, ἐς τὸν ὕπερθεν ἅλιον κείνων ἐνάτωι ἔτεϊ
> ἀνδιδοῖ ψυχὰς πάλιν, ἐκ τᾶν βασιλῆες ἀγαυοί
> καὶ σθένει κραιπνοὶ σοφίαι τε μέγιστοι
> ἄνδρες αὔξονται.   (fr. 133. 1–5 M)

It is impossible to tell whether the penalty, ποινά, of this passage is the same as the ποιναί of the second *Olympian*, although the testimony of Philolaus (see above, p. 291) suggests that there is a close link between the present passage and Pythagorean beliefs; while parallels with contemporary Italian and Thessalian funerary texts[53] suggest that the doctrine of the present fragment may have taken shape through the myth of the dismemberment and resurrection of Dionysus, whose experience was repeated in that of the initiate. Be that as it may, the important point is that the heart of the doctrine in Pindar's words is the movement of souls, ψυχαί, which first go to Hades and are sent back to the mortal world by Persephone. As each ψυχή moves between worlds, it carries the identity of a human being with it, and its quality in the world beyond death seems to determine that of the mortal man in whom it will next be placed. Throughout this process the soul alone is the essence of what it means to be a human being.

If the soul carries the self of man with it at every stage of life, death, and resurrection, it follows that the body of man will be accidental to his spiritual core. This sends us on to Pindar's

---

[53] Pending systematic study of the lore of the growing body of gold leaves and other funerary texts, see esp. Janko (1984), Lloyd-Jones (1985). Lloyd-Jones (1989) prints the texts of two further golden *lamellae* from Thessaly which make an explicit link between the story of the resurrection of Dionysus and the doctrine of the soul expounded in the Pindaric fragment. On the theme of the purification of the soul during the cycle of death and reincarnation see also Parker (1983), 299–307; West (1983), esp. 21–2. According to West's hypothetical reconstructions there was an account of the reincarnation of souls in the 'Rhapsodic Theogony' (1983: 75), which derived in turn from the 'Protogonus Theogony' made for Bacchics in Ionia about 500 BC (see 98–101, 110).

most explicit enunciation of the dichotomy between body and soul:

> σῶμα μὲν πάντων ἕπεται θανάτωι περισθενεῖ,
> ζωὸν δ᾽ ἔτι λείπεται αἰῶνος εἴδωλον· τὸ γάρ ἐστι μόνον
> ἐκ θεῶν . . .   (fr. 131b. 1–3 M)

The body is subject to death, but the αἰῶνος εἴδωλον remains free. Here as in Homer an εἴδωλον must be an insubstantial image, and although αἰών in Pindar is usually the time span of life it occasionally retains its Homeric meaning as an essence or fluid that encapsulates life (see Ch. 4, pp. 113–14).[54] If this is the meaning here, the αἰῶνος εἴδωλον is a wraith representing the living man's vitality and identity; but however it is defined, the crucial point for us is that Pindar identifies it both as the survivor of death and the spiritual core of the living—'the part that comes from the gods'. During life it acts as a conscience, guiding its owner in making moral decisions:

> . . . εὕδει δὲ πρασσόντων μελέων, ἀτὰρ εὑ-
> δόντεσσιν ἐν πολλοῖς ὀνείροις
> δείκνυσι τερπνῶν ἐφέρποισαν χαλεπῶν τε κρίσιν.   (3–5)

When the man is awake it is dormant in the body, but during sleep it communicates the truth to him in dreams.[55] Here at last we see the dualistic structure giving clear shape to a doctrine of personal morality. In this fragment, still more clearly than in the other passages, Pindar acknowledges the core of man as a psychological and spiritual soul, named typically but not

---

[54] Pindar once uses αἰών for marrow. Someone has bludgeoned someone else to death and crushed his body so that the marrow is dashed out of the bones, αἰὼν δὲ δι᾽ ὀστέων ἐρραίσθη (fr. 111. 5 M; cf. ix. 458–9). This suggests that for Pindar the full range of meaning of the word may be similar to what it is for Homer. Otherwise the best attestation of αἰών as an essence rather than a time span comes, significantly, in a passage about the emptiness of bodily life: σκιᾶς ὄναρ | ἄνθρωπος. ἀλλ᾽ ὅταν αἴγλα διόσδοτος ἔλθηι, | λαμπρὸν φέγγος ἔπεστιν ἀνδρῶν καὶ μείλιχος αἰών (*Pyth.* 8. 95–7). See also Degani (1961), 45–51.

[55] Compare Hippoc. *Vict.* 86, for the concept that the soul is subject to the body when man is awake, but acts of its own accord when he sleeps (cited by Regenbogen (1948), 26–7). The Derveni papyrus perhaps refers (in col. V) to an Orphic doctrine that the truth is revealed in dreams (see West (1983), 81).

exclusively as ψυχή,[56] which is distinct from the body both in mental life and in life after death. In this way his doctrines imply or depend upon the concept of soul which was suggested, if no more, by the semantic range of ψυχή observable throughout Archaic poetry.

Dialogue between the poet and his soul

The most striking feature of the αἰῶνος εἴδωλον is that it communicates truth to man: and as such it presents a mirror image of the just man in the second Olympian who keeps his ψυχή away from evils, ἀπὸ μάμπαν ἀδίκων ἔχειν | ψυχάν (*Ol.* 2. 69–70). If we put the two images together we can generalize that Pindar sees the relationship between body and spirit as a dialogue passing between them in both directions. Here it is vital to see that the same image appears in a less overt form in passages where no special doctrine is brought into play: witness the introspective address to the ψυχή which we saw not only in Pindar's self-warning against excessive ideas (*Pyth.* 3. 61–2) but also in some lines of his predecessors—Simonides' οὐ δύναμαι, ψυχή, πεφυλαγμένος εἶναι ὀπηδός (fr. 21W) and possibly Sappho's address to ψυχὰ ἀγαπάτα (fr. 62. 8 L–P). As we look for further examples of this pattern, we will no longer need to restrict ourselves to the word ψυχή alone: since we have shown that in the context of reflective thought ψυχή tends to be inseparable from the θυμός family, it will make sense to take all these words together to see how Pindar conceives of the inner dialogue.

Although earlier Archaic poets (as well as Homer himself) often represent pondering thought as an address by self to θυμός,[57] in Pindar the inner dialogue between self and spirit is peculiar to the inspired prophet or poet. Just as Cassandra's heart prophesies the fall of Troy,

---

[56] On the range of Pindar's names for the inner self, see also Claus (1981: 116–18), comparing philosopher's names for the transmigratory soul; and cf. Zuntz (1971), 85.

[57] See esp. Archil. fr. 128. 1–4 W; Ibyc. fr. 317b P; Terp. fr. 697 P; and Thgn. 213, 695–6, 825–6, 877–8, 1029–30, 1070a.

> ... ἔκλαγξέ ⟨θ'⟩ ἱερ[
> δαιμόνιον κέαρ ὀλοαῖ-
> σι στοναχαῖς ἄφαρ,
> καὶ τοιᾶιδε κορυφᾶι σά-
> μαινεν λόγων ... (*Pae.* 8a, fr. 52i(A). 10–14 M)

so the poet himself can communicate in the converse direction, addressing his spirit as he moves along the path of his song. We have seen the one surviving example where the word ψυχή is used: μή, φίλα ψυχά, βίον ἀθάνατον | σπεῦδε (*Pyth.* 3. 61–2); here ψυχή is the appropriate noun because of the solemnity of the sentiment and its reference to mortality.[58] More lightly he addresses his θυμός in a spirit of 'carpe diem', telling it to enjoy love while youth lasts:

> χρῆν μὲν κατὰ καιρὸν ἐρώτων δρέπεσθαι, θυμέ, σὺν ἁλικίαι.
> (fr. 123. 1 M)

Similarly, he urges himself not fall into love at the wrong time:

> εἴη καὶ ἐρᾶν καὶ ἔρωτι
> χαρίζεσθαι κατὰ καιρόν·
> μὴ πρεσβυτέραν ἀριθμοῦ
> δίωκε, θυμέ, πρᾶξιν. (fr. 127 M)

Since the address to the spirit is linked to the poet's mysterious sense of divine inspiration, it comes to the fore several times at a turning-point in the flow of ideas of a song. Thus his spirit chooses a new theme:

> εἰ δ' ἄεθλα γαρύεν
> ἔλδεαι, φίλον ἦτορ ... (*Ol.* 1. 3–4)

Similarly his heart will never admit that it has told a tale to discredit a hero's memory:[59]

[58] Similar in spirit is the unusual passage where Euxantios declines the offer of dominion over extra territories because too much prosperity might provoke divine anger. He tells his own mind to relinquish the cypress-tree and the meadow: ἔα, φρήν, κυπάρισσον, ἔα δὲ νομὸν Περιδάιον (*Pae.* 4, fr. 52d. 50–1 M).

[59] If H. Pelliccia's emendation to οὔ ποτ' ἐφήσει is right—a question which I am not qualified to judge—it does not change the sense significantly as far as our argument here is concerned (see Pelliccia (1995), esp. 334–54).

τὸ δ' ἐμὸν οὔ ποτε φάσει κέαρ
ἀτρόποισι Νεοπτόλεμον ἑλκύσαι
ἔπεσι. (*Nem.* 7. 102–4)

His θυμός aims his song at a target like an archer aiming an arrow,

ἔπεχε νῦν σκοπῶι τόξον, ἄγε θυμέ· τίνα βάλλομεν
ἐκ μαλθακᾶς αὖτε φρενὸς εὐκλέας ὀιστοὺς ἱέντες;
(*Ol.* 2. 89–90; cf. *Isthm.* 5. 46–7)

It steers his song as a helmsman steers a ship:

θυμέ, τίνα πρὸς ἀλλοδαπάν
ἄκραν ἐμὸν πλόον παραμείβεαι; (*Nem.* 3. 26–7)

In the strangest example of this kind of imagery, Pindar hears the music of the Castalian spring as he approaches Apollo's territory at Delphi—an image, perhaps, of poetic initiation as much as of setting the scene for the Delphic paean—and follows his ἦτορ as a child follows its mother:

ἤτορι δὲ φίλωι παῖς ἅτε ματέρι κεδνᾶι
πειθόμενος κατέβαν στεφάνων
καὶ θαλιᾶν τροφὸν ἄλσος Ἀ-
πόλλωνος. (*Pae.* 6, fr. 52f. 12–15 M)

Note that elsewhere Pindar addresses the Muse herself as his mother, μᾶτερ ἁμετέρα (*Nem.* 3. 1): the parallel suggests that in the present fragment he is guided by his spirit in the same way as he might be guided by the deity of song. The simile recalls the dichotomies of body and soul which we have seen in the overtly mystical fragments: just as the αἰῶνος εἴδωλον is divine, ἐκ θεῶν, and thus able to communicate moral truth to man, so the poet's inspiration comes from the hidden spirit that is his ἦτορ. The precision of the parallel suggests that there is nothing novel or outlandish about the structure of body and spirit implied by the αἰῶνος εἴδωλον fragment: in fact it is only a particularly overt expression of a dichotomy which is deep in Pindar's understanding of mental life, creativity, and life after death, and which is implied on the simplest level by the way he uses the soul-words throughout his work.

σῶμα *as the body of the living man*

A final capstone can now be fitted to our argument. When we saw in Chapter 4 that Homer has no word for the body of the living man, this was explained by saying that without the concept of a mind or soul the body cannot be distinguished from the total human being, the 'I' who lives and acts and thinks as a unity. If I am right to argue that the Archaic use of ψυχή implies such a concept and signals a new and un-Homeric model of identity, it follows that the new category of 'soul' will march with a new category of 'body'; and indeed we have already seen the word σῶμα helping to articulate one of Pindar's dualistic images of man:

σῶμα μὲν πάντων ἕπεται θανάτωι περισθενεῖ,
ζωὸν δ' ἔτι λείπεται αἰῶνος εἴδωλον ... (fr. 131b. 1–2 M)

The spirit survives death, but the body is brought away by Death. Here at a pinch the word σῶμα might be glossed as 'corpse', as in the Homeric usage; but the reference to the living body is unmistakable in another fragment where Pindar contrasts the immortality of the soul with the mortality of the body's death:

ἀθάναται δὲ βροτοῖς
ἀμέραι, σῶμα δ' ἐστὶ θνατόν. (*Parth.* 1, fr. 94a. 14–15 M)

Similarly, in less marked contexts Pindar speaks of the σώματα of defeated wrestlers (*Pyth.* 8. 81–2) and the body of a living baby is its ἁβρόν | σῶμα (*Ol.* 6. 55–6); while Bacchylides says that poetry keeps men's great deeds intact as the body declines:

ἀρετᾶ[ς γε μ]ὲν οὐ μινύθει
βροτῶν ἅμα σ[ώμ]ατι φέγγος, ἀλλὰ
Μοῦσά νιν τρ[έφει]. (3. 90–2)

A wrestler holds down the bodies of his opponents, γυια[λκέα σώ]ματα (9. 38); Heracles' sword fails to penetrate the σῶμα of the Nemean lion (13. 51–2); and Minos tells Theseus to plunge into the sea by 'throwing his body down', δικὼν θράσει σῶμα πατρὸς ἐς δόμους (17. 63), a phrase which seems to make a mannered conceit of the antithesis between body and self. In earlier literature there are a handful of examples to show that this usage of σῶμα was already well established before the time of Pindar and Bacchylides. Witness Archilochus when he describes himself seducing or sexually assaulting a girl:

μαλθακῇ δ[έ μιν
χλαί]νηι καλύψας, αὐχέν᾽ ἀγκάληις ἔχω[ν,
. . .]ματι παυ[σ]αμένην
τως ὥστε νεβρ[
μαζ]ῶν τε χερσὶν ἠπίως ἐφηψάμην
. . .]ρέφηνε νέον
ἥβης ἐπήλυσιν χρόα
ἅπαν τ]ε σῶμα καλὸν ἀμφαφώμενος
. . . .]ον ἀφῆκα μένος
ξανθῆς ἐπιψαύ[ων τριχός.   (fr. 196a. 44–53 W)

Despite the lacunae the sense is clear: excited by the bloom of youth, ἥβης ἐπήλυσιν, on her skin, χρόα, he embraces her whole body, σῶμα, and spills his seed on her loins.[60] Theognis articulates the dichotomy between body and spirit still more starkly when he complains to Poverty that she disgraces both his body and his νόος, which we can now confidently translate as 'mind':

ἆ δειλὴ Πενίη, τί ἐμοῖς ἐπικειμένη ὤμοις
σῶμα καταισχύνεις καὶ νόον ἡμέτερον;   (649–50)

The contrast somewhat resembles Homer's description of Odysseus' men transformed by Circe, who had their own thoughts but the limbs and faces of swine; here, however, the new sense of the word σῶμα informs an image beyond what was possible in the language and lore of the epic poet.

---

[60] In their original edition of the Cologne fragment, Merkelbach and West (1974: 111) followed Snell on σῶμα and held that, with Hes. WD 540, this is the earliest example of σῶμα used for the living body rather than the corpse. Merkelbach (1975) went on to produce an elaborate new interpretation. He compared the Archilochus passage with the σῶμα simile of Iliad III. 23–6, which he took to refer to a lion fastening on the body of a living animal; and using the letters ὥστε νεβρ in the Cologne fragment (l. 47), he held that Archilochus was remodelling the Homeric simile by likening himself to a predatory beast and the girl's body to that of its (living) quarry. I have argued (Ch. 4, p. 117) that there is no pressing reason to take the Homeric simile in that way; and S. R. Slings (1975) has shown that Merkelbach's reconstruction was unnecessary and that it is both simpler and more likely that Archilochus is using σῶμα in what was for him an everyday sense, with no Homeric allusion.

Conclusion: ψυχή and σῶμα in Hesiod

The evidence, then, is that the language and lore of Archaic poetry bears witness to a structure of body and soul which is in sharp contrast with the undifferentiated unity of Homeric man in life and death. When a word for 'body' and a word for 'spirit' appear at about the same time and in the same authors, it would be perverse not to look in the history of ideas to explain these new and unprecedented symbols of a dichotomy between inner self and outer flesh. But the linguistic evidence tells against the conclusion that the concept of the soul sprang into existence fully armed from the head of a single philosophical or religious movement. Although Pindar's revelations show that it has become possible for a lyric poet to listen to the dualistic doctrines of religious innovators, none the less there is enough evidence from the usage of ψυχή among the Archaic poets *before* Pindar to show that these doctrines merely give concrete form to something that had already happened in the microcosm represented by the meaning of a single simple word. It is not the whole truth to say that the poetic language is feeling the repercussions of esoteric religion; it is better to surmise that both the language and the doctrines bear witness in their different ways to a deeper cultural movement. In this sense a sea change has taken place on each level of Greek culture, and the innovation in language runs in tandem with an innovation in the realm of ideas. This means that there is good reason to suppose that the extension of the semantic range of ψυχή was at once culturally and linguistically significant, and correspondingly that its different Homeric meaning represents a different way of thinking about man.

One last doubt remains. Because the epic vocabulary and repertoire may have crystallized long before the *Iliad* and *Odyssey* were composed, it is possible that what we have seen in Homer's depiction of man is no closer to the mainstream of eighth-century thought than is what we find in the Archaic poets, even in Pindar's most mystical revelations. This means that we are left with two possible conclusions: either the Homeric epics bear witness to an earlier stage of the development of the Greek world-picture, or else they represent a view of man that was peculiar to the epic genre in terms of both language and image-making.

How can we choose between those alternatives? The only suggestion of an answer, as far as I can see, is provided by the scant examples of ψυχή and σῶμα in what survives of the early epic tradition *outside* Homer.[61] Here the evidence suggests that Hesiod stands very close to the lyric poets.[62] Although the subject-matter of the *Theogony* and the *Works and Days* means that they offer no instance of the loss of the ψυχή in death, we once find a ψυχή given to the living man in a way that contrasts sharply with the Homeric norm. Men risk their lives when they go to sea to trade, because they think money is the same thing as life itself:

> χαλεπῶς κε φύγοις κακόν· ἀλλά νυ καὶ τὰ
> ἄνθρωποι ῥέζουσιν ἀιδρείηισι νόοιο·
> χρήματα γὰρ ψυχὴ πέλεται δειλοῖσι βροτοῖσιν.
> δεινὸν δ᾽ ἐστι θανεῖν μετὰ κύμασιν.   (*WD* 684–7)

Although the context distantly implies the risk of drowning, recalling some instances in the *Odyssey*,[63] nevertheless the shift in the positive direction is more marked here than in any Homeric example: men take risks because they equate money with life, that is with life cultivated and enjoyed.[64] Alongside

---

[61] The evidence of the earlier Hymns is trivial: the few examples of ψυχή either reproduce Homeric formulae (*h. Ap.* 455 = *Od.* iii. 74, ix. 255) or conform to the usual patterns of Archaic verse. The pattern is similar in the Hesiodic *Shield of Heracles*: to die is to lose ψυχή and to kill it is to take it away, ἀπουράμενοι ψυχάς (173), and in the heightened imagery of this poem the separation of ψυχή from corpse is articulated more sharply than is usual in Homer: τῶν καὶ ψυχαὶ μὲν χθόνα δύνουσ᾽ Ἄιδος εἴσω | αὐτῶν, ὀστέα δέ σφι περὶ ῥινοῖο σαπείσης | Σειρίου ἀζαλέοιο κελαινῆι πύθεται αἴηι (151–3; sim. 254–5). The foes of Heracles are slain and their ψυχαί go to Hades, but their bones rot in the mortal world: the passage obviously resembles the proem of the *Iliad* but marks out a starker contrast between corpse and wraith. Similarly the *Catalogue of Women* offers an instance so close to one of our Homeric passages that it seems to be a deliberate reminiscence. Hippomenes' race with Atalanta is a matter of life and death for him, τῶι δε περὶ ψυχῆς πέλε[το δρόμος, ἠὲ ἁλῶναι | ἠὲ φυγεῖν (fr. 76. 7–8 M–W), just as Hector and Achilles raced each other for life or death around Troy, περὶ ψυχῆς θέον Ἕκτορος ἱπποδάμοιο (XXII. 161).

[62] On σῶμα, ψυχή, and the question of a body–soul dichotomy in Hesiod, see also Krafft (1963), 24–35.

[63] Cf. West ad loc., with a collection of parallels in other poets.

[*See opposite page for n. 64*]

this hint that Hesiod sees ψυχή as the foundation of life stands the fact that he definitely uses σῶμα for the body of a living man. He bids the listener wear a cloak so that his hair will not stand up on his body,

ἵνα τοι τρίχες ἀτρεμέωσι
μηδ' ὀρθαὶ φρίσσωσιν ἀειρόμεναι κατὰ σῶμα. (*WD* 539–40)

This is enough to show that for Hesiod the semantic development of σῶμα and ψυχή has gone a step further than for Homer;[65] and this in turn suggests that it is not simply because of the conventions of hexameter verse-making that we have been able to contrast the Homeric usage with that of the later poets working in other genres. Unless Hesiod is significantly earlier in date than Homer,[66] this encourages a suspicion, if no more, that the Archaic poets bear witness to a semantic and conceptual change which happened after the *Iliad* and *Odyssey* took shape.

[64] Compare Thgn. 229–30: τίς ἂν κορέσειεν ἅπαντας; | χρήματά τοι θνητοῖς γίνεται ἀφροσύνη.

[65] Krafft (1963: 35–50) also surveys Hesiod's use of δέμας, φυή, and other words translatable as 'body', and contrasts Hesiod's sense of physical body with the uses of the same words in Homer. The shift is less clear than in the case of σῶμα.

[66] As argued by West (1995).

REFERENCES

ADKINS, A. W. H. (1960), *Merit and Responsibility: A Study in Greek Values* (Oxford).

—— (1969), 'Threatening, Abusing and Feeling Angry in the Homeric Poems', *JHS* 89: 7–21.

—— (1970), *From the Many to the One* (London).

ALSTER, B. (1980) (ed.), *Death in Mesopotamia* (Copenhagen).

ALY, W. (1914), 'Lexikalische Streifzüge', *Glotta*, 5: 57–79.

ANDERSON, M. J. (1997), *The Fall of Troy in Early Greek Poetry and Art* (Oxford).

ANDRONIKOS, M. (1968), *Totenkult* (= *Archaeologia Homerica*, pt. III.w) (Göttingen).

ARBMAN, E. (1926–7), 'Untersuchungen zur primitiven Seelenvorstellung mit besonderer Rucksicht auf Indien', *Le Monde Oriental*, 20 (1926), 85–226; 21 (1927), 1–185.

AREND, W. (1933), *Die typischen Scenen bei Homer* (Berlin).

ARIÈS, P. (1981), *At the Hour of our Death* (London; tr. from *L'Homme devant la mort* (Paris, 1977)).

ATHANASSAKIS, A. (1971), 'An Enquiry into the Etymology and Meaning of ἴφθιμος in the Early Epic', *Glotta*, 49: 1–21.

AUSTIN, N. (1975), *Archery at the Dark of the Moon: Poetic Problems in Homer's Odyssey* (Berkeley and Los Angeles).

—— (1994), *Helen of Troy and her Shameless Phantom* (Ithaca, NY).

BADER, F. (1991), "Autour de ϝιρις ἀελλόπος", *RPh* 65: 31–44.

BAKKER, E. J. (1997), *Poetry in Speech: Orality and Homeric Discourse* (Ithaca, NY).

BANNERT, H. (1978), 'Zur Vogelgestalt der Götter bei Homer', *WS* 12: 29–42.

BARFIELD, O. (1928), *Poetic Diction: A Study in Meaning* (London).

BARNES, J. (1979), *The Presocratic Philosophers*, 2 vols. (London).

BECKER, A. S. (1990), 'The Shield of Achilles and the Poetics of Homeric Description', *AJPh* 111: 139–53.

BECKER, O. (1937), *Das Bild des Weges* (*Hermes* Einzelschriften, 4; Berlin).

BEEKES, R. S. P. (1969), *The Development of the Proto-Indo-European Laryngeals in Greek* (The Hague).

—— (1998), 'Hades and Elysion', in J. Jasanoff *et al.* (eds.), *Mér Curad: Studies in Honour of Calvert Watkins* (Innsbruck), 17–28.

BENVENISTE, E. (1932*a*), "Grec ψυχή", *BSL* 33: 165–8.

—— (1932*b*), 'Le Sens du mot κολοσσός et les noms grecs de la statue', *RPh* 6: 118–35.

—— (1937), 'Expression indo-européenne de l'éternité', *BSL* 112: 103–12.

—— (1971), *Problems in General Linguistics* (Miami; tr. from *Problèmes de linguistique générale* (1966)).

—— (1973), *Indo-European Language and Society* (London; tr. from *Le Vocabulaire des institutions indo-européennes* (1969)).

BERNSTEIN, A. E. (1993), *The Formation of Hell: Death and Retribution in the Ancient and Early Christian Worlds* (London).

BIANCHI, F. (1953), *ΔΙΟΣ ΑΙΣΑ* (Rome).

BICKEL, E. (1926), *Homerischer Seelenglaube* (Berlin).

BLACK, M. (1955), 'Metaphor', *Proceedings of the Aristotelian Society*, 55: 273–94.

BLACKER, C., and LOEWE, M. (1975) (eds.), *Ancient Cosmologies* (London).

BLANC, A. (1985), "Étymologie de ἀπηνής et de προσηνής", *RPh* 59: 255–63.

BLÜMEL, R. (1927), "Homerisch ταρχύω", *Glotta*, 15: 78–84.

BOASE, T. S. R. (1972), *Death in the Middle Ages* (London).

BOEDEKER, D. (1984), *Descent from Heaven: Images of Dew in Greek Poetry and Religion* (Chico, Calif.).

BÖHME, J. (1929), *Die Seele und das Ich im homerischen Epos* (Leipzig).

BOLTON, J. D. P. (1962), *Aristeas of Proconnesus* (Oxford).

BOTTÉRO, J. (1987), *Mésopotamie: L'Écriture, la religion et les dieux* (Paris).

BRASWELL, B. K. (1971), 'Mythological innovation in the *Iliad*', *CQ* 21: 16–27.

BREMER, J. M. (1990), "Pindar's Paradoxical ἐγώ", in Slings (1990*a*), 41–58.

—— DE JONG, I. F. J., and KALFF, J. (1987) (eds.), *Homer: Beyond Oral Poetry* (Amsterdam).

BREMMER, J. (1983), *The Early Greek Concept of the Soul* (London).

—— (1987) (ed.), *Interpretations of Greek Mythology* (London).

—— (1988), 'La Plasticité du mythe: Méleagre dans la poésie homérique', in Calame and Bérard (1988), 37–56.

BÜCHNER, W. (1937), 'Probleme der homerischen Nekyia', *Hermes*, 72: 104–22.

BURKERT, W. (1960), 'Das Lied von Ares und Aphrodite', *RhM* 103: 130–44.

—— (1961), 'Elysion', *Glotta*, 39: 208–13.

—— (1972), *Lore and Science in Ancient Pythagoreanism* (Cambridge, Mass.; tr. from *Weisheit und Wissenschaft* (1962)).

—— (1979), *Structure and History in Greek Mythology and Ritual* (Berkeley and Los Angeles).

—— (1985), *Greek Religion* (Oxford; tr. from *Griechische Religion der archaischen und klassischen Epoche* (1977)).

—— (1992), *The Orientalising Revolution: Near Eastern Influence on Greek Culture in the Early Archaic Age* (Cambridge, Mass.; new version of *Die orientalisierende Epoche in der griechischen Religion und Literatur* (*SHAW* 1984, Abh. 1; Heidelberg).

BURNETT, A. P. (1983), *Three Archaic Poets: Archilochus, Alcaeus, Sappho* (London).

—— (1991), 'Signals from the Unconscious in Early Greek Poetry', *CPh* 86: 275–300.

BUSHNELL, R. W. (1982), 'Reading "Winged Words": Homeric Bird Signs, Similes and Epiphanies', *Helios*, 9. 1: 1–13.

BUXTON, R. (1994), *Imaginary Greece: The Contexts of Mythology* (Cambridge).

CAIRD, G. B. (1980), *The Language and Imagery of the Bible* (London).

CALAME, C. (1977), *Les Chœurs de jeunes filles en Grèce archaïque*, i (Rome).

—— and BÉRARD, C. (1988) (eds.), *Métamorphoses du mythe en Grèce antique* (Geneva).

CALHOUN, G. M. (1935), 'The Art of Formula in Homer—ἔπεα πτερόεντα", *CPh* 30: 215–27.

—— (1937), 'Homer's Gods: Prolegomena', *TAPhA* 68: 11–25.

CARTER, J. B., and MORRIS, S. P. (1995) (eds.), *The Ages of Homer: A Tribute to Emily Townsend Vermeule* (Austin, Tex.).

CASWELL, C. P. (1990), *A Study of θυμός in Early Greek Epic* (*Mnemosyne*, Suppl. 114; Leiden).

CESTUIGNANO, A. (1952), 'Ancora a proposito di πορφύρω/πορφύρεος', *Maia*, 5: 118–20.

CHANTRAINE, P. (1933), *La Formation des noms en grec ancien* (Paris).

—— (1942), *Grammaire homérique*, 2 vols. (Paris, 1942–53).

—— (1954), 'Le Divin et les dieux chez Homère', in *La Notion du divin depuis Homère jusqu'à Platon* (Entretiens Hardt, 1; Geneva).

CHEYNS, A. (1979), 'L'Emploi des verbes βάλλω, βλάπτω et δαΐζω dans la poésie homérique', *AC* 48: 601–10.

—— (1981), 'Considérations sur les emplois de θυμός dans Homère: *Iliade* VII.67–218', *AC* 50: 137–47.

—— (1983), 'Le θυμός et la conception de l'homme dans l'épopée homérique', *RBPh* 61: 20–86.

CHEYNS, A. (1985), 'Recherche sur l'emploi des synonymes ἦτορ, κῆρ, κραδίη dans l'*Iliade* et l'*Odyssée*', *RBPh* 63: 15–75.

CHRISTMANN-FRANCK, L. (1971), 'Le Rituel des funérailles royales hittites', *RHA* 29: 61–111.

CLARKE, M. J. (1995*a*), 'Aeschylus on Mud and Dust', *Hermathena*, 158: 7–26.

——(1995*b*), 'The Wisdom of Thales and the Problem of the Word *hieros*', *CQ* 45: 296–317.

——(1996), review of Austin (1994), *JHS* 116: 190–1.

——(1997), 'Gods and Mountains in Greek Myth and Poetry', in A. B. Lloyd (ed.), *What is a God?* (Swansea), 65–80.

CLARKE, W. M. (1974), 'The God in the Dew', *AC* 43: 57–73.

CLAUS, D. B. (1981), *Toward the Soul: An Enquiry into the Meaning of ψυχή before Plato* (New Haven).

CLAY, J. S. (1981), 'Immortal and Ageless Forever', *CJ* 77: 112–17.

COLDSTREAM, J. N. (1976), 'Hero Cults in the Age of Homer', *JHS* 96: 8–17.

COMBELLACK, F. M. (1975), 'Agamemnon's Black Heart', *GB* 4: 81–9.

—— (1984), 'A Homeric Metaphor', *AJP* 105: 247–57.

CRANE, G. (1988), *Calypso: Backgrounds and Conventions of the Odyssey* (Frankfurt).

DALLEY, S. (1991), *Myths from Mesopotamia* (Oxford).

DARCUS, S. M. (1977), "The -φρων Epithets of θυμός", *Glotta*, 55: 178–82.

——(1979*a*), 'A Person's Relation to ψυχή in Homer, Hesiod and the Greek Lyric Poets', *Glotta* 57: 30–9.

——(1979*b*), 'A Person's Relation to φρήν in Homer, Hesiod and the Greek Lyric Poets', *Glotta*, 57: 159–73.

——(1980), 'How a person relates to νόος in Homer, Hesiod and the Greek lyric poets', *Glotta*, 58: 33–44.

as DARCUS SULLIVAN, S. (1980), 'How a Person Relates to θυμός in Homer', *IF* 85: 138–50.

——(1981), 'The Function of θυμός in Hesiod and the Greek Lyric Poets', *Glotta*, 59: 147–55.

——(1987), "πραπίδες in Homer", *Glotta*, 65: 182–93.

——(1988), *Psychological Activity in Homer: A Study of φρήν* (Ottawa).

DAVIES, M. (1989), *The Epic Cycle* (Bristol).

DEGANI, E. (1961), *Aἰών da Omero ad Aristotele* (Padua).

DIETRICH, B. C. (1965), *Death, Fate and the Gods* (London).

DIHLE, A. (1982), 'Totenglaube und Seelenvorstellung im 7. Jahrhundert vor Christus', in *Gedenkschrift A. Stuiber* (Münster), 9–20.

DILCHER, R. (1995), *Studies in Heraclitus* (Spudasmata, 56; Hildesheim).

DIRLMEIER, F. (1967), *Die Vogelgestalt homerischer Götter* (*SHAW* 1967, Abh. 2; Heidelberg).

DODDS, E. R. (1951), *The Greeks and the Irrational* (Berkeley and Los Angeles).

DOYLE, R. E. (1984), Ἄτη, *its Use and Meaning* (New York).

DUHOUX, Y. (1992), *Le Verbe grec ancien* (Louvain).

DURANTE, M. (1968a), " Ἔπεα πτερόεντα: die Rede als 'Weg' in griechischen und vedischen Bildern", in R. Schmitt (1968), 242–60.

——(1968b), 'Die Terminologie für das dichterische Schaffen', in R. Schmitt (1968), 261–90.

EDMUNDS, L. (1990) (ed.), *Approaches to Greek Myth* (Baltimore).

EDWARDS, M. W. (1986), 'The Conventions of a Homeric Funeral', in J. H. Betts (ed.), *Studies in Honour of T. B. L. Webster* (Bristol), 84–92.

——(1987), *Homer, Poet of the* Iliad (Baltimore).

——(1988), 'Homer and Oral Tradition, Part II', *Oral Tradition* 3: 11–60.

——(1991), Introduction to vol. 5 of *The* Iliad: *A Commentary* (Cambridge).

ELIADE, M. (1964), *Shamanism: Archaic Techniques of Ecstasy* (London; tr. from *Le Chamanisme et les techniques archaïques de l'extase* (Paris, 1951)).

ELIOT, T. S. (1921), 'The Metaphysical Poets' (orig. pub. 1921; cited from *Selected Prose* (Harmondsworth, 1975), 59–67).

ELLIGER, W. (1975), *Die Darstellung der Landschaft in der griechischen Dichtung* (Berlin).

EMPSON, W. (1930), *Seven Types of Ambiguity* (London).

ERBSE, H. (1972), *Beiträge zum Verständnis der Odyssee* (Berlin).

——(1980), 'Homerische Götter in Vogelgestalt', *Hermes*, 108: 259–74.

——(1984), 'Zur Motivation des Handelns bei Homer', *Perspektiven der Philosophie*, 10: 207–28.

——(1986), *Untersuchungen zur Funktion der Götter im homerischen Epos* (Berlin).

EVANS-PRITCHARD, E. E. (1956), *Nuer Religion* (Oxford).

——(1965), *Theories of Primitive Religion* (Oxford).

EVERSON, S. (1991) (ed.), *Psychology* (= *Companions to Ancient Philosophy*, no. 2; Cambridge).

FARRER, A. M. (1972), 'An English Appreciation', in H. W. Bartsch (ed.), *Kerygma and Myth: A Theological Debate* (London), 212–23.

FENIK, B. (1968), *Typical Battle Scenes in the* Iliad (*Hermes* Einzel-schriften, 21; Wiesbaden).

—— (1978*a*) (ed.), *Homer: Tradition and Invention* (Leiden).

—— (1978*b*), 'Stylisation and Variety: Four Monologues in the *Iliad*', in Fenik (1978*a*), 68–90.

FERNÁNDEZ-GALIANO, M. (1992), Introduction to *Odyssey* xxii, in vol. 3 of *A Commentary on Homer's* Odyssey (Oxford).

FESTUGIÈRE, A. J. (1949), 'Le Sens philosophique du mot αἰών', *PP* 11: 172–89.

FOCKE, F. (1943), *Die Odyssee* (Stuttgart).

FRAME, D. (1978), *The Myth of Return in Greek Epic* (New Haven).

FRÄNKEL, H. (1960), *Wege und Formen frühgriechischen Denkens*, 2nd edn. (Munich).

—— (1975), *Early Greek Poetry and Philosophy* (Oxford; tr. from *Dichtung und Philosophie des frühen Griechentums* (1962)).

FRAZER, J. (1922), *The Golden Bough*, abridged edn. (London).

FRIEDRICH, W. H. (1956), *Verwundung und Tod in der Ilias* (Göttingen).

FRISK, H. (1966), *Kleine Schriften* (Göteborg).

VON FRITZ, K. (1943), "*Νόος* and *νοεῖν* in the Homeric Poems", *CPh* 38: 79–93.

GARBRAH, K. A. (1977), 'The Scholia on the Ending of the *Odyssey*', *WJA* 3: 7–16.

GARLAND, R. (1981), 'The Causation of Death in the *Iliad*: A Theological and Biological Investigation', *BICS* 28: 43–60.

—— (1984), "*γέρας θανόντων*—an Investigation into the Claims of the Homeric Dead", *AncSoc* 15: 5–22.

—— (1985), *The Greek Way of Death* (London).

GASKIN, R. (1990), 'Do Homeric Heroes Make Real Decisions?', *CQ* 40: 1–15.

GENTILI, B. (1988), *Poetry and its Public in Ancient Greece* (Baltimore; tr. from *Poesia e pubblico nella Grecia antica* (Rome, 1985)).

GERMAIN, G. (1954), *Genèse de l'Odyssée* (Paris).

GIBBS, R. (1996), *The Poetics of Mind* (Cambridge).

GILL, C. (1990) (ed.), *The Person and the Human Mind* (Oxford).

—— (1996), *Personality in Greek Epic, Tragedy, and Philosophy* (Oxford).

GIPPER, H. (1964), 'Purpur', *Glotta*, 42: 39–69.

GLADIGOW, B. (1968), "Zwei frühe Zeugungslehren? Zu *γόνυ*, *γένυς* und *γένος*", *RhM* 111: 357–74.

GNOLI, G., and VERNANT, J.-P. (1982) (eds.), *La Mort, les morts dans les sociétés anciennes* (Paris and Cambridge).

GOODY, J. (1977), *The Domestication of the Savage Mind* (Cambridge).

—— (1987), *The Interface between the Written and the Oral* (Cambridge).

GOULD, J. (1973), 'Hiketeia', *JHS* 93: 74–103.

—— (1985), 'On Making Sense of Greek Religion', in P. Easterling and J. V. Muir (eds.), *Greek Religion and Society* (Cambridge), 1–33.

GRAF, F. (1974), *Eleusis und die orphische Dichtung Athens in vorhellenistischer Zeit* (Berlin).

—— (1993), *Greek Mythology* (Baltimore; tr. from *Griechische Mythologie* (Basel, 1987)).

GRIFFIN, J. (1976), 'Homeric Pathos and Objectivity', *CQ* 26: 161–87.

—— (1977), 'The Epic Cycle and the Uniqueness of Homer', *JHS* 97: 39–53.

—— (1980), *Homer on Life and Death* (Oxford).

—— (1986), 'Homeric Words and Speakers', *JHS* 106: 36–57.

GURNEY, O. R. (1952), *The Hittites* (Harmondsworth).

HAINSWORTH, J. B. (1968), *The Flexibility of the Homeric Formula* (Oxford).

—— (1993), Introduction to vol. 3 of *The* Iliad*: A Commentary* (Cambridge).

HALKBART, K. W. (1796), *Psychologia Homerica* (Zullichau).

HANDLEY, E. W. (1956), 'Words for "Soul", "Heart" and "Mind" in Aristophanes', *RhM* 99: 205–25.

HARRISON, E. L. (1960), 'Notes on Homeric Psychology', *Phoenix*, 14: 63–80.

HAVELOCK, E. A. (1963), *Preface to Plato* (Oxford).

—— (1972), 'The Socratic Self as it is Parodied in Aristophanes' *Clouds*', *YCS* 22: 1–18.

HEANEY, S. (1980), 'Feeling into Words', in id., *Preoccupations: Selected Prose 1968–1978* (London), 41–60.

HELBIG, K. G. (1840), *Dissertatio de vi et usu φρένες, θυμός similiumque apud Homerum* (Dresden).

HERINGTON, J. (1985), *Poetry into Drama: Early Tragedy and the Greek Poetic Tradition* (Berkeley and Los Angeles).

HERSHKOWITZ, D. (1998), *The Madness of Epic* (Oxford).

HERTER, H. (1957), "*Σῶμα* bei Homer", in K. Schauenberg (ed.), *Charites: Festschrift E. Langlotz* (Bonn), 206–17.

HEUBECK, A. (1963), "*KIMMEPIOI*", *Hermes*, 91: 490–2.

—— (1972), 'Nochmals zur "innerhomerischen Chronologie"', *Glotta*, 50: 129–43.

HOEKSTRA, A. (1965), *Homeric Modifications of Formulaic Prototypes* (Amsterdam).

HOIJER, H. (1954) (ed.), *Language in Culture* (Chicago).

HOOKER, J. T. (1980), Ἱερός *in Early Greek* (*Beiträge zur Sprachwissenschaft, Vorträge und kleinere Schriften*, 22 (Innsbruck).

——(1987), "Homeric φίλος", *Glotta*, 65: 44–65.

HOUSMAN, A. E. (1933), 'On the Name and Nature of Poetry' (lecture delivered in 1933 and repr. in *Selected Prose* (Cambridge, 1961)), 168–95.

HUDSON, R. A. (1980), *Sociolinguistics* (Cambridge).

HUFFMAN, C. (1993), *Philolaus of Croton* (Cambridge).

HUGHES, D. D. (1991), *Human Sacrifice in Ancient Greece* (London).

HUNTINGDON, R., and METCALF, P. (1979), *Celebrations of Death: The Anthropology of Mortuary Ritual* (Cambridge).

HUXLEY, G. L. (1958), 'Odysseus and the Thesprotian Oracle of the Dead', *PP* 13: 245–8.

IMMERWAHR, S. (1995), 'Death and the Tanagra Larnakes', in Carter and Morris (1995), 109–22.

INGENKAMP, H. G. (1975), 'Inneres Selbst und Lebensträger: Zur Einheit des ψυχή-Begriffs', *RhM* 118: 48–61.

IRELAND, S., and STEEL, F. L. D. (1975), "Φρένες as an Anatomical Organ in the Works of Homer", *Glotta*, 53: 183–95.

IRWIN, E. (1974), *Colour Terms in Greek Poetry* (Toronto).

JAEGER, W. (1947), *Theology of the Early Greek Philosophers* (Oxford).

JAHN, T. (1987), *Zum Wortfeld 'Seele-Geist' in der Sprache Homers* (Zetemata, 83; Munich).

JANKO, R. (1982), *Homer, Hesiod and the Hymns* (Cambridge).

——(1984), 'Forgetfulness in the Golden Tablets of Memory', *CQ* 24: 89–100.

——(1992), Introduction to vol. 4 of *The* Iliad: *A Commentary* (Cambridge).

——(1997), 'The Physicist as Hierophant', *ZPE* 118: 61–94.

——(1998), 'The Homeric Poems as Oral Dictated Texts', *CQ* 48: 135–67.

JARCHO, V. N. (1968), 'Zum Menschenbild der nachhomerischen Dichtung', *Philologus*, 112: 147–72.

——(1990), 'Das poetische "Ich" als gesellschaftlich-kommunikatives Symbol in der frühgriechischen Lyrik', in Slings (1990*a*), 31–9.

JONES, D. M. (1949), 'The Sleep of Philoctetes', *CR* 63: 83–5.

DE JONG, I. F. J. (1987), *Narrators and Focalizers: The Presentation of the Story in the* Iliad (Amsterdam).

JOUANNA, J. (1987), 'La Souffle, la vie et le froid: Remarques sur la famille de ψύχω d'Homère à Hippocrate', *REG* 100: 203–24.

KAHANE, A. (1994), *The Interpretation of Order: A Study in the Poetics of Homeric Repetition* (Oxford).

KAHN, C. H. (1979), *The Art and Thought of Heraclitus* (Cambridge).

KARL, W. (1967), *Chaos und Tartaros in Hesiods Theogonie* (diss. Erlangen).

KIRK, G. S. (1962), *The Songs of Homer* (Cambridge).

——(1970), *Myth: Its Meaning and Functions in Ancient and Other Cultures* (Cambridge).

——(1974), *The Nature of Greek Myths* (Harmondsworth).

——(1985), Introduction to vol. 1 of *The* Iliad*: A Commentary* (Cambridge).

KITTAY, E. F. (1989), *Metaphor: Its Cognitive Force and Linguistic Structure*, 2nd edn. (Oxford).

KOLLER, H. (1958), "Σῶμα bei Homer", *Glotta*, 37: 276–81.

KRAFFT, F. (1963), *Vergleichende Untersuchungen zu Homer und Hesiod* (Hypomnemata, 6; Göttingen).

KRANZ, W. (1938), 'Gleichnis und Vergleich in der frühgriechischen Philosophie', *Hermes*, 73: 111–13.

KRISCHER, T. (1984), "Νόος, νοεῖν, νόημα", *Glotta*, 62: 141–9.

KULLMANN, W. (1956), *Das Wirken der Götter in der Ilias* (Berlin).

——and REICHEL, M. (1990) (eds.), *Der Übergang von der Mündlichkeit zur Literatur bei den Griechen* (Tübingen).

LAKOFF, G., and JOHNSON, M. (1980), *Metaphors We Live By* (Chicago).

——and TURNER, M. (1989), *More Than Cool Reason: A Field Guide to Poetic Metaphor* (Chicago).

LAMBERTON, R. (1988), *Hesiod* (New Haven).

——and KEANEY, J. J. (1992) (eds.), *Homer's Ancient Readers: The Hermeneutics of Greek Epic's Earliest Exegetes* (Princeton).

LANDFESTER, M. (1966), *Das griechische Nomen φίλος und seine Ableitungen* (Spudasmata, 11; Hildesheim).

LANIG, K. (1953), *Der handelnde Mensch in der Ilias* (diss. Erlangen).

LATACZ, J. (1965), "ΑΝΔΡΟΤΗΤΑ", *Glotta*, 43: 62–76.

——(1966), *Zum Wortfeld 'Freude' in der Sprache Homers* (Heidelberg).

——(1968), "Ἄπτερος μῦθος—ἄπτερος φάτις: Ungeflügelte Wörte?" *Glotta*, 46: 27–47.

——(1977), *Kampfparänese, Kampfdarstellung und Kampfwirklichkeit in der Ilias, bei Kallinos und Tyrtaios* (Zetemata, 66; Munich).

——(1984), 'Das Menschenbild Homers', *Gymnasium*, 91: 15–39.

LEFKOWITZ, M. (1969), 'Bacchylides' Ode 5: Imitation and Originality', *HSCPh* 73: 45–96.

——(1991), *First-Person Fictions: Pindar's Poetic 'I'* (Oxford).

LESKY, A. (1950), review of second edition of B. Snell, *Die Entdeckung des Geistes*, *Gnomon*, 22: 97–106.

——(1961), *Göttliche und menschliche Motivation im homerischen Epos* (*SHAW* 1961, Abh. 4; Heidelberg).

——(1967), *Homeros* (Stuttgart).

——(1985), 'Grundzüge griechischen Rechtsdenkens', *WS* 19: 5–40.

LÉTOUBLON, F. (1983), 'Défi et combat dans l'*Iliade*', *REG* 96: 27–48.

LEUMANN, M. (1950), *Homerische Wörter* (Basle).

LÉVY-BRUHL, L. (1918), *Les Fonctions mentales dans les sociétés inférieures*, 3rd edn. (Paris).

——(1931), *La Mentalité primitive* (Oxford).

——(1949), *Les Carnets de Lucien Lévy-Bruhl* (Paris).

——(1952), 'Letter to E. E. Evans-Pritchard', *British Journal of Sociology*, 3: 117–23.

——(1963 [1927]), *L'Âme primitive* (orig. pub. Paris, 1927; cited from reissued text (Paris, 1963)).

LIENHARDT, G. (1961), *Divinity and Experience: The Religion of the Dinka* (Oxford).

——(1966), *Social Anthropology*, 2nd edn. (Oxford).

LLOYD, G. E. R. (1966), *Polarity and Analogy: Two Types of Argumentation in Early Greek Thought* (Cambridge).

——(1975), 'Greek Cosmologies', in Blacker and Loewe (1975), 198–244.

——(1987), *The Revolutions of Wisdom: Studies in the Claims and Practice of Greek Science* (Berkeley and Los Angeles).

——(1990), *Demystifying Mentalities* (Cambridge).

LLOYD-JONES, H. (1971), *The Justice of Zeus* (Berkeley and Los Angeles).

——(1985), 'Pindar and the Afterlife', in *Pindare* (Entretiens Hardt, 31; Geneva), 245–79.

——(1989), 'Pindar and the Afterlife: Addendum (1989)', in *Greek Epic, Lyric and Tragedy: The Academic Papers of Sir Hugh Lloyd-Jones* (Oxford).

LOCHER, J. T. (1963), *Untersuchungen zu ἱερός, hauptsächlich bei Homer* (Bern).

LOCKHARDT, P. N. (1966), "φρονεῖν in Homer", *CPh* 61: 99–102.

LORD, A. B. (1960), *The Singer of Tales* (Cambridge, Mass.).

LORETZ, O. (1993), 'Nekromantie und Totenevokation in Mesopotamie, Ugarit und Israel', in B. Janowski *et al.* (eds.), *Religionsgeschichtliche Beziehungen* (Freiburg), 285–318.

LOVIBOND, S. (1991), 'Plato's Theory of Mind', in Everson (1991), 35–55.

LYNN-GEORGE, M. (1978), 'The Relationship of Σ 535–40 and *Scutum* 156–60 re-examined', *Hermes*, 106: 396–405.

McCARTHY, M. (1957), *Memories of a Catholic Girlhood* (London).

MacCARY, W. T. (1982), *Childlike Achilles: Ontogeny and Phylogeny in the* Iliad (New York).

McGIBBON, D. (1964), 'Metempsychosis in Pindar', *Phronesis*, 9: 5–11.

McKINLAY, A. P. (1957), "On the Way Scholars Interpret ἀμαυρός", *AC* 26: 12–39.

McMANNERS, J. (1981), *Death and the Enlightenment* (Oxford).

MARCOVICH, M. (1967), *Heraclitus* (Merida).

MARG, W. (1938), *Der Charakter in der Sprache der frühgriechischen Dichtung* (Würzburg).

——(1942), 'Kampf und Tod in der Ilias', *Die Antike*, 18: 167–79.

——(1957), *Homer über die Dichtung* (Münster).

MARTIN, R. P. (1989), *The Language of Heroes: Speech and Performance in the* Iliad (Ithaca, NY).

MERKELBACH, R. (1951), *Untersuchungen zur Odyssee* (Zetemata, 2; Munich).

——(1975), 'Nachträge zur Archilochus', *ZPE* 16: 220–2.

——and WEST, M. L. (1974), 'Ein Archilochus-Papyrus', *ZPE* 14: 97–113.

MEULI, K. (1935), 'Scythica', *Hermes*, 70: 121–76.

MONDI, R. (1986), 'Tradition and Invention in the Hesiodic Titanomachy', *TAPhA* 116: 25–48.

——(1990), 'Greek Mythic Thought in the Light of the Near East', in Edmunds (1990), 141–98.

MOREUX, B. (1967), 'La Nuit, l'ombre et la mort chez Homère', *Phoenix*, 21: 237–72.

MORRIS, I. (1987), *Burial and Ancient Society* (Cambridge).

——(1992), *Death-Ritual and Social Structure in Classical Antiquity* (Cambridge).

MOULTON, C. (1977), *Similes in the Homeric Poems* (Hypomnemata, 49; Göttingen).

——(1979), 'Homeric Metaphor', *CPh* 74: 279–93.

MUELLER, M. (1984), *The* Iliad (London).

VON DER MÜHLL, P. (1938), 'Zur Erfindung in der Nekyia des Odyssee', *Philologus*, 93: 3–11.

MURRAY, P. (1981), 'Poetic Inspiration in Early Greece', *JHS* 101: 87–100.

MYLONAS, G. E. (1948), 'Homeric and Mycenaean Burial Customs', *AJA* 52: 56–81.

NAGLER, M. N. (1967), 'Towards a Generative View of the Homeric Formula', *TAPhA* 98: 269–311.

——(1974), *Spontaneity and Tradition: A Study in the Oral Art of Homer* (Berkeley and Los Angeles).

NAGY, G. (1979), *The Best of the Achaeans* (Baltimore).

——(1983), 'On the Death of Sarpedon', in C. A. Rubino and C. W. Shelmerdine (eds.), *Approaches to Homer* (Austin), 189–217.

——(1990a), *Greek Mythology and Poetics* (Ithaca, NY).

——(1990b), *Pindar's Homer* (Baltimore).

——(1990c), 'Death of a Schoolboy: The Early Greek Beginnings of a Crisis in Philology', in J. Ziolkowski (ed.), *On Philology* (University Park, Pa.), 37–48.

——(1992a), 'Mythological Exemplum in Homer', in R. Hexter and D. Selden (eds.), *Innovations of Antiquity* (New York), 311–31.

——(1992b), 'Homeric Questions', *TAPhA* 122: 17–60.

——(1996), *Homeric Questions* (Austin, Tex.).

NALBANTIAN S. (1977), *The Symbol of the Soul from Hölderlin to Yeats: A Study in Metonymy* (London).

NEHRING, A. (1947), 'Homer's Description of Syncopes', *CPh* 42: 106–21.

NICKAU, K. (1977), *Untersuchungen zur textkritischen Methode des Zenodotos von Ephesos* (Berlin).

NIENS, C. (1987), *Struktur und Dynamik in den Kampfszenen der Ilias* (Heidelberg).

NIKITAS, A. A. (1978), 'Bemerkungen zum Lexikon des Liddell–Scott–Jones', *WJA* 4: 75–90.

NILSSON, M. P. (1941), 'The Immortality of the Soul in Greek Religion', *Eranos*, 39: 1–16.

——(1967), *Geschichte der griechischen Religion*, i, 3rd edn. (Munich).

NISETICH, F. J. (1989), *Pindar and Homer* (Baltimore).

NOCK. A. D. (1972), 'Cremation and Burial in the Roman Empire', in Z. Stewart (ed.), *Essays on Religion and the Ancient World* (Oxford), 277–307.

NOTHDURFT, W. (1978), 'Noch einmal πεῖραρ/πείρατα bei Homer', *Glotta*, 56: 25–40.

NOTOPOULOS, J. (1949), 'Parataxis in Homer', *TAPhA* 80: 1–23.

NUSSBAUM, A. (1986), *Head and Horn in Indo-European* (Berlin).

NUSSBAUM, M. C. (1972), "ψυχή in Heraclitus", *Phronesis*, 17: 1–16, 153–70.

ONIANS, R. B. (1951), *The Origins of European Thought about the Body, the Mind, the Soul, the World, Time and Fate* (Cambridge).

O'NOLAN, K. (1978), 'Doublets in the *Odyssey*', *CQ* 28: 23–7.

OTTEN, H. (1958), *Hethitische Totenrituale* (Berlin).

OTTO, W. F. (1923), *Die Manen, oder von den Urformen des Toten-glaubens*, 2nd edn. (cited from new edn. (Darmstadt, 1958)).

PADEL, R. (1992), *In and Out of the Mind: Greek Images of the Tragic Self* (Princeton).

PAGE, D. L. (1955), *The Homeric* Odyssey (Oxford).

——(1956), *Sappho and Alcaeus* (Oxford).

PAGLIARO, A. (1956), 'Il proemio dell'Iliade', in *Nuovi Saggi di Critica Semantica* (Florence), 3–46.

PARASKEVAIDES, H. A. (1984), *The Use of Synonyms in Homeric Formulaic Diction* (Amsterdam).

PARKER, R. (1983), *Miasma: Pollution and Purification in Early Greek Religion* (Oxford).

PARRY, A. (1956), 'The Language of Achilles', *TAPhA* 87: 1–7.

PARRY, A. A. (1973), *Blameless Aegisthus* (*Mnemosyne*, Suppl. 26; Leiden).

PARRY, M. (1971 [1928]), 'The Traditional Epithet in Homer' (orig. pub. as *L'Épithète traditionelle dans Homère* (1928); cited from M. Parry (1971 (below)), 1–190).

——(1971 [1933]), 'The Traditional Metaphor in Homer' (orig. pub. 1933; cited from M. Parry (1971 (below)), 365–75).

——(1971 [1937]), 'About Winged Words' (orig. pub. 1937; cited from M. Parry (1971 (below)), 414–17).

——(1971), *The Making of Homeric Verse* collected papers, ed. A. Parry (Oxford).

PATZEK, B. (1992), *Homer und Mykene: Mündliche Dichtung und Geschichtsschreibung* (Munich).

PELLICCIA, H. (1995), *Mind, Body and Speech in Homer and Pindar* (Hypomnemata, 107; Göttingen).

PENN, J. M. (1972), *Linguistic Relativity versus Innate Ideas* (The Hague).

PERRY, B. E. (1937), 'The Early Greek Capacity for Viewing Things Separately', *TAPhA* 68: 403–27.

PETZL, G. (1969), *Antike Diskussionen über die beiden Nekyiai* (*Beit-räge zur klassischen Philologie*, 29; Meisenheim).

PINKER, S. (1994), *The Language Instinct* (Harmondsworth).

POHLMANN, E. (1990), 'Zur Überlieferung griechischer Literatur vom 8. bis zum 4. Jh.', in Kullmann and Reichel (1990), 11–31.

PORTER, J. I. (1992), 'Hermeneutic Lines and Circles: Aristarchus and Crates on the Exegesis of Homer', in Lamberton and Keaney (1992), 67–114.

PÖTSCHER, W. (1959*a*), 'Ares', *Gymnasium*, 66: 5–14.

PÖTSCHER, W. (1959*b*), 'Das Person-Bereichdenken in der frühgriechischen Periode', *WS* 72: 5–25.

——(1960), 'Moira, Themis und τιμή im homerischen Denken', *WS*
73: 5–39.

——(1965), 'Die "Auferstehung" in der klassischen Antike', *Kairos*,
7: 208–15.

——(1978), 'Person-Bereichdenken und Personifikation', *Literatur-
wissenschaftliches Jahrbuch*, 19: 217–32.

PULLEYN, S. (1997), *Prayer in Greek Religion* (Oxford).

PULLUM, G. K. (1991), *The Great Eskimo Vocabulary Hoax and other
Irreverent Essays on the History of Language* (Chicago).

RAHN, H. (1953), 'Tier und Mensch in der homerischen Auffassung
der Wirklichkeit', *Paideuma*, 5: 277–97, 431–80.

RAMNOUX, C. (1959), *La Nuit et les enfants de la nuit* (Paris).

RANK, O. (1971), *The Double: A Psychoanalytic Study*, with introd.
and notes by H. Tucker (Chapel Hill, NC; tr. from *Der Doppelgänger* (1914)).

REDDY, M. J. (1993), 'The Conduit Metaphor', in A. Ortony (ed.),
Metaphor and Thought, 2nd edn. (Cambridge), 164–201.

REDFIELD, J. M. (1975), *Nature and Culture in the* Iliad: *The Tragedy
of Hector* (Chicago).

——(1979), 'The Proem of the *Iliad*: Homer's Art', *CPh* 74: 95–110.

REEVE, M. D. (1973), 'The Language of Achilles', *CQ* 23: 193–5.

REGENBOGEN, O. (1948), "*Δαιμόνιον ψυχῆς φῶς*: Erwin Rohdes Psyche
und die neuere Kritik" (orig. pub. 1948; cited from Regenbogen,
Kleine Schriften (Munich, 1961)), 1–28.

REICHLER-BÉGUELIN, M.-J. (1991), 'Motivation et rémotivation des
signes linguistiques', *RPh* 65: 9–30.

REINHARDT, K. (1948), 'Die Abenteuer der Odyssee', in his *Von
Werken und Formen* (Godesberg), 52–161.

——(1960), 'Personifikation und Allegorie', in his *Vermächtnis der
Antike* (Göttingen), 7–40.

RENEHAN, R. (1975), *Greek Lexicographical Notes* (Hypomnemata, 45;
Göttingen).

——(1979), 'The Meaning of σῶμα in Homer', *CSCA* 12: 269–82.

RISCH, E. (1974), *Wortbildung der homerischen Sprache*, 2nd edn.
(Berlin).

RIX, H. (1965), "Homerisch ὀρώρεται und die Verben ὄρνυμι und
ὀρίνω", *IF* 70: 25–49.

ROBB, K. (1994), *Literacy and Paideia in Ancient Greece* (Oxford).

ROBERTSON, D. S. (1940), 'The Flight of Phrixus', *CR* 54: 1–8.

ROBERTSON, N. (1980), 'Heracles' *katabasis*', *Hermes*, 108: 274–300.

ROBINSON, D. (1990), 'Homeric φίλος: Love of Life and Limbs, and

Friendship with One's θυμός', in E. M. Craik (ed.), '*Owls to Athens*' (Oxford), 97–108.

ROBINSON, L. (1927) (ed.), *The Golden Treasury of Irish Verse* (London).

ROBINSON, T. M. (1970), *Plato's Psychology* (Toronto).

ROHDE, E. (1925), *Psyche* (London; tr. from 9th Ger. edn. of work orig. pub. 1893).

ROUX, G. (1960), "Qu'est-ce que un κολοσσός?", *REA* 62: 5–40.

ROWE, C. J. (1983), '"Archaic Thought" in Hesiod', *JHS* 103: 124–35.

RUESCHE, F. (1930), *Blut, Leben und Seele* (Paderborn).

RUIJGH, C. J. (1957), *L'Élément achéen dans la langue épique* (Assen).

——(1971), *Autour de τε épique* (Amsterdam).

RUSSO, J., and SIMON, B. (1978), 'Homeric Psychology and the Oral Epic Tradition', in J. Wright (ed.), *Essays on the* Iliad (Bloomington, Ind.), 41–57.

DE RUYT, F. (1932), 'Le Thanatos d'Euripide et le Charun étrusque', *AC* 1: 61–77.

RYLE, G. (1949), *The Concept of Mind* (London).

SACKS, R. (1987), *The Traditional Phrase in Homer* (Leiden).

SANSONE, D. (1975), *Aeschylean Metaphors for Intellectual Activity* (*Hermes* Einzelschriften, 35; Wiesbaden).

SAPIR, E. (1921), *Language* (Oxford).

SCHADEWALDT, W. (1965), *Von Homers Welt und Werk*, 4th edn. (Stuttgart).

SCHMITT, A. (1990) *Selbstañdigkeit und Abhängigkeit menschlichen Handelns bei Homer* (Abh. der geistes- u. sozialwiss. Klasse, 1990. 5; Mainz).

SCHMITT, R. (1967), *Dichtung und Dichtersprache in indogermanischer Zeit* (Wiesbaden).

——(1968) (ed.), *Indogermanische Dichtersprache* (Darmstadt).

SCHNAPP-GOURBEILLON, A. (1982), 'Les Funérailles de Patrocle', in Gnoli and Vernant (1982), 77–88.

SCHNAUFER, A. (1970), *Frühgriechischer Totenglaube: Untersuchungen zum Totenglauben der mykenischen und homerischen Zeit* (Spudasmata, 20; Hildesheim).

SCHOECK, G. (1961), *Ilias und Aethiopis* (Zurich).

SCHOFIELD, M. (1991), 'Heraclitus' Theory of Soul and its Antecedents', in Everson (1991), 13–34.

SCHRADER, W. (1885), 'Die Psychologie des ältesten griechischen Epos', *Jahrbücher für classische Philologie*, 31: 145–76.

SCHRETTER, M. K. (1974), *Alter Orient und Hellas* (*Beiträge zur Kulturwissenschaft*, Sonderheft 33; Innsbruck).

SCHULZE, W. (1892), *Quaestiones epicae* (Güterslow).

SCHWABL, H. (1954), 'Zur Selbständigkeit des Menschen bei Homer', *WS* 67: 46–64.

——(1955), 'Zur Theogonie des Hesiod', *Gymnasium*, 62: 526–42.

——(1990), 'Was lehrt mündliche Epik für Homer?', in Kullmann and Reichel (1990), 65–110.

SCULLY, S. (1984), 'The Language of Achilles: The *ΟΧΘΗΣΑΣ* Formulas', *TAPhA* 114: 11–27.

SEAFORD, R. (1994), *Reciprocity and Ritual: Homer and Tragedy in the Developing City-state* (Oxford).

SEEL, O. (1953), 'Zur Vorgeschichte des Gewissens-Begriffes im altgriechischen Denken', in *Festschrift F. Dornseiff* (Leipzig), 291–319.

SEGAL, C. (1971), *The Theme of the Mutilation of the Corpse in the* Iliad (*Mnemosyne* Suppl. 17; Leiden).

SHARPLES, R. W. (1983), 'But why has my spirit spoken to me thus?', *G&R* 30: 1–7.

SIHLER, A. S. (1995), *New Comparative Grammar of Greek and Latin* (Oxford).

SILK, M. (1974), *Interaction in Poetic Imagery* (Cambridge).

——(1983), 'LSJ and the Problem of Poetic Archaism: From Meanings to Iconyms', *CQ* 33: 303–30.

SIMON, B. (1978), *Mind and Madness in Ancient Greece: The Classical Roots of Modern Psychiatry* (Ithaca, NY).

SLINGS, S. R. (1975), 'Three Notes on the New Archilochus Papyrus', *ZPE* 18: 170.

——(1990a) (ed.), *The Poet's 'I' in Archaic Greek Lyric* (Amsterdam).

——(1990b), 'The I in Personal Archaic Lyric', in Slings (1990a), 1–30.

SNELL, B. (1952), *Der Aufbau der Sprache* (Hamburg).

——(1953), *The Discovery of the Mind* (Oxford; 1953; tr. from *Die Entdeckung des Geistes*, 2nd edn. (Göttingen, 1948)).

——(1954), 'Die Welt der Götter bei Hesiod', in *La Notion du divin depuis Homère jusqu'à Platon* (Entretiens Hardt, 1; Geneva), 97–126.

——(1969), *Tyrtaios und die Sprache des Epos* (Hypomnemata, 22; Göttingen).

——(1975), *Die Entdeckung des Geistes*, 4th edn. (Göttingen).

——(1978), "*φρένες/φρόνησις*", in his *Der Weg zum Denken und zur Wahrheit* (Hypomnemata, 57; Göttingen), 53–90.

SNODGRASS, A. M. (1982), 'Les Origines du culte des héros dans la Grèce antique', in Gnoli and Vernant (1982), 107–20.

SOLMSEN, F. (1965), 'Ilias Σ 535–40', *Hermes*, 93: 1–6.

——(1979), 'Symphytos Aion (A. *Ag.* 106)', *AJPh* 100: 477–9.

SOURVINOU-INWOOD, C. (1987), 'Myth as History: The Previous Owners of the Delphic Oracle', in Bremmer (1987), 215–41.

——(1991), *'Reading' Greek Culture* (Oxford).

——(1995), *'Reading' Greek Death* (Oxford).

SPENCER, A. J. (1982), *Death in Ancient Egypt* (Harmondsworth).

STALLMACH, J. (1968), *Ate: Frage des Selbst- und Weltverständnisses des frühgriechischen Menschen* (*Beiträge zur klassischen Philologie*, 18; Meisenheim).

STANFORD, W. B. (1936), *Greek Metaphor* (Oxford).

STEINER, G. (1971), 'Die Unterwelts-Beschwörung der Odyssee im Lichte hethitischer Texte', *Ugarit-Forschungen*, 3: 265–83.

STERN, J. (1967), 'The Imagery of Bacchylides' Ode 5', *GRBS* 8: 35–43.

STINTON, T. C. W. (1990), 'The Apotheosis of Heracles from the Pyre', in his *Collected Papers on Greek Tragedy* (Oxford), 493–507.

STOKES, M. C. (1962–3), 'Hesiodic and Milesian Cosmogonies', *Phronesis*, 7 (1962), 1–37; 8 (1963), 1–34.

TAPLIN, O. (1992), *Homeric Soundings* (Oxford).

TAYLOR, C. (1989), *Sources of the Self: The Making of the Modern Identity* (Cambridge).

THALMANN, W. G. (1984), *Conventions of Form and Thought in Early Greek Epic Poetry* (Baltimore).

THIEME, P. (1968), 'Hades', in R. Schmitt (1968), 133–53.

THOMAS, R. (1992), *Literacy and Orality in Ancient Greece* (Cambridge).

THOMSON, J. A. K. (1936), 'Winged Words', *CQ* 30: 1–3.

THORNTON, A. (1970), *People and Themes in Homer's* Odyssey (London).

TICHY, E. (1981), 'Hom. ἀνδροτῆτα und die Vorgeschichte des daktylischen Hexameters', *Glotta*, 59: 28–67.

TILLYARD, E. M. W. (1943), *The Elizabethan World Picture* (London).

TRIER, J. (1931), *Der deutsche Wortschatz im Sinnbezirk des Zustandes: die Geschichte eines sprachlichen Felds* (Heidelberg).

TSAGARAKIS, O. (1977), *Self-expression in Early Greek Lyric, Iambic and Elegiac Poetry* (Palingenesia, 11; Wiesbaden).

——(1982), *Form and Content in Homer* (*Hermes* Einzelschriften, 46; Wiesbaden).

TSANTSANOGLOU, K. (1997), 'The First Columns of the Derveni Papyrus', in G. Most and A. Laks (eds.), *Studies on the Derveni Papyrus* (Oxford), 93–128.

TURNER, M. (1991), *Reading Minds* (Princeton).

TYLOR, E. B. (1903), *Primitive Culture*, 4th edn. (London).

VERMEULE, E. (1979), *Aspects of Death in Early Greek Art and Poetry* (Berkeley and Los Angeles).

VERNANT, J.-P. (1985), *Mythe et pensée chez les grecs*, 2nd edn. (Paris).

—— (1990), *Figures, Idoles, Masques* (Paris).

—— (1991), 'Psuche: Simulacrum of the Body or Image of the Divine?', in his *Mortals and Immortals* (Princeton), 186–93.

VEYNE, P. (1983), *Les Grecs ont-ils cru à leurs mythes?* (Paris).

VIAN, P. (1968), 'La Fonction guerrière dans la mythologie grecque', in J.-P. Vernant (ed.), *Problèmes de a guerre dans la Grèce ancienne* (Paris), 53–68.

VIVANTE, P. (1955), 'Sulla designazione del corpo in Omero', *AGI* 40: 39–50.

—— (1956), 'Sulle designazioni omeriche della realtà psichica', *AGI* 41: 113–38.

—— (1975), 'On Homer's Winged Words', *CQ* 25: 1–12.

—— (1980), 'Men's Epithets in Homer', *Glotta*, 58: 157–72.

—— (1982), *The Epithets in Homer: A Study in Poetic Values* (New Haven).

VOIGT, C. (1934), *Überlegung und Entscheidung: Studien zur Selbstauffassung des Menschen bei Homer* (diss. Marburg; repub. as *Beiträge zur Klassischen Philologie*, 48; Meisenheim, 1972).

WACE, A. J. B., and STUBBINGS, F. H. (1962), *A Companion to Homer* (London).

WACKERNAGEL, J. (1916), *Sprachliche Untersuchungen zu Homer* (Göttingen).

—— (1926), *Vorlesungen über Syntax* (Basle).

—— (1953), *Kleine Schriften*, i (Göttingen).

WARDEN, J. (1969), "Ἴφθιμος: A Semantic Analysis", *Phoenix*, 23: 143–58.

—— (1971), "Ψυχή in Homeric death-descriptions", *Phoenix*, 25: 95–103.

WEBSTER, T. B. L. (1954), 'Personification as a Mode of Greek Thought', *JWI* 17: 10–21.

—— (1957), 'Some Psychological Terms in Greek Tragedy', *JHS* 77: 149–54.

WENDER, D. (1978), *The Last Scenes of the* Odyssey (*Mnemosyne* Suppl. 52; Leiden).

WEST, M. L. (1961), 'Hesiodea', *CQ* 11: 130–45.

—— (1974), *Studies in Greek Elegy and Iambus* (Berlin).

—— (1983), *The Orphic Poems* (Oxford).

—— (1985*a*), *The Hesiodic Catalogue of Women* (Oxford).

—— (1985*b*), review of Bremmer (1983), *CR* 35: 56–8.

—— (1988), 'The Rise of the Greek Epic', *JHS* 108: 151–72.

—— (1990), 'Archaische Heldendichtung: Singern und Schreiben', in Kullmann and Reichel (1990), 33–50.

—— (1993), *Greek Lyric Poetry, Translated with Introduction and Notes* (Oxford).

—— (1995), 'The Date of the *Iliad*', *MH* 52: 203–19.

WHITMAN, C. H. (1958), *Homer and the Heroic Tradition* (Cambridge, Mass.).

WHORF, B. L. (1956), *Language, Thought and Reality* (Cambridge, Mass.).

VON WILAMOWITZ-MOELLENDORF, U. (1931), *Der Glaube der Hellenen*, i (Berlin).

WILLCOCK, M. M. (1964), 'Mythological Paradeigmata in the *Iliad*', *CQ* 14: 141–54.

—— (1970), 'Some Aspects of the Gods in the *Iliad*', *BICS* 17: 1–10.

WRIGHT, M. R. (1990), 'Presocratic Minds', in Gill (1990), 207–26.

ZUNTZ, G. (1971), *Persephone* (Oxford).

INDEX OF WORDS

Index of Words 345

INDEX OF PASSAGES

Parmenides (KRS):
fr. 288.17 154 n. 45

Pausanias:
2.10.12 235 n. 8
2.31.2 235 n. 8
5.18.1 235 n. 8
5.19.6 260 n. 63
6.6.3 188 n. 64

Philolaus:
fr. B14 D-K 291
frs. 450–5 KRS 291

Pindar (M):
Isth. 1.68 150 n. 35, 306–7
Isth. 4.37–42 265 n. 4
Isth. 4.71 306
Isth. 5.46–7 314
Nem. 1.47 306–7
Nem. 3.1 314
Nem. 3.26–7 314
Nem. 7.102–4 313–14
Nem. 8.44 307
Nem. 9.32–3 306
Nem. 9.38 306
Nem. 10.80–2 110 n. 124
Ol. 1.3–4 313
Ol. 2.56–80 294, 308–9
Ol. 2.69–70 312
Ol. 2.89–90 314
Ol. 6.55–6 315
Ol. 8.39 306–7
Pyth. 1.47–8 306
Pyth. 3.40–1 306
Pyth. 3.60–2 306, 312–13
Pyth. 3.101 306–7
Pyth. 4.122 305–6
Pyth. 4.159 307
Pyth. 8.81–2 315
Pyth. 8.95–7 311 n. 54
Pyth. 11.20–2 307
fr. 33d.1 250 n. 43
fr. 52d.50–1 313 n. 58
fr. 52f.12–15 314
fr. 52i(A).10–14 312–13
fr. 72 91 n. 78
fr. 94a 309 n. 51
fr. 94a.14–15 315
fr. 111.5 311 n. 54
fr. 123.1–9 306
fr. 123.1 313
fr. 127 313

fr. 129 294, 309 n. 52
fr. 130 294
fr. 131b 45, 294, 311–12, 314–5
fr. 133 294, 308 n. 50
fr. 133.1–5 309–10
fr. 137 294, 309 n. 52

Plato:
Cra. 400c 290
Grg. 493a1–3 290
Lg. 891e–896e 287 n. 6
Lg. 899b 262 n. 68
Tim. 78b ff. 291 n. 17

Sappho (L-P):
fr. 22.3 133 n. 4
fr. 42.1 99 n. 96
fr. 55 199 n. 83, 205 n. 90, 300
    n. 36, 303 n. 41
fr. 62.8 301, 312
fr. 132 301 n. 37

Semonides (W):
fr. 1.13–14 301 n. 38
fr. 4 101 n. 105

Simonides:
no. 12 PEG 27 n. 65, 296
no. 15 PEG 300
no. 70 PEG 301
fr. 508.2 P 86 n. 62
fr. 531.4–5 P 192 n. 71, 199 n. 83
fr. 553 P 296
fr. 20.11–12 W 299
fr. 21 W 301, 304, 306, 312

Solon (W):
fr. 13.46 297
fr. 24.8 301 n. 38

Sophocles:
Ant. 20 87 n. 66
Ant. 529 133 n. 4
El. 242–3 155 n. 45
OC 621–3 216 n. 3
OT 174–8 5 n. 7
Tr. 9–23 276 n. 31
fr. 725 N 33 n. 77

Stesichorus (P):
fr. 185 272 n. 21
frs. 192–3 196 n. 78
fr. 233 125 n. 161

GENERAL INDEX

Authors of secondary literature cited in footnotes are not included

Yeats, W. B. 40–41
Youth, as deity 223 n. 15, 267

Zenodotus 175–6

Zeus 34, 65, 125, 165, 174 n. 28,
178–9, 233, 238–9, 247 n. 36, 252
n. 49, 254 n. 52, 255–6, 260, 267
n. 9, 273, 280–2, 291–2, 308

DATE DUE

MAY 3 0 2019			